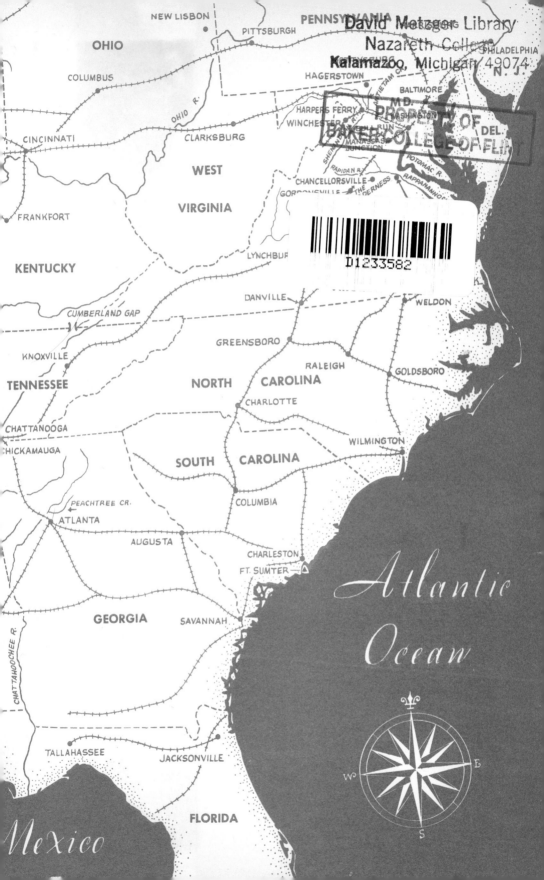

OHIO

NEW LISBON

PITTSBURGH

PENNSYLVANIA

PHILADELPHIA

N.J.

COLUMBUS

HAGERSTOWN

BALTIMORE

MD.

DEL.

OHIO R.

HARPERS FERRY

WINCHESTER

WASHINGTON

ANTIETAM CR.

SHEN. R.

BULL RUN

MANASSAS JUNCTION

POTOMAC R.

CINCINNATI

CLARKSBURG

WEST

VIRGINIA

GORDONSVILLE

CHANCELLORSVILLE

THE WILDERNESS

RAPIDAN R.

RAPPAHANNOCK

FRANKFORT

LYNCHBURG

KENTUCKY

DANVILLE

WELDON

CUMBERLAND GAP

GREENSBORO

KNOXVILLE

RALEIGH

GOLDSBORO

TENNESSEE

NORTH   CAROLINA

CHARLOTTE

CHATTANOOGA

WILMINGTON

CHICKAMAUGA

SOUTH   CAROLINA

PEACHTREE CR.

ATLANTA

COLUMBIA

AUGUSTA

CHARLESTON

FT. SUMTER

Atlantic

Ocean

CHATTAHOOCHEE R.

GEORGIA

SAVANNAH

TALLAHASSEE

JACKSONVILLE

W

E

S

FLORIDA

Mexico

Mainstream of America Series ★

EDITED BY LEWIS GANNETT

The Land They Fought For

By Clifford Dowdey

The Land They Fought For

THE STORY OF THE
SOUTH AS THE CONFEDERACY
1832–1865

By Clifford Dowdey

DOUBLEDAY & COMPANY, INC., GARDEN CITY, N.Y., 1955

LIBRARY OF CONGRESS CATALOG CARD NUMBER 54-7321

PRINTED IN THE UNITED STATES

THE COUNTRY LIFE PRESS, GARDEN CITY, N.Y.

FIRST EDITION

For
ROBERT R. BROWN
my friend and rector
St. Paul's Church, Richmond, Virginia

Contents

SECTION FOUR: "STRIKE THE TENT"

Section One

THE COLD WAR

The Battleground

THE CIVIL WAR was fought for thirty years before the mounting antagonisms between the sections exploded in the clash of arms. From Nullification in 1832 until Fort Sumter in 1861 constituted a long period of cold war, even by today's standards. Men who opposed one another in the opening phases of the conflict had gone to their rewards when the shooting began, and the generation in the South which was to die had not been born when South Carolina first defied the Union. The quarrel was passed on, like a baton in a relay race, from generation to generation, until the men who settled it in the bloodiest violence had little notion of what had started it.

Indeed, the causes of the war were so involved that people haven't agreed yet what the fighting was about. In 1955 historians are as much at odds as sectional leaders were a hundred years ago.

The interpretations of the causes have changed from generation to generation as the climate of opinion changed, and the need continued for Americans to understand the revolution that shook this nation when democratic processes failed.

Immediately after the war, both sides acted under a compulsion to fix the "war guilt" on the other. Because the North had the nobler slogans, "freedom" and "preserving the Union" (and also because it won), slavery and union became fairly well fixed, with whatever variations, as the basic causes. From the beginning the slavery part brought indignant denials from the Southerners, who had been taught that their fathers or grandfathers had *not* fought for slavery. But, however few Southerners owned slaves—less than ten per cent—the institution was inextricably involved in the long conflict.

Then, around the turn of the century, under the motives of reunion and reconciliation, the "Nationalists" eased off the stigmatizing and interpreted the conflict in terms of a clash between divergent civilizations. Later, as "economic determinism" became a fashionable way of interpreting history, the war was explained in terms of rival economies: Northern capitalistic powers sought to exploit the South as a colony—which, after the war, they did.

More recently, the "revisionists" decided that the conflicts need not have been resolved by war at all; the rival sections were driven at each other's throats by the extremists of both sides. In that theory, passion replaced reason and the men of good will became ineffective.

Currently, there are the anti-revisionists. Their viewpoint is that extremists could not arouse such passions unless the sectional consciousnesses were receptive, and they stress the moral aspects of the slavery issue.

By now a whole secular priesthood has arisen to assume authority for the dogmas of the interpretations of the war. To the confusion of the laity, no group recognizes the authority of another, and manifestly they cannot all be right. It is more likely that, if no agreement has been reached by now, they all are at least partly wrong. They are like a group of medical specialists with a dying patient: each doctor finds something that is wrong, but no one can diagnose the fatal disease. Like the specialists in Shaw's *The Doctor's Dilemma*, each one rides his hobby while the patient dies.

There can be no question that each of the elements was present. The sections *had* diverged into patterns of life which became increasingly antithetical; antagonisms and rivalries grew in intensity. The industrial North *did* wish to buy cheap and sell dear at the expense of the South, while Northern money powers needed the South in a colonial status for exploitation. Slavery *did* exist in the South, and there *was* a high moral tone in the issue of freedom, held by a small minority. Extremists on both sides *did* inflame passions. There was, as an amalgam of all this, the nationalistic sweep of the new industrial middle-class society represented by the North, in alliance with the expanding, democratic West, and against these the South stood as an anachronistic, arrogant feudal culture in the path of manifest destiny. All of this defines the elements of duality within the corporate body of the nation; yet, put them all together, with equal emphases or any single emphasis, and the element of explosion is missing.

That element was similar to the violence inherent in the split personality of the schizophrenic. There the separate parts are locked in a struggle which must be resolved if the corporate body is to function. If this warring duality cannot be resolved, an explosion is inevitable. But this inherent element in the schizoid, this catalyst of violence, defies definition because it is essentially an unknown quantity.

As it is, the mass of interpretations over the past ninety years, as well as the popular myths, tend to impose a rationale on the events leading up to the explosion and aftermath. Instead of that, the country was more like the schizoid in a violent cycle, where he is driven by the warring parts, with no guiding intelligence to direct the whole. One illogical act of violence led to others of even less logic and more violence, until the nation was swept along by a concatenation of events which had become a force in themselves.

As men were caught up in this force, few in positions of power could foresee the end to which the concatenation was building. Fewer still would have deliberately designed anything of the nature of civil war.

In the forty-six years from the beginning of the conflict in 1831 to the end of Reconstruction in 1877, not only did generations of leaders die off but men changed under the impact of events. The thirty years of the cold war caused shifts in attitudes and in the deepening of passions. Men changed during the fighting years, as did Lincoln, and men changed as a result of the war, as did Lee.

Then, as always, words were said. Words were spoken in anger and in expediency, in the intemperateness of excitement and in the irresponsibility of personal ambition. Words spoken in Illinois changed the minds of men in Virginia, and words spoken in Alabama affected the thoughts of men in New York.

Political parties changed too. Parties died and parties were formed with the usual motives.

Even the separate societies within the nation were in various stages of flux. There were no clearly drawn lines between Northerners, as solid Unionists, and Southerners, as solid slaveholding secessionists.

Northerners, for instance, moved into the South to become successful slaveholders and extreme secessionists; Southerners moved out in opposition to the institution of slavery, and roughly fifteen per cent of the population of the expanding Middle West were native-born Southerners. Within the South the first emancipation movements were started (and ironically ended by the abolitionists) and within the North were some of the slaveholders' stoutest friends—financially, politically, and socially. Southerners attended all the major Northern universities and Southern politicians worked with Northern allies to form non-sectional parties designed to end the national strife. Until the eve of secession, probably the majority of all Americans could not believe it would happen.

By then, the chain of events had formed its own grim illogic of action for both sections. Hate and distrust, involved with personal ambitions, formed the atmosphere of government. In the South people's pride was affected, their honor at stake, and they had been on the defensive a long time. People under forty had no memory of life without pressure coming at them from the North. They had had enough of it.

2

In all the torturous events of the thirty years of the cold war, it was the South that had been on the defensive. Its whole course was counteraction, even secession. The South, the legendary and allegedly solid South, was formed slowly and spasmodically in that defensiveness, and the assertive individualism of the people and the states never approached anything remotely "solid." Even the Confederacy represented the apogee of the awesome lack of unity which historically characterized the Southern people.

The nearest "the South," so called, ever came to solidarity was *after* the war, during the twelve years of that military occupation called, with humorless irony, "Reconstruction," and during its subsequent decades as an exploited province. This total postwar period colors all Southerners' thinking of the war and sharply differentiates their interpretations from Northerners'.

The reason for this is the Southerner's painful knowledge of what the North did with its military victory in contradistinction to the avowed purposes of the war—"freedom" and "preservation of the Union." As opposed to these noble abstractions, *the Southerner had visited on him by the conquerors the very worst of all the things he had feared from the beginning of his defense.*

From the beginning, slavery—which became the catchall for the whole complex of antagonisms and rivalries, the political bone of contention, the "issue"—was no abstraction in the South. Obviously the champions of "freedom" stand in an impregnable position in the course of mankind's history. But the "fanatics of freedom" could not, on the stand of liberty alone, have antagonized the ninety per cent of Southerners who did not own slaves and the many who (like Lee and Jackson) disbelieved in the institution. From 1831 to 1861 Southerners were aroused to defense by the vindictiveness of the fanatics who were as callously indifferent to the means as they were irresponsible for the ends.

To the Northern abolitionist, the emancipation of slaves achieved the end of "freedom"; to all Southerners, four million black people in a society of five and a half million whites created an appalling problem. It was a problem that Lincoln, contrary to the myth of a logical progression toward human liberty, understood very well. He wrote on slavery, "I think no wise man has yet perceived how it could be at once eradicated without producing a greater evil even to the cause of human liberty itself."

As even such a humanitarian as Lincoln did not believe in equality of the races, the average non-slaveholding Southerner shrank from the chaos inevitable in the freeing of former black slaves in a white society. Where to the abolitionists the "high moral note" was on the issue of slavery, to the Southerner the issue was the Negro.

From the inception of this "issue," the Southerner felt that the abolitionist assumed no responsibility for the Negro in the nation. New Englanders had never objected to the institution of slavery as long as they made a profit out of selling captured Africans to planters. As Southerners in Washington, like Georgia's Bob Toombs, constantly pointed out, the Union was founded and the Constitution was written on the existence of slavery. If slavery was to be legalized out of existence, there should be some way for the country as a whole to assume the responsibility for dissolving the institution without putting either the burden or the stigma on the one section where slave labor happened to form the basis of its economic system.

The slave-labor economic system in the South did not arise because the Englishmen who settled in Virginia were particularly committed to the enslavement of fellow human beings. It arose for the same reason and at the same time that the slave trade arose in New England—because it was profitable. Slavery came to the South for the same reason that cattle raising came to Texas, cattle slaughter to Chicago, the exploitation of Okies to California, and the exploitation of immigrants to Northern factory owners. It came because, in a new and vast land where everyone had come for opportunity, the soil and the climate of the South were peculiarly adapted to the use of chattel labor imported from a hot country.

This did not mean that everybody owned or wanted to own slaves; it meant that the ownership was legal where it was practical. It was most practical on a plantation which, with all the romantic connotations, was basically large-scale farming devoted to one money crop. In Virginia this crop was primarily tobacco, in South Carolina rice and cotton, in Louisiana sugar and cotton, in Georgia and the new states of the lower South almost entirely cotton. The slave-labor system was essentially mass-production agriculture.

On the larger and more successful plantations, resourceful planters supplemented the money crop with total farming and stock raising, developed artisans of all kinds, and achieved virtually self-sufficient domains. It was this lavish and isolated self-sufficiency, along with the planter's absolute mastery of all he surveyed, that gave the lordliness and enchantment to plantation life. The plantation came to represent an ideal of a civilization as well as the structure of its economic life. It was the cachet of the semitropical nobility, the symbol of the white-column class.

While less than one per cent of Southerners achieved the true baronies—such as those of Wade Hampton in South Carolina and Howell Cobb in Georgia—the plantation stood for a pattern of life. Planters of modest gifts and small establishments emulated the pattern of the grandees, sub-

scribed to the codes, customs, and manners of the ruling class, and considered themselves of it. For the plantation enabled the people who
emigrated into the Southern states to fulfill their dream of belonging to
an "aristocracy."

Though the Southern aristocracy was, as are all aristocracies, self-
created, it was truly a *ruling* class—openly and proudly avowed as such,
with no shilly-shallying about "equality." To it all aspirants brought far
more than acquisitiveness. The original princes of Virginia might have
been chiefly ruthless, capable men of ambition who "got there fust with
the most acres," but it was always required of a planter that he possess
more than "land and niggers."

As early as 1660 in Virginia, a newcomer to the ruling class was praised
for living "bravely," for the hospitality of his home, for his sense of honor
and love of *that* land. The codes of honor became formalized, hospitality
traditionalized, and a pattern of manners stylized. Suspiciousness in social
or business intercourse became the deadliest of sins, as it reflected on a
man's honor and on the honor of his society. Men would impoverish
themselves to avoid even a taint of shadiness in their dealings. In turn,
graciousness became a prime virtue, at the basis of all courtesy.

Since the planters dominated Southern culture, their codes and customs,
manners and values, sifted down throughout the whole society, making it
at once homogeneous and parochial.

Men totally outside the plantation system from choice—such as soldiers,
lawyers, doctors, academicians, and the like—equally subscribed and were
devoted to the culture which evolved around the center of the plantation.
The stout yeomanry, that unsung two thirds of the Southern whites who
were non-slaveholding farmers, were warp and woof of the total society
characterized by the planter. Even the canebrake casuals, the red-hill poh
whites and the mountaineer castaways, all shared the personal assertiveness
and individualism of the planter.

Currently there is a fashion to resurrect these forgotten Southerners
who, outside the legend, bore the brunt of the war and were victims of
the aftermath. In the long struggle between the North and South, these
were not the people either the Northern money powers or the fanatical
do-gooders wanted to get at. This vast majority of Southern whites,
largely innocent of slaveholding or secessionist tendencies, were drawn
in by the parochial nature of their society—with its immediacy of love
of their land and respect for the ruling class—and by the all-inclusive
nature of the attacks on their society from without.

With little inkling of the amalgam of forces which historians have been
analyzing for ninety years, they understood that "Yankee" had come to
mean enemy and that Negro slaves might be turned loose among them.
But their resentments and fears were played upon by the planters' political
representatives. For it was the planters who recognized that *they* were the

class who would be destroyed, along with their civilization, if the North gained power over them.

With all the subsurface power struggles between the sections that had nothing to do with slavery and all the political dogfights that used slavery as an "issue," the planters' defense against the encroachments from the North was essentially of their property and the life of splendor built upon it.

3

It was not that all planters believed in the institution. Many had changed with the shift in world opinion since their system had developed, and Virginia particularly was influenced by Jefferson's humanism. They simply did not know how to get rid of slavery. In the first place, the slaves themselves (worth approximately a thousand dollars each) represented a lifetime's investment. Then, even where the planters were willing to impoverish themselves, there was no place in a white agricultural country for freed Negroes without cash.

When John Randolph of Roanoke, without heirs to worry about, manumitted four hundred slaves, worth roughly half a million dollars, he happened to possess the cash to deport them to Africa. Lincoln believed deportation was the solution. Obviously, most planting families would not have the cash for that after giving away all their property, and the shrill advocates of freedom were notably silent on either any plans for compensation to the planters or the future of the freed Negro.

Many families of modest circumstances—with children to educate—lived with the single goal of freeing their slaves and transporting them. So many others simply freed their own slaves that in a few Virginia *counties* there were larger populations of freed Negroes than there are in some New England *states* today. Virginia and Maryland had tried abortive plans of deportation and in 1832, in the Virginia Assembly, Thomas Jefferson's grandson offered a bill of gradual compensatory emancipation which, if passed, would have begun practical abolition in 1861!

As it turned out, some Virginians solved the dual problems of compensation and the freed Negro by the cold pragmatism of selling slaves South. As land worn out by tobacco made large-scale planting impractical, Virginia was actually drifting away from slavery. As this affected the institution in the South, however, it meant only that plantation power was shifting from the old coastal states to the new states of the lower South.

This shift in itself brought a complexity to the slavery issue within the South. Those planters in the first flush of power and prestige could scarcely be expected to feel philosophic about the means of their rise. The fact that a *new* slave power was in the ascendant when the South went on the defensive indicates a flux within the Southern states that is not suggested by the acceptance of the South as "static and feudal."

The individualistic Southern states were static in terms of the dynamic North, as the people—not only the planters—were passionately devoted to the *status quo*. But within the feudal concept there was restless change. New sections arose as others declined, new fortunes were founded as others vanished and, most of all, new powers won their way into the plantation nobility in positions of control. Most of the movement centered in the new land of the now-called Deep South.

While this lower South has come down through history as a lush land where decadent aristocrats practiced miscegenation behind white columns, actually those states were just emerging from the frontier stage when the cold war began in 1831. Anything but static or feudal, they were the scene of one of the most tumultuous and certainly the strangest pioneering movements in history.

Along with the usual assortment of adventurers and riffraff, of dispossessed families and stout yeomanry seeking to improve their positions, came wagon trains of the great plantation families. Leaving their worn-out lands in the coastal South, they were transporting their aristocratic pattern *in toto*—slaves and furniture, animals and equipment—to the new rich lands of Alabama and Mississippi, to the territories of west Florida and Arkansas, and to the vast Mexican empire that became Texas. This gold rush, for the white gold of cotton, presented the spectacle of the pre-forty-niners marching forth with coats of arms—or to get them. Unlike any other opening frontier in America, the lands of the lower South were settled in a duplication—really an extension—of an existing society. Because the blueprinted societal structure so quickly emerged from the times of tumult, it gave the illusion of an old South.

It was a very new South and a very brief one. Within the span of a mortal lifetime, the civilization of the lower South emerged from the frontier, flowered in its dramatic brevity, and was destroyed by invading armies.

The effect on the conflict of the newness of this society was that it gave the newly sprung Bourbons more impetuosity and less *noblesse oblige* than had characterized the patriarchs, such as George Washington, in the older and generic Southern society. These lordly parvenus were glorying in the first headiness of the feudal power that had come to Virginia nearly two centuries before. They had the optimism of the new.

The coastal South, with a mellowed disenchantment about success, luxuriated in the shade of its long twilights, and perhaps was flattered to see its manners imitated. But the upper and lower South had little in common, much less than is believed.

Yet what they did have in common, though it could not unite them, could unite an enemy against them. They had the Negro, and they had the enchanting legend.

4

The Southern legend was unique in that it was formed almost in equal part by the glorifiers of the South and by its attackers, even vilifiers, from the North. It was begun innocuously by a young Baltimorean, John P. Kennedy. After visiting the plantation of his mother's Virginia kin, he wrote a charming book called *Swallow Barn* (1832)—a series of sketches of a past time on plantations as it had come down to him through the pathos of distance and sentiment. Kennedy went on back North, where he cut something of a figure in the practical world of money and its society, while the byplay of his imagination became the genesis of that glamorous plantation world that never was.

From this model grew a body of glowing literature whose composite impression soon passed into folklore.

At the same time, the images created by the apologists were curiously complemented by those evoked in the Northern works which followed Garrison's anti-slavery *Liberator*, first published in 1831.

Writing even more from imagination than had Mr. Kennedy, the abolitionist authors drew a gaudy picture of harems of bright-skinned girls from the Potomac to the Gulf, being slavered over by a goateed colonel with a whip in one hand and a julep in the other. A composite character developed of this colonel, a sort of Cottonfield Caligula, who lived in imperious and splendid sin. The colonel was invariably lazy and proud, self-indulgent and quick-tempered, pleasure-loving and courtly, an utterly thriftless wastrel who squandered the wealth (which, despite these traits, he had somehow acquired) in ostentatious and ruinous hospitality.

The apogee was reached in *Uncle Tom's Cabin*, published in 1851, and the figures of Mrs. Stowe's vivid imagination entered American folklore on the other side.

To complement Mrs. Stowe, in turn, also in 1851, Stephen Foster (as ignorant of the South as the authoress) came to the romanticists' rescue with "Old Folks at Home." *Still longing for the old plantation.*

Since the plantation was the center of Southern life, it was natural for the apologists to idealize it. On the best of them, there were undeniably a magnificence and a graciousness of life. In the Southern legend, the best was attributed to all plantations.

From the enemy's side, the worst was attributed to all. Much that European travelers found charming, Northern observers found deplorable,

invariably attributing the conditions to Southern lack of get-up-and-go
and a slothful incapacity for material well-being.

The Northerners made a fundamental mistake: they measured the
South by the yardstick they brought from home. To the Northerner,
his factories represented "progress." Upon this industrial progress were
based the standards of an acquisitive competitive society which valued
material possessions, the physical symbols of success—"conspicuous con-
sumption"—and the traits and habits that directed a life toward these
things. The observers, unable to conceive of a people without those
values, cited the lack of factories as indicating backwardness and judged
the people as failures for not achieving something they never wanted. As
with Americans ever since, they could not believe that people different
from themselves actually *liked* their own way of life.

The Southerner not only liked his life; it had evolved through a conscious and articulated ideal whose genesis had begun in Virginia two
centuries before. The ideal was based on enjoyment of *the land*. Part
of the South's resistance to industry was the people's abhorrence of indoor
—hence, factory—work. Winters were brief and mild, spring came early
and lush, and the long, hot summers with the mellow, sweet-smelling
nights brought languor to the body and the pleasure-principle to the
mind. The people possessed an earthy, immediate love of and identification with their slumberous land. Their conversation was colored by com-
parisons with things of their land: things were measured or described by
their likeness or unlikeness to the minutiae of their immediate, physical
world. In that world, what they valued more than anything made by man
was *time*—not to be used profitably, but to enjoy.

This was the same all the way to the top. While in the capitalistic
North power fed on power—men who made money pooling their wealth
with other money men, forming combines of power for wider spheres
of exploitation, toward the ultimate power of government control—the
Southern planter wanted to enjoy what he had. To him the doctrine that
"time is money" would have been incomprehensible and monstrous. Time
belonged to man, not to the bank: it was his heritage from God.

It was the complete mastery of their own time that made all Southerners, not only the planters, self-assertive and personally inviolable individualists. This individualism in a parochial, agricultural society, dominated by the imperious planter, was at the basis of the Southern states'
belief in a loose national confederation as opposed to a strong centralized
government. "States' rights" as a political theory really articulated the feelings of the people in regard to their land. The county, the ultimate extension of their neighborhood, comprised their political unit. The state was
their *country!* That was as far as they could imagine, or wanted to.

Where Northern leaders regarded the Union as a nation of *people*,
Southerners regarded it as a confederation of semiautonomous principali-

ties. In their confederation with other states, no member of the ruling class ever dreamed of placing a strongly centralized government over himself. No planter-aristocrat could conceive of another will imposed on his own. Even Jefferson, when old and dying, wrote his highest praise to Judge Spencer Roane for his outraged stand against a central government which presumed to encroach on the rights of the Commonwealth of Virginia.

When these encroachments on Southern power persisted, growing in intensity and intemperateness, as slavery became *the* "issue" to becloud all others, over the thirty years the planter class stiffened and grew more violent in defensiveness.

The economic threat that the plantation class feared could not in itself have aroused the bulk of Southerners to any sense of danger. The average Southerner was aroused slowly, by a threat to his own land, to the familiar life he loved.

The first alarm struck in 1831. It had nothing to do with abolitionists, with economic determinism or the nationalistic sweep of empire. It concerned only some humble white and colored people who lived in Southampton County, Virginia, and who were totally unaware of their place in history. In all the analyses of the causes of the Civil War, you will look in vain for the name of Joseph Travis, coachmaker and small planter, of Southampton County.

All unwittingly this honest family man provided the first "event" in the concatenation that led to civil war.

CHAPTER I

"The First Shall Be Last . . ."

NOTHING was more untypical of the legendary picture of slavery on a plantation than life on Joseph Travis' farm. Southampton County was not a part of the Old Dominion from which the legends came. It was one of six soundly though modestly prosperous counties which had spread south of the James River from the original settlements across from Jamestown. Its southern border was contiguous with North Carolina, and its people had more in common with their friendly Carolinian neighbors than with the Tidewater grandees. They were what might be loosely called the middle gentry.

The county was agricultural, with diversified farming rather than concentration on the one money crop which characterized plantations. It was good country for orchards, and so many family stills produced cider and brandy that these beverages could be counted as a small money crop. From their hogs and peanuts came a combination destined to become nationally famous as the Smithfield ham.

With no large plantations, there were no large slaveholders, and the county typified those older communities where slavery was passing by personal manumission; the slaves and freed Negroes outnumbered the whites to make a potentially dangerous problem. To 6500 whites, there were 7700 slaves and 1500 freed Negroes. Slave and free, all Negroes lived in intimate proximity to the whites, a situation that did not exist on large plantations, where overseers came between the masters and field hands. Field hands in that sense scarcely existed in Southampton County.

The most successful plantations were operated avocationally by professional men, doctors and lawyers, since the plantation represented the aspiration of everyone. In the same way, many of the plantation-conscious farmers supplemented their agricultural incomes by working as artisans in small enterprises. Such a man was Joseph Travis, the honest coachmaker.

He had apprenticed to him a sixteen-year-old boy, who shared the bedroom of Mr. Travis' foster son, Putnam Moore. Mrs. Travis, whose first husband had died, had a baby by Joseph Travis. This small family had no house servants as such. The few colored families of slaves lived in the single cluster of buildings around the farmyard and there was no distinction between house people and field hands. There the whites and blacks, working together and virtually living together, shared an hourly and constant companionship, and knew one another with the casual intimacy of members of the same family. Though everybody worked hard, the slaves were held to a fairly rigid schedule.

Working five days a week from roughly sunup until sundown, they had Saturday afternoons and Sundays off. They were encouraged to grow garden crops for themselves on allotted plots of ground, either to fill out their diets according to personal tastes or for use in trade and barter. Skills were taught them and, as in other families like the Travises, who could not afford to free their lifetime investment, sometimes a Negro worked out his freedom at a trade.

Great attention was given to their religious education. They went to the whites' churches, where the Methodist and Baptist preachers of the people's religion evoked fiery and wondrous images, and they developed their own preachers, who supplemented the whites'. Such a Negro preacher acted as Joseph Travis' "overseer."

The overseer of this little family plantation, bearing not even unintentional similarity to Simon Legree, merely acted for the owner with the few Negroes who worked the farm. With Joseph Travis busy at his coachmaking, somebody had to be in charge of the work, though The Preacher extended his leadership over the total lives of the three families in the Travis farmyard, and exerted considerable influence over other Negroes in the scattered community.

He always said that Mr. Travis was a very kind man, maybe even too indulgent with his people, and Mr. Travis regarded The Preacher as something of a privileged character. He had been born in the county of an African mother and a slave father, who ran away when The Preacher was a child. He had been raised by his grandmother, who worked on his religious education, and by his mother, who was deeply impressed with the child's gift of second sight.

When the owners' attention was called to his precociousness, they encouraged him to read and gave him a Bible. He culled the Bible for predictions and prophecies which he used to impose his visions on his fellow slaves. He found portents in the sun and moon, portentous hieroglyphics in leaves and suchlike, and in general created of himself a mysterious figure of supernatural gifts.

The Preacher did not regard himself as a humbug in imposing on his fellows. He actually believed he could read signs in the sky. "Behold me in the heavens," the Holy Spirit said to him, and he beheld and he knew.

He knew the signs were directing him toward a holy mission. In the spring of 1828, he heard a loud noise in the heavens and, he said, "The spirit instantly appeared to me and said the Serpent was loosened, and Christ had laid down the yoke he had borne for the sins of men, and that I should take it on and fight against the Serpent, for the time was fast approaching when the first should be last and the last should be first."

The time came in late August of 1831, when The Preacher was thirty-one years old.

2

The twenty-first of August was a Sunday, in the season when the white people spent the day away at camp meetings. The weather was not hot for the season and the day was lazy on the quiet Travis farm. In The Preacher's cabin, his wife was fixing Sunday dinner for their child. In the woods below the fields, six of The Preacher's disciples were gathered in a glen, where to a Sunday feast they added some of the apple brandy which was always handy to acquire. Only one of them belonged to Mr. Travis—Hark Travis, a magnificently and powerfully built black man. Two others, Sam and the ferocious Will Francis, belonged to one of Mrs. Travis' brothers. As farms were relatively few in the sparsely settled and wooded country, all the Negroes were intimately acquainted.

The Preacher, after his custom of keeping himself aloof, joined the frolic in the middle of the afternoon, when several hours of feasting and drinking had his followers in receptive humor. From then until full night he coached them in the details of his predestined mission in which they were to be allowed to participate.

At ten o'clock they left the woods and silently approached the dark farmyard of the Travis house. All lights were out in the house where the family, tired from their trip to the camp meeting, were asleep. In the farmyard stood a Negro named Austin, who joined them, and brought The Preacher's band to eight.

The seven followers went to the unlocked cider press while The Preacher studied the situation. When the silent men returned, The Preacher directed Hark, the Apollo, to set a tall ladder against an upper-story window sill. The Preacher climbed the ladder, stepped through the open window, and tiptoed through the familiar house down to the front door. When he opened it, his disciples crept in. The fearsome Will Francis held a broadax and one of the men gave The Preacher a hatchet. Without any other weapons, the eight men crept into the master bedroom, where Mr. and Mrs. Travis were asleep.

When The Preacher stood over them, he paused, looking on the face of the kindly man who had given him so many privileges. The other Negroes told him that the leader must strike the first blow. After another pause, The Preacher struck suddenly and awkwardly down at the sleeping man.

The hatchet glanced off, giving a blow on the side of the head. Mr. Travis, startled into wakefulness, struggled out of bed, sleepily calling to his wife. When his bare feet touched the floor, Will Francis, with no confusion of purpose, brought the broadax down on his head in a single long stroke. Without another sound, Mr. Travis fell dead to the floor. Whirling, Will came down with the broadax again, and Mrs. Travis died in her bed without ever coming fully awake.

The sounds had not aroused the two sixteen-year-old boys—Mrs. Travis' son, Putnam Moore, and the apprentice, Joel Westbrook—asleep in the same bed in a room in another part of the house. They were killed before they were awakened.

Last The Preacher went into the baby's room. He had often played with the child and fondled it, and the baby smiled at him when he woke up. The Preacher backed out, unable to touch the child, and sent in Will and another follower to knock the baby's brains out against the brick fireplace.

With the house theirs, they took four shotguns, several muskets, powder and shot, and exchanged their clothes for garments of the dead men. To give a dash to the new costumes, they got some of the red cloth with which the top of the gig was lined and tore that into sashes to go around their waists and over their shoulders. The material gave out and they made other strips from sheets, which they dyed in the freely flowing blood. The Preacher felt that this unit was now ready to serve as the nucleus around which all the slaves of the county would rally.

With some of the force mounted on the Travis horses, they went to the small farm owned by Mrs. Travis' brother, who was also the brother of the owner of Sam and Will. This younger Mr. Francis, a bachelor who lived with his one slave in a single-room house, came to the door when Will and Sam called to him that they had a message from his brother.

When he opened the door they grabbed him. He was a strong man and he fought, calling to his loyal slave for his gun. One of The Preacher's men shot Mr. Francis' slave, Nelson, who managed to stagger to the back door and escape in the darkness to the woods. He started out to give the alarm to his master's brother, the owner of Will and Sam, but he didn't make it that far. Mr. Francis was finished off before Nelson had reached the woods, going down under repeated blows from the hatchet.

From there The Preacher's band walked on through the night to the home of Mrs. Harris, a widow with several children and grandchildren. Unbeknownst to themselves as they slept, this family was spared through the agency of their slave, Joe, who joined The Preacher on the condition that his people be spared.

With their first recruit, the band descended on the home of the widow Reese, whose front door was unlocked. They killed her in her sleep, her son as he awakened, caught the white farm manager who tried to escape in the darkness. He got off with his life by feigning death, though he was forever after crippled.

By then other slaves, too frightened to defend the whites but unwilling to join the insurgents, had fled before the band, and nearby plantations were warned. Not willing at that stage to risk losing any of his eight followers, The Preacher changed his course.

At sunrise on Monday morning they reached the substantial home of the widow Turner, set in a grove and flanked by a row of outbuildings. Mrs. Turner's manager was already at work at the distillery beside the lane to the house. He was shot and stripped, his clothes going to the last recruit, the Joe who had saved his own people. Mrs. Turner and a kinswoman were awakened by the shot and came downstairs to bolt the door. The fearsome Will battered the door down with several strokes of his ax, and the two women were grabbed in the hallway.

While they pleaded for their lives, Will went about his skillful work of execution on Mrs. Turner, and The Preacher pulled Mrs. Newsom, trembling violently, out of the door. He kept striking her over the head with a sword he had acquired. The edge was too blunt to kill the screaming woman and Will, turning from the corpse of Mrs. Turner, methodically finished off The Preacher's victim with his ax.

They got silver there and more decorations for their costumes, and when they left the silent plantation at full daylight their number had spread to fifteen.

They divided, those on foot under The Preacher swinging by the Bryants', where they paused to kill the couple, their child, and Mrs. Bryant's mother, before joining the mounted force at the pleasant establishment of Mrs. Whitehead.

When The Preacher's force got there, Mrs. Whitehead's grown son had already been hacked to death in a cotton patch while his own slaves looked on. Inside the house three daughters and a child, being bathed by his grandmother, were dead. Will was dragging the mother of the family out into the yard, where he decapitated her, and a young girl who had hidden was running for the woods. The Preacher caught her and, his sword failing him again, beat her to death with a fence rail. Another daughter, the only member of the family to survive, had made it to the woods where she was hidden by a house slave.

When they left the seven dead and mutilated bodies at the Whiteheads', The Preacher's band had grown and acquired more weapons and horses. They had also drunk more cider and brandy, and they moved boldly ahead to continue the massacre although they knew that the alarm was out by then. Several of the next small plantations in their line of march were deserted. The band divided again, with Will the executioner leading the mounted force toward the house of his own master, Nathaniel Francis, the brother of The Preacher's Mrs. Travis and of the bachelor whose slave, Nelson, had been among the first to give the warning.

Though the warning had not reached the Francis plantation, a Negro boy had told Mr. Francis a wild tale of the slaughter of his sister's family. Having heard nothing of The Preacher's band, Mr. Francis and his mother were on the way to investigate the grisly scene awaiting them at the Travis household.

Two of Mr. Francis' nephews, eight- and three-year-old boys, were playing in the lane as the Negroes rode silently toward them. The three-year-old, seeing the familiar Will, asked for a ride as he had many times before. Will picked him up on the horse, cut off his head, and dropped the body in the lane. The other boy screamed and tried to hide, but they were too fast for him.

Henry Doyle, the overseer, seeing this, ran to warn Mrs. Francis. He was shot dead in the doorway of the house, but not before he had warned Mrs. Francis. A house slave hid her between the plastering and the roof in one of the "jump" rooms, and kept The Preacher's band away from her hiding place by pretending to hunt for her. When the Negroes had gone on, the house slave of necessity with them, Mrs. Francis came down to find the other house women dividing her clothes, including her wedding dress. One attacked her with a dirk and another defended her. She escaped to join her husband and be taken to safety.

When the band left the Francis plantation, the alarm by then was general and the Negroes were beginning to get drunk. They headed for the road to the county seat. They found more deserted houses, where faithful slaves had left to hide their masters, and met other slaves who had waited to join the insurrectionists. At young Captain Barrow's the warning had been received and the overseer had escaped, but Mrs. Barrow, a woman of beauty, had delayed to arrange her toilet before appearing abroad. She tarried so long that the Negroes reached the house before she left. Her husband called to her to run out the back door while he fought from the front.

In leaving, Mrs. Barrow had the same experience with her house slaves as had Mrs. Francis. A younger one tried to hold her for the mob, while an older one freed her and held the young Negro woman while her mistress escaped. In front, Captain Barrow emptied a pistol, a single-shot rifle, and a shotgun, and fought with the butt of the gun across the porch, through the hall, and into the front room. He was holding them off when a Negro on the outside reached through the window and, from behind, sliced his throat with a razor.

The Preacher's men had a great respect for Captain Barrow's bravery.

They drank his blood and spared his corpse mutilation. Instead, they laid him out in a bedquilt and placed a plug of tobacco on his breast.

It was ten o'clock Monday morning when they left there, and the two bands soon reconverged. They then numbered over fifty. The Preacher's vision of a mass insurrection was coming true. White men were trying to form a force ahead of the band but some of the men, on seeing the bleeding and mutilated bodies of women, hurried back to their farms to hide their own wives and children. Hundreds of women and children were gathering in the county seat at Jerusalem, unaware that the band's winding course was directed there.

On the way The Preacher's formidable force passed more deserted places, but got its biggest haul at Waller's, a country corner. A children's boarding school was there and a large distillery, a blacksmith shop, and the wheelwright, and it had taken some time to gather all the people in the neighborhood. Before they could start for Jerusalem, the Negroes were on them. Some escaped to the screams of those being chased and butchered. More than ten were killed there, mostly children.

From the Waller massacre, the band headed directly for Jerusalem. By then eighteen white men had gathered with arms at some distance from the town, where four hundred unarmed people had collected. The Preacher's band of sixty would have reached the town first except that his lieutenants overruled him when they passed the famous brandy cellar at Parker's deserted plantation, three miles from town. They tarried there to quench their thirsts.

The eighteen white men came on them in Parker's field and opened fire. In a short, pitched battle the boldest Negroes, leading a charge, fell, and most of the insurrectionists fled. The Preacher escaped with twenty of his most faithful followers, and headed toward the Carolina border.

He was seeking new recruits then. They were slow coming in and victims were getting scarce. Late in the afternoon The Preacher, still supported by the Apollo-like Hark and Will with his broadax, allowed a single armed planter to hold off his band from a lady with two children. That planter's family had already escaped to safety. In that family was a fifteen-year-old boy who, thirty-odd years later, was to duplicate his father's indomitable stand—at Chickamauga—and immortalize the Southampton County name of Thomas among the Union's heroes.

Below the Thomas' fine plantation home, near dusk, The Preacher's faithful score of followers turned back north and at night made camp in the woods. At dawn, The Preacher started for the large and handsome home of Dr. Blunt, one of the county's few plantations of the legend, and on the edge of the district of yesterday's triumph. Not seeking victims then, The Preacher wanted fresh supplies and recruits to put heart and strength back into the insurrection.

His band of twenty reached the Blunts' yard fence just before daylight.

Unlike the smaller houses, Dr. Blunt's house was set back in a grove a hundred yards from the front fence—a stout affair, with a locked gate. A precautionary shot was fired to determine if the darkened house was deserted, as expected. Then the powerful Hark broke down the gate, and the group advanced toward the house, looking for slaves to join them. The band was within twenty yards of the house when firing broke out from the front porch.

Hark Travis, one of the original conspirators and one of the bravest of the subleaders, fell wounded in the first volley. When The Preacher, shaken but grown desperate, tried to rally his force for an attack, another volley dropped two more. His men broke. At that moment Dr. Blunt's slaves came swarming out of hiding places, armed with grub hoes, and rushed the insurrectionists. The Preacher fled with his men. Dr. Blunt's slaves rounded up several prisoners, including the wounded Hark, crawling toward a cotton patch.

Dr. Blunt, his fifteen-year-old son, and his manager had done the firing, while the women loaded single-shot rifles and shotguns. Before The Preacher's men arrived, Dr. Blunt had given his own slaves the choice of fighting with his family or leaving. They chose unanimously to fight.

The Preacher had been disappointed earlier when other Negroes, more than had joined him, had helped hide their white people or escaped with them. When his own people *fought* against him, The Preacher lost faith in his insurrection.

More in desperation than purpose he led the dozen remaining followers to retrace their triumphant steps of the day before. At the first plantation, the Greensville County cavalry militia rode them down. They killed Will, the ax-executioner, and killed or captured all except The Preacher and two others. The insurrection was over then, though the alarmed neighborhood did not know it.

Following the Greensville cavalry, other militia units poured into the county during the next two days, and U. S. Marines from Norfolk. At Fortress Monroe Robert E. Lee, a young army officer, prepared to leave with his company if needed. No more forces were needed. The two men who had escaped with The Preacher were captured. Many who followed the leader during the successful stages of Monday had returned to their homes. They were hunted down, some killed and others taken to jail. But The Preacher eluded them until the beginning of October.

While changing hiding places on another Sunday, he encountered a poor farmer in some woods. Like his neighbors, this Mr. Phipps was carrying a gun when he came upon the ragged, emaciated, and wretched-looking Preacher, who immediately surrendered.

No demonstration was made against The Preacher when he was brought to jail or when he and fifty-two others were brought to trial. Of these, seventeen were hanged and twelve transported. Of five free Negroes among them, one was acquitted, the others sent to Superior Court, where one more was acquitted and three convicted. All convictions were based upon cross-evidence given by white people and the Negroes participating. The Preacher confessed fully to his leadership and to the details of the murder of more than fifty white people.

With The Preacher's execution, the case was closed and entered the record books as Nat Turner's Rebellion.

In history, the unelaborated reference to "Nat Turner's Rebellion" has been made so casually for so long that the tag has no association with the terror and horror of mass murder. Also, to the population of the United States today the slave insurrection in Haiti is a remote thing, part of the inevitable and the just march of events. But to the South, where white refugees had fled—at least one to Southampton County—the Haiti massacre was the dread reminder of what could happen to them. With Nat Turner, it *had* happened. The deep fear of the blacks' uprising against them had been implanted. It was never to leave.

3

The fears following the mass murders did not turn into recrimination against Negroes, though slaves and freed Negroes were treated with a new strictness. Primarily the effect in Virginia was an aroused demand for abolition *and* deportation. Southern emancipationists wanted the alien and potentially hostile race removed from its borders.

In the 1831–32 session of the Virginia Assembly, which convened four months after the insurrection, the passionate debates between planters and yeomen over slavery foreshadowed at a state level, and prophesied in detail, the way the whole sectional struggle would center on slavery with the onus on the South. A legislator from the democratic, non-slaveholding Western counties gave the ominously accurate warning that slavery would provide the rest of the country with a crusade "in the name of liberty but with the purpose of plunder . . ." in which the South would be held up ". . . as the common enemies of men whom it will be a duty to overthrow and a justice to despoil."

Despite the warnings and the zeal of the native emancipationists, their movement within the South was given a sharp check by Garrison's abolitionist *Liberator*, first published in the same year as the insurrection. To the horror of the Virginia governor who read it, and the legislators to whom he passed on the small paper, the *Liberator* approved of the Negroes' race warfare against fellow Americans. Later abolitionist broadsides urged the slaves to do more of the same. Once the native emancipationists could be tarred with the same brush as the hostile outsiders, their movement became suspect to a people grown so nervous that practically every stranger in the neighborhood was arrested as an agent of Northern saboteurs. Some of the arrested men were accused by the Negroes of having tried to incite them. At the beginning, on a local level, reason became dominated by fear, and passions inflamed by hatred.

Simultaneously the big planters, aroused to defense of their baronies by both the local and the "foreign" emancipationists, found an eloquent spokesman for their own cause in the unlikely person of a scholarly recluse. Young Thomas R. Dew was a gentle and likable professor at, of all places, William and Mary—the college of Jefferson and of the enlightened humanism of George Wythe and St. George Tucker.

Though born in a plantation background, Professor Dew had no personal stake in slavery and the series of articles he wrote for a Richmond paper were purely an intellectual exercise. Influenced by his studies in Germany, where he had gone for his health, the tubercular young scholar based his defense of slavery on the Germanic theory of superiority of the race. Going along with Jefferson on the ideal of a society producing superior individuals—as his own small colony had produced in the great Virginia dynasty—Dew gave economic, biblical, and philosophic reasons to support his theory that a slave-based society was best fitted to achieve this ideal. It was the Greek ideal, where a society would avoid the turmoil of a restless proletariat (the bugbear of the planter) and the superior individual would be given the best opportunity to emerge.

Until 1831, the South had not been particularly self-conscious about slavery. With the collection into book form of Professor Dew's articles, the philosophy was first articulated which identified Southern civilization permanently with slavery. Dozens of professors rallied to Dew's support and spread his doctrines. Outstanding among his disciples was Beverley Tucker, also at William and Mary, the son of the great humanist and the half brother of Mad Jack Randolph, the Randolph of Roanoke who manumitted his own slaves. Tucker's passion was the Southern aristocratic republic. In defending slavery as necessary for it, he wrote a polemical novel, *The Partisan Leader*, in which he correctly prophesied the national split and the coming war. (The book was later used in the North as an expression of Southern secession sentiment.)

From 1832, professors began to inculcate students with the defense of slavery as the basis of their superior, hedonistic civilization, which repudiated the industrialized, money-dominated, Puritan-influenced democracy of the North. With all the other elements of division between the sections, the disciples of Thomas R. Dew distilled the essence of the differences in an ideal of vivid appeal to young men of the ruling class.

The South, with its contempt for the wisdom of majorities, did not believe in common education, and at the school age had proportionately fewer children in school than the North; but, in its belief in educating the aristocracy for rule, it had proportionately more students in college than the North. Since their education was almost entirely in the classics, the young princelings were familiar with Plato's Greek Republic—founded securely on a slave class—and they were proud to belong to a civilization based on the Greek ideal.

At the bottom of everything in the South, as the cold war was joined, was a fear of the Negro, while the youth of the ruling class was aroused with the need to defend slavery in order to sustain their stabilized civilization against the surgent, antithetical power of the North.

Other elements were developing at the same time to deepen the division between the sections. The stream of immigration started to pour in to provide pools of cheap labor for Northern manufacturing; the use of the Erie Canal and the building of railroads would connect and ally the Northern money combines with the growing Midwest; and all over the North a rash of isms broke out with a vague messianic urge to cure the ills of mankind, all of which were ultimately to unite in the single cause of "freeing the slaves." Most directly of all, the Northern manufacturers, in their design of exploiting the agricultural South, had already caused tariff measures to be passed which were harmful to the Southern economy—particularly in South Carolina.

There was one man in the South who did clearly understand the nature of all the gathering forces that would threaten the planters' semitropical Greek Republic. But he too, though born outside the plantation world, had fallen under its spell and ultimately he staked his life on the slavery that supported it. This was John C. Calhoun, that tormented contradiction—a South Carolina Puritan.

With Calhoun, the power in the South shifted from conservative Virginia, with its Jeffersonian humanizing influences, to the imperious city-state of Charleston, South Carolina, and to the Bourbons of the new Cotton Kingdom along the Mississippi and the Gulf.

CHAPTER II

"The South . . . the Poor South . . ."

JOHN C. CALHOUN has been pinned on history's wall as the leader of a doomed cause, but it was more the Southern statesman himself who was doomed. The dour and ambitious Scotch-Irishman from South Carolina's upcountry had no affinity for lost causes. There was none of the quixotic romanticism of the rebel in his disciplined and logical mind, no flair for colorful action ever revealed in the tortuous course which events forced him to follow. From first to last, it would seem that Calhoun was a man who had very little fun in his life.

One of the outstanding figures in Washington for more than three decades, he served his country as senator, Secretary of War and of State, and twice as Vice-President—the only man in American history to hold that office under two Presidents—but three times failed of the top prize for which his heart yearned. One of the country's great Nationalists, truly dedicated to the young nation's expansion, he was tapped by fate to handle the issue that formally opened the cold war between the sections.

The issue presented Calhoun by his constituents was to defend a state's nullification of a federal law, with the implication of secession. Though his issue was unrelated *as an event* to the effects in Virginia of Nat Turner's Insurrection, those aroused supporters of the aristocratic republic, such as Beverley Tucker at William and Mary, recognized that Calhoun had joined the same defensive fight and rallied to him. In his forty-ninth year, at the peak of his powers and national prestige, Vice-President to Andrew Jackson and heir apparent to the succession, John C. Calhoun was forced to turn and lead the South's long rear-guard action, which began with South Carolina.

He was a complex of contradictions. This political leader of the South's most forthrightly aristocratic state was born in modest circumstances in the back country that was frontier when he grew up in the post-Revolutionary years. A spokesman for the planter class, he had worked hard for his education at Yale and in law at Litchfield, Connecticut. The slaves he later acquired from his earnings in law signalized his arrival in the ruling class rather than represented a true personal interest in plantation economy. In the same way his home, a glorified frame farmhouse, was decorated with the symbolic white columns. Finally, married into the Charleston society famed for its gracious and cosmopolitan living, Calhoun neither drank, danced, nor smoked, never read for pleasure or attended the theater; though his somewhat monologuist conversation was brilliant, Mrs. Jefferson Davis remembered that he seldom laughed.

Without formal religious affiliation, he led what was called a godly life and was a devoted family man. Essentially, however, his private life was absorbed in his public life. There could never be the personal anecdotes about Calhoun which flavored the careers of his rivals—New Hampshire's Daniel Webster, with his persuasive rhetoric, and Kentucky's Henry Clay, with his wanton charm. Yet, coming along in an age of giants, the Palmetto Puritan stood among them as an equal.

His political mastery of South Carolina was so complete that it was said, "When Calhoun took snuff, South Carolina sneezed." Yet, as a state historian has pointed out, "he had to be careful of the brand." He could only guide the course of the baronial rulers, not lead them. Nobody could.

The Britishers who adventured, mostly by way of West Indian plantations, to the South Carolina low country—that 160-mile strip from the coast inland for fifty miles—had come with the same aristocratic dream that motivated the settlers at Jamestown. The much-publicized Huguenots who came later for religious freedom were largely people of superior backgrounds who readily subscribed to the prevailing tradition. The democratic philosophizing of the Virginia Jeffersonians made little impression on the baronies of rice planters in the water-drained, malarial lowlands of South Carolina.

There existed the plantations of the legend—like that of Nathaniel Heyward, descendant of the Signer, who owned over two thousand people. Those isolated and slumbrous domains, where the planter was the only law, made of the South Carolinian a power peculiarly unadaptable to subservience to another's will. Since his group produced a magnificent society, it also made him scornful of the will that sought to impose itself on him.

His society was centered in Charleston which, unlike any other city in American history, was similar to a city-state composed of small duchies. For Charleston was the planters' city. It was not a city to which they came: they owned it. The planters' houses were there, half their time and all their social seasons were spent there, and the businesses of the city, factorage and shipping, were operated for them. The wharves were on the rivers that flanked the city, and a wide promenade, the famed Battery, faced the bay which sent its salt breezes to mingle with the fragrance of the gardens.

Northern visitors were apt to find the city exotic, with its pastel-colored houses facing sidewise to the street and their walled gardens. But Charleston never set out to be the America of factories and immigrants and nationalistic sweeps. It set out to provide a center for its plantation masters. With a total lack of hypocrisy about democratic dreams and equality, the city expressed their rare and urbane culture, characterized by gaiety and learning and gracious manners, and of course proud independence of spirit.

John C. Calhoun was not born to this bland and privileged society. He had won his way into it from his beginnings as a representative of the back country, and all was not moonlight and roses between the proud city-state and Calhoun's native frontier country. Dissatisfaction with the planters' rule was so great among those yeomen that by mid-century forty per cent of South Carolina's native stock was to migrate out of the state. Then, many brains in the low country perceived other alarming portents of the state's decline. Charleston was being passed by New Orleans as a port. Even in planting, with rice growing permanently limited to the waterways, the dynamic crop of South Carolina cotton was being left behind by the crops of the new states to the lower South. Everything pointed to the need of change, except the perfected idyl of plantation life.

Against this idyl came a direct threat from the central government, in the form of high tariff on imports protective to Northern manufacturing. President Jackson's ruinous "tariff of abominations" would virtually force the agrarians to exist for the financial well-being of factory owners. This discriminatory tariff became the amalgam of all other external grievances and internal problems, and the rulers set themselves to resist its application to South Carolina.

When Calhoun was handed the explosive issue of nullifying a federal law while serving as Vice-President, he also suffered a division within his state between the planters of his acquired class and the yeomanry of his native section. This division was both sharp and violent, for while the moderates were "Unionists," the "Nullifiers" stood ready (some eager) for secession in 1831.

In the low-country plantations there were no mystic bonds with the forty-two-year-old Union, younger actually than Calhoun himself. Certainly the "democratic" hordes who descended like the Goths on Washington with Andrew Jackson were scarcely calculated to kindle any affection for the central government. Even before the advent of the President with his harmful tariff, a liberal educator had said, "It is time to calculate the value of the Union." Since Jackson, newspaper articles had urged resistance, armed if necessary, to federal encroachments; and Robert Barnwell Rhett, vehement editor of the *Mercury*, and obsessed with the vision of an independent South Carolina, stormed the country-side like a road-company Patrick Henry.

It was this extreme view, essentially of the planter interest rather than of the state, which Calhoun, the great Nationalist, was required to represent. Though, like all those under the spell of the land, his native soil was his first love, the Palmetto Puritan was no secessionist. Also he was supposed to represent the whole state, and he had his presidential aspirations to think about. Yet he could not ask the grandees to adapt to national measures for the commercial benefit of other sections, nor did he believe that they should. His analytical brain must have recognized that the assignment was an impossible one, for of all things Calhoun was logical—and the situation was not.

2

In trying to temporize at home and to tread softly in Washington, so as not to endanger his own career, Calhoun lost all his usual adroitness. The skill of long experience in politics deserted him. He turned his gift for finespun abstractions to a tenuous constitutional defense while uneasily waiting on that dictatorial pragmatist, President Jackson.

As demands from South Carolina grew more violent and talk of the rights of Nullification became the critical topic in Washington, there were ample evidences that the wind was blowing against him. Calhoun persevered in the face of the warnings which his intelligence must have shown him, waiting with mounting anxiety for his boss, the President, to reveal his feelings on Nullification.

Jackson showed his hand with dramatic suddenness, and cruelly to Calhoun who, as Vice-President, stood in line of presidential succession. At a large dinner party in a public place famous in the times, the tough-bitten ex-frontier hero faced Calhoun directly as he proposed a toast.

"Our Union," he said, "it must be preserved."

That was his answer to the secession implied in Nullification: without that threat, to nullify a federal law would be an empty protest.

Calhoun took it manfully. He answered, "To our Union, next to our liberties, most dear."

It no longer mattered what he said. The stand on which he represented his state had been denied, and Jackson soon made his meaning even more explicit. Dismissing Calhoun's brilliant logic, he said he simply would not tolerate nullifying, and if South Carolina attempted secession, he would conquer the state by force.

From this shattering defeat for his state, Calhoun then watched the castle of his presidential aspirations tumble around his head. Everything turned against him. His wife, bringing to Jackson's "democratic" Washington the social standards of Charleston's Battery, cut a former tavern-keeper's daughter, the celebrated Peggy Eaton, whose husband was a close personal friend of the President. Political rivals raked up old scores to poison the mind of Jackson, a dedicated hater, against Calhoun. The South Carolinian himself fumbled from one maladroit act to another, sealing his doom as the President's successor.

With his position lost, Calhoun's poise went with it. He climaxed his series of untypical blunders by the unheard-of act of resigning as Vice-President of the United States.

Under the terrible ordeal, the Nationalist and back-country defender of the planters' class broke physically. Before the strain he had presented a striking figure in the capital. Standing six feet two, lean and erect, he moved in vigor and pride. Though no beauty, he had a full, resolute mouth, dark hair, and fine bright eyes, looking confidently and directly at the world in an intensity then described as "lustrous." Within two years, he was stooped, pale, and tortured-looking, on the way to becoming the specter by which history knows him. The smooth black hair became a gray mop on his head, the formerly lustrous eyes stared fiercely out of sunken sockets, hollows ravaged his cheeks, and his mouth, thinned into a wide line, turned down at the edges above newly sprouted chin whiskers.

This physical break reflected the collapse not only of his presidential ambitions but of his career as an American Nationalist. In the crisis, he had been forced to choose between his state and his nation in one of the most fateful and symbolic choices in American history. For Jackson's denial of the abstract rights of Calhoun's state was based on the principle of force and not, as Calhoun saw it, on constitutional interpretations of the young confederation of united states groping toward self-understanding and mutuality of interests.

Jackson sent men-of-war to Charleston Harbor and threatened that within forty days he could invade South Carolina with fifty thousand men. This application of might, in enforcement of a law harmful to Calhoun's home state, defied all the intellectual reasoning on which Calhoun had built his nationalism. To him always the government was to protect all members of the confederation, not some at the expense of others.

If the Minute Men of South Carolina had had their way, over the opposition of the unionists within the state, the Civil War would have started right then, in 1832. Calhoun took no important part in the resolution of the deadlock between Jackson and the Bourbons.

Henry Clay, the Virginian who went to Kentucky for opportunity and found it, solved the problem short of shooting. Clay, the brilliant and warmhearted presidential aspirant, reflected the views of the border states in the conflict between the North and the South. Always believing in a union in which no section rose at the expense of another, as a neutral

Clay always advocated compromise. He proposed a reduction of the tariff, which would save South Carolina's face as well as economic situation, in exchange for the state's rescinding of the Ordinance of Nullification.

When this was done (March 15, 1833), Calhoun breathed no sigh of relief. Then returned to Washington as South Carolina's senator, the broken man recognized that nothing had been solved by the application of might to a principle. South Carolinians would never forget it. The seed of disunion there had been firmly planted. Worse, the principle of might for the majority definitely threatened the culture of the South, then becoming a numerical minority.

"The struggle," he said, "far from being over, is only beginning."

3

For that struggle, at fifty-one John C. Calhoun dedicated his remaining years to a defense of his beloved minority within the whole. In his vision of the industrial, competitive North existing happily with the agrarian, aristocratic South, like the lion lying down with the lamb, Calhoun possessed a gorgeous if impractical concept of union. His ideas on minority rights were extremely advanced, but he put the South essentially on the defensive when he identified its culture with an institution against which public opinion was rising

Born of the eighteenth-century world of the old, passing America and in thrall to the plantation ideal, Calhoun saw no wrong in the institution which supported his civilization. With his logical mind limited by this provincialism, Calhoun set out to develop sectional allies for his state—to form, what had never existed in the South, a sectional political party.

Calhoun's natural allies were in the new states of the lower South, then bursting from the frontier into its full, lush, and, as it was to happen, brief bloom. Though the span of a mortal would more than cover the birth, flowering, and death of the fabled Cotton Kingdom, then the new Bourbons thought it would last forever. In the flush of their new power the Cotton Princes had no interest in the Democratic Party—Jackson's frontier "democrats" and big-city politics. They joined the Whig Party which, led by Compromiser Clay, allied gentlemen of property from both sections. For them the moderately states' rights Whig, planter, and Episcopalian stood as the pillar of aristocratic conservatism.

But Calhoun was given a national "issue"—the first of the grim concatenation—which served to unite Southerners regardless of political parties. The issue was Texas (1836), that republic, won from Mexico, which wanted to enter the Union as a Southern (i.e., slaveholding) state. While the Southern leaders welcomed a new state, which would maintain their numerical equality in the Senate, the Northern powers, wanting to break the balance, fought it on the ground that it would extend "The Slave Power"—one of the most effectively sinister phrases ever attributed to "Anon." They had no constitutional ground for objecting, since the Missouri Compromise (1820) had established the legality of slavery in all new territory west to the Pacific and south of the lateral from the southern boundary of Missouri.

At the time of the Missouri Compromise, anti-slavery Thomas Jefferson, old and dying in his debt-ridden hilltop mansion, had warned the Southerners in Washington that they were making a mistake. Jefferson said that if the South allowed a precedent which admitted the restriction of slavery anywhere, a principle would have been established and the North would use it in gradual encroachments for the restriction of slavery everywhere. Only sixteen years later, his prophecy came true over the admission of Texas and with the rise of an anti-slavery bloc in Washington.

Calhoun fought for the admission of Texas as a Southern state for eight years, 1836 to 1844, and won. He was returned to power by Virginia's Tyler, whose Secretary of State he became in 1844. Then in his sixty-third year, Calhoun was old for his time, half sick and haunted, like a man whom death is upon. However, he recaptured his earlier adroitness. Freed of the divisions of the Nullification fight, he spoke more frankly and more passionately of secession—though this was essentially a threat. He still worked for a South secure within the Union.

Calhoun, as a skillful maneuverer, had operated on solid ground in bringing in a Southern state to maintain the political equilibrium. Then the issues began to come too fast for him, as the undeclared struggle swept more into the open over the increasingly used question of slavery. Actually the next issue caught him, and all Southerners, unaware.

It came about during the Mexican War, in the administration of Tennessee's Polk (1845–49), which was dedicated to national expansion. The Westerners thought Polk had been less aggressively interested in their expansions, in Oregon and California, than in the Southerners' movements in the Southwest. The Westerners held a long resentment anyway, because the Southerners chronically opposed internal improvements at government expense for the Midwest and free lands to immigrants. To retaliate, the Westerners made a new issue over slavery in order to create trouble for Southern projects.

As their hatchet man the Westerners selected David Wilmot, and you will look in vain for national monuments to this political hack from Pennsylvania. Yet, with one unexplainable gesture, he contributed more to the sectional war than any dedicated patriot. As Wilmot had been an administration wheel horse, his independent act is obscure as to motive, except that he was aware of carrying out the Westerners' spitefulness.

Specifically (in 1846), to an appropriations bill for the purchase of territory from Mexico, the former wheel horse attached a "proviso" which forbade slavery in *any* of the new territory to be obtained from Mexico. This territory included what is today New Mexico, Arizona, and southern California, and the exclusion of slavery there clearly violated the Missouri Compromise. But ominously this bill passed in the House, and in the Senate only the aroused Southerners narrowly prevented its becoming law.

This Wilmot Proviso alarmed and enraged Southerners of all persuasions. It showed the most Union-loving Nationalists that they were in a fight against containment. The Southern states were to be restricted to their present territory while the North gained new states which would give it majority power. However, when the younger men perceived what Calhoun had long before understood, the aging South Carolinian could not create any united purpose or action among the fiercely proud individualists.

At that stage, his long absorption in abstractions began to carry him into the realm of constitutional principles. In his defense, he was not uniting his section in practical terms but trying to force its leaders into a political counteroffensive. He explained his tactics in a letter to an Alabama legislator.

If the South had backed him in 1835, he wrote, "when the spirit of abolitionism first developed, to any considerable extent, I would then have forced the issue on the North. It is a true maxim in politics as well as war to meet danger on the frontier. . . . We must look far beyond the Wilmot Proviso. It is but one of many acts of aggression . . . and I would regard any compromise . . . which did not meet . . . the danger in its whole length and breadth, as very unfortunate for us."

This belated recognition of Jefferson's warning of 1820 was a desperate effort to turn back the clock. His counteroffensive must suddenly demand slavery *any*where, since the Wilmot Proviso—disregarding all former agreements—would prohibit it *every*where. If the Wilmot Proviso said, in effect, that the North's way must obtain in all the new territory of the common country, the Southerner must answer that his way had as much right anywhere. Though this position might appear just in the abstract, as long as Calhoun accepted slavery as the natural order, it was out of tune with the times.

In the twenty-six years since Jefferson had warned Southerners against the Missouri Compromise, a generation of Northern politicians had developed who accepted the restriction of slavery as a fact, and a breed of politician had arisen to use the issue for personal, party, and sectional advantage. The territory north of the slave-free line was not designed by nature to support a slave-labor economy, and most of the immigrants shifting westward above the Ohio River were forthright advocates of social democracy. As it was not possible that any of those territories would enter the Union as slave states, Calhoun's "issue" over slavery became essentially a Southern principle.

In committing the South's defense to this principle, Calhoun, with all his impressive structure of constitutional legalities, actually committed the South to the abstract right of slavery everywhere. With that, any enemy could cloak his motives in the mantle of "freedom" and appear as a crusader.

Though younger Southern leaders were not unmindful of that, they had nothing constructive to offer. They were all working as individuals, conditioned by their own states. Despite Calhoun's long effort to unite his section, there was no agreement on either strategy or tactics when the next issue—both a practicality *and* a principle—was thrust upon them.

4

Though the southern part of the new territory of California lay undeniably within the limits of legal slavery, the inhabitants of southern California voted with the rest of the territory to enter the Union as a single free state. With the sectional lines then sharply drawn, the Northern powers immediately sought to admit the whole territory as a single state on their side. With this Calhoun, even without unity among Southerners, decided the showdown had come.

He was back where he had started the long rear-guard action, at the height of his powers and beckoning future in 1832. In 1848–49, ill and feeble, approaching his sixty-eighth year with all his personal dreams ashes behind him, the South's first sectionalist determined that he would not die in defeat over the cause to which he had dedicated his later life. He stood ready at last to execute the long-held threat of secession, if California was admitted as a single free state in denial of all former sectional agreements.

With his failing strength, he tried desperately to arouse Southern leaders to their danger, accurately predicting that if the South conceded California the North would never cease encroachments until the Southern states were contained and their civilization legislated out of existence.

Many leaders and individuals were aroused by Calhoun, but the people could not be unified. Cotton was high. For some plantation powers of the New South, threats to their system seemed remote and unreal against the tangibles of following a big crop of cotton down the river to New Orleans for a blowout in town and some fancy shopping for the family. In the Old South, where economy was shifting from the big crop to a more diversified system (including even the dread industry), ties remained strong with the Union. Throughout the area the yeoman, without stake in slavery, saw no threat to his life. If a Southerner first, he was an American too.

In politics the younger leaders, then emerging, represented all shadings of the Southern position, largely though not entirely determined by the viewpoint of their immediate region. The three who were to become outstanding, all in their thirties, were in Congress in 1845—Georgia's Bob Toombs, Mississippi's Jefferson Davis, and Alabama's William Lowndes Yancey. Of these, only the handsome Davis gave a full discipleship to Calhoun, while the golden-tongued Yancey completely repudiated the old leader, and the hearty, extroverted Toombs operated somewhere between the two.

Though all three had received at least part of their education in the North and each represented the planter interests, the men were never intimate. Indeed, after the Davises had shared a "mess" with the Toombs, those two men became definitely unfriendly; and Yancey soon left Congress to begin his own messianic and for a time virtually solitary course devoted to Southern independence.

This Yancey was a strange man, the nearest of the Southern leaders to fanaticism, a zealot who renounced political ambition. He had grown up in the South Carolina upcountry of Calhoun, with whom his father had once shared a law office. At an early age, on the death of his father and remarriage of his mother, Yancey had been taken to Troy, New York, a community thriving on the new prosperity from the Erie Canal and a hotbed of the current isms. From there he went to New England's fine conservative Williams College but, as soon as he was on his own, the young Yancey fled to his native country, whose spell had never left him.

A brilliant trial lawyer and a newspaper editor, Yancey married a young lady of means and joined the trek to the new frontier in the Alabama canebrake country. Unlike Calhoun, Yancey did have fun. He always loved good horses, liked to live in style, and thoroughly enjoyed the avocational plantation he acquired as the frosting of his cake of success.

Yancey would have succeeded at anything. He was self-contained, industrious, and highly disciplined. He worked quickly up the planters' scale to a wisteria-, honeysuckle-, and wrought-iron-enclosed house on Perry Street in Montgomery, the state capital, with his plantation out of town. He was soon a voice of influence in planter politics—quite literally a "voice." In a region in which the spoken word was revered above all earthly things, in which all the political powers were great speechmakers, Yancey was recognized as the golden voice beyond compare.

In his phlegmatic self-containment and quietly courteous manner, there was nothing to suggest the orator. There was a foursquare solidarity about the man, with the level gaze of his eyes, the mouth wide and straight, the flat-topped head erect on his shoulders, and his hair, worn full over the ears, parted on one side and brushed across the scalp with a curl in the front like a bartender out of the nineties. Not tall, he was well developed and always neat about his person.

With a few drinks before a speech, some inner fire was released to bring a magic to his usually stolid presence. Outwardly he did not change. He made none of the theatrical gestures, as did Henry Clay, which were commonplace in his day, and could speak for hours in a space of one square yard. It was the words he spoke, and the voice, that magnetized an audience. Yancey spoke at those barbecues where the country people gorged themselves on hogmeat, slowly emerged from their torpor by cheering on participants in horse races, foot races, and like exercises, until they were receptive to the day's speakers. After these canebrake crowds had been spellbound by his magic, they rushed him through the state legislature to the U. S. Congress when he was only thirty.

There Calhoun, to befriend his old friend's son, offered him advice. Yancey had his own ideas. He soon became convinced that the difference between the sections, with the abolitionist bloc determined to destroy the Southern society, could not be resolved within the structure of the Union. He repudiated Calhoun's constitutionalities, with their design of maintaining an artificial balance, and believed the various compromises were merely makeshifts which did not reach to the core of the conflict.

Yancey left the Washington arena and Calhoun's rear-guard action with a dedication to the independence of the cotton states. He was too extreme for his fellow Alabamians at that time, but the stocky, stolid man worked skillfully and waited patiently for the people to catch up with him. He proselyted for converts at the various commercial conventions then meeting through the South to strengthen Southern economy and break the dependence upon the North. With the California dispute growing more acrimonious and tense, as neither Calhoun nor the anti-slavery men gave an inch, Yancey went further than Calhoun's position of secession *if* California was admitted: he stood for forthright Southern independence *then*.

5

Bob Toombs was of another breed altogether. With nothing fanatical about him, he most typified the planters' society and the joyous native love of their land. His only similarity to Calhoun was that he also began his political life as a Nationalist—only by 1845 it had come to be called "Unionist." As passionate as any of them for Southern rights, Toombs believed (as Calhoun had started by believing) that protection could be secured in the Union. He placed his faith for his section's safety in what he hoped would be the non-sectional Whig Party. This party of men of property was natural to Georgia planters, and Toombs was one of the few Southern leaders who was, as the saying goes, to the manor born.

He came from that fine plantation country up the Savannah River and, after a round of colleges (Georgia, Union in New York, University of Virginia), soon succeeded on his own in law and politics. He was a big fellow with big appetites, for food and drink, work and play, people and books, and he possessed a lot of the charm of vitaliy. Toombs might have traded at times on his somewhat overpowering personality, but he was smart. His weakness lay in the undisciplined quality of his assertive energy, a mixture of hormones and plantation privileges—what Mrs. Davis called a "lawlessness"—and he sometimes spoke with intemperateness.

When he came to Washington at thirty-five, a Whig Unionist, Bob Toombs scorned Calhoun's sectional party along with the old man's "principles" concerning slavery. He directed his awesome energies toward national financial matters and toward nationalizing the Whig Party. His first turn came over the Wilmot Proviso (1847), though even then he would have nothing to do with Calhoun's tortured logic on government compacts and minority rights.

Speaking for all moderate states' rights Southerners, he said simply that his people only "asked for an honest and honorable union . . ." and they "would remain on a ground of perfect equality with the rest of the Union, or they would not stay at all."

The very casualness of his mention of disunion showed how far the South had drifted toward sectionalism since Calhoun had begun his defense fifteen years before. It also showed how far apart the sections had drifted when this casualness made no deeper impression. Either the Northerners who continued what Southerners called "agitations over slavery" did not take seriously the talk of secession or they were themselves indifferent to disunion.

In either case, Toombs grew gradually alarmed for his section's safety within the Union and lost faith in the Whig Party's nationalism. By the time the issue over California reached its climax at the end of 1849, the genial Georgia Unionist had been driven almost as far as Calhoun—almost, but not quite. Toombs still would not secede over any issue, not even California's admission. But he said, "I am for disunion," if the North refused to make concessions and continued the aggressive acts which differentiated the South from the rest of the country, sectionalized it, and drove its people into defensiveness against the whole.

As the amalgam of warring forces concentrated on the issue of California in the early part of 1850, Toombs said vehemently, "This cry of the *Union* is the masked battery from behind which the Constitution and the rights of the South are to be assailed."

He stressed that the South "took the Union and the Constitution together—and we will have both or we will have neither. . . . We had our institutions when you sought our alliance. . . . We have not sought to thrust them upon you, nor to interfere with yours. . . ." When it is "demonstrated that the Constitution is powerless for our protection; it will then be not only the right but the duty of the slave-holding states to resume the powers which they have conferred upon this government, and to seek new safeguards for their future security."

Northern moderates believed Toombs, believed that he spoke for the Southern moderates who were open to compromise. But the moderates were not in power in either section; nobody was in power anywhere. The conflict, like a senseless argument that grows more serious on the exchange of words, was gathering its own momentum and nobody seemed to think of the consequences.

6

Trying to check what amounted by then to a force of nature, Calhoun had in Jefferson Davis a disciple with a strong natural affinity for the dying leader. Neither born to the purple like Toombs nor succeeding on his own like Yancey, Davis lacked the genial Georgian's tumultuousness and the golden-tongued's messianic zeal. The Mississippian was a product of the study, a triumph of disciplined will directed toward an ambition as cold as Calhoun's and along the mentor's line of political theory, constitutional abstractions, and principles of the rights of the plantation South. For Davis, without choice or intention, was a composite of that newly flowering cotton South—so new that in his own Mississippi not a leader was a native of the state and half of them were Northern immigrants.

Davis' own grandparents, Welsh immigrants, had migrated into the South from the Philadelphia area, and his father, typical of the unsuccessful yeomanry, wandered about until he settled his family briefly in Kentucky around the turn of the century. There, in 1808, Jefferson was born in modest circumstances not far from where Lincoln was born the next year. When he was still a child, the family moved to Mississippi, where his father, with the help of Jefferson's older brother, enjoyed more prosperity, though his farm was in no sense a plantation. Davis was sent for a while to a Dominican school in Kentucky, then to a school near home, and at thirteen he returned to Kentucky's Transylvania College, at that time boasting the largest enrollment in the country.

When Davis was sixteen, his father died and he came under the guardianship of his forty-year-old brother. Joseph Davis was just then reaching the peak of his own success in planting and speculation. An intelligent and shrewd man, with a taste for learning and plantation society, he held

vast ambitions for his appealing younger brother and sent him to West
Point. The appointment was signed by John C. Calhoun, then Monroe's
Secretary of War, back in the days of his own vaulting aspirations.

Though a mediocre student at the Point, Davis found the military life
to his liking, and formed lasting friendships with Albert Sidney Johnston
and Leonidas Polk. He also knew, without intimacy, two Virginians—
Joseph E. Johnston and Robert E. Lee.

As a young lieutenant, Davis performed the usual service at frontier
posts and would probably have continued in the army except for falling
in love with the commanding general's daughter. Zachary Taylor, a
planter aristocrat, didn't like the young officer as a son-in-law, and Davis
resigned from the army, taking his new bride to a Mississippi plantation
provided by his brother.

The couple were scarcely settled in the new life when she died of a
malarial fever which almost carried Davis off too. After a long recupera-
tive trip, Davis returned to his lonely paradise and there, at twenty-seven,
for the first time knew plantation society. At school during his family's
struggles and in the army during his brother's rise, Jefferson Davis entered
the planter world full-blown without roots in Mississippi or in any Southern society.

Unlike the other leaders, he could not know the structure of its life
from the inside out, the nature of its people. While Davis was as insulated
from the people as if he had been born in a highly protected aristocracy,
to him the aristocrat was a concept of the mind—and the planter class
which his brother opened to him was composed of new powers.

Many of these were people of native breeding, but some were pretty
crude customers. Whatever the cultural backgrounds of individuals and
the planters' code to which all subscribed, their society represented no
political-economic continuity—only an arrogant determination to defend
the semitropical splendor they had just achieved. Davis became their representative without having made the achievement.

He became their representative virtually as an idealistic amateur in the
world of tough-bitten men of affairs and politics—led by John Quitman
from New York, Jacob Thompson from North Carolina, and Albert Gal-
latin Brown, a son of one of those South Carolina yeomen who migrated
west for fortune. Though Whiggery was still the fashionable party for
planters, Davis, probably under the guidance of his astutely realistic
brother, joined the Democratic Party of these new Bourbons. Before he
became active, the young widower had spent his solitude in study, absorbing the ready-made Calhounian doctrines on the defense of the South.

When Davis emerged as a spokesman for his brother's practical friends,
he was an engaging personality, an imposing presence, and he looked
"quality." He was tall and lean, with a fine military carriage, and his well-
formed features were sharply defined. In his mid-thirties, he then pos-

sessed a natural buoyancy. The ideas in his speeches were well arranged and carefully thought out, and he spoke with a ringing sincerity. He had married again, a handsome, intelligent woman of fine background (her grandfather had been governor of New Jersey), and when the young couple went to Washington, it was obvious that the new congressman was on his way to a brilliant career.

The Mexican War gave the first big jump to this promising career. Resigning his seat in Congress, he led a regiment of Mississippi Volunteers, as whose colonel he performed so handsomely in action that General Taylor—his former, reluctant father-in-law—cited him for conspicuous courage and gallantry. Davis' political crony, Albert G. Brown, was then governor, and he sent their imposing spokesman back to Washington to fill an unexpired term in the Senate. Returning to Washington as a hero on crutches (he had been wounded in the foot), the new senator was drawn into the bitter conflict over California and all the implications of this test.

It was a time of great changes in the country. Mrs. Davis had paid, as she said, her "two bits, to see Mr. Morse's machine make the wires talk." She had also heard of a new sewing machine "that stitches like the handwork." They heard of all manner of new inventions—the rotary press and typesetting machines, electric motors and Otis elevators, power looms and Goodyear rubber patents.

Most significant of all for the South was a machine invented by a young Virginian with the help of one slave in a shed outside the little Shenandoah Valley town of Lexington (where another ex-Mexican War hero, Major Thomas J. Jackson, U.S.A., had taken a professor's job at V.M.I.). McCormick's reaper with machine farming was making a grain empire of the Midwest to rival the slave-farmed cotton empire of the South. Also, where the Cotton Kingdom extended in individualistic waves from the worn-out lands of the coastal slave states, the new grain empire extended from *and interrelated with* the money powers of the East, in their new growth in textile mills, coal production, interlocking railroads and in the application of automatic machinery and interchangeable parts.

These were the portents of the future America, of a scientific and mechanical democracy in vast and complex interrelation of money power, where there could be no room for a slave-based, agricultural aristocracy. Against this grim outlook, Jefferson Davis unhesitatingly threw his support to Calhoun, of the old, passing order which supported their idyl. Adopting the old man's strategy of "holding the enemy at the frontier" by refusing to concede the prohibition of slavery anywhere, he opposed the admission of California as a free state or any compromise involving it.

As Calhoun's spokesman, Davis demanded that the originally agreed-upon boundary of 36° 30′ for slavery continue to the Pacific, including southern California; that a slaveowner could take his property into any

U.S. possession; and that "agitation" over slavery in the District of Columbia and over interstate slave trade within the South must cease. His summaries, while adding nothing new, went to the core of the issue.

"It is a struggle for political power [where] concession has been ever the precursor of further aggression, and the spirit of compromise has diminished as your relative power has increased. The sacrifices which the South has at other times made to the fraternity and tranquility of the Union are now cited as precedents against her rights."

Then Davis joined those voices which calmly accepted the alternative of secession to further compromise. "If the folly and fanaticism and pride and hate and corruption of the day are to destroy the peace and prosperity of the Union, let the sections part like the patriarchs of old and let peace and good will subsist among their descendants."

As the spokesman for Calhoun's doctrines, Davis showed how far apart the sections had drifted in the two decades since Nullification. That the conviction behind his words went unheeded showed that the conflict was gathering between forces which daily grew more antithetical.

In the winter of 1849-50, the voices of Yancey and the other demagogues bugled through the warm afternoons in the cotton South. Even in the old, conservative upper South newspapers blazoned appeals for secession as alternatives to accepting a Union with sections that waged an undeclared war on their civilization. These papers and leaders, like Toombs, were still open to compromise. The Northern powers were not offering any.

Against this adamant attitude over California, the issue which Calhoun had decided was the showdown, the aged leader made a last desperate appeal to the South. Stooped and bent, moving slowly in his lank, dark clothes, shivering in the damp blasts from the Potomac when he needed the healing warmth of his plantation, Calhoun urged the formation of a bloc for the purpose of considering secession. Then Mississippi called a Southern Convention to meet in June in Nashville to discuss the course of action. Calhoun had not united his people even yet in a single purpose, but they were aroused to sectional consciousness and to their danger.

Suddenly it looked as though, without some concessions from somewhere, the sixty-one-year-old Union was ready to be dissolved.

7

At this deadlock, seventy-two-year-old Henry Clay stirred from the retirement which he had already begun in Kentucky. Once Calhoun's ally as "young war hawks" in the long-ago War of 1812, long his political rival and personally contemned by the hot-country Puritan for his lascivious turns, the warmhearted Clay came once more to Washington to offer a compromise between Calhoun's section and the others—for the good of the whole.

As a border-stater and virtually a neutral, Clay suggested that California should come in as a single free state, since that was the manifest will of the inhabitants. By the same token, slavery should not be prohibited in the territories of New Mexico and Utah, but their inhabitants should decide. Further to placate the South, Clay suggested the continued legality of slaveholding in the District of Columbia, continued slave trade within the Southern states, and more stringent fugitive slave laws to prevent Northerners from helping runaways and stolen Negroes to escape.

The Compromise of 1850 offered the South nothing in practical terms, and Calhoun knew it. Daniel Webster, his friendly sectional rival and spokesman for New England, also knew it. But, convinced that Calhoun was fighting over an empty principle and confident that the future belonged to his own industrial world, Webster wanted to avoid the showdown.

In one of his greatest speeches he supported Clay's Compromise, knowing that it resolved nothing. He said that no Wilmot Provisos were needed to permit slavery where it was against nature, and time would resolve the issues. He spoke in friendly terms and so eloquently of "Union" that even Southerners were moved.

Northerners were not. Webster was excoriated in New England for offering the South any concessions. The extremists (expressing their cold confidence in the cynicism, "look at the census returns") revealed the uncompromising attitude which Calhoun had predicted the North would show when it felt sufficiently strong.

Calhoun could look at those census returns too, and he knew another compromise would only postpone the hour of doom for his land. When he prepared his answer to Clay and Webster, the clarity of his logical mind was breaking under the prolonged strain. In fear of his civilization's being engulfed in the tidal wave of industrial democracy and unable to conceive that others could not recognize the necessity for preserving his stabilized agricultural society, the dying South Carolinian spoke for a past dying with him. Not only rejecting Clay's compromise, he wanted constitutional amendments to restore sectional equilibrium. In his last struggle for his minority, he sought to undo by legislation what geography had done in giving the North a controlling majority.

He was too ill to read his own speech and came wrapped in blankets to the chambers which had been like a home to him. His words were received with great respect, and changed nothing. Calhoun tacitly accepted defeat in this, his last, act in the U. S. Senate.

Back in his room in Mrs. Hill's famous boardinghouse on F Street, where his long friend Webster visited him for the last time, the master of abstruse logic seemed to wander off into fantasy. He wrote memoranda

suggesting two presidents—one from the slave states, one from the free—
each with a veto power. That was nearly one hundred years before the
United Nations set up machinery for the protection of minority states.

Then to his friend, James Mason of Virginia, he said, "The Union is
doomed to dissolution. . . . The probability is that it will explode in an
election within twelve years."

On the last day of March, when death came to the long-suffering
Nationalist who had turned to the defense of his land, the back of resistance was broken for the Southern non-compromisers. Basically the people
were still Unionists. State legislatures adopted the Compromise and routed
the secessionists. In Mississippi, Jefferson Davis resigned from the Senate
to lead the non-compromisers locally, and was defeated for governor, as
well as vanishing from Washington. The June Nashville Convention,
where Yancey went, was a futile anticlimax. The Southern people settled
back with relief and, in a false sense of security, refused to see beyond
the high price of cotton.

Calhoun, in his final hour of defeat, regarded their shortsightedness
with infinite pity. Dying, he murmured, "The South . . . the poor
South . . ."

CHAPTER III

The Incidents

CALHOUN'S successor in Washington was forty-four-year-old Jefferson Davis, rescued from the temporary political oblivion, where the Mississippi compromisers had thrust him, by President Franklin Pierce (1853–57). When Davis was returned to Washington as Secretary of War by his White House friend, he said that the Compromise vote had showed him the will of the people and he assumed his new position with concentration on the national welfare rather than on sectional defense.

As Secretary of War, no appointee ever served the nation in peacetime better than the West Pointer from Mississippi. He loved the work, and the post, requiring neither flexibility of mind nor adaptability to situations as they arose, needed his type of disciplined mind which gave attention to details and operated smoothly in tables of organization. It required a bureaucratic rather than an original or intuitive mind, and Davis' intelligence—as well as his nature and training—were ideally suited to the War Office.

For Davis' intellect was basically a "made" product, as opposed to something that grew organically from its nature. It was an acquired product of his self-concept, a learned expression of his pride, a trained implement of his ambition, a part of his total concept of the aristocracy—which, in turn, he had been made through the circumstances of his brother's success and his own predilections. Many of the attributes of the aristocrat, such as a deep sense of honor and personal courage, were native to Jefferson Davis, and few patricians were more punctilious in the formalities of courtesy. Yet his character had not grown from the inside out, as an expression of the social structure which he represented.

Dedicated to the ideal of the planter South, which he (with many others) sincerely conceived of as a knighthood, Davis had first come to Washington as its spokesman for another man's ideas. With Calhoun's uncompromising stand politically repudiated, Davis turned to his new job as if the 1850 Compromise had settled the issue. At his physical and mental peak, he became the most powerful man in Pierce's administration.

At this pinnacle of his swift rise in national affairs, as all through his Washington career, Davis was blessed with a wife designed by nature to help a public personage. A handsome, even striking-looking woman rather than pretty, she was not petite and her features were large, though well formed. She had fine, dark hair, beautiful eyes, and a good figure. She and her husband set each other off well, and there was an air of pride about them as a pair.

Sometimes Mr. Davis grew touchy about his dignity, and Mrs. Davis, with a low threshold of tolerance for fools and bores, sometimes had the quality of her tact strained. Among friends they were a pleasing, interesting couple, and enjoyed many gay evenings in Washington society.

Varina Howell Davis came along at a time when Southern wives, with their trained social gifts, conducted salons of intimate political gatherings where a great deal was accomplished on policy and strategy levels. The native intelligence of Mrs. Davis was highly cultivated, she possessed a deep and knowledgeable interest in national affairs and a capacity for entertaining good minds. The antithesis of the legendary, wilting belle, Varina Davis was forthright and forceful, an energetic woman of strong character, and in her great, admiring love for "Banny" (as she privately called Mr. Davis) there was nothing of the clinging vine. Though eighteen years his junior, Varina Davis was truly the helpmate of her husband in the finest sense of the word, and never consciously failed him.

Where she failed him was in never turning her analytical gaze on the man she regarded as perfect, virtually godlike. She saw Jefferson Davis, without reservation, precisely and as largely as he saw himself.

2

While Davis was conscientiously performing his duties as the man closest to the President, the ill feeling between the sections grew and extremists maneuvered as if the 1850 Compromise had never happened. Clay and Webster died soon after Calhoun and, with the passing of the three great statesmen of an old America, no powerful voice spoke for the Union. Representatives from both sections seemed more interested in attacking the other side than in trying to resolve the difficulties; instead of avoiding incidents, they created them. In the North, sincere if fanatical abolitionists and opportunists alike used the slavery issue for political advancement. In the South, the voices of the zealots grew more passionate in their crusades for independence. Northern agitators gave them the ammunition.

When the Southern states had adopted the Compromise of 1850, the Georgia legislature summarized the attitude of them all. Serving notice that the preservation of the Union depended on the Northern states' faithfully abiding by the terms of the Compromise, the Georgia delegates stressed its particular application to the federal laws regarding fugitive slaves. This was a very real issue to the planters, and nothing so impressed the individual Southerner with Northern hostility as the protection given runaways in the North and the actual attacks on federal officials trying to enforce the laws on stolen property. No matter who was right, taking a man's livelihood away is a serious thing to do. On this last point, the Georgians stated, *"It is the deliberate opinion of this convention that upon the faithful execution of the fugitive-slave bill depends the preservation of our much loved Union."*

Yet, in the North, many people continued to repudiate and defy the fugitive slave laws, which constituted about the only thing the South got out of the Compromise. To the Southerners trying to promote secession, this breach of faith served to illustrate the little regard in which the North held Union.

Then Northern literature erupted into what amounted to an anti-Southern propaganda mill. In 1851 appeared *Uncle Tom's Cabin*, that inflammable work of the imagination, to start the decade in a spirit of recriminations. With the pamphlets and literature which took up where Mrs. Stowe left off, newspapers joined in the denunciations of their fellow Americans. To support the fictional pictures of the benighted Southerners, the New York *Tribune* stated flatly that plantations were "little else than Negro harems," and that, of Washington, Jefferson, Madison, Monroe, and Tyler (who was then still living) "hardly one has failed to leave his mulatto children."

Even Virginia, which produced these Presidents, had been brought to ruin by "pride and folly and . . . [Negro] concubinage . . ." while South Carolina, with its "chivalry-ridden inhabitants," like the other states, "is a full thousand years behind the North in civilization." Emerson and Longfellow, Lowell and Whittier, the new literary pillars of that civilization, conjured up pictures of the vileness of their Southern neighbors.

The Northern attitude warned all Southerners that, as Calhoun had contended, no peace had been made by the Compromise. The South remained on the defensive. Since the leaders had identified their total defense with slavery, nothing remained for them except to fight their counteroffensive with increasingly extreme demands based on the principles laid down by Calhoun.

By then these principles, of slavery in all territories, were definitely unrealistic and arrogant, as the agitations from the North became spiteful and frankly anti-sectional. It was the time when the national schizophrenia was nearing the point of explosion, and the President who was elected in

1852, the virtuous Franklin Pierce of New Hampshire, was scarcely fitted for the role of national psychiatrist.

Pierce had come in on the strange political alliance of Northern workers and the Southern planters who, finally giving up on the Whigs as a nationalistic party, had joined the Democrats. The President they agreed upon—by nature a conservative, rural New Englander—was close to the agricultural ideals of the South. Slavery as a support of Southern agriculture was more understandable and less obnoxious to him than the industrialization that was changing his old America as well as the South's. He was one of the non-abolitionists of the North (one of the men of tolerance who also opposed anti-Catholicism) and, like Southern Unionists, less effectual than the extremists. Trying to save a vanishing America, Pierce allowed himself to be influenced by the Southerners whom he understood personally—a switch in practical politics from the Whig effort of men of property working together across all borders.

The Southerner with the greatest influence, his friend Jefferson Davis, was acting only in naïve innocence when he used his personal influence with the President on what became a fateful measure. Completely without intention, Davis collaborated in setting in motion the incidents which carried the verbal issues of the complex quarrel into the physical conflict.

3

It all started when Davis planned what later became the Southern Pacific Railroad. To this end he had South Carolina's Gadsden purchase from Mexico for $10,000,000 the strip of land in southern Arizona and New Mexico through which a railroad would run connecting the new non-slaveholding state of California with New Orleans and Vicksburg or Memphis. Though in his plan Davis considered the advantages to the South, it was—as proven—sound for the nation.

Into this non-political venture came a joker, presented by a Midwest politician who was to figure as significantly in the South's history as any dedicated Southern patriot. This was Stephen A. Douglas, Democratic senator from Illinois, presidential aspirant, and Davis' unwitting collaborator in providing the incident which hastened the nation's duality toward the breaking point.

Senator Douglas was married to a Southern girl (niece of the later famous Confederate spy, Mrs. Greenhow), whose father had died in 1848 and bequeathed her his slaves. The Illinoisan took no political stand against the institution of his Democratic allies, though personally he wanted nothing to do with slaveholding. His investments were in land in the Chicago area, where the center of east-west commerce was shifting by way of the

Great Lakes tie-up with the Atlantic coastal cities, as the balance of power between the sections shifted north of the Ohio River from Clay's Kentucky to Douglas' Illinois.

With no more intention of provoking an incident than Davis, though with far more guile, Douglas suggested another railroad to the Pacific, which would have Chicago as its terminus. Though Douglas' interests in the northwestern railroad might have considered his constituents, as well as his family's security, both railroads were practical—indeed, inevitable. However, as a Democrat who wanted his mail delivered to the White House, Douglas could not risk antagonizing his political ally, Davis, and a dozen Southern states, by seeming to compete with their project. To show the Southerners that he had their interests at heart, Douglas offered them a sop.

The Illinois senator had evolved as his own contribution to compromise an idea called "popular sovereignty." Under that doctrine, each territory would come into the Union as a state, slave or free, according to the dictates of its own votes—a principle opposed to the abolitionists' prohibition of slavery *every*where. His sop to the South, then, would be a bill introducing popular sovereignty in the Nebraska territory, then being settled, and providing for two territories instead of one—Kansas and Nebraska.

It was a meaningless sop and the South needed nothing less than a reopening of the slavery issue. In this period (1854), Salmon P. Chase, the presidential-minded political abolitionist, wrote a friend, "Anti-slavery men should be constantly warned of keeping the anti-slavery idea paramount. There is *danger* of its being shoved aside."

As long as the individualistic South continued its struggle without a leader or a commonly held purpose, Chase's issues were in no danger of dying. When Douglas drafted his popular sovereignty bill for Kansas and Nebraska, two non-fire-eating Southerners, remote from history's pages, decided to make it stronger. They insisted, over Douglas' objections, that his bill specifically repudiate the Missouri Compromise and permit *no* boundary lines to apply to slavery.

Since Douglas and his foolish friends wanted the explosive bill to be an Administration measure, on a Sunday morning they called on Davis, the President's friend, to present it to Pierce. The devout Pierce never did business on Sunday, and Davis was asked not only to offer the bill to his friend in the White House but to presume on the friendship to gain an audience on the Sabbath.

It was at this moment in the quiet Sunday parlor that Davis revealed the limitations of acquired learning as against the instinct, the *feeling*, for a situation, which comes with a native flexible intelligence. For Douglas' sop, while flattering the followers of Calhoun's principles, was anything except a principle to that population in the new, the third, section of the country in the Midwest.

Composed of Swedes and Germans, migrant Easterners and three quarters of a million native-born Southerners (many of whom had migrated out of their region in opposition to the planter rule and slavery), this new population, unlike the strident abolitionists who were against slavery as they were against sin, opposed extending slavery into territories because of the practical risks of slave barons blocking off free land and of blacks' stigmatizing honest labor. With their dreams of a working democracy, the very idea of slavery was distasteful, and the presence of a slave society meant to them the proximity of the "concubinage" and loose morals depicted in the abolitionist literature.

These people, far more than the personally uninvolved Easterners, would react violently to any principle which considered the extension of slavery into territories, and these people comprised the bloc which swung the balance of power in the country. This balance of power arose when, with migration out of the South and foreign immigration into the Northern and Western sections, 6,000,000 of the 8,500,000 increase in the national population occurred *outside* of the Southern states.

Of all times the numerically inferior South, in its inelastic geographical boundaries, needed allies in addition to the Northern Democrats, and not the resurrection of a "principle" to alienate them. Jefferson Davis, perhaps with his human vanity flattered, missed the reality and took the abstraction.

He was pleased to call on his friend in the White House on a Sunday morning, where the genial President gave Administration support to the measure which entered history as the Kansas-Nebraska Bill. A Southern leader and a Midwest politician had inadvertently combined to give the abolitionists the issue they wanted, and that issue (the bill was passed in May 1854) resulted in the first actual incident of the cold war.

4

Neither Kansas nor Nebraska was practical for slave-labor plantations and few slaveholders lived in those territories. However, as many Southerners in Missouri, to the east of Kansas, would be active in Southern interests, the abolitionists selected Kansas as the battleground and left Nebraska to its fate. "The Crime against Kansas," they called it, as New England emigrant societies sent families out to prove that the territory belonged to freedmen. Between them and the pro-Southern men in the general area, the natural antagonisms led to ugly minor incidents. As each side included some tough customers, the incidents progressed into outbreaks of actual violence. When the usual assortment of transient ruffians common to all Western territories took sides more or less impartially, the clashes were exaggerated into minor holy wars.

When election time came, thousands of pro-Southern Missourians trekked across the state line to vote (as pro-Northern Iowans did in Nebraska) and their numbers were enough to elect a pro-slavery government. Not to be outdone, the anti-slavery men held an equally fraudulent election and came up with a "free" government. Thus, Kansas had two governments, neither representative of anything except the dishonesty with which a Washington "issue" was being fought on the land of innocent settlers. But with the two governments, things began to get out of hand.

A pitched battle was narrowly averted in Lawrence near the end of 1855, and then in May 1856 nearly a thousand armed pro-slavery men invaded the "treasonable" town, burning buildings and threatening the terrified citizens. The wanton act of hoodlumism made grist for the national anti-slavery propaganda mills and redounded to the discredit of the Southern "leaders" (who knew nothing about it) and to the Southern people as well.

At this time, the political machine long sought by the Eastern money powers took shape in the Republican Party. A hodgepodge of ex-Whigs, Free Soilers, Know Nothings, anti-Southern Democrats, abolitionists, the party was united by sectionalism and hostility to Southern interests. When the Lawrence raid was avenged by murders on Pottawatomie Creek, Republican newspapers, often propaganda outlets for the Kansas Free Staters, suppressed the facts.

While the raid on Lawrence had been no part of a "slave power" plot, the Kansas murderers were morally supported by New England abolitionists who felt that in this case at least they served the cause of Negro freedom by condoning the killing of Southern white people. The group they fostered was led by a paranoiac named John Brown.

This chronic failure, dishonest businessman, passer of bad checks, and repudiator of debts had a huge brood which he did little or nothing to support, while he read abolitionist literature and the Bible for inspiration for his vengeful crusade against slaveholders. Envenomed by failure and lack of recognition, the fifty-six-year-old fanatic focused all his hatred on people associated with slavery (they did not have to own slaves) and became Jehovah's sword against the wicked Southerners.

With his older sons as the nucleus of his band, John Brown began his crusade in Kansas. At Pottawatomie Creek, in a section which never before had experienced a killing in the "bleeding Kansas" strife, they descended on two pro-slavery families and killed five men and boys, mutilating their bodies.

In retaliation, pro-slavery men formed in a group and attacked the murderer's headquarters. In the shooting, one of Brown's sons was killed while guarding some stolen horses, and their place was burned. At this "unprovoked" crime against his kin, Brown swore eternal vengeance on the *whole* South and went back North with his grievances. There he held admirers spellbound with his bloodthirsty tales, and prepared for larger fields. The failure had found himself as a murderer, in the cause of abolitionism.

From the bloodletting of John Brown, the incidents began to snowball. In the same week (late May 1856), a Southerner gave the anti-slavery people more grist by one of those impulsive acts which the individual forever repents but which, in the case of Preston Brooks, became another act of the "slave power" aggression.

It began with Charles Sumner, of Massachusetts, a senator noted for his intellectual arrogance, illimitable pride, and nastiness of tongue. All during the Kansas issue, he had spoken of "The Crime against Kansas," using without editing the propaganda supplied by the Free Staters. Sumner struck out at the whole South on the basis of biased coverage of the ruffianism in Kansas, and then made his attacks personal on one of the defenders of the Southern position.

The object of his spleen was old Senator Butler, of South Carolina, the son of a Revolutionary soldier and a devout follower of Calhoun. Senator Butler, with hair as white as cotton and black eyebrows, was absent from the Senate because of an illness, which was to prove fatal. In referring to the venerable senator, Sumner said, among other insulting things, "he has chosen a mistress to whom he has made his vows, and who, though ugly to others, is always lovely to him—though polluted in the sight of the world, is chaste in his sight: I mean the harlot slavery."

In view of the abolitionist literature about Southerners' black concubines, this carried a personal connotation, and Preston Brooks, Butler's nephew, so took it. Brooks was thirty-seven years old, a graduate of the University of South Carolina and a successful lawyer, a veteran of the Mexican War (as captain of volunteers) and then a congressman. On him centers a real difference of the sections. In the self-conscious Southern code of honor, an insult to a kinsman from an equal was answered by a duel. Since the nature of Sumner's insult could not be dignified as an act which called for an affair of honor, Brooks rebuked the insulter with the humiliation of physical punishment, as he would an inferior. In acting by the code of his land, for national consequences Preston Brooks served his land very badly.

Since it was poor form to strike an inferior by hand, he bought a light gutta-percha cane which would break on contact. Brooks accosted Sumner in the empty Senate chambers and, after telling him why he was being punished, struck him about the head. The light, hollow cane broke, but Sumner made a great to-do about the injuries suffered from it and "retired" for three years.

When the young congressman became the symbol of the vicious South, Brooks knew he had hurt his section by an impulsive act, and he regretted it until he died, less than a year later in Brown's Hotel in Washington.

While the "Crime against Kansas" and the act of "Bully" Brooks (as he was labeled) still hung in the air, another issue heightened and spread the ill feeling in the North against the slave South—though in this case not one Southern leader was involved in any way. The famous Dred Scott affair was a Supreme Court decision of a case which had been dragging for ten years through the lower courts of Missouri, where a few abolitionists had been making a "test" case over an illiterate Negro who showed little interest in the whole thing.

The affair broke on the public just when matters were quieting down in Kansas and after the vote in the presidential election of 1856 showed that the country, as a whole, North and South, preferred peace between the sections. This was the first election in which the Republican Party put up a candidate, that posturing and foolish adventurer, Fremont. He ran on a radical anti-sectional platform against Pennsylvania's James Buchanan, a conservative representative of the nationalist Democratic Party. Though the Republicans made an ominously good showing, they were rejected in the North. At the same time the South's own extremists were rejected, though Yancey also ominously had gained power in Alabama.

The new man in the White House was untouched by any of the extreme views. He wanted peace, national peace and personal peace. James Buchanan, a career politician whose industrious use of his modest gifts led him to the fulfillment of his life's ambition, happened to occupy the seat of power in his country at a time when the pressure of circumstances forced all his weaknesses to the surface and called on a few of his limited strengths.

As a senator, he had served long, honorably, and without distinction; as minister to Russia and England, he had served ably; and, in another era, he would have joined our list of undistinguished Presidents who, as a reward for party loyalty, were given a few years in the White House. It was Buchanan's misfortune to reach his earthly rewards when the thirty years of sectional conflict had reached the moment of convulsion. Events demanded of the personally decent and deeply religious bachelor a decisiveness which God had not given him. Under stress, he lacked self-confidence, he floundered for guidance, was betrayed by his desire to placate and his tendency to vacillate. History has given him a hard name in general, though he was really a victim of bad timing in realizing his life's ambition.

Buchanan got off on the wrong foot by announcing, in his inaugural address, that the Dred Scott case, then months in the Supreme Court, was going to be satisfactorily decided—thus revealing that a justice or justices had given him advance notice. Since the decision seemed favorable to the

South, Buchanan was excoriated for collusion with the Southern justices and damned from the start as pro-Southern.

Regarding the whole Dred Scott affair, no one is the wiser for knowing the tortuous details. The high point was that Dred Scott, as a slave, was taken by an army doctor, who had bought him, into a free state, where he lived with the doctor for four years. After the doctor died and after changes of ownership by and residence with various of the doctor's heirs, the Negro was transferred to the ownership of a brother of the doctor's widow. She had meanwhile married a Massachusetts abolitionist. The slave did not instigate any fight for his freedom. In fact, after failure to support his family by sporadic efforts at work, Dred Scott was living off the bounty of his original owner's sons in St. Louis.

In the "test" case, a group of abolitionists sued Scott's legal owner, the widow's brother, J. F. A. Sanford of New York, for the slave's freedom. Sanford's defense was that Scott was not a citizen and could not sue in a federal court. When the U. S. Circuit Court found for Sanford, the abolitionists carried it to the Supreme Court on the plea that four years on free soil established Scott's freedom. That was all the Court was asked to decide. The majority decided against it on the grounds that, since Scott had returned to and lived in a slave state, he was subject to its laws. Originally, this majority decision had no implications beyond the specific case and avoided the larger "territorial question."

At this point, two Northern justices dissented and forced the territorial question into the decision. Opinion is divided on their motives but, whatever their reasons, Curtis and McLean followed the line of abolitionist Chase in keeping the "idea" paramount.

When the revised decision was made public, Chief Justice Taney made an error in judgment. In deciding that Negroes (not only slaves) were not citizens, he fixed their non-citizenship on their "inferior race." As property, and not citizens, slaves could be transported anywhere, slave or free state, without change of status. This ill-considered generality in the Court's decision went further than repudiation of the Missouri Compromise: it said, in effect, that the Compromise was unconstitutional from the beginning. This was a match falling into the powder keg of the territorial controversy, set before the public by the propaganda on "bleeding Kansas."

Northerners branded old Taney a "Southern slaveholder." Justice Taney was a Marylander who had inherited slaves and freed them all except two old ones of whom he personally took care. He was eighty years old, with more than twenty years of honorable service in the Court behind him, and he had recently suffered the death of his wife and daughter. At his age, the blow of the loss of his family might well have rendered the judge less astute in his judgments. But he became then, and loosely comes down in history, as, one of the real villains of the "slave power."

Innocent though the Southern states were in the Dred Scott decision and the accompanying furor, the building tensions affected Southerners too. Yancey and his allies, through their Southern Rights Associations, cited expressions of Northern hostility to turn the deepening sectional consciousness into secession sentiments. Two glib phrases of campaign oratory especially caused the people's apprehension over Northern intentions to grow. As the Southerners took the words at face value, they were alarmed as well as angered at Lincoln's "house divided" speech and Seward's provocative "irrepressible conflict."

While Seward's phrase, "the irrepressible conflict," rings down through history like one of America's resounding challenges ("54° 40′, or fight"), the New Yorker recognized instantly that he had gone too far for his political good and tried to change the impression left by his campaign oratory. It is probable that his implied threat cost William H. Seward the Republican nomination in 1860, as it frightened off the less radical members of the new party.

With all the contradictions in the conflict, Seward was neither a South-hater nor a warmonger. This brilliant, opportunistic protégé of Thurlow Weed, a corrupt political boss, was a charming and cynical gentleman, vastly ambitious and the ultimate realist. He held an uncompromising position against Southern minority rights and slavery solely on the practical ground that the obsolete institution was doomed by the economic progress surrounding it and that the only rights were those of the majority. Where Calhoun had been behind his times on slavery and ahead on minority rights, Seward belonged precisely to his times on both counts, and his assurance had made him a little careless with words.

Lincoln, the rising Illinois lawyer (who had been wont to visit the Senate to study the clear logic of Calhoun's speeches), also repudiated the ringing words he had used in a campaign speech against Douglas; but the damage had been done. More significantly than the alarm cry which Lincoln gave the Southern extremists, his campaign against Douglas caused another event—the strangest and most complex of them all—which affected the Southern leaders in Washington, especially Jefferson Davis.

For the end of Davis' unguarded historical moment with Douglas on the spring Sunday morning was not yet. His inadvertent collaboration with Douglas on "The Crime against Kansas" was to turn into a political struggle to the death with his former ally. It was this feud, involving the course of the Southern states with it, that made Douglas, against all his desires, a key figure in the South's destiny.

5

Douglas, as ambitious as all the big ones, was called the "Little Giant" because of the greatness of his intellect and his small stature, though he was a well-formed man. He comes down in history largely as Lincoln's opponent in the momentous debates over a Senate seat, but he was more the dupe of his own cleverness in throwing the South that sop over his railroad. Since then he had experienced nothing except trouble over his "popular sovereignty" in Kansas, and the climax was reached over a forgotten "issue" called the Lecompton Constitution.

This was the Constitution of the pro-slavery people in Kansas, rammed through with the usual frauds and with the Free Staters abstaining from a vote because the "issue" of bleeding Kansas was worth more to the Republicans than a settled territory. President Buchanan, under pressure from the Southern politicians who believed in the theoretical rights in territories, tried to admit Kansas to statehood on the Lecompton Constitution.

Douglas was caught in the same untenable position where Calhoun had squirmed nearly thirty years before. His Illinois constituents would not have Kansas admitted as a slave state in any such fraud as the Lecompton Constitution and, to secure his votes at home, Douglas was forced to turn against the Democratic administration. Unlike Calhoun, when he saw what he had to do, Douglas went whole hog. With his help, the anti-Administration forces got another Kansas election held (August 1858), which rejected the pro-slavery Constitution. Finally the Kansas issue was bled dry, but Douglas' chances were finished with the Democratic Administration and its Southern supporters.

It was while the Illinois senator had split with the Administration, though retaining his own presidential aspirations, that he was forced into the arena with Lincoln—that astute politician and eloquent phrasemaker, then going after Douglas' Senate seat. Lincoln used both his wiliness and his phrasemaking in taking against Douglas the aggressive tactics of the moral wrong of slavery. Outside the lunatic fringe of the abolitionists, the feeling that slavery was morally wrong had grown slowly with new generations and changing climates of opinion, and Lincoln became the most evocative spokesman of this new principle. His superlative gift was to *suggest* action without promising any.

In his most famous speech in the campaign against Douglas, "I believe this government cannot endure permanently half slave and half free," any Southern planter would see reason to fear his intentions and any abolitionist would find cause to expect action. With their fears and passions, both sides failed to define Lincoln's carefully inserted word, "permanently."

No abolitionist (he said that he had no purpose of interfering with slavery where it existed: "I believe I have no right to do so"), Lincoln was committed only to containment of the institution. This would in time cause slavery to pass without dislocation to either race or to their total society. He looked beyond his time to a solution which would not involve any form of the racial equality in which he disbelieved.

As he wrote, "I am not, nor ever have been, in favor of bringing about in any way the social and political equality of the white and black races . . . and I will say in addition to this that there is a physical difference between the white and black races which I believe will forever forbid the two races living together on terms of social and political equality."

In dealing with the hot political issues, however, Lincoln did not shout his private opinions from the housetops. His purpose was primarily to defeat Douglas and secondarily to strengthen his own and the Republican Party's positions. To this end he put on the badgered Douglas the burden of defending his popular sovereignty theme which permitted slaves in new territories. Operating on his knowledge of Douglas' split with the Democratic Administration, Lincoln had him coming and going.

If Douglas repudiated his position on the rightful existence of slavery in all territories, he would permanently alienate the Southern Democrats, already chilled toward him. If he did not, he would antagonize his constituents. The Little Giant tried to play it cozy, and outraged the Southern leaders more than their worst enemy ever had.

Theoretically retaining his position on the "rights" of the territories concerning slavery, he confessed to his own people that it was really an empty claim. While, he said, any citizen could *legally* take his slave property anywhere, that was "a barren and worthless right unless sustained, proclaimed and enforced by appropriate police regulations and local legislations."

With these words he became to his former Southern Democratic allies the reincarnation of Judas Iscariot and Benedict Arnold combined. The fact, that he won his election (with no increase in prestige) merely made him a more open target to attack. For his admitted chicanery to the South, violating all their codes of honor, the leaders determined to defeat him for President, regardless of the cost to themselves and the intersectional Democratic Party.

As slavery provided a common issue for Northerners of all stripes and sizes, so Douglas provided a common issue for many Southerners of divergent plans and purposes. There was, however, a significant difference between the sectional leaders. In the North the practical-minded men of ambition held the common, realistic purpose of containing the South and gaining control of the government through the surgent, sectional

Republican Party. In the South, not only was there no common or realistic purpose, but dark forces were released under cover of the Douglas feud.

Jefferson Davis, as Mississippi senator in Buchanan's administration and recognized as the South's representative spokesman, served the ends of a gathering power he did not comprehend. For as Douglas became the dupe of his own cleverness, Davis became the dupe of his intellectual pride in the abstract principles of the South's defense. As Douglas had acted as Lincoln's foil, Davis acted as the pawn of arrogant leaders who were rushing their region toward self-destruction.

The inherent violence in the country's division—set in motion on that unhistoric Sunday morning in Davis' parlor when he had gone for the bait of Douglas' popular sovereignty—was gaining momentum that carried the conflict beyond the Calhounian principles which Davis had grown so adept at defining. Only he did not understand that danger when he emerged as the titular leader of the South for the climactic phase of the struggle.

CHAPTER IV

"Though We Must Part . . ."

AS MISSISSIPPI senator in Buchanan's administration (1857–61), Jefferson Davis carried over the prestige from his power with Pierce and he spoke for a section that, at least on the surface, was more unified than ever in its previous history. But when the drums began to roll offstage in 1858, Davis, in his fiftieth year, had passed the peak of his own powers.

There was no decline in his intelligence. There was simply no maturation, and the theories he had learned fifteen years before in his tropical sanctuary no longer applied. Though not recognizing this, Davis was profoundly disturbed at the size and the intensity of the warring forces. They were dragging him out of his depth and physically, like Calhoun, he broke under the strain.

Also like his mentor, Jefferson Davis had no healthy outlets, no relaxations. He loved his family, but children are not notoriously restful, and to his passionately devoted wife he brought the problems of his titular leadership. Only for brief interludes, without change, could he leave the burdens of the defense in his office. A deeply conscientious man, Davis, without admitting his limitations, seemed goaded to accomplish by effort, by toil, what did not come naturally. When his overstrained nature broke under the pressure, his un-self-analytical type of intelligence failed to read the signposts.

Jefferson Davis was not physically a weak man. When all responsibilities were finally removed from him after the Civil War, he lived on for a quarter of a century, into his eighty-second year, even after undergoing a harsh imprisonment. He simply placed on his organism a strain for which nature had not designed it and, in his pride, he could not accept the limitations even of the flesh. His physical break was what today we call psychosomatic.

The break came in the winter of 1858–59, when the mounting tensions had so deepened that personal strains developed between Northerners and Southerners in Washington. Men and families who had enjoyed long friendships began to avoid one another. When they met in social groups, controversial subjects of their sections were so studiously ignored as to bring a general restraint over the gathering. This was the first session of Congress where Republicans held a majority.

Davis' break started with a cold, went into laryngitis, and before that passed he suffered the excruciating agony of a procidentia of the pupil. When Dr. Hayes, an "eye specialist" from Philadelphia, was brought in by Washington colleagues, Davis' left eye was blinded and in danger of bursting.

Glaucoma, as a disease of the eye, was not then known in America, but Dr. Hayes's medical descriptions of the symptoms coincide with the eye pathology now diagnosed as glaucoma. This affliction can be closely associated with or related to emotional stress. With Davis, it would seem fairly certain that this attack of glaucoma was so induced, since the only previous attack had occurred during the bitter 1850 campaign in Mississippi, when he was running for governor against the vituperative compromiser who won.

While Senator Davis was recovering from the Washington attack of glaucoma with his sightless eye blindfolded, he was visited by one Northern friend who had not let sectional strains bother him personally—the Republican leader, "Irrepressible Conflict" Seward. This easy-mannered and easy-conscienced social being held an affectionate respect for the Southern leader and thoroughly enjoyed Mrs. Davis. He showed it, too, for with the charming New York senator she took conversational liberties which she would not have thought of with another.

On Seward's visit, since the usual social restraints did not apply, Mrs. Davis asked him how in the Senate he could make "those piteous appeals for the Negro," when she was sure he didn't believe what he said.

Smiling without the least abashment, Seward answered, "I do not, but these appeals, as you call them, are potent to affect the rank and file in the North."

Shocked, Mrs. Davis then asked him if he never spoke from conviction alone.

"Never," he said, with humor lighting his secretive eyes.

At this, Jefferson Davis was aroused to lift his blindfolded head, and heatedly said, "As God is my judge, I never spoke from any other motive."

Seward put his arm about the Mississippian and gently returned his head to the pillow. "I'm sure you do not," he said, "I'm always sure of it."

Mrs. Davis said, as she recalled the incident long afterward, that the New Yorker spoke with "great tenderness."

It was probably the tenderness that a cynical realist feels for an idealist in the affairs of men. Seward perceived, as he said, that political strife was a state of war, and in war all stratagems were fair, including that first principle of subverting truth to the end to be served. Seward knew precisely what end he wanted served: the control of the government by the Republican Party.

Against Seward's pragmatic realism, Davis' commitments to honorable principles were virtually beside the point. Even in the South principles were being used, rather than shared, by a small group of Southern leaders who seemed to be as anxious for a sectional break as were the extremists in the North.

In a time when no man in the nation spoke for the Union, a small group, with determination, adroitness, and clarity of purpose, could advance their own ends behind the façade of a dedicated spokesman. Behind the still outwardly imposing façade of Jefferson Davis, a few Southerners in Washington were going along with Davis' feud with Douglas for reasons quite beyond the mere defeat of Douglas as a Democratic nominee.

To insure Douglas' defeat among Southerners, these men planned to use against him his very denial of "police protection and local legislation" to slaveowners in the territories. To their other abstract rights, they were to add the demand that protection *must* be provided slave property in the territories.

This was something which had never existed before, not even in the South, and Toombs called this new and impractical demand what it was. "It is the very foolishness of folly," he said, "to raise and make prominent such issues now."

These were not foolish men. Self-made planter barons and planter aristocrats, all political powers, they were not likely to act in arrogant folly without awareness of the consequences. In blocking Douglas, the likeliest national candidate of the cross-sectional Democratic Party, they blocked their chances of continuing in power the one national party that protected them. At the same time they opened the way for the new anti-Southern Republican Party, their avowed enemy. The only way the election of a Republican President could be regarded as desirable would be if it led to secession.

These men were a part of or attached to a powerful cabal of Southern leaders in Washington, who held President Buchanan practically captive. While not all of this group was scheming to defeat Douglas or directly to promote secession, they were all uncompromising champions of a planter South free of Northern interference of any kind.

Of these, the strong man in the Cabinet (as Davis had been in Pierce's) was Howell Cobb, Secretary of the Treasury. This blandly intelligent Georgia grandee was a planter of the legend, owning more than a thousand slaves. Like his political ally Toombs and so many others, he had shifted slowly from his original Unionist position into unyielding sectionalism.

The Secretary of War was John Floyd, former governor of Virginia, who had been an anti-slavery man during the 1832 slavery debates; he had also shifted toward the extremists. Virginia's R. M. T. Hunter, a highly respected senator, was a moderate secessionist as befitted the cautious industry with which he had followed his ambitions, but he could be counted on where he felt a threat to the slaves he had acquired in a lifetime of work and frugality.

Then there were Davis' old political cronies from Mississippi—tough-bitten Jacob Thompson, Secretary of the Interior and forthright extremist, and Senator Albert G. Brown, the "democratic" demagogue who had originated the scheme of making an issue of Douglas' "barren rights."

The Louisiana senators were both successful adventurers in the Cotton Kingdom—the shrewd intriguer, John Slidell, Columbia-educated New Yorker, transplanted to cosmopolitan New Orleans, and Judah P. Benjamin, the West Indian émigré with a cloudy record at Yale and a brilliantly subtle mind. They were adroit behind-the-scenes manipulators for the independence of the land where they had won power and found pleasure.

A dependable states' righter of the Calhoun school was Alabama's senator, C. C. Clay, whose charming wife provided a social background for politicking.

South Carolina's senator, the eccentric James H. Hammond, a literate planter and political power, was an aggressive voice for Southern rights. With no pussyfooting about it, and scorning abstractions, the intemperate Hammond exulted in the empire where cotton was king and defied anybody to interfere.

These men, too, could read the census returns as well as Seward could. They recognized that the New Yorker's cold confidence in the triumph of numbers was justified by the trends, and they hadn't the slightest intention of holding still to be fitted for the role of colonials by Northern banker-industrialists.

Outside of Washington, and growing in power every day, Yancey trumpeted tirelessly for an independent Cotton Kingdom. He had a zealous and energetic ally in Virginia's venerable Edmund Ruffin, progressive planter and publisher, as passionately committed to complete independence as South Carolina's Rhett. At Ruffin's suggestion, Yancey started to beat the drums for a new pressure group, the League of United Southerners, and he stated his unequivocal position in a letter which was made public.

"No national party can save us; no sectional party can do it. But if we do as our fathers did, organize 'Committees of Safety' all over the Cotton States (and it is only in them that we can hope for any effective government), we shall fire the Southern heart—instruct the Southern mind—give courage to each other, and at the proper moment, by one organized concerted action, *we can precipitate the Cotton States into a revolution.*" (Not his italics.)

That position of Yancey's was the essence of the radicals' belief: they wanted their own country, just as European nations split off from a larger group. In our time, this has been recognized as the right of self-determination.

Davis neither shared Yancey's forthright purpose nor perceived the meaning of the gathering forces as did the realists fighting for the plantations which they had won on their own energies. Still the amateur whom the Mississippi political powers had sent to Washington in the forties, he had little notion that the extremists on both sides were playing in deadly earnest, and carrying the country along with them. He really believed in his words on "rights," and believed the conflict would be resolved on that basis.

Typically Southern, Davis went on talking—in New England, as well as in Washington and the South—while up in Peterboro, New York, a group of abolitionists were outfitting a guerrilla band to invade the South as a means of forcing the civil war they wanted.

2

Among the consistently Unionist areas in the South, Virginia's capital, Richmond, had been a stronghold. Though the city had its secessionists ("fire-eaters"), control was in the hands of able, energetic moderates. Yancey, whose organizations were feeble in the Old Dominion, was right in thinking that no "effective government" for his independent cotton empire would come from Virginia or the neighboring state of North Carolina.

Along with political ties with the Union went personal ties in the North. Since the nineteenth-century shift from England, Virginia's sons were frequently educated at Yale, Harvard, Princeton, Columbia, and Pennsylvania, and North-South intermarriages were commonplace. Richmond's businessmen exchanged visits with their Northern colleagues, and Virginia families spent summers at Northern spas as well as at their own Springs. (In 1859, a Saratoga hotel man complained of the decline of business, since the lavishly spending Southerners were scared away by Negro-stealers.)

Richmond was the most advanced city in the South in evolving a pattern of commerce-industry-banking, while retaining the flavor and characteristics of a planters' capital. Rising on its series of hills from the James River and branching out from its beautiful Capitol grounds—dominated by the imposing and columned Capitol designed by Thomas Jefferson—the city had started life as a frontier trading post for the tobacco of both the grandees of the James River plantations and the back-country yeoman farmers. Its growth, steady, never spectacular, and nearly always sound, was an organic development around the core of tobacco.

It had various manufactories, the largest ironworks in the South, the largest flour mill in the world; it was a thriving wholesale center for the produce of its countryside, for imports from everywhere, and its exports were shipped over the whole world. In this balanced economy, the city was a banking center, a railroad center (with railroad manufacturing), and a shopping center.

For a century, Richmond had enjoyed a highly distinguished bar. Its newspapers were good, its *Southern Literary Messenger* (once edited by Poe) ranked with national magazines, its printers published all manner of books and its bookstores were not only well patronized but focal points of the downtown city life. It had fine hotels, with first-rate dining rooms and bars, a theater district for the *haut monde* and a sporting section in the tenderloin. Basically, as in the plantation world from which it evolved, homes were the center of Richmond's social life, and on the wide, tree-lined streets its handsome homes with their walled rear gardens ("villas," as Dickens called them) were remarked upon by all visitors.

For population growth the city drew largely on its own countryside, as planters moved into town from worn-out land and yeoman families came in for better opportunity. With this influx bringing to the city essentially the character of country life, and with the natives' continuation of the ideals of plantation life, Richmond was spared those evils of urbanization feared by Southerners. It remained parochial, conservative, and leisured. Its people valued good manners, an inflexible code of honor, derogated suspiciousness, and their indifference to money was praised by a Bostonian, who found their civilization superior to anything in the North, except for the blight of slavery.

Slavery was passing. With no importations to replace the slaves being sold south, as large plantations continued to cease the slave-system operation and few yeomen held aspirations to slaveownership, the time would come when there would be no more slaves. As it was, most of the slaves in Richmond were house people. But, though on the way out, slavery existed. Along with a population of freed Negroes, there were nearly half as many colored as white people in the state. Since these were mostly concentrated east of the Blue Ridge Mountains, many counties still had a density of colored population equal to or numerically superior to the white.

In Richmond, free Negroes and slaves comprised a third of the population, and in cities there were no slave quarters: servants lived in wings attached to the house. Also, nearly everyone visited country kinfolk who owned slaves. Thus, for all its comparative "modernity" and ties with the Union, Richmond was still a Southern city in that its life—its values, customs, and mores—was interrelated with the Negro. Its people were conditioned by the presence of Negroes in their community, in their homes, and in their consciousness.

In October 1859, Richmond was proud that its Episcopal churches were the hosts of the General Triennial Convention of the Episcopal Church of the United States. At St. Paul's, St. James's, and Monumental, they held the ceremonies for the consecration of new bishops—the bishops-elect of New Jersey, Texas, Minnesota, Alabama, and the assistant bishop-elect of Ohio—and the sermons were preached by the bishops of Delaware, of Maine and Vermont, and Virginia's Bishop Meade.

Sectional strife was remote from the minds of Richmond's citizens on the Monday afternoon of October 17, when the first rumors began to carry the most dread words in the Southerner's tongue. "Negro Insurrection!"

Women out shopping hurried home to their children. Men left offices and bars and warehouses, hurrying to their homes. Some ran up the steeply hilly streets to the red brick Bell Tower in Capitol Square, where militia rifles were stored. More details came with the fear spreading among the people.

Abolitionists had invaded the northern tip of the state, Harper's Ferry, seized the U. S. Arsenal, captured whites and held them as hostages, murdered others, and they were freeing and arming Negroes for an invasion of the state. The leader was a wildly bearded fierce-eyed old man named Andrews or Anderson, nobody seemed to know which. This was Nat Turner's Rebellion all over again, only organized and led by invading abolitionists. Nobody could guess at the number. Five hundred, some said. The wires had been cut at Harper's Ferry and no accurate information went out.

Men of the small *corps d'élite*, militia Company F, ran to their houses to dress in their fine uniforms of cadet-gray frock coats, lined with Virginia fire-gilt buttons and gold braid on the collar, and a black stripe down the trouser leg. They knew nothing except that they were to meet Governor Wise at the depot. They had heard that a militia company near Harper's Ferry and an armed band of farmers were fighting the abolitionists and apparently holding them in the little town.

Men of the company of howitzers, so recently formed that they had not gotten uniforms yet, let alone cannons, were given rifles from the Bell Tower armory, and in their street clothes hurried to follow Company F. When those companies left the city and night fell, all the other militia companies formed, and stood ready to control any violence on the dark streets or to follow the other companies. All through the darkened city doors were bolted, shutters pulled over windows, and men sat up with all kinds of arms—from shotguns to dueling pistols.

On Tuesday, the news straightened out. The leader was John Brown, the Kansas mass murderer, with twenty-one followers. He had held among his hostages old Colonel Lewis, a kinsman of George Washington, and killed a freed Negro and a workman on his way to a morning job. The Negroes he freed had not joined the insurrectionists; they had huddled in terror among the white hostages. No recruits, colored or white, had joined the murderers. Instead, the whole countryside had erupted with armed men who besieged Brown's band in the captured arsenal.

Monday afternoon, President Buchanan had sent out from Washington a marine company under Colonel Robert E. Lee, who had also been alerted during Nat Turner's Insurrection. Colonel Lee had taken with him a young cavalry lieutenant who happened along—J. E. B. Stuart, also a Virginian, who could never resist a fight. Young Stuart, whose wife was a Richmond girl, led the assault which finished off the abolitionists, killing most and capturing five with Brown. A United States marine was killed in the attack.

Thirty-six hours after Brown's attempt to lead a mass Negro insurrection, the action was over. But for Virginia, and the South, the effects were just beginning.

The more the details came in, the more the South felt the monstrousness of the attack from the North. Responsible citizens of New York State and Massachusetts, knowing the kind of criminally insane egotist they were dealing with, had supported his scheme of loosing on Southern whites—non-slaveholders as well as slaveholders—a race war. When the mad plot miscarried, only one of the eight plotters had sufficient moral courage to admit his part in it. After burning the incriminating papers, the others fled in all directions—Gerrit Smith, the leader, fittingly going into a lunatic asylum.

When several of them were tracked down to Ohio and Iowa, the governors of those states refused to extradite them for trial, on the ground that the South was responsible for the attempted insurrection because of its part in the Kansas troubles. In the East, the New York *Tribune* found no reproach to Brown and his "compatriots"; Boston papers awarded him the "crown of martyrdom," and Louisa May Alcott called him "St. John the Just." When the fanatic was sentenced to be hanged, Emerson said "he would make the gallows glorious like the cross."

This ascension of St. John was not a typical attitude of the North, and many conservatives deplored the crime. Yet the fact that he was supported at all, even glorified, and this by the enlightened intellectuals, aroused the Southern masses to a sense of physical and imminent danger from their neighbors in the Union.

For several years there had been rumors of conspiracies to incite slaves. Along with the inflammatory denunciations of abolitionist publications, these kept alive the fear of another and larger version of Nat Turner. Now it had come—and from their fellow countryman. In those thirty-six hours, the murderous maniac had accomplished what the Southern radicals had not been able to in thirty years: the people believed the North was the enemy.

Then, as whenever the South was sinned against, some home-grown hot-head managed to give the enemy a practical advantage out of its own aggression. In this case it was the Honorable Henry Wise, then governor.

The Wises cut a big figure in Virginia and nobody was more aware of it than Henry. In addition, he was a high-spirited self-glamorizer who, since he did have brilliant turns of mind, fancied himself as successor to the great Virginians of the earlier era. Unfortunately, he also had turns of mind anything but brilliant—erratic would be a generous euphemism—only in his vanity, all of his thought belonged with the wisdom of the ages. This Governor Wise, instead of commuting Brown's mandatory sentence of hanging (for treason) to life imprisonment, allowed the sentence to go through, and out of a murderer created a martyr.

The people of the South were not thinking then of the effects in the North of the governor's stupidity. They were thinking of themselves in a Union where such things as Brown could happen to them.

Militia units multiplied as young men rushed to enlist. In Richmond, sixteen infantry companies, seven artillery companies, and a mounted guard were formed. Merchants met and decided to establish a direct ship-ping line to Liverpool, to be independent of the North. Over one hundred students left the University of Pennsylvania medical school to return South; they were escorted by the militia and local college students to a great crowd waiting for them in Capitol Square. The legislature appropri-ated $30,000 to enlarge the Medical College in Richmond.

Most significant of all, the dormant Southern Rights Association of Richmond and Henrico County became revivified. The people had at last been put in the mood for William Lowndes Yancey.

3

When the golden-tongued Yancey reaped the fruits of his single-pur-posed dedication, Jefferson Davis was not present to witness the zealot's hour of triumph. It came in a hot April in Charleston, when the Demo-cratic National Convention crowded into the Institute Building on Meet-ing Street and overflowed the rooming accommodations to the extent that steamers were moored at the wharves to serve as floating hotels. Visitors from the North had always found South Carolina's city-state exotic, with the palmettos rustling in the walled gardens and the heavily scented fragrance of the flowers mingling with the salt breeze from the bay. In that hot spring of 1860, the visitors also found Charleston hostile —for Yancey's followers had come to the convention with terms they knew the national party could not meet.

They had come prepared to force into the platform a new and extreme stand on the slave code. This not only denied the right of either Congress or a territorial legislature to prohibit slavery in a territory, but demanded the government protection for slaveholders without which, as Douglas had told his constituents, rights were empty legalities. Yancey and his followers knew that Douglas and his Northern backers would never accept it. In forcing the issue their only possible motive could have been to split the Democratic Party between the Southern sections and the larger sections from the rest of the country.

The Northern delegates, as realistic as Northern Republicans, and wanting only to maintain their party in power, made all reasonable concessions on the assumption that their fellow Democrats also wanted to win the election. But the aroused Southern emotions were responsive only to Yancey's passion. With reason forgotten, a majority were stampeded toward the end of defeating Douglas—their likeliest candidate.

After a week of acrimonious harangues, Yancey met his long-deferred hour in the hot dusk of the hall, where the lamps and the crowds in the balcony intensified the sultry heat that fans the emotions. At the age of forty-five, with two decades of campaigning behind him, the confident, stolid man faced the audience with a slight smile on his wide, tight mouth, his hair fluffed like a bartender's, and the "luminous" eyes ranging over the galleries. Then came the golden voice calling to the people's awakened sectionalism. Reviewing their grievances, stirring their pride and their passions, he filled Southerners with an exultance of regional fervor.

After that, the convention had no chance. The Southern states' delegations walked out over the slave code and jubilation filled the Charleston streets. Their delegates had broken with the North! Except to a few, it was all emotion.

The fantastic slave-code issue could have no real meaning to most of them. Not in any rationality could the people cheer the smiling Yancey because he had split the one party which protected their interests in Washington. They never considered why Yancey had wanted to defeat Douglas. They cheered because they had broken from Northerners. Even though they were political allies, the visiting delegates represented what in the overcharged atmosphere had become the enemy.

Far away from this hysteria on Charleston's scented streets, Jefferson Davis did no cheering. His own learned speeches against Douglas' perfidious denial of "protection" for slavery had helped make it possible for Yancey to get the "few" determined followers who, as Rhett had written, could force a bolt over the slave code. When the Democratic Party split, however, Davis belatedly perceived the consequences of the Southern leaders' fight with Douglas: the Republicans would come in.

When Douglas was nominated by the Northern Democrats, the Cotton States selected the handsome Vice-President of the United States, John

Breckinridge, while the border states—Breckinridge's own Kentucky, along with Virginia and Tennessee—nominated still a third Democrat. For the first time a momentous consequence had caught up with Davis' words; only he did not see it that way. He saw only that the Democrats must then unite in order to defeat the Republican candidate, Abraham Lincoln.

Then, from having failed to see in time the possible consequences of his damning words about Douglas, in deciding what to do about the consequences, Davis showed he also failed to read the hearts of men. In his fortune-favored rise, Jefferson Davis had never been forced to manipulate people or to avoid manipulation. In his self-concept of the plantation aristocrat, such behavior perhaps seemed base and ignoble. In dealing with others, he stood rather stiffly on his own dignity, and could be acutely sensitive about it, though almost totally blind to the dignity of others. In this blindness, he approached Douglas.

He made the Illinois senator the incredible proposition that Douglas, at the pinnacle of his career, withdraw from the Democratic nomination in order that the three factions might agree on someone else. On the ground that if he withdrew so would his supporters, Douglas refused any part of the naïve scheme.

As the final consequence of his carefully reasoned arguments against Douglas on "principle," Davis watched with deep depression the election of the first Republican, on a minority of the popular vote. Though he received the largest popular vote of any of the candidates, Lincoln went in on less than half the national vote, largely on the system of counting electoral votes as a unit. In New York, for instance, where Lincoln drew 362,000 votes to 312,000 against him, instead of getting 19 electoral votes and losing 16, the Republican got all 35. His electoral votes were entirely in the North on a straight sectional vote all across the country. The divided South (upper and cotton) went for two Southerners, and Douglas got only Missouri.

4

With the election of a Republican, all those words of campaign speeches, such as "house divided" and "irrepressible conflict," began to assume a dread reality to people in the cotton states. To them, the word "secession" had been bandied about for so long as to achieve current acceptance. Only its procedures and timing seemed the question with the Republicans, symbol of Northern aggressions and hostile intents, coming to Washington. To turn the fears into affirmative action, Yancey's Cotton Kingdom gave the people a dream and a goal.

To all this, too, Jefferson Davis was a disturbed spectator. With the secession urge gathering impetus every December day, the titular leader of the South's defense began to try to hold the Union together. While South Carolina's senators resigned (Hammond, in the excitement, against his better judgment) the Mississippian joined a Senate "Committee of 13," to try to evolve a last-ditch compromise.

Georgia's Toombs and Virginia's Hunter were on it, with Crittenden of Kentucky, Douglas with several other Northern Democrats, and Seward with Northern Republicans, including three aggressive Radicals. Finally, old Senator Crittenden proposed what was to be the country's last effort at compromise. Including all the details of exacerbation, it essentially returned to the principles of the Missouri Compromise. The Radical Republicans wrote privately to Lincoln for his advice, and he privately advised rejecting Crittenden's compromise. As Calhoun had predicted, when one majority felt it did not have to compromise, it would not.

When long-Unionist Toombs (who ten years before had helped swing Georgia for the 1850 Compromise) faced the adamant Republican attitude, even he began sending messages home that the Union was over for the South and urged his people to prepare withdrawal from the compact of States.

By then (December 20, 1860) South Carolina had opened the ball with its formal ordinance of secession. Rhett's *Mercury* proclaimed in an extra:

The
UNION
is
DISSOLVED!

Though Unionist voices had been drowned out by what one South Carolinian called "the passions of that mad hour," no fire-eater was selected to write the state's Declaration. The honor went to humorless, conscientious C. G. Memminger, the self-educated son of a German foot soldier, as innocent of fiery Gascon blood and mulatto descendants (he owned no slaves) as of previous disunionist utterances.

In his clear and measured document, Memminger stressed, along the lines of the disregarded warning of the Georgia Compromise Legislature, that Northern citizens had been allowed "to disturb the peace and eloign the property" of fellow Americans and "incite to servile insurrection." Then, "as the South shall be excluded from the common territory [and] the judicial tribunals shall be made sectional," the guarantees of the Constitution were lost.

South Carolina's clearly stated "Declaration of . . . Secession" was broadcast throughout the Southern states, followed by tracts—such as *The South Alone, Should Govern the South*—appealing to the sister states to form a Southern confederation.

During all this upheaval, in Washington the shocked Davis met with other Southern senators while their own states were debating on secession, and poor President Buchanan, the peace-loving Democrat, tried to hold the ship together until the new captain relieved him.

Being a Unionist with Southern sympathies (notably attentive to Southern ladies), Buchanan was badgered from both sides and from within. Disbelieving in secession, he also disbelieved in coercion if secession happened. Radical Republicans urged him to "do something," while the planters' powerful cabal—still intact—urged him to "do nothing." Between the two groups "Irrepressible Conflict" Seward, the Republican power until Lincoln arrived, maneuvered for compromise now that his party was in office. Working realistically with the President and Douglas to contain the secession movement, he did everything possible to make the conflict "repressible." To that end, Seward helped Virginians establish a Peace Convention, roughly designed to act as peace-making neutrals between the secessionists and the Radical Republicans.

By then, other Southern states were following South Carolina. In Georgia, the Unionist movement was strong, and all of Howell Cobb's bland skill and Bob Toombs's fiery eloquence were required to move their fellow Georgians "to reconquer liberty and independence." Toombs thundered, with all the examples fresh in the people's minds, "I do not know why the abolitionists should object to [secession] unless they want to torture you and *plunder* you."

Unionists were still plentiful in all the Southern states, but the secessionists had the known leaders, the determined purpose, the party organizations, and they acted in concert. Most of all, they acted.

In the midst of that winter of turmoil and heartache, Senator Davis was ill again when he was notified of the withdrawal from the Union of the "state from which he was accredited." Mississippi was the second to go, precipitating the rush of the other five cotton states (Florida, Alabama, Georgia, Louisiana, and, late, Texas). Time had brought the long-dreaded hour to Davis, who regarded the South's independent future with a pessimism unshared by the enthusiastic secessionists.

Mrs. Chesnut, the sharp-eyed and sharp-tongued wife of the resigned South Carolina senator, wrote in her diary, "We separated from the North because . . . we have hated each other so."

Davis feared that hate carried to the extremes of disunion would not be resolved by peaceable separation. The fight had been too long building to a climax. The Northern fanatics would no more let the South go than the Southern extremists would remain in the Union with them. There was too little concern with "*the* Union," which even anti-Southern Henry Adams said "was a sentiment and not much more."

It was a sentiment to Southerners too. When Jefferson Davis worked on his farewell address, his mood was similar to the sadness in which Calhoun, ten years before, had composed his final speech.

Davis was still sick when he went for the last time to the Senate, and he cast a sorrowing glance over the full chambers and the packed galleries. Though he had never been more than the titular leader of the disunited Southern section, and was not even that any more, still the imposing gentleman of unimpeachable honor was the leading representative of the Southern defense. The crowd listened in profound silence, except for bursts of respectful applause, as he made one of his least Calhounian and most forthright of speeches. He stated without elaboration the rights of secession, and the "pressing necessity" of it for their own protection, but "not in hostility to others."

"I am sure I feel no hostility to you," he said, and "there is not one of you . . . to whom I cannot say now, in the presence of my God, I wish you well; and such, I am sure, is the feeling of the people whom I represent toward those whom you represent. I, therefore, feel that I but express their desire when I say I hope and they hope for peaceful relations with you, though we must part."

He apologized for any offense he might have given "in the heat of discussion," and said, "I go hence unencumbered by the remembrance of any injury received . . . [and] having made the announcement which the occasion seemed to require, it only remains for me to bid you a final adieu."

His wife, who'd had a seat held for her since seven in the morning, hoped that some could see behind his reserve "his deep depression, his desire for reconciliation, and his overweening love for the Union." But, when he left the Senate with Mrs. Davis, she said, ". . . we felt blood in the air."

While other Southerners were leaving Washington excitedly, going to their independent states as if joining the nobility of a monarchy, the Davises packed in deep grief and said their personal good-bys to old friends.

The seven seceded states—with Virginia and the other powerful border states voting to remain in the Union—were then electing delegations to meet in the Deep South to form a new nation on the continent. Davis continued to remain outside the crucial movements in the lower South, as he had since Yancey assumed control at the Charleston convention. He and his family were simply going home, to "the cat-and-clayed" affair which Davis had built with a Negro helper in a wan imitation of Thomas Jefferson serving as his own architect.

Their unpretentious home lay in a deep grove, where the air would be sweetened by the early-blooming Delta flowers, and the ill man could recover from the strife of the national convulsion. He and his wife were pleased at least by the assignment that would come to Davis as Mississippi's leading citizen soldier. He would be major general in charge of state volunteers.

But his dread of war hung over everything. Though Davis was not then a communicant of any church, the last words the defender of the South's rights said on his last night in Washington were in a prayer:

"May God have us in His holy keeping, and grant that before it is too late peaceful councils may prevail."

Section Two

". . . I'LL TAKE MY STAND . . ."

CHAPTER V

The Blow Is Struck

WHEN the delegates from the six seceded states (soon to be seven, when the Texans arrived) gathered in Alabama's pleasant, small capital at Montgomery to form their Cotton Kingdom, no electricity of rebellion charged the air. The gathering had more the festive, yet somewhat apprehensive, atmosphere of setting up an old business at a new stand.

Except for a few pessimists, the majority believed they would be allowed to leave the Union in peace (as the President opposed coercion and many Northerners thought "the erring sisters" should be allowed to depart). At worst, a halfhearted attempt at their subjugation would be quickly repelled by patriots fighting for their land. Leaving such contingencies to the future, the delegations busied themselves about setting up the legal structure of a nation on the model of the familiar one.

They must get a name for themselves, write a Constitution, elect officers, then attend to such delicate and unprecedented items as dividing up the postal service, customhouses and arsenals, defining "borders," and finally get to the larger matters of finance and taxation, diplomacy and national defense, and the complex plans and infinite details of establishing their group of states among the race of nations.

As if to assure everyone of their moderation, as well as to adhere to the familiar routine, the delegations largely eschewed the more rabid secessionists. Yancey was passed over in Alabama when the visitors gathered in his own home town. He was to render no useful service to the Confederacy and died during the war.

South Carolina also passed over Rhett, the *Mercury* editor who had trumpeted independence for twenty years. To placate the strong Unionists at home, the Georgia delegation included Alexander Stephens, an avowed anti-secessionist who had fought Toombs and Cobb to keep the state in the Union. Thompson and Brown, the secessionist manipulators in the Southern cabal in Washington, went on back to Mississippi, as did Davis, and their state sent an undistinguished collection of representatives. For the most part, all the delegations were composed of politicians, and they gave their languid energies to those things they knew best. They formed committees. . . .

To the people it was different. They had listened to the words of the Yanceys, read in the newspapers what the Northerners thought of them, talked over their corn likker through the hot, murmurous nights about John Brown and inciting the Negroes, and they didn't think it was going to be peaceful. They were not concerned, like the politicians, with procedures and establishing the formal structure of government. A personal people, of immediate and personal love for their land, they wanted first to be sure that their land was safe. In the lonely farms of the non-slave-holding yeomen, they remembered stories from their grandparents about the British soldiers coming through, trying to keep them with England, and they wanted to be prepared if it happened again.

The merchants and artisans and businessmen, also with no stake in slavery, worried about invaders too.

"If the Yankees can't sue us," they said, "I reckon they'll fight over a dollar. That's why they want to keep us with them, ain't it?"

"Leastwise, we ought to get ready."

To the imperious young plantation princes, who were to be liquidated as a class, the threat of invasion was no menace. They were eager to ride as Prince Ruperts against a nation of shopkeepers and mill hands who had the ill-mannered insolence to threaten the planters' civilization. And the camellia-skinned, soft-voiced belles, who were to become a generation of widows, were busy making silk flags to flutter as banners above the lancers.

In the cities and in the towns where the train came through once daily, on the isolated plantations reached only by small boats creeping up the jungle-banked streams, in the canebrakes and pine barrens and hill country, where neither boat nor train came, the people wanted to get ready for whatever happened to their land.

Travelers toward the new capital noticed the excited confidence bubbling at the top, with alert determination underneath, and they saw that the people *wanted* action. The travelers noticed, too, that there was no leadership to give the people action—or anything else.

In crowded Montgomery the delegations were followed by office seekers and sight-seers, pickpockets and adventurers, men of all ages offering their services to non-existent armies and women offering theirs to men. The two hotels overflowed and visitors complained of the food and accommodations. From the river up the wide street to the Capitol on the hill, bands played, slave auctions went on, and men fought to get in and out of the packed bars. Cursing in slow, liquid drawls, sizzling streams of tobacco juice in all directions, talking horses and "niggers" and Yankees, talking guns and dogs and personalities, the confused crowds were almost a caricature of the concept of the ante-bellum South.

In the Exchange Hotel the delegates of six states who went about the business of framing a Constitution for their confederation had less sense of the reality of their situation than the young ladies and their beaux who were dancing away the nights while awaiting the call to arms. There were high-minded men among them, and some not, but basically they all had been for too long an opposition party in the United States.

Having entered politics when the Southern states were on the defensive, their thinking was conditioned to defending their states against a larger body of states. They had defended with issues, against abolitionists and Free Soilers and Northern Whigs, and their consolidation in the Republican Party. Suddenly there was nobody to defend against and no issues. Even the last issue of the rights of slavery in territories—over which the states of the lower South broke the Democratic Party and at least helped the Republicans in—ceased to exist, because they had no territories.

Drafting a Constitution, the delegates could work on something constructive. Southerners had been great constitutionalists since pre-Revolutionary days and, since some of their best brains for the past thirty years had been interpreting the U. S. Constitution for their own protection, the delegates had trained scholars to put on their document. The framers of their Constitution produced a fine and learned work which expressed, in concept and detail, an ideal credo for their civilization.

Aside from making explicit the protection of slavery (with the "right" to take slave property into territories), the authors of the Confederate Constitution made no changes to indicate that they wanted a different kind of country from what they had left. The changes they made were designed to correct evils in detail in the old government and to constitutionalize those principles, protective of Southern life, for which their representatives had fought since Calhoun.

Being agricultural, they prohibited duties for the protection of special industries; being state-minded, they frowned on government subsidization; being poor, they authorized a self-supporting post office; being politicians, to avoid the pitfalls of politicking, they limited the President's tenure to one six-year term.

However, the drafting of this Constitution—with no steps taken to ensure the existence of the country for which it was adopted—implied a stable society co-existing with its former partner and now neighbor. In constitutionalizing their course out of the Union, the new Confederates obviously expected to continue to exist in relation to the United States.

When they went from the Constitution to the election of a President (by state delegations), the delegates looked to none of their revolutionaries, great soldiers, or practical politicians. They elected their representative *spokesman* in their former relation to the United States.

The unsought honor fell on Jefferson Davis like a blow, and his wife was dismayed. "He did not know the arts of the politicians," she said, "and would not practice them if understood." Politics implied that manipulation of people, that flexible give-and-take, which Mrs. Davis contemned for her husband. She said, "As a party manager, he would not succeed."

She saw him as a war leader. Educated at West Point, with service on army posts, he had displayed great personal bravery with volunteers in Mexico and as a peacetime War Secretary left an enviable record. All of this, with his passion for the military, added up for Mrs. Davis to the conviction that "his genius was military."

However, a dozen generals on each side, with similar training and experience, were disastrous failures as leaders. Webster's New International Dictionary gives a detailed explanation of that tricky word, "genius," which reveals Mrs. Davis' delusion when analyzing her husband. The lines read in part: "the intuitive and spontaneous, in opposition to the merely disciplined and trained; . . . inspired, over against what works in the main by rule and line."

Of all things, Davis worked by rule and line, by discipline and main effort. Thomas Cobb, the younger brother of Georgia's grandee and power in Buchanan's Cabinet, thought that Davis had reached his eminence by will alone. Certainly, neither by vision nor by timeless phrase did he ever seem inspired. He had many fine qualities of character, and neither moral nor physical fear was in him—but neither was humility.

He completely shared his wife's delusion as to his military genius, and this he brought with him to Montgomery on assuming the presidency of the Confederacy of the cotton states.

2

When Jefferson Davis arrived in the capital, he looked pale and harried. His features had sharpened, his lips tightened, and he revealed the strain of the will which young Cobb observed. He had been pleased to write his children of the ovations he received along the way. When his wife joined him, a transient sanctuary was provided in a corner house, which admirers every day filled with flowers. None of this removed the gnawing burden of his anxiety for the new little country, for all the things to be done, and of his gloomy apprehension that the United States would not allow them to get done.

His inaugural speech (February 18), a milk-and-water recital of Southern rights, was obviously intended more for the United States and the world than for the new Confederacy. In assuring everybody that their intentions were peaceful, and "no reason or justice" existed for the United States to violate that peace, he really appealed to the world that the new nation be permitted its destiny.

From inaugurals and appeals for the Confederacy's safety, Davis perforce turned to the practical procedures of forming an Administration.
On this, he never conceived of anything beyond the political practices
he had known and which existed in Montgomery on his arrival. No more
than any of the others did he think in terms of their specific needs, though
it was obvious that his (Provisional) Congress seemed unaware that any
specific needs existed.

As DeLeon, that sharp-eyed observer, said, the Confederates "looked
like the Washington Congress, viewed through a reversed opera-glass.
The same want of dignity and serious work; the same position of ease,
with feet on desk and hat on head; the same buzzing talk on different
subjects; often the very same men in the lobbies. . . . No point in Montgomery was remote enough—no assemblage dignified enough—to escape
the swoop of the lobby vulture. . . . The South had, in most cases,
chosen party hacks to legislate for and lead her on this great crisis, rather
than transfused younger blood and steadier nerves into her councils. . . ."

Along with the "party hacks" the South, through the state delegates,
made a far costlier choice in its Vice-President, Alexander Stephens. He
was chosen because of the delegates' desire to represent the anti-secession-
ists in the government and, along with the exclusion of their revolutionaries, to give the appearance of a sectionally unified, non-revolutionary
movement. With this unrealistic reasoning, they selected a sickly, undersized pedant, with an oversize vanity in his intellect and the infallibility
of his judgments, who had spent most of his political life in a personal
retreat from reality.

Born of poor dirt farmers and ascending by his own efforts into the
planter class, Stephens was anything except seignorial. In some need for
absolutism, he clutched at the American Constitution like a savage at his
charm, and his sense of infallibility was based on his expertness as a constitutionalist. Disbelieving in the whole Confederate movement from the
beginning, the Vice-President came to Montgomery with his large eyes
searching for weaknesses in the leaders and he was soon writing carping
criticisms home to his brother.

Between him and the President there was neither warmth nor antipathy,
but Davis, naturally assuming some dedication and intelligent purpose in
the Vice-President, at first sought Stephens' counsel and suggested assignments to him. Stephens soon failed him and Davis gradually withdrew
from the Vice-President, which aroused his spite and created an unhealthy
condition at the center of the administration.

Davis inherited Stephens and the Congress, but he selected his own
Cabinet. This he did through political considerations which would have
been applicable only to a going concern, plus the consideration of the
sensitivity of the separate states. Each of the seven must be represented
if the new nation was to begin life with any accord at all.

The best mind in the South was the highly successful and widely cultured Judah P. Benjamin, of Louisiana, who was personally unpopular. This was partly because he was an alien type (a West Indian Jew) of sybaritic tastes and mellowed, disenchanted realism, and partly because of jealousy for the ease with which he did so many things and never lost his smile. Davis' history with Benjamin had the usual episode of a sharp exchange, nearly a duel, but unusually the dissimilar men gained mutual respect and became friends. Wanting Benjamin, and knowing high office for him would antagonize the people, Davis made him Attorney General.

In a confusion over appointments, Memminger, the German orphan from Charleston, got the Treasury Department instead of Toombs. The Georgian, a financial expert in Washington, would have been bolder. Memminger, while shrewd, well trained, and methodical, lacked force and the courage to fight for his convictions. He executed with exemplary attention to detail a financial policy of paper money which he knew to be ruinous. In this Memminger typified a curious state of mind in the Southern Confederacy, where men in responsible positions went dutifully about their jobs whether or not the job accomplished the designed—or, indeed any—purpose.

Robert Barnwell, a gifted, Harvard-educated, and gracious South Carolinian, then refused the State portfolio because he objected to two cabinet members from the same state. To get Toombs in the Cabinet, Davis offered him the State Department. The Georgian did not want it, and Stephens and other friends were needed to persuade him to accept a post which he feared would amount to nothing under a President who could not delegate authority and to whom he was personally antithetical. For years in Washington, Toombs and Davis had been barely on speaking terms, and only that because of the good offices of friends who wanted the South to give the appearance of solidarity.

Stephen Mallory, Florida's outwardly phlegmatic senator who had served on the Naval Committee in Washington, was appointed Secretary of the Navy. Perhaps because of his humble beginning, growing up in the Key West boardinghouse of his widowed Irish mother, Mallory enjoyed living high at home and liked the companionship of the self-indulgent Benjamin. In his own department, considering the awesome handicaps against the U. S. Navy, Mallory accomplished as much as was possible with imagination and audacity. Though nothing of a secessionist, he operated his Navy Department more as a revolutionary than any of the others, and conceived of a plan from the beginning. Perceiving that his department could not hope to match the U. S. Navy in numbers, he constantly strove for the invulnerable sea monster that would nullify numerical superiority and was ahead of the enemy on ironclads.

From Texas came plain Judge Reagan, a poor boy from Tennessee who had done well in the West. Though he was little known, there was little interest in his department—the post office. In any event, the U. S. Post Office was still operating. He proved to be as capable as anyone could have under the impossible conditions, kept the post office self-supporting, and was a Confederate of selfless and unswerving loyalty.

To the public the one inexplicable appointment was the War Department, which everyone perceived to be the most vital post. There went a lank Alabama lawyer, Leroy Pope Walker, the gentleman who had the honor to announce the withdrawal of his state's delegation at the Charleston Democratic Convention. He was unfitted in all ways for the office, and some people soon suspected that Walker had been chosen as a "straw man," because Davis intended to run the War Office himself.

With this Cabinet, without either grandees or revolutionaries, and which was representative of the cotton states only politically, the Administration turned toward its first major problem—and made its first and irreparable major blunder. The blunder was made partly because the men believed the way to prove their existence as a sovereign power was to act like one. It was made partly because the men, believing in those "rights" they had so long defended, believed that England would also subscribe to them. It was made, finally, because the men had grown to their power and privilege on cotton and, a parochial people, they believed that their "king" was as important to everybody as to them.

If the new Confederacy was forced to defend itself from armed aggression, it needed money of all things—and of all things money was what it lacked. Only $25,000,000 in bullion existed in the seceded states and there were few ways of getting more. What those states had, indeed *were*, was cotton. In a momentous decision, the Administration decided not to use cotton for the cash it desperately needed but as a diplomatic weapon.

The United States declared a blockade on the Confederate ports, which was at that time unenforceable. This the Administration seized upon as a legality for its own use. The Cabinet decided to withhold cotton from the insatiable mills of England on the theory that England, in order to get the cotton, would break the blockade and recognize the new nation. So the Administration declared an embargo on the shipping of the only wealth it possessed.

This fateful and ruinous policy was caused by the lack of one true revolutionary who could conceive of *winning* independence. Nobody in Montgomery was psychologically disassociated from Washington.

When some of the old timeservers got to Montgomery, like the old fire horse at the sound of a bell, they went through the same paces as in the Washington Congress and continued to spout on about Southern rights as if the seats were filled with bored Yankees instead of bored Southerners.

Actually, everybody was waiting to see what the United States was going to do when Lincoln came in. Among those who feared armed force, Davis, having served as U. S. Secretary of War, knew better than most the frightening lacks of the new confederation of states in contrast to the old Union.

In the cotton states there were either not made at all or made only in insignificant amounts: gunpowder, percussion caps, rifles, cannons, ships. Nor was there any appreciable store of them in the South at the time. Scattered through the states were thousands of old flintlock muskets and revolvers and knives, in which the people had abundant faith, but Davis knew their inadequacy against modern rifles, let alone artillery.

The United States had a nucleus of an army and trained personnel from West Point, then out of the army, like Grant, Sherman, and McClellan. The South was getting a trickle of West Pointers coming home from all over the world, but the hot-blooded patriots distrusted them, as Davis shared the West Pointer's distrust of militia, with which the country abounded.

At the state university of his own home state, students had formed a militia company before Mississippi seceded, the University Greys, and the town boys of Oxford formed a rival company, the Lamar Rifles.

In December 1860 the University of Mississippi was only twelve years old, though the original faculty had been distinguished and cosmopolitan. Its students brought their own horses, with Negro hostlers and valets, and lived as young princes. Nineteen-year-old William Lowry, who brought a horse for himself and one for his body servant, along with his own bird dogs and guns, was elected captain of the university company because he had had some military training at a school in Kentucky. Lowry was a tall, slender, good-looking boy, described as "a courteous and refined gentleman." Most serious about the militia company, Lowry carried on a running fight with the college authorities over his absences for the purpose of drilling until the university gave him forty-eight hours to get out of Oxford.

By then the student company and the Lamar Rifles had been mustered into the state militia, with Lowry duly commissioned, and the young captain defied the college to remove him from his company. The state gave the two Oxford companies 120 muskets, and at the Cumberland Presbyterian Church the Lamar Rifles were presented with a company banner. With this, they paraded through Oxford to the music of fife and drum. Then the ladies of the town gave a band concert to raise money for the University Greys to get a banner—while the chancellor of the university was petitioning the governor to remove Lowry from the company. The young captain hung on.

In all the Southern states were similar units of high-spirited and physically fine young men, eager for action and in deadly earnest. The reason these partially trained and at least organized militia units were not brought immediately into the provisional army was only partly for lack of the arms for which Davis had purchasing agents scurrying off to Europe. The more basic reason seems to be that Davis, rejecting their revolutionary status, did not believe in "peacetime" armies and was afraid that a large army might be interpreted in the North as indicating a warlike disposition in the Southern states. Of all things Davis wished to avoid even the appearance of aggression.

While the young and the old champed impatiently for action, and the embargoed cotton bales gathered on the wharves, the political hacks pursued their craft in the friendly atmosphere of Montgomery, and the cabinet members set up shop in a building, with offices partitioned off, where they received petitioners for place and glory. The President, working at his office in the same building from nine to six, and coming home exhausted with fatigue, received for his main attention a familiar "issue." It must have seemed like old times, taking up where he left off, to have all ready-made and waiting for him another issue with the Republicans.

To his old stamping ground at Washington, while Buchanan was in his last days as President, Davis had dispatched three "commissioners" to deal with the United States Government over the disposition of the unfinished fort in Charleston's harbor. With the unanimity mania, he picked an old Louisiana Whig, a Georgia states' righter, and an Alabama Douglasite. Even this did not satisfy his Vice-President. Already giving a forecast of the tortured anti-Administration course he was to follow, Stephens had personally refused to go to Washington on the grounds that it would serve no useful purpose. Then he sat back and criticized the men Davis picked.

Soon self-righteous Stephens was to complain bitterly that Davis no longer sought his advice. However, little notice was taken of the Vice-President then. Lincoln had just been inaugurated, and the commissioners had waited to present their petition to him. With the hostile Republicans at last in power, the new Confederates recognized that the showdown had come over their status in relation to the United States—and it centered on the issue of Fort Sumter.

3

When Abraham Lincoln was inaugurated as President, there was no suggestion of the aura in which history has clothed him, and Southerners as well as many Northerners held a low opinion of him. Seward, who had lost the Republican nomination to Lincoln, confidently expected to control the Administration of a President who was privately called by powerful Republicans everything from buffoon to baboon.

Lincoln had been a compromise candidate whose stand on the slavery "issue" was mild enough not to alarm the moderates and eloquent enough to please all except the most fanatical abolitionists. However, when he came to Washington, slavery was not the issue confronting him. His very real problem was the secession of seven states, which had formed a new nation, and the tenuous position of the four powerful border states of Virginia, North Carolina, Kentucky, and Tennessee.

The country behind him was by no means solid, with attitudes varying from those Republicans who were snorting to get at the Southern states then and there to Democrats and others who strongly opposed armed coercion. Of this the Southerners were well aware and they were careful not to antagonize their friends in the North.

Lincoln possessed that "genius" for politics which his rival's wife scorned for her patrician husband. No man to show his hand, he was not given to those ringing statements, so dear to the hearts of the Southerners, which declared his intentions. During the months before his inauguration, when he acted as the behind-the-scenes manipulator of his party, Lincoln frequently tried out "feelers" by having others introduce ideas as "probably" representing the viewpoint of the President-elect. If the trial balloon was shot down, he could repudiate any connection with it.

In line with this went a genius for speaking, as the Indians say, with a forked tongue. As with his "house divided" speech, he could make a moving statement that could mean everything to everybody and, broken down, no impartial judge could say exactly what it did mean. So with his inaugural address.

". . . no State, upon its own mere motion, can lawfully get out of the Union . . . and . . . acts of violence, within any State or States, against the authority of the United States, are insurrectionary or revolutionary, according to circumstances. . . . [Then] I shall take care, as the Constitution itself expressly enjoins upon me, that the laws of the Union be faithfully executed in all the States. . . . [But] in doing this there needs to be no bloodshed or violence; *and there shall be none, unless it be forced upon the national authority.*"

The italics are not his, but those words, "unless it be forced upon . . ." could be interpreted almost any way anyone wanted to. To the Southerner, this could mean peace between the sections, unless the South committed an act of violence. On the other hand, it might mean the national authority could be forced to act in execution of the laws. He clearly implied the last interpretation by saying, "The power confided to me will be used to hold, occupy, and possess the property and places belonging to the government, and to collect the duties and imposts. . . ." But, to confuse that statement, he added, ". . . beyond what may be necessary for these objects, *there will be no invasion* [not his italics]—no using of force against or among the people anywhere." Yet how could properties be occupied and duties collected except by using force "against or among the people"?

After puzzling over these words, the new Confederate government knew no more than it had before—except, as Davis had suspected, Lincoln had no intention of accepting the secession of the states. In his implied coercion, the U.S. President apparently had decided on no course of action. With the divided country behind him and the importance of saving the border states for the Union, he was going to move cautiously and be guided by events.

In the preceding thirty years, the Southerners could usually be depended upon to force issues, but since the states had seceded the leaders were showing an unwonted guilefulness. They were doing absolutely nothing to provide any excuse for Lincoln's applying "such force as may be necessary." Though the South Carolinians were champing to get at Fort Sumter, the Confederate Administration restrained them too, in their determination not to commit an act of aggression.

It was obvious that the hot spot of Sumter was to be the "issue" over which side would strike the first blow. That federal fort became *the* issue purely by circumstance. During the last months of Buchanan's administration, the seceded states had occupied peaceably enough the other federal properties within their borders, such as forts, arsenals, and navy yards, post offices and customhouses, the mint at New Orleans, and suchlike. But Fort Sumter, out in Charleston Harbor and heavily gunned, could not be occupied without an armed attack. In their non-aggressive policy, South Carolina sent commissioners to Buchanan to request its evacuation—from their viewpoint, a perfectly reasonable request.

This harbor fort occupied the same position in relation to Charleston and South Carolina that a British fort off the tip of Manhattan would have occupied in relation to New York after the American Revolution. To South Carolina the United States had become an alien power, and the fort was not only within the territorial confines of the state but a menace to the harbor and Charleston.

Charleston Harbor is very roughly like a horseshoe, with Charleston at the base and the bay between two hooks of land. Though divided from the mainland by the network of waterways which makes that stretch of coast a succession of sea islands, the tips of the hooks are for practical purposes extensions of the mainland. About midway between the two hooks of land and in the opening of the horseshoe, Fort Sumter rises abruptly out of the water, facing the ocean outside the bar.

On James Island to the south were positions for a series of batteries and some installations, the group called Fort Johnson; on Sullivan's Island to the north was an old sea fort in poor condition, Fort Moultrie. Near the city was a small fort, Castle Pickney, and in the city a U.S. arsenal. The four forts and the arsenal comprised the command of a permanent U. S. Army base, quartered at Fort Moultrie.

This sea fort of Moultrie was virtually open on the inland side and in such a state of neglect that drifting sand had piled up to the top of ramparts and formed an inclined parade ground for cows. The garrison was extremely small, seventy-five men and officers, including a nine-piece band, and army life had been pleasant on Sullivan's Island, where there were many summer homes for Charlestonians and some year-round places. Edgar Allan Poe described Sullivan's Island in *The Gold Bug*, after his one-year hitch at Fort Moultrie, 1827–28.

In addition to the garrison at Fort Moultrie, some engineering officers supervised civilians on the work to complete Fort Sumter; a caretaker's staff occupied Castle Pinckney and an army storekeeper was in charge of the arsenal.

When South Carolina first seceded, the United States and the state agreed on a "truce" regarding the harbor forts. Though Buchanan refused to evacuate the forts, he promised not to commit any act of aggression. South Carolina's new Governor Pickens did not know how to handle such an unprecedented situation, but he was thoroughly outraged at having the armed forces of an alien power in his territory and his growing militia units were straining to get at the forts.

The newly appointed commander, Major Robert Anderson, of Kentucky, was that most painfully divided of men—a Southern sympathizer and staunch Unionist. Under orders to avoid collision and anxious himself to avoid war, Major Anderson grew alarmed at the threatening attitude of the South Carolinians. On his own responsibility, he secretly moved his small forces at dusk to a consolidation on Fort Sumter, abandoning all the other positions.

The South Carolinians, in a state of agitation anyway, regarded this as a breach of faith and made a highhanded representation to Buchanan. By then the Southern influences had left the President's Cabinet, to be replaced by firm coercionists, and, disillusioned with his former secessionist friends, old Buchanan got his back up. He took a very stiff attitude toward South Carolina, and supported his attitude by sending a relief ship, *Star of the West*, with supplies for Fort Sumter. The ship was driven off by cannon fire from the two land forts, Moultrie and Johnson, both then occupied by South Carolina militia. The United States flag had been fired upon! But, since no harm was done and Buchanan was trying to avoid issues rather than seek them, the *Star of the West* did not become an international incident.

There the matter rested, with Major Anderson buying greens and fresh meat in Charleston—and sending regular reports to Adjutant General Cooper in Washington on the progress of the South Carolina militia in building up armament for an attack on Fort Sumter—until Lincoln was inaugurated and Davis' commissioners sought to present their credentials.

4

The commissioners of an unrecognized foreign power could not be received by the United States President or even the Secretary of State. But protocol had no terrors for Davis' former New York friend, William Seward. He dealt with the commissioners through the intermediary of Judge Campbell, the Alabama Unionist who still served on the Supreme Court. This began a much-discussed maze of triple dealings, in which the South received an impression, which it never lost, of a betrayal—an act of duplicity and bad faith—by the Lincoln Administration.

Seward was the villain, and that inadvertently. He outsmarted himself and caused a betrayal as a result. The Secretary of State, expecting to run the government as he had watched Southerners do with two weak Presidents, personally gave the Confederate commissioners assurances that Fort Sumter *would* be evacuated. The confusion arose from the commissioners' natural assumption that the Secretary of State was speaking for the Administration. Seward was not. He was saying what he *wanted* done and probably *believed* he could get done.

At this time Lincoln had reluctantly accepted the majority opinion of his Cabinet against supplying Fort Sumter. On his own, however, the President had sent private emissaries to Charleston to discover first-hand the sentiment of the state. Two of the men were civilian friends: one a former Charlestonian and the other one of those Virginians who had migrated west, to become a law partner of Lincoln in Illinois. They talked to Charleston friends and particularly to Petigru, the brilliant-minded lawyer who called himself "the last Unionist in the state."

Petigru sadly assured his friends that, as far as the state was concerned, the break was complete and irrevocable. Nothing that happened or did not happen at Sumter would affect its stand.

But resupplying the fort, Governor Pickens warned, would be resisted. The attempt would, he stated flatly, "mean war." The governor was given to understand that the United States was more likely to evacuate the fort.

The third emissary was Captain Fox, who had first broached to Lincoln the plan for an armed relief of the fort. Captain Fox arrived in Charleston, where with all courtesies he was taken by boat to the fort for an interview with Major Anderson. Once on the ground, Fox became more than ever convinced that his plan of an armed expedition was feasible, despite Major Anderson's obvious disbelief in such an expedition.

Major Anderson by then was suffering from the prolonged strain of living under the constant threat of the South Carolinians, the humiliation of confinement in the small fort with the necessity of asking permission to go ashore for mail, for food, for any reason, and of avoiding offense to a trigger-happy militia swelled in numbers to approximately five thousand with over fifty heavy guns. Major Anderson had about seventy guns in two tiers, the bottom inside the heavy masonry of the outer walls of the fort and the top firing through embrasures from an open barbette.

Major Anderson's ordeal was rendered at least less humiliating when, on March 1, the Charleston forces were placed under the command of a former brother army officer, P. G. T. Beauregard. The gorgeous Creole from New Orleans had been superintendent of West Point when his state seceded and, after his resignation from what the Confederates called "the old army," he was appointed brigadier general of the Provisional C.S.A. To a deep native courtesy Beauregard added a childlike love of all the forms and panoply of the military. In his exchanges with the besieged Major Anderson he verged on the operatic in his efforts to spare the major's feelings.

But Major Anderson found nothing operatic in the Creole's ceremonious solicitude. Their exchanges are unsurpassed in history for mutual consideration of the mortal dignity of man, expressed in friendly courtesy while observant of the strictest punctiliousness. Both of the officers were waiting on Washington, with Anderson frankly longing for evacuation orders. As late as April 1, on the basis of Lincoln's Charleston emissary, the major was waiting for those orders.

Lincoln had finally made up his mind to force that "issue." On March 29 he ordered his Secretary of War, then slippery Simon Cameron, to co-operate with the Secretary of the Navy and have a force ready for the relief of Fort Sumter not later than April 4. On the first of April through his grapevine (Seward to Judge Campbell to the Confederate commissioners) Lincoln passed the word to Governor Pickens that the fort would not be reprovisioned "without notification."

Then the Southerners knew something was going to happen. The three commissioners in Washington rushed around desperately trying to find out details. Well-wishers wired conflicting messages from Washington every day. In the fort, poor Anderson was harassed almost beyond endurance, and the punctilious Beauregard was now sending messages to *his* Adjutant General Cooper at Montgomery. The old Hudson River New Yorker had, as the saying went, "gone over" to the Confederates, and thus Samuel Cooper had the distinction of serving both armies during the Sumter crisis.

Finally, on April 6, all uncertainties were ended. Lincoln wrote out a message in his own hand for Governor Pickens and entrusted it for delivery to a State Department official. As Professor Ramsdell has pointed out, the message was only ostensibly for Pickens. To the people of the

North the note meant only that he was sending supplies to a starving garrison. To the Confederate leaders it was a challenge, and one he had been assured they would meet. The note read:

"I am directed by the President of the United States to notify you to expect an attempt to be made to supply Fort Sumter with provisions only; and that, if such an attempt be not resisted, no effort to throw in men, arms or ammunition will be made without further notice, or in case of an attack upon the fort."

That read innocently enough to his own side, unaware of the dealings. To the government of the new Confederacy, however, it was most threatening with that phrase "without further notice." What Lincoln said to Governor Pickens was that there would be no evacuation of Fort Sumter. The United States would continue to supply its garrison there and might even reinforce it.

However Lincoln might deny the rights of secession, he must have known that to themselves the Southerners were as much a new republic as were the American colonies in their revolt, and to this republic it was unthinkable that the fort of a foreign power should remain indefinitely in their territory.

As John Brown had Governor Wise to hang instead of imprison him, so Lincoln had the whole Confederate Cabinet, with the exception of Toombs, to catch in the trap.

Once Governor Pickens received Lincoln's note on April 8, with the relief expedition already starting from New York, the Southerners, as they had been doing for thirty years, rushed to give all benefits of the issue to their long-thinking enemies.

The details were conducted with the warm and solicitous courtesy of all the exchanges between Beauregard and Anderson. At 3:45 P.M. on April 11, two of Beauregard's staff officers were rowed out to the fort and presented the request for evacuation in almost apologetic terms. The note ended: "The flag which you have upheld so long and with so much fortitude, under the most trying circumstances, may be saluted by you on taking it down."

In forty-five minutes Major Anderson gave the two aides a polite note of refusal to evacuate, but said to them, "Gentlemen, if you do not batter the fort to pieces about us, we shall be starved out in a few days."

Acting on the added verbal line, and after communicating with War Secretary Walker, Beauregard sent just after midnight a note asking when the major might be forced to evacuate for want of victuals. After trying to delay the aides until daylight, Major Anderson replied that he would evacuate on the fifteenth, three days away, but with a provision on the Lincoln line: ". . . should I not receive prior to that time controlling instructions from my Government or additional supplies."

As the Confederates knew that ships were on their way—in fact, the first was outside the bar the early morning of the twelfth—the provision did it. At 3:20 A.M. the aides wrote on a casement of the fort this brief message:

"By authority of Brigadier-General Beauregard, commanding the Provisional Forces of the Confederate States, we have the honor to notify you that he will open the fire of his batteries on Fort Sumter in one hour from this time."

Major Anderson shook hands with the young men and they left the fort.

After thirty years, an issue in the long concatenation of events had led at last to trial by arms.

5

Rough seas kept the relief ships outside the bar during the thirty-four hours that the shore batteries fired on the fort. With ammunition and supplies low, after hot shots fired the barracks inside the bastions and other minor damage was done, Major Anderson, who never felt Sumter could be defended, decided that the formalities had been observed and surrendered the fort.

The formalities were observed to the end. With a fifty-gun salute to the flag and the band playing bravely, the garrison troops left the fort and embarked on a Confederate steamer which took them to one of the U.S. ships outside the bar. Major Anderson never recovered from the strain. Though promoted to brigadier, a nervous breakdown prevented his service.

Lincoln wrote his emissary Captain Fox, who headed the expedition, "You and I both anticipated that the course of the country would be advanced by making the attempt to provision Fort Sumter, even if it should fail; and it is no small consolation now to feel that our anticipation is justified by the result."

The result was the violent reaction of Northern Democrats against their former Southern allies. Other Northerners, who had opposed coercion, became enraged patriots at the armed assault on the United States flag and its protectors.

South Carolinians were not unmindful of the consequences of their act. But Sumter, as the last of the "issues," had exacerbated their nerves until that fort had to be theirs if the heavens fell. On the night of April 13, the Charlestonians thought only that *at last*, after a drawn-out four months, they were finally and completely free of the United States.

The most gala throng in the history of Charleston crowded the battery to watch the bombardment. Military and civil staffs were bedecked in blue capes embroidered with palm leaves, and blue frock coats had shoulder straps edged with lace. Gilt palmetto buttons glinted everywhere. Distinguished Southerners attended as if guests to a race meet or a St. Cecilia Ball, and Virginia's old fire-eater, Edmund Ruffin, was allowed to fire a shot—some say the first. Virginia had there another fire-eater, young Roger Pryor, newspaper editor, duelist, and volunteer aide to Beauregard. It was Pryor who had urged the South Carolinians to start bloodshed, as a means of bringing in his own reluctant state. Yet, when the Charleston gentlemen offered him the honor of firing the first shot, Pryor drew back and said, "I don't want to begin the war."

The South Carolinians, in accepting war as a consequence of their actions, had cherished too long a history of independence to feel any fear. Then, they had no experience with what was to become the first modern war—total war. They thought in terms of men against men, and on that basis they certainly proved to be justified in their faith in themselves.

However, lost in the enchantment of their tropically enclosed plantations, with the habit of personal self-assertion, the people had little notion of how the despised factories of the North would relate to war. The Southerners thought of themselves, with their habits of shooting and riding, against drudges of those factories. Their thinking of war had stopped, along with their political-economic thinking, in 1832. It was not to be man against man; it was to be man against machines.

Happily ignorant of the new style of war that was to come into the world against them, the people danced and sang, and except for a few die-hard Unionists and foreboders, were happier than they had been in thirty years.

CHAPTER VI

The Gathering of the Knights

WHEN the mass excitement spread from Charleston through the seven states of the new nation, the men of anxiety spoke little aloud and the men of sorrow went unheeded. From all over the country and all over the world, men and their families were leaving established positions to come home in duty to their states, in loyalty to their own land. The stream of congressmen leaving Washington was followed by government employees, some in high place, and men in diplomatic and consular service booked passage in foreign ports to bring their families home. Army officers left posts and their careers, naval officers left ships, students left colleges, and an Alabama boy named John Pelham, later to be heard from, the son of a staunch anti-secessionist, left West Point. An old South Carolina patriarch, returning to his home place, spoke for many when he said, "I have lived too long; I should have died ere these evil days arrived."

While the unarmed young knights paraded in gorgeous uniforms before the admiring glances of the belles, and the hotheads cursed the Yankee scum, the men of responsibility looked at their capacities for waging war —and found none. The happy hedonists, living in the enchantment of the hour in their agrarian world, had depended on the outside for everything.

With two exposed coasts containing endless waterways to the inland and the Mississippi River on the third side, they had no shipbuilding, few ships, and a "navy" only on paper. Without arsenals or laboratories, they had no heavy industry—iron mills, rolling mills, or powder mills of any capacity—that could be converted into arms manufacturing, nor any workmen for such. Of railroads they had a plenty, in proportion to population as much mileage as the North—only they did not connect. With typical individualism, the lines had been built without central systems, and gaps of from one to twenty miles between lines existed all over the South. A railroad simply ended at one point, and another began somewhere else. A union depot was unknown. As with everything else, there were no facilities for the replacement of locomotives, rolling stock, ties, and equipment.

Even in the manpower on which they proudly depended, the combined population of the seven states was less than that of New York State. To augment this, and gain at least *some* industrial potential, the leaders looked longingly at Virginia and the other border states. But they remained steadfastly within the Union. Many Virginians were totally out of sympathy with the cotton states. While spirited young people flaunted the South Carolina cockade, conservatives regarded the firing on Sumter as "folly and madness."

Then Lincoln, with an aroused country behind him, issued his call to arms, and the whole complexion suddenly changed for the new Confederacy. Lincoln did not declare war, as he regarded the seven states as acting illegally within the Union. He called for 75,000 ninety-day volunteers to suppress "a combination too powerful to be suppressed by the ordinary course of traditional proceedings."

As there was nothing "traditional" about the whole thing, and nothing in the Constitution to cover such a situation, the only precedent was Andrew Jackson's decision thirty years before to deny the rights of secession by force of arms. Jackson had been confronted with one state. When Lincoln applied force of arms to a whole section, the "suppression" got out of hand.

When he called on Virginia, North Carolina, Tennessee, and Arkansas to supply volunteers, Lincoln actually asked them to participate in an invasion of their sister states. Not only did they disbelieve in this extreme as a violation of states' rights (and also that the grievances of the cotton states were just), but they were outraged at the idea of making war on people of their own land. Since the alternative to participation in the invasion was to be themselves invaded, the reaction was immediate and violent.

Virginia's Governor Letcher spoke for them all when he answered Lincoln, "You have chosen to inaugurate Civil War."

The people in those four states joined the secession movement with a high and angry sense of justice on their side. The original emancipationists of the country were in Virginia, North Carolina, and Tennessee, where slavery was passing. Instead of seceding, they had fought to preserve the Union. To them, there was no need for definitions of principles, recitations of their grievances, or calling to the world to regard the justice of their position. They responded in pure and primal defense of their land against an aggressor. The poem, *The Flag of the South*, was written when the Confederate flag was raised over Virginia's Capitol.

> *Defend your lov'd soil from the proud tyrant's tread,*
> *Be fearless while living—be honored while dead. . . .*

A member of one of Virginia's foremost Unionist and emancipationist families wrote, ". . . the terrible conflict upon which we are now about to enter is forced upon us by Lincoln's administration and in ruthless disregard of our protestations and honest attempts at pacification . . . we ceased not our patriotic and blessed office of peacemakers until the call for 75,000 troops. . . . To tarry longer without the most active preparations for determined resistance is compatible with neither the safety nor the honor of Virginia. . . . We are therefore shut up to the necessity of maintaining our rights but as we may."

To maintain those rights, Governor Letcher issued a proclamation that looked neither to England nor to Northern Democrats for help. It was a call to the people to defend their own land as they had against the British. The Revolution was not remote to them. They had talked with veterans of Washington's army; Lee's father had been a cavalry leader with and a friend of George Washington. Virginia's governor said:

"The sovereignty of the Commonwealth of Virginia having been denied, her territorial rights assailed, her soil threatened with invasion by the authorities at Washington, and every artifice employed which could inflame the people of the Northern States and misrepresent our purposes and wishes, it becomes the solemn duty of every citizen of this State to prepare for the impending conflict."

In the other three states, it went the same way. Lincoln had created the Confederacy of Calhoun's dreams.

With those four states, the Cotton Kingdom got a manpower greater than its own, an industrial potential, a physical buffer, and the completeness of a nation which would make of the suppression a real war. When these people came in with a high and undivided moral purpose, there came with them the imponderables of armed force as a solution for the nation's schism.

Of the "ifs" of the armed conflict, the big "if" is: suppose Virginia had remained a neutral? With Virginia came Robert E. Lee, Joe Johnston, and Stonewall Jackson (with the Valley men who comprised his first foot cavalry), Dick Ewell, John Magruder, and Jeb Stuart (with the cavaliers and the farm boys who dominated his cavalry), A. P. Hill and George Pickett, Jubal Early and Matthew Fontaine Maury ("the Pathfinder of the Seas"), who sadly left his Washington Naval Observatory and invented the naval torpedoes which Union officers said were the Confederacy's best defense against the blockade.

With the imponderables of the leadership of such men, and their followers, came the matériel of war. Some of it was immediately available and some provided a future potential. With legalities removed and a state of undeclared war proclaimed, Virginia militia immediately seized the Norfolk Navy Yard with fifty rifled guns and sufficient powder to become, as President Davis said, "the chief store" in the Confederacy. They seized the arsenal at Harper's Ferry, the only U.S. arsenal maintained in the South and the only machinery for making rifles. Virginia's state armory in Richmond and Richmond's laboratories were converted to modernize outmoded field artillery and muskets. These items were immediately vital when only 15,000 rifles existed in the eleven seceded states (mostly belonging to militia) and less than 150,000 weapons for infantry were available, counting antiquated muskets.

For the future, Richmond had the only cannon foundry and rolling mills for bar iron; except for negligible small mills, Virginia and Tennessee had the only blast furnaces. The Tredegar Iron Works in Richmond manufactured the only field artillery at the time of secession, and the next city to produce it was Nashville, Tennessee. From Tennessee came the bulk of the niter used by the powder mill which was built in the summer of 1862 in Augusta, Georgia. Lead came almost entirely from Wytheville, Virginia.

In time, some powder came through the blockade, and two small mills in South Carolina and one in Raleigh were in operation. Later, arsenals and foundries were built in the lower South. But what future could the agricultural states have had without the matériel from Virginia and Tennessee and the physical buffers they provided which gave the lower South protection in order to develop its few scattered war industries?

The Confederacy never had to answer that question. It was in business, and its people had no intention of being physically coerced by any "suppression" to return to a Union composed of other states then preparing to invade them.

2

With all the expansion of the Confederacy and the high-running emotions of the people, it did not approach being a united nation. At the inception, motives for secession were too involved within the separate states, and the upper South had left the Union for different reasons than the Cotton Kingdom. Then, the Confederate government was unsure of exactly what states would comprise their new country, and this uncertainty created another kind of division.

They had hopes of Maryland, Missouri, and Kentucky, in the last of which Lincoln did experiment with "neutrality." Kentucky, above Tennessee, and Missouri, above Arkansas, both on the same latitude with Virginia, became divided states.

They had both Unionist and secessionist governors and legislatures, Unionist and secessionist troops. Both states were predominantly Unionist and, as political and geographic entities, for all practical purposes they operated as states of the Union. In Missouri the Rebel forces occupied some Union attention and troops, and the state sent good men to the

Confederate armies. Parts of Kentucky were an early battleground and many Kentuckians performed handsomely and faithfully with the Confederacy to the end. Both states had stars in the Confederate flag of thirteen stars.

North of the Potomac, Delaware was a completely Unionist slaveholding state, while Maryland was a slaveholding state with a considerable population of Southern sympathizers. However, except for an outburst of hoodlumism in Baltimore when Union troops passed through and some defiant talk from individuals, the state as an entity remained Unionist from the beginning. Many Marylanders fought with the Confederate troops, chiefly with Virginia's. Two complete Maryland volunteer companies with seven militia companies from Richmond composed Washington's old 1st Virginia Regiment. The state did not have a star in the Confederate flag.

The Confederacy as a political-military unit was composed of eleven states, with a white population of something over 5,500,000. Minus the divided border states of Kentucky and Missouri, the rest of the country had a population of roughly 20,000,000. If the populations of those two border states were divided equally between the two sections, the South would have 6,500,000 against 21,000,000. On paper they were outnumbered about three and a half to one.

That would assume all Southerners were loyal Confederates. This was far from the case. Many who had voted against secession remained Unionists, some of them actually "going over." Each Southern state furnished troops to the U.S. armies. Worse from the Confederate standpoint, the mountainous regions of East Tennessee and western North Carolina remained pockets of Unionism, and the mountainous counties of western Virginia remained so steadfastly Unionist that they seceded from the mother state during the war and formed the new Union state of West Virginia.

Yet, with all the Union strongholds and Union sentiment through the Southern states, with the announcement of Lincoln's invasion, there was a rush of enlistments in the South probably never proportionately equaled on this continent. From a population of something over 6,000,000, including the Southern share of the two divided border states, over 600,000 men of all ages volunteered for armed service.

The government accepted only two thirds, partly from inability to arm and equip any more, and partly because of that Grand Illusion about cotton. From secessionists to merchants, they were so confident that the pride of their empire would fight for them that the London *Times* correspondent, then in Charleston, said, "They assume that the British crown rests on a cotton bale."

Since none of the South's few international-size financiers had been brought into the government, one gritty item about their cotton was missed by the proud provincials. In England, the cotton manufacturers welcomed the blockade as warmly as did the Confederates. They happened to have a big store of cotton at the time and, with the world's cotton producer blocked off, they could raise the price of their manufactured goods. It was not only Yankees who put the dollar before Southern justice! The powerful textile bloc in England, far from pressing their government to lift the blockade, were making money beyond their wildest dreams.

Along with the Grand Illusion about cotton, the old-line politicians still fondly believed that the North meant them no serious harm. With his own state love, the Southerner could not conceive that the Union would have a stronger appeal to others than to him. Even after Lincoln's call to arms, the secessionists did not expect Northern Democrats to put much will into open warfare or Northern businessmen to support a long war that would hurt their pocketbooks.

There were many realists, even pessimists, in the South, but their attitude was unpopular during the reflowering of knighthood. Jefferson Davis was among the clearsighted who feared the South was in for more than a chivalrous tournament, and he apparently never believed the Southern states could *win* their independence. Also victimized by the Grand Illusion, his undeclared purpose was always to hold off the Union until the Confederacy's claims of nationality were *granted*.

The leaders still thought in terms of principles from their Washington days. Since the people everywhere and the governments of the border states thought of themselves repelling the invader, the new nation took up its armed defense with a basic, ineradicable, and fatal duality. This was a sad thing for all those who had taken no part in forcing any of the issues, for surely no people ever rushed more gaily to the defense of their land.

3

There was a light-opera quality about the mobilization of the Southern forces. In the beginning, they gathered as many armies as Ireland had kings. They had everything except *an* army, which, alas, they were never to have. In the first mustering, everything about the Confederacy was "provisional"—the President, the government, the army. Then, before the Provisional Army of the C.S.A., came the provisional armies of the individual states. Yet before the provisional state armies came the state volunteers, to be distinguished from recruits directly into the provisional armies. Before either came the state militia, of which there were 130,000 in Virginia alone.

The older militia units, such as Richmond's Company F, had been largely social affairs, and in New Orleans' famous Washington Artillery

Battalion new members were elected, as to a club, up to the eve of war. As these young aristocrats set the standard when the call to arms came, the men of privileged backgrounds, education, and habits of leadership volunteered as privates (as distinct from enlisted) in volunteer units—such as the Rockbridge (County) Artillery, composed of students from the University of Virginia and Washington College (later Washington and Lee University), and commanded by the Episcopal rector of Lexington.

Most of the volunteer units elected their officers, usually choosing the most popular rather than the most able. Since popularity came largely from not interfering with the young princelings' wills, this meant enforcing no discipline and attempting to instill no habits of obedience—a quality esteemed by planters only in servants and young children.

Other officers were self-appointed, where a rich or prominent man in a community "raised" a company himself. One of the most effective of these in actual fighting was the South Carolina Legion of Wade Hampton, the plantation grandee of herculean physical feats. Hampton himself became one of the few leaders without previous military experience to achieve distinction. Much of the operatic element of the early days, and some later disasters, resulted from the delusion of the lordly planters that as natural leaders they were all potential Hamptons.

After the men joined one of the thousands of individual commands, usually in their neighborhoods, they waited around to be sent to one of many mobilization centers—a center of a geographic area with railroad connections. It was purely a matter of chance as to the training the men received while waiting.

For some units the period was a prolonged barbecue, with ladies spending the day at camp and surfeiting the volunteers with fancy victuals. In others, where the officers had some military training, the men were drilled and received at least the essentials of discipline. Even the most zealous were handicapped by lack of arms, which were few and far between, and the artillery units had their pieces doled by ones and twos, as cannon from the captured U. S. Navy Yard at Norfolk were mounted on quickly made gun carriages and caissons on wagons.

Indifferent to these practical lacks, the hotspurs all over the South were clamoring for action as the belligerent in the North were clamoring for the invasion to commence. The thoughtless of both sides wanted the test over and done with and neither President told the people that the struggle might be long. Lincoln's call for "ninety-day volunteers" indicated that he was among those who believed the suppression would be a brief affair. At that, he might have been right, except for those imponderables of the resolution by arms.

The imponderable with the most effect on the armed test was a gentle Virginian, the finest soldier in the U. S. Army, who, in relinquishing the rewards of thirty-five years' service with the Regular Army to go with his state, wrote the little daughter of a Northern friend, "I cannot raise my hand against my birthplace, my home, my children."

Robert E. Lee, then fifty-four years old, also said, "A union which can only be maintained by bayonets has little charm for me."

A disbeliever in slavery and no secessionist, this flowering of one of the truly great American families brought to the defense of his land the same purity of motive that had actuated his father, uncles, and cousins in the Revolution, and his hero, George Washington, the step-great-grand-father of his wife. Colonel Lee, late U.S.A., did not join any of the Con-federate "armies." He offered his services to his native state and, very unobtrusively, assumed the responsibility for Virginia's defense as major general in command of the state's troops.

As Virginia did not enter into a compact with the Confederate States until three weeks after its secession (May 7), when Lee first set up his office across from Capitol Square, he was confronted with the task of fortifying a state against the invasion of a nation. In this unpublicized and largely unappreciated work, the quiet gentleman performed as brilliantly as later in the field. Without his heroic work on the Virginia defenses, Lincoln might well have accomplished a quick suppression.

At this stage of his life, Lee was a physically powerful and handsome man of pronounced self-composure. Though his dark hair was turning gray, his mustache was still dark and he had not yet affected the beard by which history knows him. In his carriage and manners, as well as in his classic features, he reflected the generic aristocracy from which he had sprung. As a traditional aristocrat, he possessed those qualities of *noblesse oblige* which derived from the Old South of the legend, with none of the excesses and assertiveness of the new. He was the mellowed South, of graciousness and gentleness and tact. He was going to need it all.

From the first Lee was deaf to loud-talking politicians and would-be Napoleons. He believed the war might last for ten years and he prepared for a long war. He also had to prepare for the opening invasion in a hurry, so that he was rushing defenses at the same time that he was building for the future.

The reluctantly seceding state of Virginia, destined to become the battleground of the Civil War, was designed by nature to favor the in-vader. It was literally riddled with inviting avenues of entrance. Lee's im-mediate task was to place a block in each avenue.

4

The broad rivers that had nurtured the growth of the Virginia planta-tion aristocracy became vulnerable lines that could be exploited by the

U. S. Navy. First the unhurriedly busy man in Richmond had to erect river fortifications to contain enemy boats.

Then the flatland of the fabled tidewater peninsula, between the James and the York, had to be protected because the Virginia militia had been unable to capture the U. S. Fortress Monroe on the tip, and at the outset, Virginia had an enemy implanted on her soil.

The state also had enemies in Virginians in the western counties, those who formed the new state of West Virginia. While the United States was purportedly invading the Southern states in denial of the rights of self-determination, the western counties of Virginia were encouraged to secede from their own state and assert *their* rights of self-determination.

With Washington support, Ohio's governor dickered with the western counties' officials to turn them against their own state and to justify something the disaffected people had long wanted to do—escape the domination of eastern Virginia. The whole formation of the new state was an illegal business. One third of the counties included in the secession were not represented at the Wheeling Convention, and few of their citizens voted on the movement. No citizens in the rest of Virginia were allowed to vote on the separation of their own counties. Thad Stevens, the vindictive hater of the South, said that West Virginia was admitted "under our absolute power which the laws of war give us in the circumstance . . . [but] I will not stultify myself by supposing that we have any warrant in the Constitution for such proceedings."

The fighting in Virginia's western counties has received little historical attention, partly because on looking back it seems to have been inevitable that the section should become West Virginia. Leaders of the state forces, not realizing the extent to which the westerners were anti-Virginian, wasted time and energy, equipment and men in trying to save the less remote and more loyalist counties. They had also a practical military reason, which continued throughout the war, to keep enemy forces out of the Shenandoah Valley, which was Virginia's bread basket.

A threat to the Valley which could work in conjunction with enemies to the west was a force forming to come straight down through Harper's Ferry, a northernmost projection of loyalist Virginia at the juncture of the Potomac and Shenandoah rivers.

And there was the most vital direct thrust from Washington. At Manassas Junction, such a thrust would sever the connections of northern Virginia with the Shenandoah Valley, and then stand poised to come on down to Richmond, little more than a hundred miles from Washington with no natural obstacles between.

None of these threats was theoretical. Union forces were forming to exploit each of the avenues of entrance.

In preparing for a war, as well as for immediate defense, Lee began by organizing a superb staff, some of whom served him to the finish. While soothing ruffled feelings, he organized the militia and volunteers into the provisional army for one year—this short-term concession against his own judgment. He had to supervise the production of arms, mounting for field artillery the guns captured with the Norfolk Navy Yard, turning out rifles from the captured U.S. arsenal at Harper's Ferry, converting flintlocks into percussion-fire muskets in the state armory. He supervised the procurement of equipment, for the C.S.A. lacked cartridge cases, tents, haversacks, and almost anything you could name. The arms and equipment he collected Lee apportioned to men whom he stationed at the points of entry. That was only the beginning.

The real work lay in selecting the men to command the volunteers. The commanders must quickly form the patriots into units and train them in the rudiments of soldiering and fighting. As it was manifestly impossible to make a soldier of a civilian in a few weeks, the main effort—which included drilling, mostly close-order—was to get the proud individuals to adapt to group organization.

After the proper men to command had been selected, Lee had to keep in constant communication with them, answering their calls for supplies, adjudging the needs, and compromising everywhere; answering the countless questions that arose concerning details of state armies, for which there was no precedent; advising and being advised on the places and time the enemy would be most likely to jump.

Such exacerbations as the governor's making appointments over his head, Lee simply ignored. He had a rare gift for delegating authority and a knack of non-interference with subordinates. He was a truly great man in a most troublesome and thankless position, and this too he suffered while the heroes preened themselves and the menace from the North grew more ominous.

5

Happily unaware of the details mastered by the gentle man behind the scenes, the troops began to gather according to his plans of operations. At first they were units of Virginia militia-volunteer-recruits, and then from the lower South came state troops, some in the C.S.A.'s provisional army and some not.

Some state volunteers were mustered into the C.S.A. provisional army while in transit. The University Greys, from the state university and its town of Oxford, Mississippi, went from militia to Mississippi Volunteers on April 22, with anguished parents petitioning to remove their underage sons. At Corinth (one year from the battlefield of Shiloh), the boys became Company A of the 11th Mississippi, received field equipment and tents, and started out for the Virginia frontier. When a week later they reached the pleasant city of Lynchburg in the Blue Ridge foothills, they were mustered into the Provisional Army of the C.S.A., May 13.

They went circuitously by train to the little Shenandoah Valley town of Strasburg, named by the Germans who originally settled that section. From there eighteen miles to Winchester, at the gateway of the Valley, they suffered the indignity of transportation by wagons, and complained bitterly. Worse was to come. From this point the Mississippi boys *walked*, in their fine-looking gray frock-coated uniforms, with black felt hats looped on three sides and topped with pompons, and plumes for the three lieutenants and nineteen-year-old Captain Lowry.

They began to meet other former militia and volunteer companies, in which the young bloods also were accompanied by their body-servants, many of the infantry privates had their own horses, and each mess had its wine and its colored cook. Few fared as well as New Orleans' Washington Battalion, with a corps of French-style cooks topped by François, a Creole Negro, whose progress across Virginia was marked by a line of light-of-loves. The South Carolina boys went in for champagne suppers, and they were great social favorites. The Virginia families' hospitality and the ladies' smiles seemed inexhaustible.

Also on the way northward, the Mobile (Alabama) Cadets were spreading from their line of travel new words to the minstrel tune of "Dixie." Young Henry Hotze, the Swiss-born Alabamian who became the South's great propagandist abroad, stated that "Dixie" meant south of the Mason and Dixon line. The Negroes had said, "I wish I was in the land of cotton," when they got cold in the North. The whistling and the singing of the song before the war had begun to get on people's nerves, and nobody would have thought that Dan Emmett's tune would become the national anthem of the Confederacy.

For the University Greys the end of the line was Harper's Ferry, a dread name to every Southerner since John Brown's insurrection. Northwest of Washington, at the juncture of the Potomac and Shenandoah rivers, and on the B. & O. Railroad, the little town nestled under mountain heights on three sides. It was indefensible militarily and the Virginians remained there on a temporary basis for three reasons: from the Maryland Heights they could observe the enemy; it served as a base of movements into the northwest counties; and, most of all, they had captured the U.S. arsenal. Few rifles were left by the small Union unit who abandoned the arsenal but a Virginian armorer frustrated their efforts to burn the machinery, and the pieces were removed slowly while rifle manufacturing continued.

When the militia converged at Harper's Ferry, they encountered the true panoply of war—before the shooting. "It was," one of them said, "like the Champs Elysées." It was a long parade and a party. Though there were present a militia major general, three brigadiers, and colonels everywhere, there was neither division, brigade, nor even regiment. It was a conglomeration of companies, first from the Valley of Virginia, then of Kentucky and Maryland volunteers, and finally of companies from all over the South.

From 80 to 100 men formed a company, with a captain and three lieutenants. When they were finally formed into regiments, anywhere from two to ten could be regimental strength, and from three to five regiments would make a brigade. The average regiment ran around 600 and the average brigade about 2000.

At Harper's Ferry, in those spring days, the volunteers were as innocent of these organizations as of discipline or standard uniform. The Confederacy, as a central government of the separate states, had little or nothing to do with the outfitting of volunteers. This was an affair of the states, and as there were neither time nor facilities for large-scale manufacture, the Southern states never provided uniforms for their soldiers. The men were allowed an allotment with which to purchase their own uniforms wherever they could, though in most of the first companies (all of the old militia units) the men bought their own. Frequently men bought cadet-gray cloth and had it tailored. Ladies sewed on the braid and the frogs which decorated the private as well as the general. In some of the cases where a rich man raised a company or battalion, he outfitted the whole lot of them, thus insuring his election as captain or major.

In this way, each company was caparisoned as grandly as a Graustarkian palace guard and, as each was different from the others, the total resembled an international assemblage of *corps d'élite*.

Their knapsacks, frequently packed by ladies, were things of wonder. In one of the fancier Virginia companies, the knapsack contained several pairs of white gloves, several changes of underwear, several white shirts (sometimes starch-bosomed, or as they said, "b'iled"), linen collars, neckties, white vest, socks, handkerchiefs, a fatigue jacket, writing paper and —what the men came to prize most—a needle case, with thread, buttons, and various-size needles. Outside this knapsack were extra shoes, an oilcloth, and—in Virginia for the coming summer!—two blankets. The lightest knapsack weighed thirty pounds and the heaviest fifty. If a little impractical for the field, the knapsack certainly accoutered the men superbly for the camp and its attendant social functions.

In addition to this equipment, most of the new soldiers, whether issued an old flintlock musket or nothing, carried in their belts revolvers and bowie knives. These weapons, which they confidently expected to use, were about the only warlike things among these militiamen.

In those volunteer companies fortunate enough to include members of a lower social caste ("the overseer class," as one said), the privileged ones paid the unprivileged a quarter to stand their turn at guard duty.

For the dismal stretch on the horse picket line, they simply turned that chore over to their servants.

Even the officers encouraged the laxity. Tough-bitten Colonel Arnold Elzey, a volunteer from Maryland, got mellow one night while drinking with his staff and offered a dram to the sentry on duty. At first light, the colonel was outraged to be awakened from a heavy sleep by the sentry calling into his tent:

"Gin'ral! Gin'ral! Ain't it about time we had another little drink?"

To such "soldiers" as these, General Lee sent from Richmond a recently appointed colonel of the Virginia Provisional Army to assume command at the Harper's Ferry post. All the militia commands above the rank of captain were to be revoked; the companies were to be organized into regiments and drilled for warfare; production of arms at the arsenal was to be sped up and the apportioning of the arms systematized. In short, the brilliant gathering, without General Staff or Ordnance Department, was to become transformed into a military training camp *while* guarding against invasion.

With one glance at General Lee's appointee it became obvious that, along with the passing of exalted militia ranks, the frolic was coming to an abrupt end.

The new colonel was plain enough looking by any counts, but against the array of resplendent uniforms, pompons, and plumes, he looked positively seedy. He wore high boots which seemed to emphasize his outsize feet, an ill-fitting single-breasted blue jacket, and a battered blue cadet cap tilted down to shade his eyes and obscure his face. What could be seen of his roughhewn visage was mostly covered by a rust-colored beard. When a militiaman got a clear look at the colonel's face and eyes, he wished he hadn't. The stern, unsmiling countenance was brightened only by light-colored eyes and they were half covered with drooping eyelids; but the half that was seen held an unwavering, uncompromising gaze piercing straight to the heart of whatever object they fixed on.

The colonel never spoke unless spoken to. Then his answer was slow in coming, as he thought carefully before speaking. When he finally answered, his words were few and straight to the point, sometimes brusque. To say that he made absolutely no effort to please would be an understatement. His sole preoccupation was Duty. The colonel's sole interest in any man was that he do his duty to the letter as his commanding officer saw it.

Behind the colonel's back, the first question the men asked was the same that had been asked in Richmond when General Lee appointed him. "Who *is* this Jackson?"

6

Thomas Jonathan Jackson was the outstanding illustration of those Southern people who were drawn into the national convulsion without having taken part in the thirty years' struggle. With Lee, Tom Jackson was the other great imponderable to result from a resort to arms involving the whole South. Born a poor mountain boy, he had no stake in slavery, believed in gradual emancipation, and showed his feeling toward the Negro by the close attention he gave his Sunday school class for colored children. Though, like most Southerners, a theoretical believer in secession, he disbelieved in it as a means of adjusting the wrongs to the South. In his early years, Tom Jackson had not even seen a plantation in his native western Virginia mountains (later West Virginia) and his whole struggle in life was made on the virtues of the frontier democracy.

Orphaned at seven, he grew up on an uncle's frontier farm in the Alleghenies where, like many another of the Scotch-Irish who settled the Southern mountains (such as Calhoun and Andrew Jackson), young Tom was imbued with the virtues of his forebears, their unassailable self-respect, and with an absorbing ambition to do credit to his own kind. Never robust, with weak eyes and fearing the tuberculosis that had killed his mother, Jackson used the iron self-discipline that later characterized him to develop by outdoor work the body slighted by nature. At the same time he sought such schooling as was available to prepare himself for West Point, his only hope of a college education.

He entered the class of 1846 with George Pickett, from Richmond, and George McClellan, the charming prodigy who had already attended the University of Pennsylvania at sixteen. Sam Grant was still there, kindly and well liked, noted for his horsemanship, along with Franklin and Hancock, who were later to face Jackson across the Whiteoak Swamp, and John Gibbon, of the future "Iron Brigade." Also from Virginia were generous Dabney Maury, the sensitive and intense A. P. Hill, and from South Carolina the courtly Barnard Bee who, before falling mortally wounded at the first battle of the war, was to give Jackson his sobriquet of "Stonewall."

None of these future enemies and comrades at arms was his friend at the Point, nor was anyone else. Painfully aware of his poor scholastic preparation, his physical awkwardness and lack of social graces, the proud mountain boy developed a cold impassivity as a protection, while he concentrated all of his energies on his single purpose of excelling. Starting at the bottom of a class of fifty-nine, he finished seventeenth (on the basis of his four years' grades). In the early years he went to the blackboard in such an agony of embarrassment that his uniform was covered with sweat and chalk. To the end, he studied after lights were out, prop-ping his books up before the coals, until he literally, as a classmate said, burned his lessons in his brain. They stayed there. He never forgot any-thing.

"You can be what you resolve to be," he wrote in his maxim book.

He graduated from West Point indifferent to the fact that he had never been elected so much as corporal, that he had not made a friend or become a good horseman. He made up for it all in the Mexican War when, under the test of fire, his fearless brilliance attracted the kind of attention his heart hungered for. It would help his advancement in life.

Finding advancement too slow in the peacetime army, he resigned to become professor of natural philosophy and artillery at the Virginia Mili-tary Institute. In the charming post-Revolutionary town of Lexington, at the southern end of the Shenandoah Valley, ex-brevet Major Jackson found such happiness as was to come to his lonely and harshly disciplined life.

Though his students regarded him as a dull eccentric, and other faculty members referred to him as "Fool Tom," he was as indifferent to opinions as ever. Among the Scotch Presbyterians of the southern Valley, Jackson found his religion. Despite his much-discussed devoutness, Jackson had not grown up in formalized religion. He received the religious impulse from his mother, but it was not until the Mexican War that he interested himself in church. He was baptized by an Episcopal clergyman, who as-sured him that he was baptized as a Christian and not as an Episcopalian. At Lexington he became a communicant of the Presbyterian Church so well suited to his stern self-discipline.

At Lexington also he found his love. After his first wife died, Jackson met Miss Anna Morrison through the marriage of her sister to his friend D. H. Hill, a professor at neighboring Washington College. She was one of the "four fabulous Morrison sisters" of North Carolina, three of whom were to marry Confederate generals—Stonewall Jackson, Harvey Hill, and Rufus Barringer.

With the former Anna Morrison, Professor Jackson lived in a modest red brick house off the main street of the hilly little town, and walked the half mile to the one building of barracks and classrooms facing the V.M.I. parade ground. It was to his wife that Jackson revealed without reservation the phase of his character which few even suspected. Always addressing her by some affectionate diminutive or pet word, he opened his heart in complete trust and gentle tenderness, and showed along with his sweetness of nature a playfulness which no one would have associated with the iron-visaged rustic with the stiff ungainliness of manner.

Even one of his brothers-in-law perceived no more in the dully earnest professor than did his students. He was a rich man, who married the fourth of the Morrison sisters, and, after the custom of the day, he had portraits painted of his wife's sisters and their husbands—all except Major Jackson. When asked later about this oversight, the rich Mr. Irvin said, "At the time, Jackson didn't seem worth having his portrait painted."

Except for the interlude of fighting in the Mexican War, Jackson had never impressed anybody, and that is significant. For if God's will worked as Tom Jackson believed it did, he was designed by his Maker for warfare. In the devout religious spirit which Jackson developed in manhood, his prayers were not pleas for personal help but for the strength to do the will of God.

When his state seceded, though Jackson believed the South should "fight for its rights in the Union," he also believed that as a Virginian he had no personal choice. "If I know myself," he said, "all I am and all I have is at the service of my country."

The day after Virginia's secession, Jackson resigned from the Institute. Accompanying a group of V.M.I. cadets to Richmond, where they were to drill militia, he offered himself for duty. He was sent to the little hill-enclosed town of Harper's Ferry at the end of April and at first took a room in the small hotel. From that day until his death, he never took a furlough or spent a night away from army duty.

7

Colonel Jackson's first staff consisted only of Major Preston and Colonel Massie, both from the V.M.I. faculty, plus two young men who came along to serve as drillmasters. After a week he wrote his wife that he and Major Preston were sharing a room "in an elegant mansion." His staff grew slowly, since he demanded, with aptitude and fine character, the strictest punctuality, exactitude in work, secrecy, and a blind devotion to duty which made the body tireless and the mind questionless.

With the collection of magnificently uniformed civilians who were to be his troops he must work. Unlike many other old army men, he was not appalled at their lack of discipline. He did not expect that. Instead, he looked at their fine physiques, the bearing and movement of men who had lived out of doors, and the resolution in their eyes. He would make soldiers of them.

There were between 3000 and 4000 when he arrived, with the numbers increasing daily, until in late May they numbered 8000. At first they were mostly half-armed infantry, with the artillerists for a dozen or so light-caliber old cannons without horses, and several raffish companies of so-called cavalry.

These loosely organized groups of hard-riding Valley cavaliers were led, as distinct from commanded, by the later and briefly famous Turner Ashby, about whom the legends were to grow. An old-fashioned beau sabreur, the slightly built, black-bearded Ashby was the ideal of what most Southerners in those early days conceived as a military chieftain. His riding experience in the hunting field and not in cavalry, his leadership moral, as the clan chief, and not as a trained soldier, Ashby had neither experience nor patience with discipline for himself or his followers. He knew the country, his love of combat was native and joyous, and with such of his men as were "present for duty" (for they shared Ashby's indifference to regimentation) he was vigilant and audacious in reconnaissance.

Turner Ashby's men at this stage—and they never got entirely beyond it—were actually "partisan rangers." Their virtually semi-independent command only represented the extreme of the attitude of most of the high-spirited men in decorative uniforms gathered at Harper's Ferry. Only the infantry's lack of mobility in taking off across the blue hills tended to curb their expression of independence. They were all indignant when their militia officers (old friends) were summarily removed by a Richmond order executed without explanation or apology by the stiff-mannered scarecrow of a Colonel Jackson.

The outraged princelings immediately held mass meetings to discuss the measures to take to redress this indignity. Colonel Jackson was probably saved from mutiny in his first Virginia command by the appeals of some of the militia captains to their friends and equals in the ranks. They suffered themselves to be mustered into Virginia's Provisional Army, and soon many of them wished they hadn't.

In Jackson they encountered a disciplinarian the like of which they never dreamed could exist in any relation to them. Since Jackson had achieved his purpose by diligence of application and mastery of details in dedication to duty, he expected the men to learn to become soldiers by the same methods. No excuses were tolerated. Men performed according to orders, to the letter of orders, and to the maximum of the standards set by Jackson.

He could not have been an easy man and he was not at all times just. His judgments were seldom tempered with mercy, and he rarely considered extenuating circumstances. As he made no effort to win the affection of the men and his appearance was unprepossessing to the point of embarrassing them, the troops understandably chafed under a harsh regime imposed by the officer set above them. These men thought of themselves not as having entered army life but as having simply banded together, like Ashby's troopers, to repel an armed thrust into their land.

Though the young hotbloods could not appreciate the methods imposed upon them at Harper's Ferry, from the day of his first command Jackson emerged as the total soldier with all the military characteristics, by which history knows him, then present. As the fire-eaters of the South became the forgotten men who had made their contribution toward promoting the war and were useless in it, so the peaceful professor who feared disunion found in the actual fighting the destiny for which he had been preparing unconsciously all his life.

At Harper's Ferry, Jackson, more than any other outstanding Southern leader, civil or military, perceived the true nature of the struggle into which they had been drawn. Completely opposite from the government at Montgomery, he dismissed all consideration of the abstract "rights" of the issue, the history of the issue, and the involved relations of the Confederacy to the United States. He applied himself solely and totally to the problem as it existed: to maintain the independence of the Southerners' land against an enemy trying to destroy that independence by force.

Since that was the issue to the South, Colonel Jackson concentrated on it as he had concentrated on his studies at the Point. Going straight to the core of the problem, he eliminated such practical irrelevancies as threats of attack when reports indicated that these threats were far from materialization.

Certainly he knew as well as the next that he could be flanked out of his position at Harper's Ferry from crossings of the Potomac to both sides of him. Discounting these possibilities as long as they were not probabilities, Jackson sent small cavalry units to observe at the crossings. When Maryland Unionists made threatening movements at the Point of Rocks, he reinforced his cavalry with one (1!) gun.

In preparation for thrusts from the larger Union Army of volunteers gathering under Patterson in western Pennsylvania, Fool Tom occupied the Maryland Heights at the risk of antagonizing a state which the Confederacy still hoped might become an ally. His reason for occupying the advanced position illustrated his perception of the nature of the total situation in his area: holding this northernmost point of loyalist Virginia would exert a moral effect on the loyal elements in the nearby disaffected western counties as well as restrain the actions of the Unionists in them. Also, of course, the arsenal was turning out needed rifles, and Jackson had already had 480 Kentucky volunteers scornfully refuse the old muskets he offered them.

Though realizing the essentially poor nature of his position for defense, Jackson realized also that Patterson's green three-month volunteers would be ineffective on attack and he had confidence in the men he was molding into soldiers. He wrote Lee: "I am of the opinion that this place should be defended with the spirit which actuated the defenders of Thermopylae, and, if left to myself, such is my determination."

In fact, Jackson was so aggressive-minded in defending his exposed position that even Major General Lee, in Richmond, sent cautionary notes. In a revelation about both their characters, Lee also cautioned Jackson against interfering with "the legitimate commerce of our citizens." What Jackson had done was this: since the "army" had no wagons of its own, the quartermasters hired them from wagoners. When the quartermasters complained to Jackson that local merchants paid double to get the wagons for themselves, Jackson said simply, "Impress them." When he discovered that freight cars he needed for transporting machinery from the arsenal were being used by the Valley merchants to send their barrels of flour to New York, he impressed the cars *and* the flour.

On his own, in learning of the urgent need of train engines and rolling stock, he collected some from the B. & O. By a stratagem, he got the railroad to run on a schedule by which twenty-two miles of double track would be filled with east-west traffic at the same time. He shut off both ends and removed the cars and engines to the railroad going south in the Valley. When they reached the inevitable end of the line, in Winchester, Jackson had teams pull the engines down the Valley Pike to where the Manassas Gap Railroad began at Strasburg.

All the time he was collecting small arms, guns, and ammunition, drilling his men, and observing the enemy. In this vigilance, he was vastly helped with the arrival of three companies of Virginia cavalry, armed with sabers and pistols, under Lieutenant Colonel J. E. B. Stuart. Recently resigned from a captaincy in the U. S. Cavalry, the twenty-eight-year-old Virginian was returning to the scene of his capture of John Brown.

If there was ever an illustration of the attraction of opposites, it was the affection between the grim Presbyterian and the laughing cavalier.

Stuart has always come easily across the pages of history, and through the tales the old-timers used to tell. The gaudy uniforms, with the golden spurs jingling, the laughing eyes and singing voice (a banjo player on his staff), the fabled raids and the nights of dancing, these were details men would remember about a natural leader who in his branch of the service was as good as they came.

Stuart possessed legendary energy, from a stocky physique conditioned by outdoor life and with no drains of tobacco, alcohol, nerves, or worry. He could lie down and sleep instantly, like an animal, and come fully awake at a touch. He was superb at reconnaissance, aggressive, meticulous, and intuitive, and a fine fighter of troops, personally glorying in combat.

As a man he was vain and showy. His animal spirits, the vast exuberance and unbounded self-confidence, were those of a very young man who would have been rather less than welcome in a gathering of mental types.

Yet the less pleasing aspects of this simple, man-of-action personality became qualities of high color to troops who saw him gallop past with his red-lined cape flowing behind him, the breezes ruffling the great mustaches above his full beard, and heard his mellow voice calling like a bugle, "Follow me!"

Jeb Stuart was a bright gonfalon to the Southern troops in Virginia, with rare exceptions a dependable arm to the infantry, and a resourceful and tireless aggressor who rendered the enemy considerable damage and unease.

Like Jackson, he had a horror of losing any of their scant equipment and was ever vigilant to garner supplies from the fat larder of the other side. Also like Jackson, his devotion to their cause and to duty was absolute. With all his vainglory, his rough jokes and long hours of dancing, on the job Stuart was all business.

The two dissimilar men respected the soldierly qualities in each other and shared a devoutness in their religious worship. Beyond that, perhaps Jackson needed someone to take affectionate liberties with him. Stuart never stopped his jokes around Jackson; instead he got the cold warrior to laughing. This unlikely pair formed at Harper's Ferry a personal attachment and a mutually admiring understanding of each other's qualities for war which was to last until their deaths.

8

They had not long to work together on their first assignments before Jackson was superseded in command (May 24) by Joseph E. Johnston, a brigadier general in the Confederate provisional army. A highborn Virginian and lieutenant colonel in the old army, on his resignation to go with his state, Joe Johnston showed his concern over rank by waiting until a commission came through from Montgomery. His first orders, to assume command at Harper's Ferry, were signed by Leroy Pope Walker, the C.S.A. Secretary of War.

The force at Harper's Ferry had been growing steadily, reaching 10,000 in June, and the Virginians were joined by leaders and troops from North Carolina, South Carolina, Georgia, Alabama, Mississippi, Tennessee, and a Maryland battalion. The few guns without horses or caissons had become five equipped batteries in one of which was a twenty-two-year-old lieutenant from Alabama, John Pelham, recently resigned from his senior year at West Point. Turner Ashby's cavalry, after their leader resisted serving under Lieutenant Colonel Stuart, became more or less officially a semi-independent command, strengthened by a fine battery under nineteen-year-old Preston Chew of V.M.I. Though the quartermasters still struggled along without wagons, the commissary without victuals, and engineers were not to be had, though the sick were taken care of in private homes and no provision had been made for taking care of wounded men, the collection of militia companies from seven states were the nucleus of an army when General Johnston took over.

The troops were formed into four brigades, with Colonel Jackson commanding the 1st brigade, composed entirely of Virginians from the Shenandoah Valley. Each of the colonels commanding the other brigades had experience as a professional. But, with all those unseen and unsung workers who, starting from nothing little more than a month before, had labored to execute the details of the patient Lee and his struggling staff—getting gun carriages here, percussion caps there, giving everyone less than he asked for, less than he needed, apportioning, allotting, and keeping order while evolving a defense system and pacifying politicians and patriots—with all the tedium and nerve-racking accomplishment of these unheroic assignments, Joe Johnston had no experience.

He looked at his troops and instantly complained. They were raw, crude, undisciplined, unfit for anything except the least taxing defense. Harper's Ferry was too exposed. He called up all the possibilities of disaster which Jackson had ignored. Tactfully Lee wrote him that they were not unmindful of these possibilities and they were doing their best to remedy the situation. Their best was not good enough. Johnston started his career as he finished it, by retreating.

General Johnston was a highly trained, intelligent, and skillful general. But, unlike Jackson, the fifty-four-year-old Virginian never thought in terms of the Confederacy's specific situation. Though he was proud of his father's Revolutionary sword, Johnston acted as if he were still in the Regular Army of a rich, established nation.

He was wantonly wasteful of supplies, just as though he had an inexhaustible flow at his beck and call. He gave up ground with the same abandon, always with the most logical military reasons. Probably the continent had no soldier who could trap Johnston into a serious mistake. He never trapped anyone else either. He lacked the larger vision of correlative action and the will to strike boldly for success. He made war as he might play chess, without stakes.

Johnston looked like a soldier—a small, sprightly man, with an almost cocky carriage, well-cut features, and a piquantly pointed beard, then gray. His manners were engaging, he was a good conversationalist with a literate humor, and his equals and subordinates found him charming. His men liked the cut of him and liked his treatment of them. He was mindful of their welfare, did not make excessive demands of them, and never fought them too hard. He inspired a confidence in them by his presence, the sort of thing which Jackson inspired only by performance. At this stage, as Johnston ranked Jackson, he was not jealous of his subordinate. In June, when the Virginians were mustered into the Confederate armies, he recommended that Old Jack be promoted to brigadier general, C.S.A.

It was with superiors that Joe Johnston had trouble. Something of that inherited sense of privilege made it difficult for him to bend the knee. He was overmindful of his reputation too, of his prerogatives, and not of a generous spirit with rivals. But on June 14, when he began his retreat from Harper's Ferry, these character traits were unknown and Johnston was regarded highly in the system of defense which had then evolved.

9

In other parts of the state, a Union advance had already been repulsed. Led by the Boston Democrat, Ben (later "Beast") Butler, Union troops had left their Fortress Monroe base and marched up the Peninsula until they encountered Virginia troops led by "Prince" John Magruder, the resplendent gourmet from the old army. That small action at Big Bethel, with the Richmond Howitzers trying out their new fieldpieces, was the first armed action of the conflict.

There had also been action in the disaffected mountain country to the west, where Confederate militia had fallen back before the Unions. A new force was being hastily formed there to protect the approaches to Staunton in the middle Shenandoah Valley, and to lead it, Lee had sacrificed his adjutant general, Robert S. Garnett, another of the Virginians from the Regular Army and eager for the glory of warfare.

On the Potomac, half-deaf Theophilus Holmes, another old army man, waited patiently for events with a small force and a few guns at Aquia Creek, the northern terminus of the Richmond, Fredericksburg, and Potomac Railroad.

Right in the center, on the Virginia plains southwest from Washington, the main Confederate force facing the main Union threat was gathering under the South's Hero of Fort Sumter, Pierre Gustave Toutant Beauregard.

General Beauregard, through America's need of heroes, had been blown up from the "conqueror" of Fort Sumter to the Confederacy's first national, full-fledged Hero. In a triumphal passage from the South to the front, he had been hailed as magnificent and invincible, a Creole military genius whose Latin looks suggested one of Napoleon's marshals. The middle-sized Louisianian with the brooding eyes found no reason for disagreement with these estimates.

When he reached his Manassas line Beauregard, like most of the others, became alarmed at the paucity of forces and sent up pleas for reinforcements along with promises to sell his life as dearly as possible. He confronted the one Union army which had actually penetrated Virginia's soil —directly south of Washington to George Washington's old town of Alexandria—and which held the obviously serious intent of getting on to Richmond.

Beauregard's opponent, Irvin McDowell, was his own age, forty-three, and had been a classmate at West Point. A trained soldier of no vaulting ego, McDowell was naturally not eager to commit his green troops to a major offensive battle. But Lincoln's Chief of Staff was persuaded by popular clamor to take Richmond. This Chief of Staff, General Winfield

Scott, a Unionist Virginian, was a pompous old hero of the Mexican War who'd been a figure around Washington until he was like a monument, and he had a personal hatred of Jefferson Davis that made taking the capital of his own native state anything but a chore.

By late May the Confederate President was in Richmond because, for a variety of reasons involving prestige and politics and pressure, the Confederate capital had been shifted to that city. Richmond was never the capital of the Confederacy as Washington was of the United States, in that government properties belonged to the nation. The city remained a state capital whose facilities were used by the Confederates, and its local defense troops (a home guard) were mostly Richmond citizens. For the handsome private home which the city bought to present to the Confederacy for a White House, President Davis insisted that the government reimburse Richmond with rent, and at least that was Confederate property by lease.

As a White House it was gray, stucco over brick, three stories and basement, with large airy rooms of fine proportions and an outside kitchen. Most kitchens of the large houses were then outside, both as fire prevention and because of the heat in summer from cooking by wood range. Typical of Richmond houses, its wide columned balcony faced a walled garden, and the whole establishment was magnificently situated on the crest of a high bluff, overlooking Shockoe Valley and across to the old part of the city.

Davis had only three blocks to walk to Capitol Square and down its shaded brick paths to the Government Building, recently the U. S. Custom House. His executive office was in there, along with the offices of the other cabinet members except the Secretary of the Navy and the Secretary of War. But his attention turned one block away to the offices of the War Department, built with terrible racket in the Mechanics' Institute. From his arrival in the old planters' capital, the Deep South leader showed that he meant to take literally his title of Commander in Chief.

From the beginning, too, this placed Lee in an anomalous position. He had organized all the work of preparation and was still theoretically responsible for it. Davis, less sensitive about the perquisites due others than those due him, was no more troubled with self-doubts than Beauregard when it came to soldiering. The two of them began to write back and forth as if General Lee did not exist. In this headless fashion, the separate parts of the Confederate defenses operated half independently through a loose series of communications, on the inescapable assumption that the main test of their defense would be in the Beauregard-McDowell area.

The curious point about this Virginia testing ground was that each side knew precisely what the other side must do and was trying to do.

The pathway that McDowell must take from Alexandria to Richmond of necessity tended toward the Orange and Alexandria Railroad on its southwesterly course toward Manassas Junction. A Federal victory at Manassas would deal a heavy blow to the state's effort at self-defense, since the Manassas Gap Railroad ran west across the Blue Ridge to the Valley town of Strasburg and formed the *one* east-west connection of northern Virginia with the vital Shenandoah.

In the Valley, Joe Johnston had fallen back to Winchester, within a day's march of this Manassas Gap Railroad. Since Johnston and Beauregard were both outnumbered by the forces opposing them, and a communicating railroad existed between them, their obvious strategy was for Johnston to reinforce Beauregard and achieve numerical supremacy at that one point. From the Union side, since their forces had superiority at each point, their obvious strategy was to prevent Johnston's reinforcing Beauregard before McDowell fell upon him.

On the level of command, the maneuvering for the battle to suppress the combination was sound and soldierly on both sides. What the volunteers might do under fire was something else. All that could be done in three months to equip a group of states to withstand the assault of a nation had been done. Chivalry had assembled in the country's original colony to prove its right to exist. The young gallants were not only ready, they were eager to get at the people who presumed to impose a foreign will on them by physical means.

CHAPTER VII

"Manassas Polka"

THE BATTLE OF FIRST MANASSAS (named for the railroad junction) or Bull Run (named for the stream) has been written about probably more than any other Civil War action except Gettysburg. Yet only technically was it a battle of the Civil War as the long struggle came to be fought. First Manassas was what we call today a "police action."

In essence, as the Union conceived the action, the seceded states were lawbreakers, and the armed and deputized men sent into their territory were enforcement officers.

Southerners felt that, having separated from the Union, its laws did not apply to them, its enforcement officers held no authority, and the Southerners' purpose was to resist the armed presence of foreign law officers who had no right to trespass on their land.

After all the preparations for the showdown by conscientious McDowell and Beauregard with his dreams of grand strategy, the battle was to be decided by the men from the non-slaveholding section of the Shenandoah Valley trained by Jackson, a non-secessionist ex-mountaineer.

In the first maneuvering for advantage, the Unions had failed to hold the Valley army at Winchester away from juncture with Beauregard. General Patterson, the Union Commander against Joe Johnston, was an old man whose military experience dated back to the War of 1812. He was bothered both by his ninety-day volunteers, who vowed to quit the army when their term expired, and by orders from Commanding General Scott to keep Johnston in the Valley by "demonstration." Demonstration is a fine art, which unhappy Patterson's raw recruits had not mastered, and Johnston was one of the generals least likely to be imposed upon by unconvincing threats.

At 1:00 A.M. on the morning of July 18 (just over three months after Fort Sumter), Johnston received the news from Richmond, brought originally to Beauregard by the Washington espionage ring of Mrs. Greenhow (who had been recently courted by President Buchanan), that

McDowell was moving out to attack the Southern defenders. On the afternoon of the same day Johnston's newly styled Army of the Shenandoah left Winchester.

First the troops marched southward to confound the Union spies lurking around the towns. The troops themselves thought it another evacuation, and they presented a spectacle of gloom to equal that of the citizens waving tearful good-bys as they prepared themselves for the expected occupation by the enemy. A few miles south of town the dispirited troops were halted, and read the order that they were marching secretly to reinforce Beauregard against McDowell's attack. Then the men cheered, and in their elation they almost ran, as they started the march toward the mountain. Jackson's 1st Brigade led the way.

His men had marched only once before under full equipment—rifle and bayonet, knapsack and haversack, canteen and blanket, and such makeshifts as they used to carry caps and powder-topped cartridges. Most still carried their ammunition in their pockets. As they walked at route step over the climbing road, General Johnston regarded their lack of discipline with discouragement and feared they'd never reach Beauregard in time. Unaware of their general's disapproval, and cheered on by ladies who came down to the roadside, the men moved on through the falling light and reached the Shenandoah River at dark.

The ford was waist-high. The men stripped below their shirts, made bundles of their clothes and equipment which they held on their heads, and stepped out in the cold, fast-running water. On the other side, dried down as best they could, they started the steeper climb between the timber and rough rock formations of the Blue Ridge, which blend into a blue haze at a distance. The hard-surfaced road climbed straight ahead, clear in the night light. They crossed the mountain at Ashby's Gap at midnight and reached the eastern slope at two in the morning. They had done better than twenty miles, climbing much of the way, and, as soon as they halted, the men fell to the ground wherever they were into instant sleep. An officer reported to Jackson that no sentries had been posted.

"Let the poor fellows sleep," he said, "I will guard the camp myself."

At first light he had them up and down the slope on a soft road to Piedmont Station on the Manassas Gap Railroad. While they were being loaded into freight cars, cattle cars and flatcars, ladies came to the station with home-cooked food and fresh lemonade, and the boys left the mountains in a sentimental mood.

That night the men climbed stiffly down from their cramped positions at Manassas Junction. On the morning of the eighteenth they had been in Winchester, facing Patterson. On the night of the nineteenth, they were ready to face McDowell across Bull Run.

At McDowell's first advance, Beauregard had fallen back from the ridge at Centreville across the sluggish stream of Bull Run to a defensive position earlier selected by General Lee. While Jackson's brigade was en route, one of McDowell's large divisions had tried to force a crossing at one of the fords. The Unions had been easily beaten off, and the Confederates got a fine lift in morale.

To Jackson's men, awakening on Saturday morning (July 20) in a pine wood near where this action had taken place, the scene of battle was quite sobering. They looked silently at the fresh graves, the trees mangled by shells and perforated by minie balls, the chocolate-colored stains on the short grass, and the men huddled closer together, drawing comfort from the group spirit that had grown in three months.

During the day other troops from Johnston's army kept arriving at intervals. They all wanted to know if the fighting had started. They were pleased to learn they could get a crack at the invaders.

"I want to shoot all the Yankees I can, and go home."

The railroad men worked frantically to bring men to the field, shuttling the cars back and forth on the single-track railroad. But not all of their troops arrived, as the trainmen refused to work after nightfall.

Jackson had his full brigade, nearly 3000 effectives; half of Bartow's brigade; and half of Bee's, plus two companies from the 11th Mississippi —the University Greys and Noxubee Rifles. General Bee was very proud of those Mississippians. He had told Johnston they "were one of the best-looking regiments" he had seen. They had drilled hard and conscientiously, they took pride in their appearance, and they had come to admire the work done on them down in Oxford by their young Captain Lowry, who'd gotten into such trouble with the college authorities by spending too much time with his company.

When the University Greys reached the scene, they felt the imminence of battle which had spread over their comrades. Each man sensed that the alarums and excursions were past, and they were face to face with the real thing. The night was silent, and one of the boys wrote home, ". . . soldier clings to soldier as brother to brother . . . and . . . I never saw such gentlemanly deportment in civil life. . . ."

Over in the 33rd Regiment of Jackson's brigade, two Valley boys were exchanging promises to bury the other in the event that one fell and the other survived.

The pleasant camp outside of hospitable Winchester already seemed far away, and their thoughts turned to home as they fell into fitful sleep. None of the 30,000 men of the combined Confederate forces would have slept as well as they did could they have known what was going on at headquarters.

Not to be outdone by Johnston's 10,000 being called the Army of the Shenandoah, Beauregard called his 20,000-odd the Army of the Potomac. On that Saturday night before McDowell's attack, the Confederate forces consisted of two armies and two leaders, both prima donnas.

Ever mindful of rank, Johnston had carefully established with Jefferson Davis and Beauregard that he was the senior officer, though his force was a third of the whole and he had just arrived on the ground. Beauregard, graciously conceding the protocol of command, countered with a battle plan he had drawn up from familiarity with the ground, the troops, and McDowell's movements. As the united armies must attack McDowell before Patterson discovered Johnston's escape and came down on their flank, and as Johnston manifestly knew nothing of the ground and little of the troop dispositions, he could only affix his approving signature to Beauregard's plan.

Beauregard's grandiose battle plan bore no more relation to the actual condition of his hastily assembled and partly trained patriots than the government's traditional structure bore to the nature of their movement. As the Confederate government acted as if it were an established power, so the gorgeous Creole acted as if he commanded its long-standing Regular Army. Beauregard indulged his love of *la guerre* by assuming the conditions of a proven field marshal with a highly trained staff and experienced officers and troops.

On the seven-mile front, his right was such a naturally strong defensive position that McDowell abandoned hope of attacking it. So Beauregard planned to leave his strong position and from it attack McDowell's left. His own left, a physically weak position, was to be held with a small force during the complicated turning movement from the other end of the line. Johnston's piecemeal arrivals were to be held in support along the long line, a line very long for a Civil War battlefield.

However, since Beauregard did not have a trained staff and was himself not experienced in high command, the six brigadiers who were to execute his maneuvers got six different meanings. Bald Dick Ewell, commanding the pivotal brigade and himself only weeks from the minor command of fifty troopers, of U.S. dragoons, never got a final order at all.

"Old Bory," as his troops called him, had completed almost flawless arrangements for Lincoln's quick suppression. With the imponderables still working, he was saved from his folly by McDowell on that hot July Sunday when the long wrangling sections finally joined in full-scale battle to settle their differences.

2

For a fight with weapons between two groups of American civilians, both militarily trained commanders were too elaborate. While Beauregard's six attacking brigades hovered anxiously, starting nervously forward and then falling back, all waiting for the order that never came, McDowell was in turn attacking the Confederate left with a complicated involution of his own.

His troops were the same ninety-day volunteers who plagued poor Patterson. Though their equipment was stamped with the letters US, their uniforms were as varicolored as the Confederates', with the outlandish Zouave costumes predominating. This show of might impressed the Washington civilians who drove out to Centreville to watch the insurrection crushed, and they were not disturbed when their heroes marched only six miles over flat country on their first advance.

McDowell sent two of these five raw divisions on a circuitous, twenty-mile night march for a dawn attack. His plan, as opposed to Beauregard's, was sound. The extreme Confederate left rested on what became that day the famous Stone Bridge, where the turnpike crossed over Bull Run. The bridge was lightly held, and beyond it was nothing. McDowell's night march brought his attacking troops across a ford of the sluggish stream a mile or more above the bridge, from which they were concealed by heavy woods. They came across on the Confederate flank and potentially in its rear. The only trouble was that instead of crossing the ford at dawn, as planned, the Union forces didn't get over until ten in the morning.

The Federals were seen by a Confederate observer, who forthwith introduced a new communications method in warfare. Captain Alexander, late of the U.S.A. Engineers, had the previous year experimented with the wigwag system of flag waving with the Regular Army. Arriving late in Virginia, coming all the way from California, young Alexander was given what he considered the ignominious assignment of observing and signaling with his newfangled system.

It happened that his signal went to the commander of the small force at the Stone Bridge, a Regular Army man named Shanks Evans. Evans had already perceived that the Union division facing him directly across the bridge was making too much racket to have any serious intent to attack, and had correctly concluded that their noisy demonstration could only be for the purpose of diverting him from the real attack coming further to his unprotected left. Assured by Alexander's flag signals, Evans on his own divided his already small force and threw 1000 men and two guns in the path of the upwards of 15,000 Federals deploying on the Confederate side of Bull Run.

He could hope for no more than to check the forces until help came, and that he did in one of the heroic stands of the war. Help came piecemeal, in the incomplete brigades of Bartow and Bee, and Wade Hampton's South Carolina Legion, recently hurried from Richmond. These officers, with no superior commander nearby, selected their own positions under the shellbursts and threw in their panting men as they came up. The seventy-nine boys of the University Greys, who three months before had left their classrooms on the faraway campus, enter the war records as "a company of the 11th Mississippi." Ten of the seventy-nine fell in minutes, four killed outright and two mortally wounded.

It was the same with all the heavily outnumbered Southerners. Under the growing pressure of the Union fire and masses, and the growing strain of their first exposure to battle, the thin line gave, wavered, broke. They came streaming back across the turnpike behind the Stone Bridge, and only then entered the area of battle as prepared by the generals. Instead of being behind the breastworks along the high banks of Bull Run, the Confederates were at right angles to the stream and uncovering their prepared positions as they fell back.

It was at this point that the Valley men under their hated martinet checked the Union tide of victory and prevented a quick suppression of the "combination." Jackson had brought his 1st Brigade up while the broken Confederates stumbled up the hill known in history as the Henry House Hill, for the widow who had lived there until a shellburst ended her life that day.

Like the earlier arrivals, "Fool Tom" Jackson had been ordered desperately and vaguely to the Stone Bridge. After surveying the field he, like the other officers, selected his own ground—in a pine thicket on the eastern edge of the plateau. It was a good defensive position, though it didn't look good to his walleyed men who watched their fellow Confederates staggering toward them, or to those venturesome enough to climb gateposts for a look down to the turnpike where "the enemy were as thick as wheat in a field." They could see the sun glint on the brass pieces of the two Regular Army six-gun batteries.

As their own men came closer, they saw the wounded, some wearing South Carolina's palmetto insignia on their hats. They came limping off with muskets or sticks as crutches, carried along by soldiers on either side (serving as volunteer medics to get to the rear), and carried in blankets darkening with their blood. The non-wounded staggered past with slack faces and haunted eyes.

Out of the disorganized mass stumbling past them, the men saw a black-eyed, long-haired officer in a blue uniform ride up to General Jackson, standing out in front of the pine thicket. It was General Bee.

"General," he shouted to his old fellow cadet from West Point, "they're beating us back."

"Sir," Jackson answered, "we'll give them the bayonet."

Turning to his demoralized men, Bee gave the call that immortalized Jackson. The precise phraseology is subject to many interpretations. No reporter took it down verbatim. But as men remembered the words after the battle, the sense was, "There stands Jackson like a stone wall. Rally around the Virginians. Let us determine to die here and we will conquer."

The poignancy of the rallying call, and the reason it entered into the popular imagination, was that Bee's men did rally, Bee was mortally wounded within an hour after the cry, and Jackson and his men did stand like a stone wall.

Jackson had been struck by a bullet on the bone of the middle finger of his left hand and the bearded brigadier, peering under the brim of his cadet cap, stood with his left arm upright from the elbow to check the bleeding, while the victorious Union tide broke against the stone wall of his brigade.

When the Union thrust faltered before the gusts of fire from that solid line, from that moment the men who had suffered under Jackson's discipline proudly called themselves the Stonewall Brigade. Throughout the army and throughout the South the eccentric professor became "Stonewall" Jackson.

With Jackson's stand, the battle, raging on throughout the day, entered the second phase. The commanding generals came to the area of action, and the movements of both armies were made under some correlating control. Joe Johnston and Beauregard, finally relinquishing his own grand assault, kept reinforcements from the Valley army coming in on the left, supporting Jackson, as the Unions kept flanking wider and wider away from Bull Run.

Jackson's men had a near thing of it when the two regular batteries of the enemy got up on the plateau to give the brigade personal and unwelcome attention. But the infantry support was driven off by Stuart's cavalry, and the 33rd Virginia under the order of their colonel ran out and shot the gunners. The guns changed hands three times on the Henry House Hill, while Johnston's men and some of Beauregard's troops got in to the widening left. Arriving from Manassas Junction after the trainmen had enjoyed a night's sleep, Kirby Smith's brigade went in for the final containing movement.

Smith was wounded going in and the brigade command devolved on Arnold Elzey, the Marylander who'd given the sentry a drink. Strangely, out of those four border-state regiments (Maryland, Tennessee, and two Virginia—one of them, the 13th, commanded by A. P. Hill) the Rebel Yell was born on that late Sunday afternoon back of Bull Run. It came spontaneously and inexplicably, but men remembered that on the sound of that high-pitched eerie hunting call the Unions began to fall back.

Of course the screeching wail had nothing to do with the Federals' falling back. Attacking all day, they had reached the point where their drive was spent. When the hitherto defensive forces struck at the moment of the battle hanging, the initiative passed to them. Jackson's fought-out men and the whole Confederate line swept forward. Both groups of uniformed civilians were by then tired, and in falling back the Unions naturally lost some of their newly acquired organization. While the old soldier huddles in a group for safety, the recruit reverts to the individual. In all truth, the Confederates had little better order themselves. But they had the ball.

The often-described rout of the Federal forces happened later and away from the field. Most versions attribute it to a shell bursting over a bridge across a little creek northward of Bull Run. The burst overturned a vehicle, temporarily blocking the road to safety, and the panic first seized the civilian sight-seers from Washington.

From them the frenzy of fear spread to the individual soldiers who had lost their commands, and from them to the more disorganized units. Though McDowell still had effective and determined units in good order, as an army his force had ceased to exist. Too many men had reverted to the civilians they still were under the uniform, and joined the other civilians in a mob flight that took the Federals beyond their base of supplies and all the way to Washington.

For them the police action was over. They were ready to go back to their homes and jobs, and let the Southerners go their own way.

To the exhausted but joyous Southern volunteers it was also all over. They had met the test and proven by arms their right to independence. The young men were so convinced of the finality of their success that, when the 1st Tennessee arrived after the battle, its volunteers were ashamed to go home and admit they hadn't fired a shot in the war.

3

The leaders on the field did not think the war was over, but they were overwhelmed with the apathy of relief. Jefferson Davis had rushed to the field from Richmond, where the Cabinet huddled anxiously around the telegraph instrument in the War Offices, where Lee waited like any clerk, and where at the new and fashionable Spotswood Hotel it fell to the lot of Mrs. Davis to go to Mrs. Bartow's room to tell her that her husband had been killed.

At Manassas, the President joined Beauregard and Joe Johnston, and they talked vaguely about pursuit during the evening. Longstreet, with a fresh brigade thrown across Bull Run, was overruled from advancing. Jackson was ignored when he asked for 10,000 men to follow the fleeing enemy into Washington. Always some reason was found for doing nothing, and the victorious army went into bivouac—with the Valley soldier from Jackson's 33rd Virginia carrying out his promise to bury his comrade.

On returning to Richmond, Davis, and the political leaders, continued the course of inaction after Lincoln called for 500,000 troops and abandoned talk about using the power confided in him "to hold, occupy and possess the property and places belonging to the government." Though the Union had failed to resolve the split in the nation by a test of arms, obviously the Lincoln Administration was not accepting that test as final.

The United States was gathering its vast potential of manpower, sea power, and industrial might to overpower the Southerners' armed resistance to being citizens of the same country.

Called "preserving the Union," the "suppression" was to change into a full-scale war which could have for its objective only conquest of the Confederacy. Yet the Confederate government gave no warning to the people that only the police action was over, and the real struggle just beginning.

The soldiers and the people reflected what seemed the satisfaction of their leaders. From the enemy's incontinent flight and abandoned camps, the Southern volunteers gathered an awesome collection of military stores. They brought off 4000 muskets with 500,000 rounds of ammunition; 29 pieces of artillery—Parrott and James rifles, boat howitzers and bronze howitzers—800 rounds of ammunition, caissons, battery wagons ("splendidly equipped") with their harnessed horses, and niceties for camp life hitherto unimagined. They pondered with some amusement over a collection of handcuffs. Though soldiers ran off with most of those as trophies, the quartermasters providently kept some against a possible future use. All these tangible fruits of victory meant more to uniformed civilian patriots than the military intangibles with which they were not concerned.

Likewise the people at home, all over the South, saw nothing beyond the inglorious return to Washington of the law enforcers sent into their country. John R. Thompson, former editor of the *Southern Literary Messenger*, expressed the people's lighthearted sense of total victory in a parody on Southey's *March to Moscow*.

> *McDowell! McDowell! Weep for that day*
> *When the Southrons you meet in their battle array;*
> *To your confident hosts with its bullets and steel*
> *'Twas worse than Culloden to luckless Lochiel!*
> *Oh, the generals were green, and old Scott is now blue,*
> *And a terrible business, McDowell, to you,*
>   *Was that pleasant excursion to Richmond.*

In the Shenandoah Valley town of Lexington, where the people waited for details of their triumph, the Presbyterian clergyman received a letter from General Jackson. On seeing the familiar handwriting on the envelope, the Reverend Mr. White told the anxious people that at last some news had come from the front. This is what he read:

My dear Pastor—

In my tent last night, after a fatiguing day's service, I remembered that I failed to send you my contribution to our colored Sunday school. Enclosed you will find my check for that object, which please acknowledge at your earliest convenience, and oblige yours faithfully,

                                 T. J. Jackson

Later Jackson soothed his wife for complaining at the lack of general recognition he had received in comparison with Johnston and Beauregard. God would look after His own, in God's time.

The few truly revolutionary leaders like Jackson had no way of knowing that time was not on their side. They had no reason to suspect that their government was not fighting the same war they were.

Some soldiers and civilians criticized the lack of action, but no serious worry was reflected as the lull continued through the summer and into the fall, with the mercurial enthusiasm of the volunteers fading with the coming of frost and the people at home returning to their affairs in a false sense of security.

The leaders, leaving the initiative with the North, went about the familiar routines of politics. The Provisional Congress (one legislative body) gathered in Thomas Jefferson's white Capitol in November and the members revealed that they had been political secessionists too long to change with the change in the nature of the conflict.

They still could not conceive that Northern businessmen and their old Democratic allies—as well as friends among political opponents—would unite with Black Republicans to wage a total war of subjugation against them. They were too close to the memories of their own service in Washington to believe that of their former fellow citizens and still fellow Americans.

At the head of the government and in complete control of all decisions involving defense, Jefferson Davis was under no illusions about the grim business from the North. But, with his hopes on cotton and England, he gave his attention to the most minute details of military affairs and neglected the people. No more or no less removed from the people as President than as Mississippi senator, he never thought they might need an appeal to their hearts to gird themselves for a long and bitter struggle for their independence.

In Richmond he made a fine appearance in his semimilitary gray suit as he rode horseback in the late afternoons to the camps. He was a superb rider, erect in the saddle, and his presence was very reassuring.

In the capital and all over the South, the people went about their ways in innocent ignorance, dancing to the new song, "Manassas Polka," and they were unprepared for the fight to the finish when the real war began.

CHAPTER VIII

The Season of Waste

JEFFERSON DAVIS' attitude of passive resistance was expressed militarily in a static defense that stationed troops at points throughout the Confederate territory, much in the manner in which the United States had been garrisoned when he was peacetime Secretary of War. For defense against invasion this dispersal of forces in fixed positions bore little relation to the needs of concentration for actual combat. Rather it reflected the bureaucratic cast of his mind, inflexibly fixed at the period when Davis' powers and prestige had been at their peak. Since then he had learned nothing and felt no need to. The Confederate President was still a fine peacetime War Secretary acting as Commander in Chief of a revolutionary movement fighting for its existence.

Taking his Commander-in-Chief title literally and insisting on the prerogatives of his office as well as standing on his own dignity, the President denied himself the advice and counsel of others. While spirited men cursed him as a despot, he became surrounded by bureaucrats and sycophants. Those few able men willing to subordinate themselves to the cause were placed under an unnatural restraint and permitted to contribute little to the whole.

In the four years of his presidency only two exceptional men possessed the tact to work closely with Davis: General Lee and Judah Benjamin. In the period of the disastrous lull following First Manassas, neither was placed in a position to help the country with his talents.

After the First Manassas victory Lee had been thrown in the shadows by the two heroes, Johnston and Beauregard, and remained in the anomalous position of "commander" of Virginia's forces. At that time, the only action in Virginia was in the western counties, where, in the central and southern sections of the mountains adjacent to what is today Virginia, affairs were going badly for the ill-equipped and poorly trained Confederate forces.

Instead of sending Lee out to command in the western counties, Davis sent the patient Virginian on the ignominious and hopeless assignment of co-ordinating the clashing egos among two political generals and an ambitious pro, each commanding his own small, private army. Advising without authority, under the general direction of the President, the finest soldier in the South was dispatched to the wilds on what a Richmond newspaper called "an inspector-general's job."

It is not after-the-fact to rate Lee highly. His pre-eminence in the old army, where he had served in the select branches of engineers and cavalry, had been recognized by the unofficial offer made to him to command the United States forces at the outbreak of the armed conflict. But there was a curious aspect in the relations of Davis and Lee. The neo-aristocrat always seemed to himself to exist in a position of superiority to Lee. This was not changed after the war. With all of Lee's record, Davis coldly stated that the general was always subject to his directions.

The only explanation would seem to lie in Lee's gentle self-effacement. The courtesy in which Southerners take such pride found its fullest flowering in Lee. He was instinctively kind, of amiable disposition; and training, association, and experience developed his native traits into a gracious consideration in dealing with others. With all his awesome self-discipline, his unbending devotion to duty, Lee was a sweet-natured person of true Christian humility. It is probable that these qualities, which caused him to suffer Davis' unconscious rudenesses for the sake of their country, caused the self-aware gentleman to feel superior and to underestimate the selfless patriot.

In his underestimation of Lee, Davis not only wasted the Virginian's great gifts for the new nation but sent him on an assignment for which he was totally unfitted. Lee's tactful consideration of others was the trait least needed in dealing with those vainglorious clowns bickering away the Confederacy's chances in western Virginia. What "Generals" Loring, Wise, and Floyd needed was a highhanded martinet indifferent to their feelings.

In his wretched and fruitless period in the mountains, the only thing of interest that happened to Lee was that he let grow the beard by which history knows him. As it came out gray, he began in that miserable phase of his career to emerge to the soldiers as "Uncle Bob" and "Marse Robert." To them the great gentleman became the clan chieftain. But the time was in the future when this affectionate trust of the soldiers was to carry the great, gentle man to his fame. In western Virginia Lee failed in a situation where his tact without authority could obviously avail nothing. The area was lost not only to the Union forces (who won by default) but to the Unionist citizens, who in October voted to secede from Virginia.

When the new state of West Virginia was received into the Union (June 1863), since the mother state was helpless, a little cheating went on. There was no argument about the section in the Pittsburgh-Ohio area. The line cut pretty sharply down the Alleghenies, where Virginia loyalists equaled or in some cases outnumbered the Unionists, and in the northeast extension of the Shenandoah Valley the two counties west of Harper's Ferry (Jefferson and Berkeley) were definitely "stolen." Old-guarders there still regard themselves as Virginians, regardless of their post office.

However, for practical purposes in the winter of 1861–62, the first thing that happened in the inaction after Manassas was that Virginia's western counties joined the enemy. Lee, whose anomalous position there had not been explained to the people, became the scapegoat. He accepted the public criticism with his usual equanimity, and with the assurances that the President still believed in him.

He was then sent down to fortify the South Carolina and Georgia coastal defenses, including Charleston Harbor. That the Charleston defenses were to endure throughout the four years of war made no difference then. Lee finished off the tatters of his first-year reputation by antagonizing the hot- and blue-blooded South Carolinians when he blighted their champagne parties with the hard labor of digging defenses. Thus the top soldier of the South was lost to leadership while the Union, angrily rid of its delusion of suppression, settled down to war.

2

Davis' other top-flight associate, Judah P. Benjamin, fared even worse than Lee.

While General Lee went off to supervise fortifications, lawyer Benjamin was made acting Secretary of War beginning in September 1861. As it happened, the military was one of the few fields not covered by the interests of the protean-minded Louisianian. The President's choice of a financial-minded lawyer to succeed another lawyer, who had failed in the vital war post, can be explained only by the need to have near him an engaging personality whom he respected and who obviously respected him. As he had kept Lee working under his orders, so he found in Benjamin what would be called today an executive officer—the man to translate his directives into action.

For Davis was his own Secretary of War as well as Chief of Staff and Commander in Chief. Indeed, as everything about the military fascinated him and he believed only he was capable of running things, the President performed tasks that belonged properly to clerks in the War Office, and even in the Adjutant General's office.

Conversely, as he squandered his time and energies in the field of his interests, Davis neglected affairs which properly belonged in the President's office. With the government committed to its egomaniacal policy of bringing England to her knees by withholding cotton, there was virtually nothing for the State Department to do and little for the Treasury except devise loans and make plans to print paper money. None of the brain power of those departments was used in correlating a total policy, since Davis was too occupied with the War Department to give much thought to correlation or policies.

Also, such vital necessities for physical defense as railroads, transportation, and disbursal of supplies were ignored. Then, the agricultural people were dislocated, as manufacturing for war, though not for civilian needs, was developed when importations from the North were largely cut off—despite the valiant and ingenious efforts of Northern businessmen to trade with the enemy in exchange for cotton.

Even within the unrelated government bureaus, the officials were left either too much to their own devices or interfered with according to the interest their department had for the President. Since the War Department was his personal province, some tremendous elasticity was demanded of the Secretary if he wanted to be effective while denied all initiative. Benjamin's predecessor lacked it.

Alabama's Walker, though an intelligent man, astute lawyer, and dauntless patriot, was simply not cast by nature for the role of titular head of a department, where he drew all the criticism for matters over which he had little control and no credit for the very real accomplishment he made through thankless detail work. It was not that Walker resented Davis' making the policy so much as that he was unable to adjust to overwhelming detail work without areas of authority.

The newly constructed office was pitifully understaffed, no organization system existed, and Walker was not gifted with organizational efficiency. It was his lot to deny all the early petitions for commissions and clamors for non-existent weapons. Being excessively polite, he must always see his equals for a little office visit or answer their letters with pages of explanations. His correspondence was Jeffersonian, though on trifles. Disorganized and badgered in his anomalous position, Walker tried to do everything himself and worked himself into physical illness. When he resigned, Davis treated him shabbily and lost any use of his by no means negligible ability and burning patriotism. The Confederacy could not afford this waste.

Then Davis, after saying that a civilian was not qualified for the War Office, appointed his friend Benjamin. Historically, Benjamin has become a cliché. To his many enemies, his smile was oily, his manners deferential and subservient, his mind for hire, and his character opportunistic. To his few friends, his smile was charming, his manners imperturbably gracious, his mind a miracle, and his character realistic. We will never know him, since he destroyed all correspondence and papers, and he comes across time as probably the most fascinating and mysterious personage in the Civil War.

Born in the West Indies of Jewish parents, of sephardic features and of the Judaistic faith, Benjamin came to a Gentile and predominantly Protestant country where no Jew had ever held a cabinet post. In his own section, the South, the church of power was the American version of the Church of England, the Episcopal Church of the United States. More vocal and more numerous were the communicants of the various Protestant faiths who, with their personal God and fundamentalist concepts, could scarcely have been more alien to the bland hedonist. In his own Louisiana, the equally alien Roman Catholics rivaled the Protestants. All in all, if he wanted to get on in the world, Benjamin had to tread softly, and of all things he wanted to get on.

The roly-poly little man, with the black whiskers framing his olive-skinned and mobile face, was all cold ambition behind that smile, oily or charming, and a lot of steel supported his agile brain. Like many another outlander, he desired the lush splendor of his adopted South and no one was more successful at attaining it. There was nothing crudely materialistic in his achievement. Actually in an exotic refinement of the planters' ideal, he used his wealth, gained through law and land speculation, to support a life of sybaritic and deeply cultured graciousness. By all accounts, he was a delightful conversationalist, a drawing-room asset, and a good companion of bons vivants.

As a War Secretary, like Walker, Benjamin was not bothered that Davis made the decisions; Benjamin recognized his own limitations. Unlike Walker, he was able to create his own spheres of authority. When he came on, Benjamin had fewer office problems to begin with, as some order had evolved and, with the false lull, there were far fewer seekers after place and glory. Then, the facile worker handled details with an amazing celerity. Freed of the nagging small problems, Benjamin was able to devote the bulk of his time and energy to effectuating the President's policies in details.

His supple adaptiveness enabled him to give such solid help without encroaching on the President's domain that Davis, trusting him increasingly, allowed the Secretary considerable authority. In particular, he allowed Benjamin authority in dealing with army personnel, and this is where the skillful operator got into trouble.

Knowing nothing of army procedure and not impressed with the military mind, Benjamin not unnaturally worked with the generals along the lines adopted by the President. There was nothing in his experience to warn Benjamin that Davis' highhanded interference with his generals was not customary. As a good Secretary, he assumed that his job was to effectuate the President's policy of extending his supreme commandership into all details affecting the armies.

About the time that Benjamin took over, Beauregard was in the Administration doghouse for publishing a twenty-page preface to his Bull

Run battle report, in which he charged the President with not following his plans for a counterinvasion. Davis was furiously engaged in collecting witnesses for his defense and, with the structure of his pride attacked, was in very bad humor with his Manassas heroes. Beauregard was soon to be banished to the West for his presumptions, and Joe Johnston was in sole command of the Confederacy's one victorious army. Seeing the way the wind blew, Benjamin concentrated first on Johnston, called, by some, "Retreatin' Joe."

There is a legend that his soldiers loved him because, under his care, one said, "We never missed a meal and never fought a battle." It is certainly true that his shrewd estimate of the evil his enemy could visit upon him made Johnston extremely skillful at avoiding armed combat. Verbal combat was another matter. Where his dignity was concerned, his perquisites and prerogatives, the peppery and highborn Regular Army man was quick to bristle and, never counting the cost, to press home the attack.

Though Lee had volunteered directly with Virginia while Johnston had waited around to obtain a Confederate commission, Johnston had written the Adjutant General that he could not accept Lee's orders because they were "illegal." Later, when Lee sent him as a staff officer Dabney Maury, a West Pointer and future Confederate general, Johnston refused to accept the able soldier and told him, "I rank Lee, and he can't place officers in my army. I won't have it."

With this smallness of spirit, Retreatin' Joe was terribly outdone in September when the Confederate Senate confirmed President Davis' order of five full generals, and he was ranked fourth, just one above Beauregard. In this instance of Davis' following the regular forms, he would seem to have acted with some judgment. He had ranked the five full generals according to their seniority in the U. S. Army. Thus the order read old Adjutant General Cooper, the Hudson River Valley fugitive; Albert Sidney Johnston, colonel of the 2nd Cavalry, who did not make his way from California until midsummer to take command in the West; then Lee, Joe Johnston, and Beauregard. Johnston, like Lee, had been a lieutenant colonel in the old army, but he had been a brevet brigadier in the Quartermaster Corps. Davis had rated him off his troop command and Johnston, naturally rating himself off his quartermaster brevet, hit the ceiling.

He wrote Davis an ill-considered and ill-tempered tome of protest, in which he included a spitefully ungenerous reference to Lee and Albert Sidney Johnston. Stating that "neither of [them] has yet struck a blow for this Confederacy," Johnston claimed that he had "served laboriously from the commencement" and "borne a prominent part in the only great event of that war." Since Davis considered A. S. Johnston the greatest living American, and was well aware of Lee's blows in Virginia while Johnston was serving laboriously for his Confederate commission from Montgomery, the President was outraged at the general's words.

Unfortunately for his cause, Jefferson Davis was not one to subordinate his feelings, any more than was Johnston, for a larger end. He put Johnston in *his* place with a short, stiff note from the Commander in Chief to a presumptuous inferior. There the matter rested for Davis, but Johnston simmered—permanently. Years after the war, whenever he thought of it, he boiled all over again.

Joe Johnston's attitude to victory and independence was scarcely calculated to increase Benjamin's estimate of the military mind, and the Secretary's own cavalier treatment of the general brought no more than puny plaints. When Benjamin blithely sent orders for troop dispositions over Johnston's head, Retreatin' Joe merely protested that the orders might *at least* be cleared through his headquarters so the illusion could be sustained that he commanded the army.

3

Misled by his dealings with Johnston and lesser commanders, Benjamin made the serious mistake of applying the same treatment to the stern-hearted Stonewall Jackson. There was no man in the Confederacy more totally dedicated to his country's independence, few men so realistic in facing its specific needs, and, despite the lull induced by the government, Jackson thought ceaselessly of ways of getting at the enemy and *winning* independence. Indeed, in perceiving the need to win, the grim-visaged soldier of the people was the antithesis of the secessionist politicians who could not disabuse themselves of the notion that they were still in some sort of argument with another party.

He was also the antithesis of those leaders who, like Davis, had once commanded small bodies of volunteer troops in action and then turned to other matters, with the memory of their heroic hour growing into the illusion of military genius. Jackson had continued his studies. At V.M.I., to rest his eyes and to keep from falling asleep, he sat erect on a stool in the darkness and worked out military problems in his mind. In those problems, different from the one-shot heroes of an old war who had no experience with larger strategy, Jackson studied in terms of armies. He studied Napoleon as he studied the Bible, both of which were ever with him.

What he had learned, that the self-deluded Confederate President was never to learn, was that troops should be concentrated for an offensive strike rather than dispersed in static defense. He wanted the initiative always. He wanted to carry the war to the enemy. To this end, in the fall of 1861 Jackson forwarded through his congressman a plan which was, in essence, attempted the following year in the Sharpsburg campaign, and once again in the Gettysburg campaign.

The difference of Jackson's plan from the later two failures was that he proposed a two-pronged invasion—one west of Washington but east of the Blue Ridge, one farther west in Virginia's western counties, where the disloyalists would be subdued and the loyalists put in control before the Confederate Army moved northward.

Though the thought of leaving all his garrisons depleted horrified the President, he did agree to a limited objective of Jackson striking into western Virginia, in the locality of his mother's grave.

At that time, November–December, the northern Virginia situation was precisely the same as it had been before hostilities opened, except for change of commanders. At Centreville, out from Alexandria, Joe Johnston instead of Beauregard faced McClellan instead of McDowell. At Winchester, in the Valley, Jackson was in command as he had been in the beginning, though a part of Johnston's army.

When Jackson was promoted from brigadier, he had been shifted from his brigade to a division command. By then, the militia and volunteers who had chafed under his early harsh discipline were the proudest brigade in the army. On leaving them, Old Jack read a farewell "address," his only speech of the war, and, as one of them said, "We returned to camp . . . considerably out of humor, for we wanted to go with him wherever he went, and be immediately under his eye. . . ." Their wishes were rewarded when the Stonewall Brigade became the 1st Brigade in Jackson's new division. That division, with some artillery and Ashby's cavalry, comprised the nucleus of the force with which he was to strike in western Virginia.

Though Jackson had wanted to concentrate all the forces in the western counties, Davis, acting through Benjamin, had compromised even locally. Jackson got only the forces from the middle-western section of the vainglorious Loring, who had given Lee such a hard time. Jackson had about 9000 men altogether when he set out on New Year's Day, 1862, for Romney (now in West Virginia), northwest of Winchester.

The enemy had been strengthening along the Potomac to the west in proportion to its concentration at Washington. But they were also adapting methods of dispersed forces. Jackson figured, accurately, that no single force would attack him nor would the enemy, while on the defensive, unite to strike against the Valley.

Virtually unhampered by the scattered enemy, though with his men suffering intensely from the cold, Jackson again interrupted the harried B. & O. lines, did some other damage, collected some stores, and occupied Romney. Then he made a mistake in the judgment of men. He left Loring with his forces in the blizzardy outpost, and returned his own troops to Winchester.

Loring's men had never been subjected to the discipline of a Jackson, and they were less than one year away from being proudly independent

Southrons. With Loring's support, his officers drew up a complaint against the outrage of being wintered in such an unpleasant environment as Romney, and their dignity demanded that they be removed. The petition added that Romney was of no consequence anyway.

This is where the brilliant Benjamin was betrayed by his ignorance of military protocol and military men. He honored the petition of Loring's officers and permitted the forces to withdraw from Romney. The reaction from Jackson was immediate and definite. He resigned from the army.

With Tom Jackson this was not a question of his personal prerogatives. For an army to have any hope of success, it was essential that strategy and the troop movements involved in it be handled through the proper channels with due regard to the authority of commanders. Without that, with civilians remote from and ignorant of the ground making decisions, all was chaos. Nothing could be planned and executed. No cause-and-effect operations would be possible.

The grim Presbyterian did not resign in a pique. He was tormented, in the house where he and Mrs. Jackson were quartered, the last comfortable period he was ever to share with his wife and friends. Shortly after his thirty-eighth birthday, he reached the decision. Knowing the Confederacy could not hope for victory under such a system, Jackson sacrificed himself that a principle might be maintained. He was cutting himself off from active work in the fight for independence, and from all hope of the glory for which he had so assiduously prepared himself. He was going back to V.M.I.

If the resignation had been accepted, probably the war would have ended in Virginia six months later. But now all hell was to pay.

Congressmen and the governor worked on Jackson to reconsider while pressure was being brought on Richmond. Joe Johnston, of whose army Jackson was a part, took the occasion to get in some licks of his own. He wrote Benjamin, "The discipline of this army cannot be maintained under such circumstances." Governor Letcher went from appealing to Jackson over the effect his resignation would have on Virginians to upbraiding Benjamin direct. The startled Secretary of War was only too happy to pour oil on the troubled waters.

To prove Jackson right, after it was too late, the Federals reoccupied Romney, gaining fertile supply ground as well as strategic position, and the Virginia-minded northwestern counties were lost as the middle-western and southwestern areas had been earlier. Jackson had been saved, after his campaign was ruined, and a jaundiced eye was turned on both Davis and Benjamin.

4

The Jackson controversy was still the subject of barroom conversation when more immediate disaster struck. This was at Roanoke Island, the first dramatic and important reverse in the Confederate East.

North Carolina is like South Carolina with its line of coastal islands which form the inland waterway to Florida. There are two huge sounds running roughly, very roughly, from west to east, toward the ocean, and connecting them and running from north to south are two small sounds. Between these two smaller sounds lies Roanoke Island. Strategically this fortified island protected from the ocean, by way of the larger sounds, the sea paths to coastal North Carolina and its inland rivers.

At the defense of Roanoke Island was Virginia's ex-governor, Henry Wise. Having learned nothing from feuding with fellow general John B. Floyd in southwestern Virginia, the vain aristocrat immediately locked horns with the commander of his new department, based at Norfolk. This was South Carolina's Huger (pronounced *you-jee*), whose aristocratic position might admit a Virginian as an equal, but certainly not as a superior on that ground. In the senseless but typically Southern conflict over authority between Wise and Huger, the émigré Benjamin had little control.

While the two gentlemen fought it out to their mutual dissatisfaction, the Union's Burnside moved in with the first amphibian force used on the Western continent and took the island. The fall of the strategic island climaxed a series of Atlantic coastal positions taken by the U. S. Navy. The navy's actions against fixed positions had gone largely unheralded while attention was centered on the invading armies, but Roanoke Island (February 6, 1862) shook the Southern *people* into startled awareness that the United States had settled down to real war—and was winning it!

The blow was felt sentimentally in Richmond because Governor Wise's son, an ante-bellum newspaper reporter and local favorite, had been killed there in service with the Richmond Light Infantry Blues. After Jennings Wise's state funeral in the Confederacy's capital, personal execrations were heaped upon the alien head of "the Jew Benjamin," as they called him.

The brilliant hedonist never defended himself, and he had a defense. It is true that, as Secretary of War, Benjamin had not stressed the building up of strength at Roanoke Island, though protestations from the area had been strong. But he was only acting as executive officer of the President, who should know such things. As for the charges of ammunition shortages, Benjamin knew that the Confederacy did not possess the powder. It was against Davis' policy to reveal these weaknesses, and Benjamin—like Lee in western Virginia—let the storms break over his head without revealing the actual situation.

Both of these extraordinary men had suffered public defamation, along with waste of their talents, by executing the policies of the President. In the case of Benjamin, a real villain was created who was to embarrass the Administration, because the President did not consider dealing honestly with the people.

Lacking the humanity to give a Churchillian appeal to the people to defend their land, Davis possessed the narrow personal pride of the neo-aristocrat which prevented him from admitting a weakness. He preferred to present a bold appearance for the sake of European recognition rather than to depend on his own people. They were *in* the real war without their government having told them. It was disillusioning when they found out, and the waste of the months after First Manassas affected the people far more deeply than merely the loss of irrecoverable time.

CHAPTER IX

The Border Shrinks

WHEN the United States commenced the real war against the Confederacy, the fighting spread from Virginia, with the objective the Confederate capital, across the Alleghenies to the Confederate "West." This involved the "neutral" state of Kentucky, Confederate Tennessee below it, and divided Missouri across the Mississippi.

Before the organized invasion began, fighting had broken out locally in Missouri. Led by Francis Blair, of the powerful Washington clan and brother of Lincoln's Postmaster General, the Union forces, without bothering about legalities, struck early and hard at the state militia and Southern volunteers gathering under the pro-Confederate governor. The state not having seceded, the pro-Confederates were confused in purpose and partially influenced by the moderates striving for peace, until Southern prisoners were massacred by Germans on the streets of St. Louis.

Even when the pro-Confederates settled down to fight, they lacked organization and matériel, and were treated like a little-regarded ally by the government then newly installed at Richmond. Missouri state troops were taken over by the former moderate, Sterling Price, an ex-Virginia lawyer, and the Confederate troops in adjoining Arkansas were commanded by a raffish hunter and former Texas Ranger, Ben McCulloch. Needless to say, McCulloch and Price were unable to co-operate on anything like a satisfactory basis. After some local successes by Price, he was forced by lack of percussion caps for his homemade bullets to withdraw to the southwest corner of the state, where he set about the vain task of collecting matériel of war.

When the fighting was all over in the fall, the legislature of the fugitive governor finally passed the ordinance of secession (November 1861) and these Southern sympathizers brought Missouri formally into a military compact with the Confederacy.

Davis, instead of embracing an ally, relieved some of the tension of responsibility by conducting a private war with the Rebel governor Claiborne Jackson. In Davis' charts of organization, the neglected and harried patriot in far-off Missouri should submit to the constituted authority as if the C.S.A. were an established nation and Jackson an integral and dependent part of it. As it was, the desperate man was striving with negligible assistance to save a part of his state *for* the Confederacy, and naturally complained of want of powder, caps, cannon and the barest essentials of warfare. Davis, with his unarticulated policy of keeping the Confederacy's lacks from his actual allies in order to impress his hoped-for allies abroad, resented the Missourian's complaints over his neglect, and showed it.

On the enemy side, a touch of high jinks was added by that foolish posturer, Fremont, whose appointment to command showed that Lincoln also had his weaker moments. Aside from courting glory with grandiose plans of conquest, Jessie Benton's husband seized history by the forelock and pronounced a personal Emancipation Proclamation for Missouri. Instead of beating Lincoln to the role of Great Emancipator, Fremont and his proclamation were forthwith repudiated by the U.S. President. Lincoln was too concerned with keeping Kentucky neutral to tamper with the institution of slavery *anywhere*.

Though Kentucky's neutrality was as important to the Confederacy as to the Union, the Southerners, as at Fort Sumter, showed their impetuosity when it came to undefined situations.

Practically, Kentucky's neutrality meant that its militia served only the state in the state, while volunteers could join either side. Kentucky, the native state of Lincoln and Davis, illustrated the ultimate division within the Union. Of the grandsons of Henry Clay, the Great Compromiser, four went with the South and three with the North. Old Senator Crittenden, Clay's less effective successor at compromise, had for sons a Union general and a Confederate general. In Louisville, Union recruits walked up one side of a street and Confederates on the other.

It was an impossible situation, as the Kentucky government was clearly Unionist, and it became intolerable to the Southerners. Though the Unions were on the point of occupying Kentucky and discarding the neutrality myth, the importunate Confederates did it first and drew the onus of invading a state.

The Confederate who assumed responsibility for this invasion was the Right Reverend Leonidas Polk, Episcopal bishop of Louisiana, who had been persuaded by his fellow cadet at West Point, Jefferson Davis, to come to the defense of his land.

Polk was a scholarly North Carolinian of privileged background who, after two years at the state university, entered West Point at the age of seventeen. While at the Point, he was converted to the Church during a religious crusade, and, over his father's objections, entered the ministry upon graduation. He rose rapidly in the Episcopal Church and was the first bishop of Louisiana and the first bishop to visit the foreign mission

that became the Diocese of Texas. He did not want the military command and accepted it under the importunities of Davis and Tennesseans on
a temporary basis.

When a friend said to him, "You throw off the gown for the sword,"
Bishop Polk answered, "No, sir, I buckle the sword over the gown."

Fifty-five years old and with no military experience beyond his West
Point training more than thirty years before, the bishop did a fine job of
organization and took in stride the usual difficulties of lack of arms and
equipment, while training civilians for the army under the eyes of the
enemy. When he learned that Union forces were about to enter Kentucky,
the new major general (like the Unionists in Missouri) discarded legalities
and moved in first. By doing so at the risk of putting the South in the
wrong abstractly, he gained the river stronghold of Columbus, at the
southwestern tip of Kentucky.

Once there, Polk recognized that the developing situation in the whole
West required a central commander, and recommended his West Point
roommate, Albert Sidney Johnston.

This Johnston, whom Davis considered "the greatest soldier, the ablest
man, civilian or military, Confederate or Federal, then living," was already
on his way from a U. S. Army post on the West Coast, and was to be
given the widest authority the Confederate President ever extended to
anybody. His impressive title was "General Commanding the Western
Department of the Army of the Confederate States of America."

2

Where Davis seemed unimpressed with Lee, even after his achievements,
he was overboard on Johnston before the latter accomplished anything. It
might have been because of something dating back to their West Point
days, when Lee was a year behind Davis and Johnston two years ahead.
Like Davis, he was a native-born Kentuckian, and it is possible that he
served as an early model to his fellow Westerner.

Albert Sidney Johnston possessed in superlative degree that old-fashioned quality called "character." As selfless as Lee, imperturbably self-
contained, and physically vigorous, he had been impressive in his youth
and he was impressive at fifty-eight, when he took command of the huge
Western area. Yet, for all his impressiveness as a character, as a soldier
Johnston had never done much. His long and honorable service with the
old army was uncolored by large-scale combat.

After routine service in the army following his graduation from the
Point, when his wife died Johnston resigned and sought action in Texas'
fight with Mexico. For a time he enjoyed the favor of that turbulent giant,
Sam Houston, and acted as Commander in Chief and then Secretary of

War of the young republic. After a parting of the ways with Houston, Johnston, remarried, was operating a cotton plantation when the Mexican War came. On that proving ground for future leaders, where so many reputations were won, he saw no action of consequence. He returned to the army as major and paymaster, from which tedious job he was saved by his admirer, Jefferson Davis.

Secretary of War in 1855, Davis gave Johnston command of the newly formed 2nd Cavalry, that regiment with the imposing list of Southern officers who were to become Civil War generals—Robert E. Lee, his nephew and future Virginia governor, Fitzhugh Lee, Hardee, Hood, Van Dorn, Kirby Smith, and the major from Southampton County, Virginia, George Thomas, who was to win fame by staying with the old army. The army had hailed Johnston's appointment in 1855 as enthusiastically as the Confederates hailed his arrival in Tennessee in September 1861, and obviously the man's heroic personality inspired confidence and trust.

His coming to the Confederacy was dramatic. In command of the Pacific coast with headquarters at San Francisco when he received the news of Texas' secession, Johnston—followed by false rumors of having headed a conspiracy to seize California for the South—made the long trip home across the Arizona desert and Apache country with thirty-odd companions, pro-Southern soldiers and civilians. Like all the big ones, he merely offered his services. His command, waiting for him, was the country west of the Alleghenies to the Mississippi, and on across the river in Missouri.

The central territory of defense—since Johnston's orders were based on resistance to aggression—was the state of Tennessee. Physically protecting the cotton states, Tennessee was a powerful state in its own right. At its southeastern tip, Chattanooga was the juncture of the South's only direct railroad from the Atlantic to the Mississippi, and on its southwestern tip, Memphis was a flourishing river port, connecting with the Confederates west of the river. In the north-central part of the state, Nashville had a production potential for war matériel. As a problem for Johnston, a strong Unionist nest existed in the eastern mountains, adjoining the Virginia and North Carolina mountaineer Unionists.

These frequently active Unionist sympathizers, however, were the only connection between the Confederate East and West. Davis, in his character of peacetime U. S. War Secretary, kept all sections strictly departmentalized, with the only center in his overtired brain.

Aside from the Unionists within his borders, the Yankees at the gates, and the sprawling, unorganized collections of Confederate patriots, Johnston was faced with a mere sprinkling of weapons for his numerically inadequate and untrained troops. Concentrating on Tennessee and appealing to the governors of surrounding states for men (though this got him in trouble with the central government), Johnston presented a bold front to the enemy. It fooled Sherman, in central Kentucky. That recent schoolmaster of a Louisiana academy was called "crazy" when, imposed upon by Johnston's threatening gestures, he demanded 200,000 men to repel the Rebel threat.

While presenting this impressive front, Johnston conceived nothing in larger strategy, nothing of the cause-and-effect action of Stonewall Jackson. He had never commanded more than a peacetime regiment and, though he proved from the beginning that he had a way with troops, Davis' hero gave no indication of those concepts of warfare which characterized the truly great. He was a brave, skillful fighter of troops, and a man of magnificent moral strength, placed in command of an area the size of European countries on a defensive assignment without the manpower or matériel for widely scattered resistance. If he possessed the imagination to conceive boldly for success, which no reports indicated, the directions from the War Office would have restrained anyone except the sheer genius who would not be denied. This Johnston was not.

Even on his defensive assignment, the details were so vast and complex that the commanding general left to subordinates the two forts vital to his defense. Though forts suggest castellated ramparts, dignified symbols of a nation's traditional power, the two river forts in Johnston's area bore no more relation to this image than did the Confederacy to the established power it assumed itself to be.

Fort Henry was the only obstacle to the Tennessee River slicing downward into western Tennessee and then eastward through northern Alabama; and Fort Donelson was the only obstacle to the Cumberland River which, paralleling the Tennessee as the rivers entered the state, swung eastward toward Nashville. The "forts" were all that opposed the invincible U. S. Navy on these inviting avenues of entrance. And Nashville was of vast importance.

In addition to being a river port, this modernized city was the hub of railroads leading to all directions of the western South, and its industries had turned to the manufacture of war matériel, particularly rifled cannons and percussion caps. Along with the city's activities, it had—with bad judgment, in view of its extreme northern position—been made a supply depot and arsenal. The Confederacy might disperse its forces, but in supplies the government committed itself to putting its eggs in one basket.

When Johnston turned over the construction of these forts to subordinates, they in turn left the details to a succession of civil engineers, army engineers, non-engineering army officers, and non-anything politicians. Each strutted his brief hour upon the riverbanks, added his part to the acrimonious confusion, and vanished into one of those obscure departments which catacombed the Southern forces. In a country where every man wanted to be king, no one wanted to assume the responsibility for a mundane though urgently necessary chore.

It was known to all that if Tennessee and Cumberland river ports were passed, the fat and temptingly offered basket of Nashville would fall into enemy hands. It was also known that the industrialized and mechanically-minded North was busily engaged in constructing gunboats for the purpose of demolishing those forts. Indeed, the U. S. Navy, in growing confidence against the C.S.A.'s wretched fixed positions, gave gunboats trial runs down the rivers and held target practices on the forts.

With every warning that it was only a matter of time before the enemy struck with gunboats in support of land masses, with Albert Sidney Johnston evincing the gravest concern, work on the forts proceeded at its halting pace while various inspectors vied with each other in denunciations of the forts' poor positions and construction.

To nobody's surprise, in early February, a seven-gunboat fleet under Commodore Foote chugged down the north-flowing Tennessee River toward Fort Henry, while a force of 17,000 with heavy artillery, which had been landed upstream, was led southward by U. S. Grant. Not that the Unions needed any luck but, as it is said that God favors the side with the strongest battalions, heavy rains raised the river waters to make perfect sailing for the gunboats and placed them practically on a level with the crudely made and unfinished fort. One of Benjamin's appointees, Tilghman, had the misfortune to be the "commander" at the moment and he did, probably, all that could be done.

Sending his small garrison with their 1812 flintlocks toward concentration at Fort Donelson, he took personal command of the fifty-four men on the fixed guns. A British observer, watching such guns at target practice, said it was safer to be near the targets than the guns. As had Major Anderson at Fort Sumter, Tilghman made a show of resistance until honor had been preserved.

With Grant's well-heeled troops still struggling through the mud, the action shifted to Fort Donelson across the flatland on the Cumberland River. At this point Sidney Johnston, with all his heroic character, failed as a commander of an area. Instead of concentrating his troops at Donelson, where he would have outnumbered Grant, Johnston ordered separate actions of retirement.

Beauregard, banished from the East and superseding Bishop-Major-General Polk on the Mississippi, was ordered to retreat to the west of Donelson. To the east, Hardee was to retreat from Kentucky through Nashville. Johnston personally followed this woebegone group, whose only purpose was to withdraw, and the crucial point of Fort Donelson was left in a fantastic command situation, without a head.

With all its inadequacies, this was a better-prepared fort than Henry and a more extensive affair. With its quarters the fort covered fifteen acres, embraced a steamboat-landing town, and the late-arriving, hard-working Colonel Gilmer had hastily erected rifle pits on the land side, facing the way Grant was uninterruptedly moving. The position was defensible if anyone had been responsible for its defense.

Of its three commanders, Simon Bolivar Buckner enjoyed the most interesting life, but Donelson was one of his drabber moments. Thirty-eight at the time, a West Pointer and Mexican War graduate, he had commanded Kentucky's militia until the neutrality myth exploded. After the war, he edited the Louisville *Courier*, later became governor of the state, and lived on until World War I. His son, also a West Pointer, was the Buckner of Pacific fame in World War II.

With him was fifty-five-year-old Gideon Pillow, a lawyer-planter, as optimistic as Buckner was pessimistic, and an old personal enemy from Mexican War days, where Pillow had commanded volunteers. To rank these two feuding soldiers came yet a third commander, John B. Floyd. Last in southwestern Virginia, where Lee had vainly tried to substitute co-operation for Floyd's private war with General Wise, the veteran politician had been sent West with the remnants of the "army" he raised on Davis' early instructions—a brigade of four Virginia and one Mississippi regiments. As Grant said, "he was no soldier." At Donelson, Floyd wavered like a weathercock between Pillow and Buckner, now full of fight, then full of surrender. This unlikely triumvirate literally talked themselves into surrendering Fort Donelson.

First came the gunboats, which Floyd immediately said would finish them off in twenty minutes. To everybody's surprise, including especially the gallant Union Commodore Foote, the gunboats were driven off—*and* by cannoneers who had their first lessons in gunnery by firing on the gunboat fleet which was knocking their own breastworks down around them. Those were very courageous and patriotic young men, the kind the South believed entirely composed its armed forces.

Heartened by this success, the three commanders dared hope to execute Johnston's defensive orders to retreat to Nashville. While Grant, without opposition of any kind, had thoroughly invested the fort, he had wrought no harm to anybody. The next morning Pillow—the manic of the manic-depressive team—took on the task of driving off Grant's right and opening the road to Nashville. Again everyone was surprised that he did! Unfortunately Pillow himself was so overcome with his local victory that instead of holding the road open, let alone following up the driven enemy, he returned to the fort and congratulations.

Meanwhile Grant, who had unaccountably been off confabing with the wounded Commodore Foote, returned to the field and ordered an attack on his left. This effected a lodgment while the Confederates were arguing over what Pillow should have done. That night (February 15), in the inn of the little town, the three Southern generals held one of those councils so dear to the hearts of the unsure. It was there that they convinced themselves that all was lost, even the road to Nashville which Pillow's men had won and which was, in fact, still open.

Though "General" Floyd was nominally in command, he asked to be allowed to escape with his brigade, since the Federals had it in for him from his Washington days. Then Pillow also asked to be spared, and the humiliating duty, involving a Northern prison, descended on Buckner. Since the Kentuckian had been a friend of Grant—supporting him during his army troubles and coming to his financial aid when Grant was embarrassed in New York—he hoped for some courtesy in performing the unprecedented American task of surrendering an army.

In Grant's curt note of reply to terms of surrender, which Buckner characterized as "ungenerous and unchivalric," the star of the stolid Unionist began its ascendant. "Unconditional surrender," Grant said. To a delighted U.S. public, his initials of U.S. prophetically stood for "unconditional surrender." Never mind that those were not the initials of the name his parents gave him but the result of the West Point registrar's mistake, "Unconditional Surrender" Grant he became to the country hungry for victory and for a hero.

On the Southern side, terms of "unconditional surrender" seemed a long way from the chivalry with which Beauregard had treated Anderson at Fort Sumter ten months before. But Southern chivalry—"the chivalry-ridden people" of the abolitionist papers—was something the Northerners wanted to get at, and they were being as businesslike about it as the South had believed they would be only in pursuit of the dollar.

The reality grew on the Southerners that they were caught up in a real war, and their land was being successfully invaded.

Of course, heads fell. Benjamin retired Pillow and Davis finally dispossessed Floyd of the command which he had given him. The two political "generals" who had lost southwestern Virginia had been placed in similar positions to lose Roanoke Island and Fort Donelson, while Lee was innocuously employed and the future great of the South's trained soldiers were restricted to line command. Davis' own god fell with the mortals—as he himself said, justly. Johnston wrote that the judgment of a general was success, and he had failed.

In the fall of Donelson, when hundreds of Confederates, including a general, simply walked away and never surrendered, one man gave promise for the future which he was to fulfill. The forty-year-old ex-slave dealer, Bedford Forrest, a semiliterate Bible reader, led his cavalry out over the road the generals had agreed was closed. Icy waters reached up to the saddle skirts as his men rode through the night. If that ferocious native military genius had been in command of Donelson, there would never have been any discussion of surrender terms. The time was not yet when untrained civilians were placed in command, unless they were politicians or planters.

However, it is by history that the small and indomitable part played by Forrest is known, and an obscure cavalry colonel who escaped with a few troops made no impression on the shocked South.

The people looked beyond local leaders for blame. They began to look to the top.

3

The people began to look to the top when Jefferson Davis' permanent inauguration took place two days before the Western disaster was completed with the Union occupation of Nashville, with loss of most of its stores and, in effect, most of the state of Tennessee. With unconscious irony the Confederates had selected for their inaugural the birthday (February 22) of that great Revolutionary leader, George Washington. Below his equestrian statue in Richmond's Capitol Square, the gaunt and suffering President addressed, in a drizzle, a crowd of shivering men and women who the year before had happily been citizens of the United States.

In the crowd who listened to Davis' uninspired speech and among his fellow countrymen who read it, there was no repining over their course. They did not need the President's denouncements of the enemy's "tyrannical despotism" to hearten them, or his assurances of the justness of their movement, with the inevitable harking back to the Revolution. Nor were they moved by his recital of their financial situation, which at the time seemed sound enough. Except for imported coffee, food prices had risen only negligibly, and their bright new paper money had not then devaluated. The people were already thoroughly committed to winning their independence and they trusted the civil operations of the young nation. What concerned them was that they were losing. They believed in their ability to win and they wanted to know why they were not winning.

The only silver to line the gathering clouds resulted from a Northern act, in which the South played but a passive role. The Confederate commissioners to England and France had been snatched from a British ship on the high seas by a U. S. Navy ship's captain evidently carried away by the successes of his service. The names of Mason and Slidell suddenly formed the basis of an international incident.

James Mason, the grandson of the author of the Virginia Declaration of Rights (who refused to sign the Constitution because it permitted slavery), had a pride in his heritage and position in Virginia's social hierarchy which made him mentally a little fatuous and personally a little pompous. But he was not without ability, having served capably in the U. S. House and Senate, and he had the sort of dignity to impress the British upper classes. In fact, he was a fair fit of the stock Southern aristocrat of legend, without of course performing as a cabin Casanova, or showing any addiction to the whip and the bottle. He was devoutly and contentedly a family man in the best sense of the word.

His companion, Slidell—the fugitive New Yorker who rose to wealth in New Orleans and to domination of the Louisiana political machine, also a U.S. senator—was variously described as "the old intriguer," "wily and devious," and given left-handed praise for his adeptness at behind-the-scenes machinations. But Slidell had a quick mind and, like his fellow import to Louisiana, Benjamin, a realistic one.

Unlike Mason, he had not left the Union to go with his state, but for years he had intrigued in Washington for a secession movement which would complete his fortune and crown the career of a most skillful adventurer. Also a family man, he did not leave his womenfolk at home, as did Mason, but took his wife and daughters along to enjoy the cosmopolitan pleasures of Paris. When old Slidell was removed from the British ship, he was pulled physically from the arms of one of his daughters.

While these two dissimilar parties rendered the greatest possible services to their country by doing time in a Yankee jail, it looked as though the long-sought intervention from Europe was at hand. England demanded the release of the Confederates and, while the U.S. refused, prepared for war. But Lincoln's Cabinet found a face-saving escape from the dilemma, Mason and Slidell were sent on their interrupted journeys, and the alarums were over. However, Southerners did feel that the contretemps had elicited European sympathies, and the people and the government felt more hopeful over recognition.

Then, wrote Slidell and Mason from Europe, the disasters in the West had cast a pall over their chances in England and France. The Confederate commissioners did not know that the British government seriously considered recognition of the new nation, and that the surface rudenesses of British officials to Mason were merely to observe international appearances and not tip their hand until a decision had been reached.

France, despite hostility in some key spots, would most certainly follow England's lead. Men powerfully placed with Napoleon encouraged the Confederates, and the Emperor himself lavished such entertainment on Slidell's wife and daughters that the old adventurer's heart swelled with joy and pride. But he was not taken in by these blandishments of royal favor. He wrote Richmond that military success was the only consideration that would bring about recognition, and a consequent break on the tightening hold of the U.S. blockade.

Instead of military successes, affairs in the West steadily worsened. On March 2, Beauregard evacuated the river stronghold at Columbus, Kentucky, in favor of river forts, over the objections of Polk, who had powerfully fortified the bluff city. A few days later, when all the Confederate forces west of the Mississippi in the Missouri-Arkansas area finally got together under one leader, they were defeated. The command had been given to dashing Earl Van Dorn, a very colorful fellow who had been a ladies' man since his West Point days (and was to die during the war from a bullet of an outraged husband). He was a natural cavalry leader in the wrong slot in infantry command.

Under him Missouri's Price and Texas' McCulloch were at last brought into concerted action, along with a force of Indians under Pike, the Arkansas philosopher—who wrote the most widely known of the various war lyrics to "Dixie."

> Southrons hear your Country call you!
> Up! Lest worse than death befall you. . . .
>
> For Dixie's land we'll take our stand,
>   To live or die for Dixie!
> To arms! To arms!
>   And conquer peace for Dixie. . . .

Earl Van Dorn, trying one of those complicated maneuvers of divided command, did not help bring peace to Dixie. When McCulloch, the old Ranger, was killed, his personally led forces broke off their action and the whole movement collapsed. Elk Horn or Pea Ridge (March 6–7), in northwestern Arkansas, brought the war in Missouri to an early and unhappy end. There would be more flare-ups of fighting, and almost continuous semiguerrilla action, but the state ceased to exist as a vital military sector.

Then, only a month after Missouri was lost to the Confederacy, the South lost its hold on the West in failing to win the first big battle of the war.

4

Shiloh was the first battle on the American continent in which 100,000 troops were engaged. While those numbers might not seem large by today's standards, in comparison to nineteenth-century armies the figures were notable, considering that it was in the first year of a war between peoples of a common country who had had no standing army to speak of at the beginning. Napoleon's army and the allies barely reached 150,000 at Austerlitz, and only 170,000 were engaged at Waterloo. Before 1862 ended, nearly 200,000 men were to fight at Fredericksburg. As the battle that fell almost on the anniversary of Fort Sumter, Shiloh was an awesome affair.

In early February the protected Southern West faced the invader across the width of Kentucky, with strongholds on the Missisippi River in Kentucky; by spring, all available troops were concentrated on the northern edge of Mississippi and near Alabama, on a line east from Memphis in the heartland of the lower South. The defense line had receded virtually due south, down the Tennessee River, from Fort Henry to Pittsburg Landing. This river landing was at the southern end of the avenue of the Tennessee River, before it swung eastward. The landing, on the western bank, was occupied by the Union gunboats and supply ships, but this was as far as the Union forces could invade southward with water support.

Twenty miles away, at Corinth, Mississippi, the forces of the Southern states were finally concentrating for a stand in defense of their territory. The town of Corinth was important as a railroad junction on the Memphis and Charleston, which ran from the Mississippi to Chattanooga and on eventually to the Atlantic. As the troops gathered from all over the Southern West, there was a feeling in the air that large-scale action was imminent. The dispersed defenses had ceased to exist and the time had come for battle.

The Unions felt it too. Grant wrote his wife, "A big fight may be looked for some place before a great while, which it appears to me will be the last in the West. This is all the time supposing that we will be successful, which I never doubt for a single moment."

Albert Sidney Johnston was equally confident. With no more dispersals over great territories, he at last had the bulk of his troops in one body. From Columbus, Polk brought two divisions (minus troops left at the river forts), Hardee brought the survivors of the punishing winter retreat from Kentucky through Nashville, and reinforcements were brought by Braxton Bragg from Pensacola. This fine drillmaster and disciplinarian had benefited by the months of idleness forced on his troops in guarding western Florida, and his 10,000 men were well conditioned and eager to fight.

A forty-five-year-old North Carolinian, Bragg was a Regular Army man, West Pointer, and Mexican War veteran ("A little more grape, Captain Bragg": Zachary Taylor at Buena Vista). His fine qualities of mind and character were equaled by his irascibility and penchant for antagonizing people. His acute and constant suffering from migraine would probably today be diagnosed as some form of psychosomatic disorder. Deeper and even more obscure personality flaws had not then been revealed, and he was welcomed with his well-trained corps, divided into two divisions.

There were also three brigades from a cross section of the western South under John Breckinridge, the handsome Kentuckian who had been Vice-President in the last Administration and leader of the forlorn hope of the Southern Democrats in the 1860 election. Though untrained, the new brigadier, who had barely managed his escape from Washington, was vigorous, intelligent, and a natural leader. He had no great future as a soldier but the true lover of good bourbon and fast horses won a large place for his loyalty. With some oddments of cavalry, including Forrest's small regiment and a Kentucky squadron commanded by another future leader, John Morgan, the formally titled Army of the Mississippi numbered 40,000 effectives.

Beauregard was second in command to Albert Sidney Johnston, a duplication of his situation at Manassas with Retreatin' Joe. As the fastidious Creole commanded the river department *within* the Western Department of Johnston, the ranking field general of the Confederacy, there was no conflict of authority. But A. S. Johnston came late to Corinth, where Beauregard had been quartered over a month, and to that extent Manassas was rehashed with a twist. Instead of Joseph Johnston's initialing Beauregard's battle plan, Beauregard, because of his familiarity with the ground, evolved the details of A. S. Johnston's plan.

This duality of responsibility was merely one of the items, though a basic one, of the controversy which continued for ninety years after the battle. With all the facts in, the half facts and biased arguments, the by no means infallible *Official Records* and the more fallible memoirs, Shiloh remains one of those crucial historical events about which only the rash would venture anything like a final conclusion.

Johnston's fundamental purpose was to surprise the invaders before their forces were as fully concentrated as his. In this he succeeded, despite the after-the-fact denials of Grant, Sherman, and their admirers. Grant's confident army, swelled to 40,000-odd (the numbers are variously estimated), reached out vaguely from Pittsburg Landing with their furthermost point in the vicinity of a country church, Shiloh Chapel. Buell's 20,000-odd, after their leisurely and enjoyable occupation of Nashville (the first Southern state capital to be captured), were on their way and close. The total force was in the Western Department of the Union's Halleck, with Grant in command on the field. As at Fort Donelson, Grant was away from the army, nine miles upriver.

His second in command, in charge of the field in his absence, was "Crazy" Sherman, restored to command through the influence of his father-in-law, a former senator, and his brother, the Ohio senator. Though Grant had found Sherman a loyal and energetic co-operationist, with his troops spread out and the river at their back the future scourge of the South showed at this stage a total absence of the elementary precautions against surprise.

Another large item in the future controversy, and in the imponderables too, was that the Confederate forces were one day, a full twenty-four hours, late in getting into position for the attack. That they were is a fact. Who was to blame—Polk, Hardee, Bragg?—is the controversy, and the effect is the imponderable. Beauregard was so certain that the Unions must know an army of 40,000 was forming for battle one and a half miles away that he wanted to call off the attack. However, Johnston was confident.

With all his serene self-containment, his refusal to make excuses or shift blame, the commanding general had hitherto been reflecting his deep worry. When he prepared his officers for the attack at Shiloh, Johnston acted as though he was freed of the nagging, immobilizing details of his earlier assignment. Finally with a cohesive army against another army in the ultimate test of combat, the imposing man clearly believed the moment had come for him to recoup by deeds the failures he scorned to explain. On the warm, clear Sunday morning of April 6, 1862, Albert Sidney Johnston was notable for his high spirits.

"Tonight we'll water our horses in the Tennessee River," he said.

Why didn't they?

If Sherman's later denial of the surprise was true, then he was crazier than the Unions had believed, to have his men preparing breakfast in an unguarded camp while 40,000 victory-starved Rebels suddenly swooped down on his army. Sherman's division at least gave a classic imitation of acting astonished. Some fired and ran, some dropped rifles and ran, but they all broke. Sherman's camp and headquarters were occupied by the Confederates for the rest of the engagement.

The exultant Southerners paused only to exchange their poor muskets for the discarded Union rifles, and other Union divisions were engulfed in the tide of retreat.

As for Grant's later denial of being surprised, if that was true, then he more than justified Halleck's poor opinion of him by doing nothing until he was interrupted at breakfast, nine miles away, by the sound of a battle which threatened to rout his army. Certainly his first message, which he later ignored, was an alarmed cry of help to "*possibly* save the day" (not his italics).

That the day was saved, and not by Grant, is the biggest bone of latter-day contention. Nobody can successfully deny that the Union troops, with hard fighting increasing in spots after the surprise, were driven back toward the Tennessee River. Officers commanding reinforcements reported thousands of them "cowering" under the riverbank and disorganized masses in "terror." Johnston's plan was to pry between the Union Army and the Landing, forcing them into the open, away from their gunboats and ship supplies, onto poor ground where surrender would be inevitable. His battle had as its intention the destruction of Grant's force as an operating army, and he seemed in a fair way to achieve his objective.

At that decisive moment which comes in all battles, the momentum of the Confederates was checked by one of those spontaneous stands unrelated to battle plans, similar to Jackson's at Manassas. At Shiloh the depression of an unused road, with ready-made abatis of thick brush and small trees, gave natural works to two compact divisions in the Union line nearest the river. Against them the victorious tide broke, and fresh C.S.A. troops went in only to stagger back.

While the Confederate line was breaking against this barrier, at half past two came high tragedy. Albert Sidney Johnston bled to death. A fragment had struck an artery in the back of his thigh and, in his excitement, he had not heeded the wound. As his physician was tending wounded, there was no one to notice the nature of the bleeding until too late. To the great soldier himself, triumph came at the hour of death. To his admirers, then and since, that triumph passed with his life's blood.

At bivouacs during the war and at reunions as long as veterans survived, around family hearths and later in steam-heated rooms, Southerners laid the loss of victory to Beauregard's failure to press the advantage after Johnston's death. By reiteration, this charge entered regional lore as fact, taking its place with such legends as that every Southerner owned slaves— or, rather, "happy darkies."

Actually, there was little advantage to press, and Beauregard did all possible. Contrary to the way the legend reached even Southern children, Johnston did not fall while his whole army was sweeping irresistibly ahead, with Beauregard immediately thereafter calling a halt. Beauregard continued the fighting from two-thirty until dark. He finally carried the pesky road position and continued to thrust forward into the punishing fire of a reserve battery of heavy artillery, supported by the first reinforcements rushing onto the confused field, and gunboats whose artillery bursts added to the confusion in the falling light. Beauregard called a halt only when the men were exhausted from twelve hours of the bloodiest fighting, their ammunition going or gone, and in the gathering gloom the units suffered the inevitable disorganization of green troops.

Beauregard was even blamed for the disorganization. On the contrary, the hastily assembled patchwork of an army behaved extremely well considering that the men were inexperienced (most of them in their first fight), the officers were handling large bodies of troops for the first time in their lives, and the units were operating together for the first time as an army. The fighting was still in the stage, too, where generals literally led their men, rushing ahead of them with wild exhortations. While this looked very gallant in lithographs of the war, it was scarcely the method for handling a division of infantry. Bishop Polk, sword in hand, was one who led his men and handled them well too.

All these natural shortcomings of a green army were exposed against a superbly equipped force with the élan of victories behind it and with some units who after the initial shock fought with the fiercest determination. Their reinforcements had an incalculable effect and darkness contributed to the Confederate disorganization. Johnston could have controlled none of these elements, any more than Beauregard could have. As for the further confusion of those Rebels who seized the fancy victuals in the Unions' bulging supply wagons, no Confederate leader—from the first chance offered the troops until the last—could keep those ravenous farmers from the Yankees' tempting feasts.

All in all, it would look as if Grant's luck held, and Beauregard's star failed him. With all his love of military panoply, his grandiose and impractical schemes which bedeviled the War Office, his unfortunate gift for controversial writing, Beauregard possessed and at times illustrated undeniable qualities of leadership. Perhaps his early glory blighted him for subordinate command at this phase, feeding his tendency to spectacular strategy. Yet, at Shiloh, he was no more truly the losing general than was Grant the winning general.

After the Confederates had won in the field on Sunday, the next day became an anticlimax for which neither general was responsible. Grant got Buell's fresh 20,000, who completed their arrival during the night—hence the importance of the Confederates' being one day late in the attack. Even with this strengthened force, Grant showed none of his famed fighting drive, not with that roughly handled army.

On the other side, Beauregard might as well have gotten reinforcements in Van Dorn's Arkansas troops, freed from their abortive effort in Missouri and anxious to join Beauregard. Instead, they idled through the spring day on their side of the Mississippi because the Louisiana governor refused them boats for transportation on the grounds that he found President Davis' treatment of him unacceptable.

On the second day, after inconclusive fighting from the Yankees' former camp (Beauregard having at least the personal satisfaction of sleeping in Sherman's bed), the Confederates decided they were losing irreplaceable men to no purpose. They retired in good order, unpursued, even packing empty caissons with muskets gleaned from the bloody field. Their total casualties were 10,000; the Unions lost 13,000.

Nobody won the field, though the Confederates withdrew to Corinth, the line they were protecting. But they failed to win. As Grant became a bigger hero than ever, the scapegoat mantle descended from Sidney Johnston to Beauregard. With Johnston's death at high tide of the battle, his recent failures were forgotten and his apotheosis begun.

Such "personal" people as Southerners could not, at that stage of their fight for independence, conceive of losing except by personal vagaries. Because Johnston died (and he had been a fine character) the battle was lost; because Beauregard lost it (as they believed) he was a humbug of a general.

Davis concurred in this. His dislike of Beauregard, begun the preceding fall, was self-feeding, and the death of his hero he regarded as "the irreplaceable loss."

At least one top-flight Confederate major general, sharp-eyed and hard-fighting Dick Ewell, thought Davis' "infatuation" for Johnston "of the blindest and most unaccountable nature."

The controversies began in the wake of the battle that had failed in its original objective, with the Confederate West in danger of quickly ceasing to exist as a military factor.

5

Beauregard's reputation was not helped by the fall of the Mississippi river fort, Island No. 10, with *its* garrison of 7000, on April 7.

Then, on June 4, the last of the river forts was evacuated. Two days later, after the powerful Union gunboats had disposed of the makeshift but ingenious Confederate "fleet," the Unions occupied the cotton-rich river port of Memphis, Tennessee's gaudy Queen of the West.

Since New Orleans, in another Southern-style farce of divided command, had already yielded to the U. S. Navy, it looked as if the Confederacy's Mississippi was about gone. After New Orleans, the Navy took Baton Rouge and Natchez in stride, leaving Vicksburg as the only Southern stronghold on the Mississippi River—and the gunboats could run past its defenses. The United States had struck the heaviest blow with the weapon an agricultural people could not quickly match, a Navy.

During this conquest of the South's great river, the opportunity existed for the United States to complete its invasion of the cotton South. In recent times analyses praise Lincoln's plan of halving and then quartering the Confederacy and then finishing up the pieces. This persuasive after-the-fact rationale is posited on the assumption that these were two countries in full alignment against each other, with the purpose of the United States clearly to invade, occupy, and destroy the alien power of the Confederacy from the beginning. Instead, plans grew as the fighting continued.

There is Grant's belief that *one* big battle, which happened to be Shiloh, would end the war in the West. It would seem at this time that Lincoln had tried for a quick end of the war in the West, as he was trying again in Virginia. The Administration had not yet been sufficiently caught up in the actual warfare to advocate total war as a means of "preserving the Union." The uncertainty, the extemporizing, were felt throughout the chains of command, where Union leaders suffered their own personality defects. Among these was Halleck, the commander of the Western Department of the United States.

In his late forties, Halleck, a West Pointer, had resigned from the Regular Army to further his ambitions some years before. Unlike most who did this, he had improved his time at army posts by studying law and was a successful attorney when the war began. His lectures on military science had been collected and were highly regarded studies, and Halleck himself was regarded as a great military mind. As with others of large reputation, the Union's Western commander did little to justify it in actual warfare.

While New Orleans was being occupied at one end of the Mississippi and the island forts falling at the other, Halleck amassed against Beauregard an army that would have been unthinkable a year before. He gathered at Shiloh 125,000 men, more than had fought the battle on both sides. With this overwhelming force, Halleck approached Corinth, less than twenty miles away, at the rate of one mile a day. After this slowest advance of the war, Halleck then laid siege.

There was nothing Beauregard could do. To the 30,000 remaining after the battle, he had added Van Dorn's force, which had finally gotten across the Mississippi. His combined force was no more than one third of Halleck's and artillery-wise it was no contest. Provisions were scarce, the enemy could operate against the east-west railroad, and Corinth was an unhealthy spot anyway.

To the thousands of wounded were added thousands of sick and the Confederate forces were not equipped for either. The rudimentary Medical Department consisted of a few doctors, helped by attendants temporarily drafted from the army, with medical supplies largely handled by those men in the procurement bureau whose qualifications consisted of a desire to avoid the stigmata of being young civilians equaled by a desire to avoid danger. Hospitals were hotels, homes, or any building with a roof on it. As in the East, nursing was done by women volunteers, mostly from the neighborhood but some coming up from lower Mississippi and Alabama.

From Mobile came a group of thirty ladies, self-yclept the "Florence Nightingale Brigade." They studied the situation of one hotel which had been turned into a hospital, with even the halls lined with suffering men, and held a meeting in which resolutions were passed condemning the mismanagement of the Tishomingo Hotel Hospital. A week later only two or three of the ladies remained.

Of these, Miss Kate Cumming emerged as a valuable hospital superintendent, became permanently attached to the hospital service, and left interesting accounts of her experiences. Ella Newsome, the daughter of a Baptist minister from Brandon, Mississippi, became so famous for her continued work with the hospital service that *others* named her the "Florence Nightingale of the South." Mrs. Newsome was the army's trusted friend, and generals wrote her personal letters of their doings. This was typical of the volunteer nursing situation, where hundreds were called and a few were chosen.

Under these circumstances it took some doing to retreat with inadequate transportation from the vicinity of a large and victorious army. Beauregard made an admirable retreat. Not only did his entire force and supplies slip away unnoticed (May 30), but Halleck had no notion where the army had gone. Even the citizens, whose homes had served as hospitals while the women served as nurses, evacuated down to a few die-hards (or perhaps resigned Unionists).

Beauregard took his hungry, sick, rebuilding army fifty miles south to Tupelo, in a fatter country, while Halleck occupied the abandoned railroad-junction town, and sat there.

At the new camp, Beauregard decided to take an overdue leave for his health. He suffered from a chronic throat inflammation, and his doctors had long ago ordered a rest. He wanted to turn over his army temporarily to Bragg, the drillmaster and second in command.

In Richmond, where Davis found the West too remote for his control, the President never relaxed his prerogatives as Commander in Chief, from details to decisions. On the detail side, when Beauregard retreated, the President sent him an insulting questionnaire of explanations to make for his shortcomings. Maintaining his perfect record for courtesy, Beauregard answered each humiliating question with reason. On the aspect of larger decisions, while Beauregard was absent on sick leave, Davis seized the opportunity to appoint his second in command as permanent commander.

Bragg had not maneuvered for the job and disliked the situation, though he knew he enjoyed Administration favor. With Beauregard brushed aside to an unimportant assignment, like some prince out of favor with the emperor, Bragg inherited an army which despised him. The migraine-suffering martinet regarded the willful volunteer troops of a revolutionary movement much as if they were peasant levies of a European nation, and matters were worsened by the Conscription Act.

The Confederate government passed this Conscription Act, which changed the status of the one-year volunteers into enlistments for the duration of the war, while the battered army was still at Corinth. Though the act was necessary, its administering needed a certain tact, as many soldiers were bitterly offended at this compulsion. Some volunteers regarded conscription as a betrayal of faith, others resented the opprobrium of conscription.

The necessity of the act was a grim illustration of the waning enthusiasm for fighting throughout the South. The eager volunteers who had been turned away the preceding spring had not answered the new calls for a variety of reasons: among an impulsive people, once the impulse had passed it was gone; the inanition of the government was reflected among the people, and they could not be roused out of it; the dreary succession of defeats and retreats, with some 20,000 Southerners dragged off to Federal prisons, was not their idea of war. An amalgam of all these causes was the fact that the new government, with no meaning to the people in itself, touched them tangibly only in the armies. At that time the Western armies were most uninviting.

For the men in Bragg's army, where the morale was already low because of retreats and poor food, a disagreeable and harsh leader turned many volunteers into active hatred for the army and everything it represented. Their case was vividly presented by Sam Watkins, of the 1st Tennessee, the same Sam who had bemoaned missing Manassas because the war would be over before he had fired a shot.

Now, he said, the men "had but one ambition . . . and that was to get out of the army." By army he meant infantry. "They wanted to join the cavalry or artillery or home guards or pioneer corps [engineers] or to be 'yaller dogs' [staff members], or anything." He said that "Bragg never was a good feeder," no extra rations were allowed the colored servants, and "no coffee or whiskey or tobacco were allowed to be issued the troops."

When deserters were shot, "the whole army was marched to the horrid scene to see a poor trembling wretch tied to a post and a platoon of 12 men drawn up in a line to put him to death." The public whippings of men who'd gone absent without leave, thirty-nine lashes on the bare back, were even more revolting to witness. They made the soldier "loathe the very name of the Southern Confederacy." Sam believed Bragg set out to crush the spirit of the men. "The more of a hang-dog look they had about them the better was General Bragg pleased."

However large the segment represented by this attitude of Sam Watkins (which he recalled twenty years later), it was certainly not purely personal with him. On the other hand, despite the hatred of his men, Bragg did mold the troops into a well-disciplined army by Confederate standards. He was allowed by Halleck most of the summer so to do.

The inaction of the vast Union horde, after Halleck inched it with ponderous caution into deserted Corinth, was similar to the Confederate inaction after Manassas the summer before. Between his army and the all-victorious fleet, the United States forces could probably have taken Vicksburg and occupied the Confederate West by summer, before the various powder and munition plants, springing up, achieved full production. To do that the army would have been required to subsist off the country, with the consequent ravages to the civilian population.

As total war was still in the future, Lincoln apparently needed briefing on his plan for halving, then quartering, the C.S.A., since attributed to him. Actually the largest army of the continent, having penetrated to the heartland of the lower South, did not know what to do about it. The South still had not thrown in the towel. In fact, in Virginia, the war was blazing.

Since he could not settle permanently at Corinth, Halleck began to break up his army in dispersed forces and the Confederacy was given a second chance to carry on its fight for independence.

CHAPTER X

The Grand Design

WITH the subjugation still in its uncertain phases, the halting of the Union forces in the West was undoubtedly influenced by the expectation of an early ending of the war in Virginia. Since the Union had made the Confederate capital its chief objective, the fall of Richmond would lose the Confederacy its only arsenal, as of then, and Union success in Virginia would break the back of the Southern defense.

With the new and awesome Union war machine, gathered under McClellan, poised to strike at the capital, the Confederate people and their Congress became frantic that Virginia would follow the Western disasters and their brief independence would be over. In their fears, citizens and government began to look critically at their leader, the President.

One learned Virginian, with four sons officers in the Confederate armies, wrote in his diary that spring: "I dare not speculate on public affairs. Nothing can exceed the imbecility of President Davis. His obstinacy and self will are dreadful. He will not have about him men of talent and force."

Newspapers did dare to speculate on public affairs, most gloomily, and Pollard on the Richmond *Examiner* denounced the President as the ultimate enemy of the South. In a Georgia weekly journal, the editor expressed the more typical disappointment and apprehension of the people.

Mentioning the high hopes held of Jefferson Davis as a military leader at the beginning and his overlong dependence on European intervention, the Georgian said, "President Davis does not enjoy the confidence of the Southern people."

Davis, "with a cold, icy, iron grasp, has fettered our people, stilled their beating pulses of patriotism, cooled their fiery ardor, imprisoned them in camps and behind entrenchments"—a reference to the idle garrisons all over the South.

Then the editor reached the core of the people's dissatisfaction, when he said, "He has not told the people what he needed. As a faithful sentinel, he has not told them what of the night." Instead, the people were forced to witness the blunders of a passive defense when the time called for bold strokes.

Congress went on from there. The leaders determined to loosen his grasp on the military and bring in a soldier either to take charge of their national defense or at least to take an active part in it. To this modest end, the original choice was to make a field general Secretary of War. This would get rid of the unpopular Benjamin and at the same time give more importance to the War Office. Many of the clerical details of the War Office could just as well be handled by Adjutant General Cooper, which would free the Secretary for policy making and a close co-operation with generals in the field. Lee, having completed his engineering job of the southern coasts, was the man Congress had in mind.

Davis, though he had been failed by two lawyers, did not want a general in the War Office, possibly because he feared strong-minded interference or attempted encroachments on his sphere. However, Benjamin did go out of the War Office in one of Davis' moves which revealed total disregard of the will of the people, through either unawareness or a stiff-necked resistance to popular pressure.

As far back as July 1861, Bob Toombs had perceived that the office of Secretary of State was no place for an ambitious man who wanted to serve his country. The latent antagonism between Davis and Toombs had flared into the open and the tempestuous Georgian took leave of Richmond in the same kind of violent flurry with which he had quit Washington six months before. Despite his wife's protest that he was physically unfit for active military service (he was over fifty and soft from his self-indulgence), and the fact that he had no experience of any kind, he entered the field where the true glory lay. As a brigadier, he was lost to any real service for the Southern states.

He was replaced by Robert M. T. Hunter, who gave Davis his chance to have late-seceding Virginia represented in the Cabinet. Hunter was a mild-mannered and soft-spoken gentleman from the fair Rappahannock River country, and the nearest to a born aristocrat in the Cabinet. He was also intelligent and successful (law and planting), a hard and methodical worker, and in Washington had quietly glowed with presidential aspirations. When Hunter left Washington with his state, he transferred his aspirations from Pennsylvania Avenue to East Clay Street in Richmond.

The solid worker needed only a little longer than Toombs also to perceive that the State Department led to a dead end. With the Administration committed to its Alice-in-Wonderland policy on cotton, there was nothing for the ambitious Hunter to devote his energies to, and he vanished from the lonely corner office in the Government Building so quietly that he was hardly missed. When the first session of the Permanent Congress met in February, he turned up in the Senate.

Since Vice-President Stephens came increasingly to absent himself from

Richmond in disapproval of the Administration, Hunter served more often than not as Speaker of the Senate. Of the 267 Southerners who served in the Confederate Congress during the whole four years, nearly one third had Washington experience, and it must have seemed like old times to Hunter, the neat, plump, cautious presidential aspirant.

For the permanent inaugural of the President, Davis had no Secretary of State. Into this vacancy, when the public clamor against Benjamin was deafening, he put the villain of Roanoke Island. This affront to the public, never forgiven by many, was completely needless. There was no place in the State Department for Benjamin's vast talents, of which the President was well aware. But he wanted Benjamin to continue as his adviser and soother, though this could have been achieved without placing him in the empty office which carried theoretically the highest prestige.

However, Davis then had the War Office vacant and he still needed a Virginian in his Cabinet. He made a happily received choice of a strange character who, for his brief time in the Confederate government, played partly inadvertently a fateful role. Of George Wythe Randolph, it was always first said that he was a grandson of Thomas Jefferson, born at Monticello, and member of the lordly and prolific clan of Randolph. That does not quite tell the story of the forty-four-year-old aristocrat.

Thomas Jefferson, despite all his political democracy and informal manners, was a gentleman who lived in grand style and very mindful of his comforts. The chatelaine of the fabulous mountaintop establishment of Monticello was his oldest daughter, Martha. To her, Papa was the head of the family, and her husband, Thomas Mann Randolph, was number two man.

Randolph suffered much at his position and took to staying more and more at his own nearby plantation, from whence came rumors of erratic conduct. He went through his share of the wealth derived from the land-rich Randolphs, and Jefferson ran so heavily in debt that public subscriptions were raised to ease his declining years. Thus, George Wythe Randolph, the son of Martha Jefferson and the embittered Randolph, was not raised in a happy household or in affluent circumstances, and grew up partly in the North after his mother remarried. He tended to his own fortune in the time-honored way of men of social position by marrying a lady of means. Perhaps because of the turbulence and instability of his childhood, he placed an unusually high value on the leisured and cultivated life of, as he said, "a gentleman."

Military-wise, he had served as a midshipman in the Navy before taking a law degree at his grandfather's university, and while practicing law in Richmond was active in the social organization of a militia company. In the war, he served briefly with the artillery but, finding military life inconsistent with his tastes, he had yearned for the more congenial atmosphere of his native Albemarle County. However, his brief war record was good. He had risen from captain to colonel of Magruder's artillery, with a promotion to brigadier coming up when he resigned. Davis could even say he had a "general" in the War Office, though Randolph was a dilettante in war as in all else.

It is no blame on the President, or the acclaimers of Randolph's appointment, that in an aristocracy natural merit was naturally attached to an aristocrat. In Randolph, as in all too many of his kidney, they had the demonstration of "what's in a name" and, more sorrowfully, what is not.

Though all these changes took care of the war department situation and Benjamin, the Confederate Congress then went further than its original demand for a change in military affairs. They passed a bill calling for a Commander in Chief, like McClellan in the United States, who would be in charge of all the armies.

This notion was more detestable to Davis than a soldier in the War Office. He vetoed that bill and very skillfully got the pressure off him at the expense of his old stooge, Robert E. Lee. Knowing that Congress had Lee in mind for Commander in Chief, he placated Congress by appointing Lee as his military *adviser*. Only this time, Lee became adviser of all the Confederate armies, "under the direction of the President."

At last, a devious and rocky way was opened for the long-suffering Virginian to save the war for the Deep South secessionists.

2

Because Lee is a god in the South, he is regarded as totally great, and it is considered *lèse-majesté* to admit he had human characteristics. Because the North regards him with detachment, Northern critics are free to point out his military mistakes, which he certainly made. Neither blind worship nor objectivity truly measures the greatness of the man's spirit. It was his heroic self-mastery of the less noble human traits which dog us all that gave to the total man a symmetry akin to the sublime in art. Indeed, in his self-concept, with his dedication to duty ("the noblest word in the English language"), the affable Virginian was by way of achieving a work of art in his own grandeur of person.

Probably no man in the South's struggle was called on for more self-mastery in the devotion to duty than the fifty-five-year-old soldier, with more than thirty years of distinguished military service behind him, who returned to an ignominious office job at the moment when the misfortunes of his native land cried out for trained leaders in the field. Worse, he had no faith that he could accomplish anything for his country.

He was the detail man on tedious chores which belonged properly in the War Office, the Adjutant General's and, in some cases, in the Commissary and Quartermaster departments. He even apportioned rifles that trickled through the blockade. His aides-de-camp said that "all papers relating to military matters of any sort received by the President, or by any member of the Cabinet, were referred to him to be answered, no matter how unimportant or purely personal. . . ."

Lee was given small, complex problems for some distant front and, before mastered, they would be snatched from him by the President. Field commanders, uncertain of Lee's position, would send him urgent telegrams regarding a decision on some movement about which the President had not seen fit to inform him. He advised where he could and, though he had no authority for his general suggestions and insufficient information for specific, some commanders sought his counsel as they would that of a kindly and wise uncle.

On his constantly interrupted, disconnected tasks, he acquired fragmentary information of every force in the South and was never permitted to absorb completely any single situation, except Virginia. There his grasp was achieved by nearness and native familiarity rather than by virtue of his nominal and meaningless "command" of forces. Yet he would be ordered from his maddening hodgepodge of duties to consult with the President on some grand strategy, on which Davis always made the decision after wasting hours of Lee's time.

It must have required the patience of Job for Lee to endure this disrespect and waste of his talents, while seeing the Commander in Chief bring his native state to the brink of a disaster which had already befallen the Atlantic coast, New Orleans, and the West. Yet the selfless man learned to bring more than patience to his distasteful and unrewarding lot.

When Lee had first resignedly accepted his fate, he was called to the bedside of dying Bishop Meade, Episcopal bishop of Virginia. The old churchman wanted to see Lee a few minutes before he passed away and he said, "God bless you, Robert; and fit you for your high and responsible position. I can't call you 'General'; I've heard your catechism so often. . . . Heaven bless you, and give you wisdom for your important and arduous duties."

As the devout Lee believed in prayers, perhaps he was heartened by the bishop's deathbed blessing. For he certainly needed help from a force larger than the strength usually allotted mortal men, to discover means of using his humiliatingly impossible job for the service of his country.

Fortunately Lee had an earlier experience with the President, when he was superintendent of West Point and Davis Secretary of War. Lee had said then to his wife that the Mississippian could be curt, and he learned in those days the methods of approach to the gentleman so sensitive about his own feelings. He perceived that the President could be persuaded by tactful suggestion. Lee perceived further that on matters of future large consequence, but involving only apparently minor details in the present, he could evolve plans in effect unbeknownst to Davis.

Then while the Commander in Chief rushed frantically from one detail to another, calling peremptorily on Lee, as though he combined in his single person a corps of office boys and a staff of yes-men, the general found that he could physically handle the details of distant places thrust upon him *and*, at the same time, concentrate on the total strategy of the familiar sector which was dearest to his heart, his home state.

At that time McClellan's fearsome armed force was ready to strike at Richmond from a point of vantage, and Lee never agreed with the latter-day critique on the folly of the defense of the capital. This critique, which passed on from one generation to the next, into legend, purports to show that the Confederacy could have won if the government had not been committed to the symbolic sentimentality of defending its capital. This critique, however, ignores several facts.

As a political center, Virginia's capital was the center of the state's life, in commerce and banking, transportation and industry. Around the core of the Tredegar Iron Works which, since the fall of Nashville, was then producing the only cannon in the Confederacy, the city had become a vast arsenal by the spring of 1862, and President Davis said that with some support in cannons and small arms from arsenals then in process of development, Richmond would completely supply the ordnance for the army.

Far more than a sentimental symbol, the capital was the center without which the Confederacy would not field an Eastern army, without which, needless to say, there would have been no Eastern Confederacy—or, indeed, any at all.

In addition, the state of which Richmond was the transportation center produced largely for the army concentrated within its borders—a vital element considering the bungling of the Commissary Department in gathering foods and the poor use the government made of the scattered Southern railroads in shipping it. Finally, the city was a hub of railroads literally to the four points of the compass, with connections to the lower South and West. With the Manassas Gap Railroad in Union hands, the Virginia Central from Richmond was the only connection of the eastern part of the state with the richly producing Shenandoah Valley. There was no possibility of Virginia continuing as a buffer territory with its center gone, and the seaboard South would have been open to the invading armies straight down from the North.

On the positive side, it has never been made clear why it was not more practical for the main army of the Southern states to contain the invader at the borders, in order that the remaining states might be free to go undisturbed about the production of food and clothing, while developing the production of the matériel of war. That was the ideal anyway. It was no fault in the basic strategy that foods, clothing and horses were not sent in proportion to the states' capacities because of venality, incompetence, want of organization, and the presence of (indeed, the ever present) individualism which never permitted co-operation for a common end.

To Lee, in Richmond, it could not fail to be obvious that the lack of co-operation, in general and in every particular, was made into a greater evil because the representatives of the people continued to play politics. Not even the shadows of the firing line at Richmond could teach those old dogs new tricks. With their bright new dream and armies dissolving around them, the collection of Southern "leaders" in Richmond's stately Capitol had come up during the winter with a basis for a Gilbert and Sullivan plot, generally called the "Bounty and Furlough Act."

This act purposed to retain the twelve-month volunteers in the army by a bounty of fifty dollars, a two-month furlough, and a choice of rejoining any outfit they wanted. As this happened when the Union armies of the West were massing for the death blow to Albert Sidney Johnston, when McClellan had gathered his awesome force to thrust at Richmond, when the unwarned Southern people were in a state of shock, it would be an understatement to say that few of the volunteers came forward for re-enlistment. Probably a majority looked forward to the day of deliverance from this terrible thing that was happening to them.

At this moment, under Lee's urging, Virginia passed what amounted to a law of compulsory military service for all white men between the ages of eighteen and forty-five. Then the Confederate Congress, emboldened by seeing no ill befall their Virginia colleagues nor any rioting among the troops, came forward finally with their Conscription Act—watered down to from eighteen to thirty-five and with the exemptions which showed mindfulness of the feelings of powerful planters. An owner of twenty slaves or more was not required to fight. Although many great planters, like Wade Hampton, fought valiantly for their civilization, the exemptions were the genesis of the later popular Confederate phrase, "A rich man's war and a poor man's fight." (Confederate Memorial Days caused most of the veterans to forget that after the war.)

With the armed forces saved from their own government, Lee could look toward saving them from the enemy—as he called them, "those people."

When Lee took over in the War Office on hilly Ninth Street, across from Capitol Square, Davis had a dispersal of forces in Virginia which, counting subdivisions of armies, had eight separate forces arranged in eight separate parts of the state. On the war map the symbolic dots would have formed a rough outline of the state. Every entrance was guarded. The Confederate forces in Virginia were ready for anything, except to fight a battle.

Fortunately they were saved from this eventuality by McClellan. A lot of hard things have been said about General McClellan, during his lifetime and since, but the South always liked him. Anti-McClellan Northerners claimed that was because Lee could always handle him. Whatever of truth that might hold, it is not the whole truth. Southerners liked Mc-

Clellan because he fought according to the lines that Lincoln said the war was about, and this was understandable to Southerners.

He fought to suppress the armed forces of dissident fellow countrymen whom it was his duty, and his desire, to return to a common Union. He did not consider it his duty, and it was certainly not his desire, to make war on those civilians among his countrymen who differed from him on the interpretation of the Constitution. He fought without hate, without cruelty, as if it were indeed a rebellion to suppress and not an alien people to conquer and despoil.

Personally the boy prodigy and successful man (retired from the army, he was president of a railroad at secession) was vain and showy, possessed of untrammeled egoism, small and mean in dealing with rivals, and among the many who considered themselves superior to Lincoln. He was also physically attractive and inspired the greatest affection in his troops. Militarily, nobody can deny his gift for training, equipping, and conditioning an army, though possibly, as his detractors have it, that's all he was good for. Certainly he was most hesitant to attack, to commit his army—and his reputation—to the ultimate test. He was a master at finding excuses for not advancing and hitting the enemy. He wanted everything just so.

However, McClellan's strategy for taking Richmond was flawless. It was the only imaginative plan ever used against the city and the only plan of any kind that nearly succeeded. What he might have done had he been allowed to follow this plan for the conquest of Richmond can never be known. He was thwarted by a strange triumvirate—Lee, Jackson, and Lincoln.

As Illinois's Senator Douglas was important in Southern ante-bellum history, so in its war history was General McClellan, thirty-five-year-old Commander in Chief of the Union armies—subject, as it turned out, to the direction of *his* President.

With a magnificently equipped and armed force in excess of 150,000, McClellan launched his long-awaited invasion to end the war in late March 1862.

The same day Stonewall Jackson, with 3600 men, attacked and was repulsed at the Shenandoah Valley hamlet of Kernstown.

The strange, and for once undeclared, pattern of events had begun to unfold in the defense of Virginia, where—between Lee and Jackson—the Confederates for the first time employed cause-and-effect strategy.

3

Before McClellan's move against Richmond, Retreatin' Joe Johnston had abandoned his winter base at Centreville, and with it a million pounds of bacon, other valuable supplies, and heavy artillery at a time when government agencies were frantically scouring the South for metal—everything from kitchen kettles to church bells—and the men at the Tredegar were working desperately and brilliantly, as virtually a self-sustaining empire, to deliver guns to the Confederacy.

He took up a stand on the Rappahannock River at the old, small city of Fredericksburg, midway between the two capitals. Stonewall Jackson, whose Valley force was in Joe Johnston's command, perforce moved south from the pleasant quarters he and Mrs. Jackson had shared during the winter at Winchester.

That old Valley town, where Washington had his headquarters in the French and Indian War and which was to change hands seventy times during the Civil War, was occupied by Banks. This political general, former governor of Massachusetts, was to gain the unflattering sobriquet of "Commissary" Banks, because of the fat supplies he involuntarily provided Jackson's troops. He was not noted for swiftness of movement, except on a retreat which was to befall him, or for accuracy of deduction. Yet he was no part of a coward, and Jackson's little Valley force was not then taking liberties with him. Banks's numbers shifted throughout the action to come but, as the two forces first lined up against each other, he greatly outnumbered Jackson.

In March these two local antagonists seemed a very distant side show to the main event. Neither knew the details of the major action; indeed, the Confederates in Richmond were at some pains to discover the course of McClellan's action. Of all the grand plan they—or, really, Lee and Jackson from here on—never knew the inner workings. The records were published after they were dead. But they acted so thoroughly as if they were privy to the exchanges of McClellan and Lincoln that their supporters attributed to them information which in fact they lacked. They made a reasonable hazard.

The immediate action inaugurated by McClellan in March, after other plans had for one reason or another been abandoned, was to send the bulk of his army (100,000) by water to Fortress Monroe, the guardian of Hampton Roads on the tip of the Virginia peninsula.

Between the James and the York rivers, the eighty-mile peninsula was the demesne of America's first plantation grandees, the country where Washington and Jefferson and many another came for their rich wives. The land is flat though attractive, in an unspectacular way. Creeks and small rivers slice across it and little valleys are lush with Virginia creeper and honeysuckle. Roadsides are flanked with sweet-smelling vines and the woods are thickly brushed with vines and creepers. Flowers grow in profusion and on the plantations still standing are some of the finest gardens in America.

In the eighty-odd miles from Richmond to Fortress Monroe, the air had never been clouded with the smoke of industry. In the early days the small planters ran their tobacco hogsheads down creeks to public ware-houses on the rivers; the big planters shipped from their own wharves, at the end of their magnificent river-front lawns. By the time of the Civil War such great planters had gone. Tobacco had used up most of the land, and the people were changing over to general farming—bringing their produce to Richmond—and power was shifting to the city. The people and their basic ways of living had changed little. As a military factor their roads had changed even less.

The main road up the center of the peninsula, today's Route 60 from Williamsburg to Richmond, then largely followed the footpath worn through the forests by Indians, and was called the Pocahontas Trail in honor of the young girl who befriended John Smith. The network of roads closer to the river and converging on Richmond, had sprung up apparently according to the whims of the planters and convenience of farmers. They were roads in name only and no living man could accurately describe their sudden appearances and mysterious vanishings as they intertwined through the fragrant brush and bottoms.

The land bore no scars and few memories of the hundred years of Indian fighting in its beginning, or of Benedict Arnold's raiders or Cornwallis' ponderously moving army. An enervating mist comes to the peninsula which brings an atmosphere of softness and shadow where outlines are blurred as in a dream.

From this dreamlike state, the peninsula country of Virginia was frighteningly awakened by the presence of an invading army the size of Wellington's at Waterloo. Such guns had never been seen outside of nightmares, and such victuals only in the memory of the old inhabitants who harked back to the great plantation days.

To confront this blue-clad mass were only the 12,000 under Major General Magruder. Magruder's force was fortified at Yorktown, at the narrowest girth of the peninsula and where his heavy guns could keep the pestilential Union gunboats out of the York River.

Excitable Prince John took one look at the reports of one laden transport following another into Fortress Monroe and immediately called a council of war. Here the alarmed officers, exactly as at Fort Donelson, talked themselves into a panic. Warmhearted and extravagantly courteous Magruder had been one of the two men who (by record) could bring himself to congratulate Lee on his wretched assignment, and Prince John forthwith wired his adviser that all was lost. Yorktown must be abandoned and he was getting out of there. Avuncular Lee quieted down the high-strung amateur thespian, advised him to avoid such councils of war, and promised him reinforcements. In the meantime, Magruder was to "impose" on the enemy.

This imposition was close to the heart of the would-be actor. While his troops dug away at fortifying, Magruder acted out such a pageant of a vast army in the process of attack that he was called "The Great Demonstrator." Against such a threatening foe, McClellan cautiously laid siege, and gave Lee precious time.

At the tip of the peninsula the James River is three miles wide, and the section of Virginia south of the James was and always had been quite separate from the northside. As Richmond dominated its area, Norfolk was the queen of the southside.

Flanked by two rivers emptying into the bay, this city faced the great Hampton Roads on the other side from the Union-held Fortress Monroe. Norfolk was important because of the U. S. Navy yards which had been captured there at the time of Virginia's secession. In the incomplete destruction of the evacuation, the Confederates had salvaged the *Merrimac*, which they transformed into the formidable iron-coated monster that revolutionized naval warfare.

The newly named *Virginia* could well have upset McClellan's invasion plans, except that a Swedish inventor had urged on the reluctant U. S. Navy the construction of a similar monster of his design, the *Monitor*. While the *Monitor* nullified the *Virginia*, it was also vice versa, and the home-grown sea beast protected the beckoning James from the ascent of the Federal fleet.

Norfolk was guarded by about 10,000 troops who'd had until then a nice thing of the war among the hospitable citizens. The department was still commanded by Huger, South Carolina's Bourbon who outlasted the feud with Virginia's Wise. With Norfolk comparatively safe from Mc-Clellan, and McClellan definitely safe from the Norfolk troops, it became clear that the Union Army's thrust would come straight up the peninsula to Richmond.

To complete the Union pattern of invasion, a third of McClellan's army, under McDowell, started a slow approach from Alexandria toward Fredericksburg, midway between the enemy capitals and fifty-odd miles due north of Richmond. His numbers varied, as troops shifted from point to point, but at the time McDowell commanded about 50,000. This alone was somewhat larger than Joe Johnston's opposing army at Fredericksburg, including various detachments.

As the Union's gigantic and well-conceived pincer movement developed, Lee was forced to guess from hour to hour what went on. Some time elapsed before he knew for certain that McClellan's main force was on the peninsula, and that the main blow would be struck from there and not overland from the north. During the period of doubt, and with no aggressive move coming from McDowell, Lee gradually caused troops to be shifted from Johnston to Magruder at Yorktown.

To accomplish this, he used a delicate diplomacy unapproached by any of the Southern civil leaders. Knowing the touchiness of both Davis and Joe Johnston about their prerogatives, he suggested to Davis so that Davis would in turn give the actual order to Johnston—who, it will be recalled, did not consider that Lee had the authority to give him an order.

By the time McClellan was concentrated on the peninsula, and ready for his movement, so were the Confederates. Fifty-five thousand in breastworks faced McClellan's 100,000, with a single brigade left near Fredericksburg as an observation force—all that stood between Richmond and McDowell's 50,000 directly from the North. Here entered the element unknown to Lee and Jackson, which they acted as if they had known:

When McClellan sailed away from Alexandria, Lincoln insisted that the general leave a sufficient force to guard Washington. By McClellan's plan, McDowell was to move directly south from Washington to Richmond and come in from the north as the main force struck from the east. With the James River to the south of Richmond and sparsely populated hilly country to the west, the capital would have been forced to withstand a siege from two sides in which, with no natural defenses, it would be doomed.

The troops left to guard Washington were second-flight, not fully trained or equipped, but adjudged by McClellan to be more than sufficient for their purpose, since the whole Confederate forces east of the Blue Ridge would of necessity be concentrated against him at Richmond. The few scattered Confederate forces west of the mountains, the largest of which was Jackson's 3000, would have their hands more than full guarding their own country against Union forces in the Valley and in the Western mountains.

Lincoln did not agree with McClellan. He was afraid for Washington and reluctant to turn McDowell loose. Though Lee and Jackson could not have known of Lincoln's fear, they did recognize that at all hazards McDowell must be kept away from McClellan and Richmond. Their juncture would make the defense of the capital just about hopeless.

To accomplish the end of keeping the Union forces separated, Lee had to persuade the President, and Lee and Jackson had to circumvent Joe Johnston. For, when Retreatin' Joe came to take personal command on the peninsula, he did not relinquish his command of northern Virginia, which included Jackson in the Valley.

First off, Johnston wanted to bring every soldier in Virginia to the peninsula and to strip the Southern coastal positions in order to concentrate all Eastern Confederate forces in one grand battle. Judging by the way strategic coastal positions had already fallen to the U. S. Navy and amphibious forces, to strip the newly and more strongly fortified positions would be inviting the Atlantic coast, essential if supplies from abroad were to be landed, to share the same fate as the Mississippi.

Even if the nation's foreign supply were to be risked, along with disheartening and endangering occupation of coastal cities and land, mathematics were clearly against Johnston's concentration plan. If all the

Southern forces came to the peninsula, so would all the Northern. As the combined Southern forces north of Richmond amounted to little more than 20,000 and the Unions had more than 60,000, with approximate superiority in heavy weapons, simple addition would show the fatuity of Johnston's plan.

Lee won the presidential support against Johnston's idea of concentration. Lee's purpose in concentration was to keep the enemy scattered, a feeling he and Jackson shared intuitively.

When Johnston was thwarted in his plan to draw all troops to the peninsula, he wanted to evacuate Yorktown immediately. This would mean the evacuation of Norfolk also, with its navy yard and the *Merrimac-Virginia*. As Johnston showed when he destroyed the supplies at Manassas, such considerations were outside his concern. More directly from a military standpoint, retreat would bring the Union armies close to Richmond, which of all things Lee wanted to avoid. Again Lee prevailed on the President (with an assist from Randolph, the new War Secretary) to get Johnston's agreement to defend at Yorktown at least as long as possible.

When Johnston agreed, he had no intention of carrying out the plans. It has been used against McClellan that Johnston found Magruder's fortifications so puny that, he said, "No one except McClellan would have hesitated to attack." Coming from Retreatin' Joe, who rarely in four years heard his own bugler blow "Charge," this remark serves as a disparagement less of McClellan than of Magruder's defenses. Johnston was giving the reasons why he could not follow the President's plans and fight. His heart was set on retreating and no power on earth could stop him. Against all wishes and again abandoning feverishly collected heavy guns —this time fifty-three—Johnston started the dreaded retrograde movement through the spring mud to Richmond.

Johnston's retreat from Yorktown began on May 4. At the same time Stonewall Jackson opened an obscure action which grew into what came to be called the Valley Campaign, and was designed to hold McDowell from McClellan in the fight for Richmond.

4

The immensely fertile and beautifully contoured rolling country of the Shenandoah Valley spans about thirty miles from the Blue Ridge Mountains to the Alleghenies; and from Lexington in the south to the Potomac (including the then northernmost county in Virginia), the Valley Pike ran along the floor for about 165 miles.

The Valley was settled by Germans, Irish, and Scotch-Irish, Quakers and Mennonites, coming down the familiar route from Pennsylvania, and by Virginia yeomanry leaving the tidewater section. The earliest settlers followed the pioneering pattern typical of the American West. Though there were a few large slaveholders in the northeastern end, the people were predominantly farmers and the section was not characterized by plantations. The people did not waste their rich, limestone soil for quick cash crops, and today, after two centuries of constant tilling, its high yield (one acre a cow for grazing beef cattle) attests to their intelligent conservation.

To victual the war population, the Valley produced grain of all kinds, beef cattle and horses, apples and poultry. With hogs and garden crops, the farms were self-sufficient as the people were self-reliant. They lived a frontier democracy as opposed to the aristocratic pattern of eastern Virginia. Yet in customs, manners, and basic standards they were Virginians—Valley Virginians. They comprised the bulk of Jackson's own division.

The place names of the Shenandoah Valley associated with Jackson's campaign belonged to little market towns and to the small cities which had grown from the original status without changing character. Some of the names that loom so large on maps were no more than crossroads, where one general store served the countryside. The military importance of most of the places was caused by their communication situation—though the hospitable tables of the townspeople served to break the monotony of the soldiers' sparse diets, and homes served as hospitals and ladies as nurses. No doubt, too, the enthusiastic affection of the people served the morale of the soldiers and kept before them the reality that they were fighting for their own land.

Jackson's campaign was centered about the range of mountains, the Massanuttens, which rise abruptly within the Valley, precisely like an island in the shape of a parallelogram. This bleak and uninhabited range runs north for roughly fifty miles between the Blue Ridge Mountains and the Valley Pike. It was crossed at only one place by a winding mountain road from New Market on the pike to Luray, the central town of Page Valley, the smaller valley within the Shenandoah.

Before Jackson opened his Valley Campaign proper, he had staged that prelude in late March at Kernstown, outside of Winchester. Acting on his own initiative, he struck for the purpose that dominated his whole campaign—to keep troops away from McDowell and immobilize him at Fredericksburg. At Kernstown, Old Jack was for once failed by his active and usually accurate home-grown spy service, and he was repulsed by superior numbers in a strong position. Even so, he served his purpose. The two heavy divisions that were supposed to leave the Valley to join McDowell in his part of the pincer movement on Richmond, were held in the Valley. A third division went west of the Valley to join the Union forces in the mountains there. Twenty-seven thousand Union troops, influenced by the aggression of Jackson's 3600, had been kept away from their part in the Grand Design on Richmond.

In May, when McClellan started up the peninsula to Richmond, Mc-

Dowell was still waiting at Fredericksburg for two of those first-line divisions to join him. Away from McClellan more than 60,000 Federal troops, with proportionate artillery, were scattered in three forces—at Fredericksburg, in the Valley watching Jackson, and in the mountains to the west.

By that time Jackson's "army" had risen to 6000 infantry through the Virginia Conscript Act. Though one third were either unarmed or poorly armed, Jackson had used the six weeks of relative Union inactivity to train the men, while observing and evading the 20,000 under slow-moving Banks.

With Turner Ashby's hard-riding if undisciplined semi-independent cavalry serving as a screen, Stonewall Jackson had his men in a fine strategic position at the foot of the Blue Ridge and at the southern base of the avenue between the Massanuttens and the Blue Ridge. Banks was at Harrisonburg, in the central Valley on the Pike, also at the base of the Massanuttens on the other side. Jackson's position gave him the opportunity to threaten Banks's rear, by going up the east side of the Massanuttens and crossing above Banks; if himself threatened, he could retreat across the Blue Ridge and join the Confederate forces building in the Fredericksburg area.

But Jackson knew that his force was too weak to carry out the threat against Banks, and that the Union's immobilization in the Valley could only be temporary. Unless he made another offensive movement, troops would soon be released to rejoin McDowell. Waiting around for eventualities and leaving the initiative to the enemy was gall to Old Jack's grimly aggressive spirit, and the scattering of other idle Confederates, also waiting, violated his ideas of warfare.

Owing to Jefferson Davis' defensive alignments in scattered "observation" units, the Confederates had, besides Jackson's, a puny force in the Western mountains, another force in front of Fredericksburg—growing but totally inadequate to contain McDowell—and another force east of the Blue Ridge between Jackson in the Valley and Fredericksburg. Since, with Jackson, the four forces combined numbered less than 30,000, and the Unions had more than 60,000, obviously as long as the opponents remained equally divided the enemy would heavily outnumber the Confederates at every point. While Jackson was restlessly brooding over some way to break this unfavorable stalemate without breaking orders, he was overjoyed to get a letter from General Lee.

With Joe Johnston, Jackson's immediate superior, occupied on the peninsula against McClellan's advance, and Davis, the ultimate superior, distracted with details, Lee took the occasion to write Jackson a suggestion. It was no more than that, since the President's adviser had no authority over anyone. But the suggestion offered Old Jack the action his heart longed for and, seizing upon it as an order, he moved before it could be rescinded. For Lee, too, loathed the passive resistance which kept scattered forces waiting on the enemy and, like Jackson, wanted always the initiative himself. His suggestion was merely that Old Jack might combine his force with the idle force east of the Blue Ridge, and strike at the enemy.

Before anybody, enemy or friend (including even Jackson's officers), knew what was in the wind, the offensive-minded mountaineer struck in a swift secrecy which completely befuddled Banks, sitting across at the opposite end of the Massanuttens.

5

The general with whom the fiercely dedicated Jackson was to co-oper-ate was "Bald Dick" Ewell, so called in consequence of the shining pate which topped the homely visage of a totally quaint figure. He was a short spry man, with thin mustachios to decorate a countenance that always appeared surprised, and slightly bulging eyes that could affix a person with balefully direct gaze. While Jackson's eccentricities have been overplayed, Ewell was really one of nature's characters.

He was born of a fine Virginia family which had fallen upon evil finan-cial times when he grew up in the Manassas area as the son of a school-teacher, and, like many another Southerner, found his education at West Point. From border service as captain of U.S. dragoons, he was as tough as a mule inside and out, and his violent tempers burst with awesome swearing, imaginative invective, and colorful exaggerations. Forty-five years old, he was the faithful suitor of a widow named Mrs. Lizinka Brown, to whom he always referred, even after they were married, as "the Widow Brown." Her son, Campbell Brown, was placed on the general's staff because he reminded Ewell of his love.

In the year when he had risen from captain of fifty U. S. Army dragoons to major general of a Confederate division of 8500 men, including artillery and cavalry, Ewell had not risen beyond his capacities. To his twenty-five years of military training and experience he brought an observant intelli-gence, a sharp practicality, and aggression. Indeed, Ewell had the most trouble controlling his personal aggression, since he loved actual combat as dearly as did Turner Ashby. He was a sound soldier and a good one, a valuable and dependable division commander. By his own nature, Ewell was probably better fitted than any major general in Virginia for the try-ing assignment of subordinate command with Jackson. A generous man, without jealousy or vainglory, his sole purpose was to serve the Southern states in their struggle for independence.

All of Bald Dick's qualities of loyalty were put to the test by the se-cretive Jackson. Ewell's troops were ordered to Jackson's abandoned camp on the western foot of the Blue Ridge, and were left there with no more notion of Jackson's whereabouts than Banks had. Ewell fretted away the time trying to prove that Jackson's V.M.I. sobriquet of "Fool Tom" really meant that he was crazy—an opinion shared by several of Jackson's officers. Ewell changed his opinion completely ("There's method in his madness," he said) when he saw the results of Jackson's extreme secrecy.

Jackson had first gotten across the Valley into the Alleghenies where, joining the small force there, his attack put the 20,000 Unions under Fremont on the defense. Leaving Fremont there, like a matador turning his back on a transfixed bull, Jackson's combined forces moved back toward the Valley from the west.

Banks, who had been assuring his War Office that Jackson was through and troops could be sent to McDowell for the Richmond plan, scurried fifty miles northward to the strategically located Valley Pike town of Strasburg. There he waited on Jackson's next move.

Leaving Banks there, as he had Fremont in the mountains, Jackson again combined forces. Drawing on his newly enthusiastic supporter, Ewell, he started swiftly up the eastern passage between the Massanuttens and the Blue Ridge—with the Massanuttens between him and Banks. There were no more observation forces and no avenues of retreat: Jackson, with 17,000 men, was going after the enemy.

Prior to this exciting moment, with the élan of action against a retreating enemy gathering in the combined forces, Jackson had received a warning letter from Lee. Joe Johnston had by then retreated before McClellan up the peninsula to Richmond and was in position to assume command of Jackson's and Ewell's combined forces. Advisory General Lee wrote, "Whatever movement you make against Banks, do it quickly, and if successful drive him back toward the Potomac, and create the impression, as far as possible, that you design threatening that line"—the Washington line. It was that sentence that caused many of Lee's admirers to believe him privy to Lincoln's fear for the capital.

Before the advice could be followed, Ewell had received an order from Johnston to leave the Valley for the purpose of joining the idle troops facing McDowell or to join Johnston at Richmond. Deeply disappointed, Ewell had generously told Jackson that he would ignore Johnston's order if Old Jack, as his immediate superior, would give him a contrary order. This Jackson did at once, on the proviso that it should be executed *unless* a conflicting order was subsequently received from their mutual superior. The conflicting order came two days later, just as Jackson and Ewell were joining forces.

Ewell must follow out of the Valley the Union division on the way to join McDowell, and Jackson must return to observing Banks. Johnston said, "My idea is to gather here all the forces who do not keep away from McClellan superior numbers."

That was precisely what Jackson was doing by strategic movement as opposed to futile concentration. In resigned despair, he said, "Then Providence denies me the privilege of striking a blow for my country, and I must be satisfied with the humble task of hiding my little army among these mountains to watch a superior foe."

He could not be satisfied that way. Aware of the muddle of high command in Richmond, and following Ewell's course with him, Old Jack appealed directly to Lee—the only one who understood the whole strategy.

As far as records show, Lee did not consult Johnston, and presumably gained the approval of the President for his return wire to Jackson to go ahead.

Lee probably was able to gain the President's support because Johnston, in his hatred of Davis, refused to confide in the Commander in Chief, and Davis was outraged by Retreatin' Joe's withdrawal to the environs of Richmond in defiance of everyone's wishes. Lee's tact had paid off. He was able to serve as a *de facto* chief of staff by circumventing the commanding general of the army and persuading the Commander in Chief to give him the authority for it. Outside of Davis' charts of organization, of Joe Johnston's jealousies and obsession with mathematical concentrations, Lee the aristocrat and Jackson the mountaineer—with the loyalty of Dick Ewell, the schoolma'am's son—combined to bring strategy to the war in spite of the Confederate government.

6

The combination of adviser Lee and audacious Jackson (with tough-bitten Ewell) might not have been as invincible as Southerners like to believe, but they achieved their purpose of preventing the juncture of McDowell and McClellan at Richmond. Though they got some help from Union blunders and inadequacies of enemy command (as did the Federals in reverse out West), with inferior manpower, greatly inferior weapons, a border-line food subsistence against lusciously prolific supplies, a collapsing transportation system against a superb one (buttressed with naval transport and a fighting fleet), they conceived largely, seized the initiative, and kept the pressure on.

From the beginning, Jackson's army grew with his maneuvers and were outfitted and supplied by immense matériel from the enemy; he created a morale in his troops which was to outlast his life, and brought a magic to his name which put heart back in the despairing Southerners.

The main phase of the Valley Campaign lasted only three weeks, from the morning of May 19 until the night of June 9. In that time his men marched 170 miles with accumulating enemy stores and prisoners, fought off, eluded, or defeated segments of forces totaling upward of 50,000 converging on them from three directions.

This "army," which constituted Jackson's "foot cavalry," was a hodge-podge of forces drawn together in barely two months' time. Along with the veterans (the oldest of whom were one year from civilian life) were raw recruits and conscripted militia companies, one of which had been snatched back bodily from a flight to the hills.

Jackson's staff was as informally gathered as the army itself. For commissary and quartermaster, he selected successful young businessmen of the Valley—a carriage manufacturer and a farmer who operated a stagecoach line. Since Jackson's methodical approach to all problems necessitated a detailed study of terrain, he selected a twenty-six-year-old surveyor, Jed Hotchkiss, to be a mapmaker. Twenty-two-year-old Hunter McGuire of Winchester was Jackson's medical director, rising as the general rose, and enjoying, after the war, a long and distinguished career in surgery.

Topping the group of virtual youths who served as aides, nearly all of whom were to be killed, was the much-loved Sandie Pendleton, later A.A.G. This young lieutenant colonel was the only staff member with military training—and that was at V.M.I., where the military courses which appealed to a segment of young Southerners served the Confederacy so well. For chief of staff at the time Jackson had a Presbyterian clergyman, the Reverend R. L. Dabney. An educated man, a devoted patriot, and unquestioningly loyal to Jackson, the humorless parson brought intelligent conscientiousness to his paper work, though later campaigns exposed his limitations for a fighting army.

The staff was completed by Jackson's personal servant, Jim, a handsome mulatto who was loyal only to the general. Though Jim approved heartily of the general's temperance views, as a staff officer said, "They did not apply to himself." Jim also liked "a quiet little game" of cards.

In Jackson's "foot cavalry," the beautiful uniforms of the first militia and volunteer companies were faded and patched, if not gone altogether. New uniforms were largely homespun, in an off-gray, brownish color, and there was a sprinkling of Union blue and civilian garments. Hats were whatever covered the uncut and frequently uncombed hair.

Gone were the handsome, compartmented leather knapsacks, containing stiff collars, white gloves, and crested linen stationery. A canvas haversack swung from a cord across the right shoulder, containing the barest necessities and—for the more elegant—a knife, fork, and spoon, a razor and a small mirror. Many men neglected to shave on the marches, many did not yet have to, and older men let their graybeards grow.

Whatever the men abandoned, each held on to his tin cup—which served as both a utensil and a dish, and was tied outside his haversack—and to his canteen, which usually swung in the middle of his back from strings looped over his head.

The haversack was supposed to carry the three days' cooked rations issued before a march. Usually the underfed men ate everything at once and depended on Yankee wagons, the messes of their more provident fellows, a stray hog or chicken, a farmer's cornfield or apple orchard. The most severe sickness to attack Jackson's columns in march was colic from stolen green apples. On his long forced marches, his troops suffered heavily from stragglers, though most of these returned to fight again. Even with the soldiers who could not stand up physically to all the marches, Jackson's troops in movement had the lowest incidence of sickness in the Confederate Army. In avoiding the sicknesses inherent in camp life of those days, action acted as a therapy while ennui lowered resistance.

A blanket roll swung from the shoulder opposite the haversack cord, crossing the body from left shoulder to right hip. At noon in the Valley the burden became so intolerable that recruits threw them away. The men experienced in the hot Valley days and cold nights endured the torment. No tents were carried in the skimpy wagon train and men slept in pairs, on one blanket and covered by another. As the field-trophy business prospered, men began to cover their blankets with a fine Federal issue of India-rubber sheets, two of which together made a cozy tent for rainy nights.

The men still carried wherever convenient their scant issues of percussion caps and paper-topped cartridges. The powder was packed in the paper top and the men tore off the paper cover with their teeth. After a battle, their mouths were ringed with black powder, adding a grim touch to their weather-stained and hairy faces.

They looked like anything except the ordinary image of an army, and they would have broken the heart, if not the mind, of a spit-and-polish general. But in Jackson's army, all their rifles and their bayonets were kept bright, and the ribald, earthy laughter was seldom silent.

In appearance, at least, all distinctions were gone between the humble yeoman and the lordly planter. In the 27th Virginia, the city aristocrats of Richmond's Company F looked no different on the march from their mountaineer companions.

The weirdest juxtaposition of ante-bellum types was in Dick Taylor's Louisiana brigade, of Ewell's division. To begin with, General Taylor himself was in the unique personal position of being the son of a U.S. President (Zachary Taylor) and brother-in-law of the Confederate President. No professional soldier, this Yale graduate was a highly literate and successful planter, of unbounded self-confidence and the natural leadership required for the strange collection of his large (3000) brigade.

There was a regiment of planters' sons and one of New Orleans toughs, one Irish battalion with its own emerald flag, and one regiment of the Acadians—from the small bayou tribe Longfellow wrote about in *Evangeline*. The New Orleans plug-uglies, called the Louisiana "Tigers" and commanded by a lovable soldier of fortune named Rob Wheat, were the only outfit in Jackson's army still wearing Zouave uniforms. Light brown jackets were opened in front to display red shirts, baggy Turkish trousers fastened below into white gaiters which topped *white* shoes. These boys shared with the Texas troops the co-championship of hen-roost foraging, and if anyone had ever bothered to tell them about the "honor of Southern gentlemen," the Tigers had not liked what they heard.

The little group of Acadians had the finest band in the army. At night the gay-hearted young men danced waltzes and polkas before their campfire, while Jackson's Presbyterians observed these goings-on with disapproving suspicion.

Jackson himself, observing the high spirits of Taylor's whole brigade, said, "Thoughtless fellows for serious work."

Taylor's brigade and Ewell's whole division, however, showed on the march the benefits of good training and physical conditioning. Anxious to get at the enemy, who had been living off the Valley people, Ewell's troops fell in with the rigid marching routine of Jackson's own division.

Each march was begun in close-order drill, and for two hundred yards the troops marched out as if on parade. Then they eased off into route step and walked precisely fifty minutes—not forty-nine or fifty-one—and rested precisely ten. A curious order, to our times, was one forbidding infantrymen to ride, except with a doctor's permission. Many of the young bloods still had their personal mounts, as well as body servants. They looked strange at the lean messes, served in tin cups, and for the wine that formerly graced their meals they occasionally and furtively enlivened things with homemade apple brandy or "mountain dew."

Along the whole line rode their unimposing general, with his relentless, monotonous, and never forgotten "Close up, men, close up. Push on, push on. . . ."

For the campaign, Jackson blossomed out in a new "regulation" gray uniform, though it fitted no better than the old blue, and he clung to his cadet cap. He still thrived on his corn-bread-and-milk diet. While some observers stress his constant sucking of a lemon—until now it is legendary —others claim that this was an exaggeration, like his hypochondria and his praying, to build up the eccentricities of his character.

The men had confidence in the strange, grim man and most of them marched lightheartedly through their exhilarating successes with no notion of the worries that beset their uncommunicative leader. For Jackson was doing at his local level what the President could never do on any— risk largely for a large end. Except for his motto, "Never take counsel of your fears," he might well have settled for less at any point and escaped with his hide.

He suffered faulty co-ordination from his hastily collected forces, he was dismally failed by the cavalry of fox hunter Turner Ashby (of whose arrogant rejection of discipline Old Jack had long and unsuccessfully complained), and some Georgia troops he left to guard captured supplies ran without firing a shot.

Yet Jackson moved from the center Valley to the northern tip, at his early training ground of Harper's Ferry, driving Banks ahead of him. When that former Massachusetts governor crossed the Potomac, minus the wagons which gained him the sobriquet of "Commissary" to Jackson's troops, there was something of a to-do in Washington.

Lincoln wired McClellan, in front of Richmond, that he was calling off McDowell's joint movement against the Rebel capital "in consequence of General Banks' critical condition."

Also acting as his own Commander in Chief (since McClellan had been reduced to command of his own army), Lincoln, in the excitement, asked McClellan, "Can you get near enough [Richmond] to throw shells into the city?" Then he ordered troops, who had gone from the Valley to McDowell, back to the Valley to intercept Jackson from the east. Fremont's troops were ordered to break their fix in the Alleghenies and to intercept Jackson from the west. A third force was gathered north of him.

Getting some overdue luck of their own (the fortune that followed the brave), Jackson's men slipped between the Union forces by no margin at all, with the assist of a freak hailstorm, and retreated back south in the Valley. Old Jack clung to his captured supplies—he would "fight for a wheelbarrow," they said—and had McDowell immobilized as far as Richmond was concerned.

He still had to fight off two pursuing Union forces in two days, with the Shenandoah River dividing his own forces. This he did against the supine Fremont, who followed him directly, at Cross Keys (June 8), and against Shields, a pugnacious and skillful Irishman trying to cut him off via the Massanuttens' eastern avenue (Port Republic, June 9).

Bald Dick Ewell got a chance to sneak away from Old Jack and get in some personal fighting of his own with the troops, while Turner Ashby— the black-bearded fox hunter of the Valley legends—ran out his own string of audacious exploits and was killed in combat. Even in Jackson's official message of condolence, he refused to call the undisciplined Ashby a soldier; he referred to him as "a fine partisan leader."

It was all over then, and so was McClellan's Grand Design against Richmond. McDowell was never coming to join the pincer movement. Jackson, beginning with 6000 partly armed men, had kept 65,000 troops away from the Federals' main objective and destroyed their plan against Richmond, while building an army of his own.

In the darkest hour of the Confederate people, their capital had been saved, at least temporarily, and they had a new hero. From the rear balconies of city villas to the front porches of lonely farmhouses, people soon recited to each other a new poem, *Stonewall Jackson's Way.*

> *Silence! ground arms! kneel all! caps off!*
> *Old Stonewall's going to pray. . . .*

CHAPTER XI

An Army Is Born

WHEN Stonewall Jackson emerged as the first solid hero of the Confederacy, the people were in desperate need of some support to their
spirits. Since their one success in the preliminary test of First Manassas,
their new country had seemed unable to defend itself in the real war of
conquest, and their former fellow countrymen as invaders showed a
harshly domineering attitude which made total defeat far more fearsome
than it had appeared a year before.

In the countrysides in the path of the enemy armies the more wanton
acts, such as the desecration of graves and tombs in search of loot, seemed
to be individual hoodlumism, and personal menace to unprotected families
came mostly from the deserters who made a constant drain on the Union
armies (200,000 in the whole war). But in New Orleans the commander
of the occupation forces adopted an official policy that belonged to
ruthless conquerors rather than to preservers of any union.

So brutal were the measures of Ben Butler, the Boston Democrat, that
President Davis declared him an outlaw, subject to execution as a felon.
Defenders of the "Beast" claimed that few women were arrested on his
notorious order which proclaimed that ladies who insulted his soldiers
would be treated as prostitutes plying their trade. If no woman was arrested, that was beside the point. It was an insult which reflected the attitude of the conqueror.

This attitude was tangibly supported by the confiscation of private
property, the eviction of people from their homes, the closing of
churches, and an application of the law of might which ended the golden
age of that colorful corner of the cosmopolitan world in America. To remove any idealism from this ruthlessness to the citizens of New Orleans,
the occupation forces were accompanied by ferret-eyed Northerners engaged in flagrant and illicit speculation in captured cotton and confiscated
goods. Beast Butler's brother made a fortune of several hundred thousand
dollars (without taxes) out of his New Orleans cotton speculations.

In other cities, without a "Beast" as commander, the people suffered less outrage and thievery by confiscation, but they knew they lived under the heel of a conqueror. In Norfolk, ladies were not permitted to sing Southern songs in their homes, or slam window blinds when occupation troops passed, on threat of having their houses burned. A strictly applied martial law required citizens to petition Union officers for passes for the personal movements Americans had always taken for granted. Almost everywhere the attitude was of a hostilely applied might, totally removed from any considerations of restoring the bonds of Union.

The people knew that the war had changed the nature of the sectional struggle if their government did not. In fact, the doings of their government were designed to increase the people's apprehension for their independence.

With their territory being gobbled up, cities occupied, and powerful armies poised to finish the work of conquest, congressmen devoted their time to voting a raise in their own pay (to $2760 a year) and doubling their traveling expenses from ten to twenty cents a mile. What else they might be up to was kept from the public by Congress' addiction to secret sessions. One item where the Confederacy did not ape an established power was on congressional records. The government denied itself the luxury of publishing the debates of Congress, which, observers said, were something less than conducive to confidence.

Even without knowing the details of the futile word exchanges, the more informed people could not fail to recognize that in the civil operation of the nation, as well as its armed defense, the government was not meeting the needs of the struggle.

After more than a year had passed and their withholding of cotton had not brought European intervention, the fatuity of the policy became evident. Worse, the Federal blockade, which had existed in name only when the Confederate government thought to use it as a legal fence for England and France to break down, had become a reality. "Running the blockade" was a phrase coming to mean a high gamble in speculation. Fortunes could be made and lost.

Old gentlemen in city clubs would pay dearly for their British magazines and French wines, and ladies wanted the fashions, even if they couldn't always get the materials. The government, wanting the matériel of war, began to compete against its own citizens.

The old men and the women in the back country, who merely wanted the necessities of life, did not promise enough profit for the speculators to bother running in their wants, and no one else thought of them. Though making no protest yet, these people were beginning to feel the first pinch of being cut off from imports from the North and the absence of compensating manufacturing in their own country.

Then the planters, who had patriotically followed the government's program of "plowing under" cotton, began to think of what they were going to use for money as the war went on longer and became more terrible than anything they had been prepared for. Nothing that the government was doing about finances was at all reassuring. Despite suggestions for the government purchase of cotton, to be used for its own credit, this measure was rejected on various grounds, including socialism. The result was that in a Cotton Kingdom the planters, without a home market, could sell neither to the government nor abroad.

In turn, the government, having deprived itself of cotton and its leading citizens of revenue from it, had floated bond loans on the proceeds from produce and, in April 1862, solved its own cotton dilemma by accepting produce in direct exchange for bonds. These government bonds were of little immediate use to the people. Even the eight per cent bonds went begging because they were never readily accepted in exchange for land, Negroes, and cotton among the people. For actual trade, the people preferred the beautifully engraved paper notes, which were supported almost entirely by faith.

To add to the confusion, since the Confederacy lacked metal for small coins, U.S. coins up to the value of ten dollars were accepted as legal tender, as were English, French, Spanish, and Mexican coins. As there were not enough of these to go around, paper money was substituted for coin. When the government's paper money failed to go around, states issued it, and counties and cities, then banks and the butcher, baker, and candlestick maker (literally).

Poor, plodding Memminger, without a thought he could call his own, and disbelieving in this financial fantasia, methodically executed the details in the ground-floor offices of the Government Building. There he was assisted by sundry ladies whose incomes had ceased when their menfolk went into the army, and by a few fugitives from the U. S. Treasury Department, some of whom had thoughtfully brought along the printed forms with which they were familiar. At least the Treasury Department still *looked* like the United States'.

That was the only thing in Richmond that did look familiar. Virginia's capital had become a war-dislocated city, and all the fears of the Southern people were concentrated and heightened in the besieged citadel.

2

While Jackson's Valley Campaign had, by keeping McDowell away, prevented the certain fall of the capital, McClellan's large army in two giant pincers was still at its gates. On the last day of May, under direct orders from the President, Joe Johnston had attacked McClellan seven miles from Richmond (Seven Pines), where, in a battle of indescribable blunders, the Confederates had been repulsed.

Joe Johnston had been wounded in the action, his friends said by riding toward the front to get away from Jefferson Davis, who brought his entourage to the battlefield. When Johnston's second in command proved psychologically inadequate to handle an army in action, and suffered a nervous collapse, there was nobody to turn to but Lee, the Faithful Rover of the Administration. In the second year of the war and with the Confederacy on the verge of total collapse, through the accident of a stray bullet, Robert E. Lee was finally given command of an army.

This brought no joy or confidence to the hearts of the people. Having been secreted away, with his painstaking and farseeing work unknown, Lee was received as virtually another calamity befalling the beleaguered people. That he introduced modern trench warfare by putting the soldiers to digging breastworks indicated to the Richmond citizens only another lack of enterprise as a fighter. The people had still not been told of the superior weapons of the Federals, especially their more numerous, more accurate, and much heavier cannons. They had not been told anything.

At Richmond, they faced not only McClellan but the fear of the Union gunboats, which had become something like supernatural monsters to the people. When Joe Johnston had made his obstinate retreat up the peninsula, in dismissal of all other considerations, he opened to the rightly dreaded U. S. Navy the fat country of the York River on the north of the peninsula, the city of Norfolk on the southside, the James River—navigable to Richmond—and the capital, possibly exposed to naval attack and landings on its river front.

That landings did not take place is an illustration of the individualism of the South working for it instead of, as usually, against it. Under the urgings of Mallory and through the resolute spirit and initiative of a few city civilians, county farmers, and a young ex-officer of the U. S. Navy working on naval gun production, a hasty defense was erected in much the same manner that individual commanders selected their positions at First Manassas.

On the south bank of the James River, the side opposite the city, several miles below Richmond there is a high ridge called Drewry's Bluff. Beneath it, the collection of patriots sank ships to narrow the channel and force the invading fleet to come directly under guns on the crest. The guns were rushed there by the young naval ordnance officer, Lieutenant Brooke, who designed the Brooke rifled gun. The successful defense by his improvised and makeshift force indicated the true extent to which the South depended on what individuals happened to assume responsibility for any action or event.

The people overflowing Virginia's ante-bellum capital did not have their fears laid by this check of the Navy—though Drewry's Bluff proved, with other later measures, to be permanently impassable. The presence of McClellan's great army was so close that the glow of its campfires could be seen against the night sky. Every afternoon at dusk, men gathered on the hill of the Jewish cemetery to watch the flicker of rifle fire to the north of the city, where the secondary claw of McClellan's army was extended from the main body to the east.

Further to awe the people, Professor Lowe's balloon ascended daily into the skies, from where unseen eyes observed their goings-on. (An interested observer was a young foreign visitor of the Union Army, Count Zeppelin.) Richmond ladies contributed their silk petticoats to provide the material for a rival air monster, but the volunteer aeronauts were less experienced than Professor Lowe. After a perilous adventure, they came to rest on the banks of the James River, still innocent of the secrets of the Union Army.

Besides the invading army, the balloon, and the gunboats, there was the timidity of their own government. Boxes and crates of records were hauled through the streets to the depot, where an engine kept up steam twenty-four hours a day. Tobacco was piled ready for the torch. President Davis sent his family down to North Carolina, and his resolute expression was set and grim. Congress adjourned and its members vied with stranded citizens for seats on southbound trains. The passport office in the War Department was so crowded with people trying to get out of the Confederacy altogether that the whole passport business was turned over to Winder, that unloved chief of a detective bureau composed of imported "plug-uglies" from Baltimore.

Winder's rough force added a sinister element to the city. Combining the functions of MPs, the FBI, and the Border Patrol, they captured deserters, hunted for spies, and guarded points of entry for civilians bringing in contraband. The U.S. had made medicine a contraband of war. While wounded men and sick people suffered fearfully for want of drugs, there were plenty of citizens eager to make a quick dollar (even a Confederate one, since it had still not dropped appreciably) out of their fellows' suffering.

With these duties, all of which they performed with more ebullience than discretion, Winder's bully boys were entrusted generally with order beyond the capacities of the local police in a city dislocated by war. For, as non-natives and some Richmonders fled the city, a motley cross section of humanity crowded in.

From the east, where McClellan's masses had passed, and from the north central sections where McDowell's units ranged, came women and children and the aged, many with their house Negroes. They called it "refugeeing" in Richmond. Also the wives and families of many officers and officials had moved to Richmond on a semipermanent basis, and others flitted in and out, according to the seasons. Prostitutes had come, and gamblers, and speculators to traffic in scarcities and in money.

From the year before at Manassas, Richmond got a permanent population of Union prisoners, in one of the most thoughtlessly stupid moves of the Confederate government. With transportation failing to provide the proper food for soldiers from the central depot at Richmond, with the city's own overblown population feeling the pinches of shortages, no logical reason could be offered for cramming thousands of enemies into confiscated warehouses in the capital. There the prisoners required more guards than they would in some distant back country where the countryside could have fed them. This was one of the more serious items for which, in the improvisation of a nation while under invasion, no provision was made.

Another similar item was the wounded, who from Seven Pines on also became a permanent segment of the city's population. Aside from the pitifully small nucleus of trained medical men, with its medical procurement bureaus of very unwarlike citizens (some of whom were speculators), the Confederacy could scarcely be said at that time to have a medical department as known today. In Richmond, most hospitals were supported and largely administered by the separate states. South Carolina alone had nine hospitals in the capital, in addition to a large hospital operated by women in Columbia—believed to be the first wayside hospital in the world.

"Hospital" usually meant a habitation in which sick and wounded were cared for, and did not imply the facilities of an actual hospital. Warehouses, hotels, and dry-goods stores were converted into extemporaneous shelters. Homes vacated by fugitives were seized and used as emergency hospitals; hundreds of private homes turned over rooms to the less seriously wounded, to the ill and convalescent.

Most of the nursing was done by the ladies of the city, the majority of whom were sincere and conscientious workers. They suffered acutely themselves from the stench of festering wounds and unburied dead, the unfamiliar sight of gore and death, and the screams of men undergoing amputations without the contraband anesthesia. Other ladies were the self-glamorizing who chiefly gave solicitude to quiet heroes.

As one convalescent soldier said to his timid comforter, "Well, ma'am, my face has been washed five times already, but if you want to wash it again, go ahead."

The belles of the privileged classes devoted their energies mostly to parlor entertainments for officers and planter princelings, who frequently regarded service in the ranks as the course of gallantry. Richmond was probably the only aristocratic capital in history where privates were socially equal and sometimes superior to generals and cabinet members. In their entertainments, the Southern ladies displayed inventiveness and adaptability with shortages in food, drink, and clothes, and at least an outwardly gay courage in providing their musicales, charades, and dance-suppers, with the rumble of guns as a background.

In the tenderloin sections—of the variety shows, bars, and bordellos—night life flourished as never before with the influx of strangers, many of whose pockets bulged with quick speculation gold.

Where pleasure ended was among the poor families, whose income ceased when the breadwinner went into the army. There were no allowances for dependents to Confederate soldiers, and their own small pay was so irregular as to make them virtually unpaid. Many of these women took jobs in the government arsenals and as regular army nurses in the burgeoning medical department. Those equally poor of a more educated class took clerical jobs with the government departments.

The new social element in Virginia's capital was formed by the families of Confederate officials and wives of officers in the field, between whom and the natives a *rapport* did not always exist. As DeLeon said, "Virginians regarded the newcomers much as Romans would regard the First Families of the Visigoths."

Many of the newcomers were required by their official positions to give public levees, where the same jealousies and little meannesses prevailed as in peacetime. The experienced hands, with a background of Washington society, naturally showed to good advantage. Amateurs in the social scene, products of the Confederacy, frequently showed an ineptitude for high life.

The wife of Judge Reagan, the Postmaster General from Texas, was such a notoriously poor hostess that she was used as a measure for inferior entertainment. When one lady wanted to derogate a social effort of Mrs. Davis ("Queen Varina"), she said, "Wasn't that a humbug of a party! Mrs. Reagan could have done better."

Basically, in the higher official and army circles cliques were formed by people who shared similar ante-bellum backgrounds and positions. No shared dangers changed the hearts of people to embrace all fellow citizens of the new country. In fact, so much inadequate work was done in responsible places by men placed there by their connections that it was said, "After this war, every tub's got to stand on its own bottom."

Where the work was really getting done, regardless of the former position of the men, was in the Ordnance Bureaus. Josiah Gorgas, the Pennsylvanian chief of ordnance, was a production genius, with power so great that he could ignore the government red tape. For his purchasing agents abroad, Gorgas demanded funds on which his men could draw direct and avoid the paper forests of Memminger's Treasury Department.

For the vital Tredegar Iron Works, its owner, West Pointer Joseph Anderson, a brigadier, was soon to be drafted *from* the army and to make his plant between the Kanawha Canal and the James River virtually the Ruhr of the Confederacy. At the peak of its power, a visitor in Richmond encountered a Negro workman for the Tredegar riding the train on a pass. When the visitor asked the workman if he was with the government, the Negro answered indignantly, "No, *suh;* I'm with the other concern."

In the Navy, phlegmatic Stephen Mallory was tireless in developing quickly made and ingenious fighting ships, and imperturbable in the face of continued losses through the losses of places—New Orleans, Norfolk, Atlantic coastal and Mississippi River positions. The roster of his navy was a melancholy roll call of ships "burned by the Confederates after the fall of ———"

At first Mallory bought up every boat he could find, from tugboats to river steamers, and sent them out with a few guns. Then he contracted for ships to be made abroad. These had to escape from the London docks to sea when United States protests became too strong for England to ignore; the great sea raider, the *Alabama,* commanded by former U.S. naval officer Raphael Semmes, made it out in the summer of '62. Mallory also started the construction of ironclads in the South, at Mobile and Charleston, along with the continuance of the quickly made contrivances bent only on destruction of the invading gunboats. These, with chronically unpredictable engines, were almost an equal hazard to their crews. He even tried a submarine which, despite sinking three times with the loss of its crews, got volunteers for a fourth attempt that finally sank a Union ship and went down permanently with that gallant crew.

With help from the reluctant Virginia seceder, Matthew Fontaine Maury, the farmers in the Confederate Navy produced floating mines, all manner of torpedoes and, in a country that had to improvise everything with makeshifts, made solid contributions to naval warfare. The fruits of Mallory's labors might have served his country better had the land forces done as well as at Richmond in protecting the sanctuaries of his ships.

At the opposite pole in Richmond from Mallory's improvisings was the commissary general, Colonel Northrop, one of those who came to be called "Davis' pets." He was "regular" and a disastrous failure. Davis defended him, as he did all of his friends, in defiance of enraged damnings and hungry wails of protest. A real patriot would have resigned when his system failed to feed the army. Instead, Northrop spent time in drawing up legalistic bills of complaint against others. It is true enough that he was not alone to blame but, righteously devoted to his bureaucratic system, he preferred to explain where he was not at fault rather than to make any effort to produce.

Against the railroads, Northrop did have a good case. There Davis, mindful of the feelings of the owners, had typically appointed a "co-ordinator," without any authority. This co-ordinator could *suggest* changes of schedules and rates, holding cars for the army, and the transfer of rolling stock from one road to another, but he could do nothing about it. With the Tredegar Iron Works devoting its entire output to war, and the new plants coming into being for the same end, there were no replacements at all for railroad equipment. Yet no railroad president could be persuaded that his line was less important than another, or that he should shift his surplus stock to where it would serve the Confederacy. For rates and schedules, human cupidity and fatuity could not be persuaded by pleas, and when McClellan's army was besieging Richmond, rows of cars were standing idle, waiting to be loaded by a flour company, an old customer.

Then, there was no one for the railroads to co-operate *with*. Through the beautiful organization charts, the railroads should have co-operated with the Quartermaster Department. This was a haven for fugitives from the armed forces, topped by General Myers, whose chief contribution to Richmond was to decorate soignée affairs with his young, Louisiana-born wife. Without any central plan or directives, the inexperienced young men rushed busily about trying to justify their appointments, and succeeded in creating a bedlam of divided and overlapping authority—to the disgust of the railroaders, the justification of Northrop, and the starvation of the armies.

The first railroad co-ordinator faded from the scene without even saying good-by, and while McClellan's steel arms were readying for the embrace, a transportation officer named Mason Morfit stared gloomily at the fantasia of railroads-commissary-quartermaster "system." Captain Morfit was a Baltimore native whose Southern sympathies had caused him to flee the jailers, and undoubtedly he wished he was back in *My Maryland*.

3

Failed from within and threatened from without, the people crowded in Richmond got a lift in their morale from another hero, closer to home. Jeb Stuart's famous "Ride around McClellan" was one of those showy gestures so dear to the horseman's exhibitionistic heart. Militarily, the twenty-nine-year-old cavalry leader exceeded his orders and put McClellan on guard. But the people were not concerned with military criticisms. The audacity of the beplumed Stuart riding his lightly armed cavalry around the whole Union Army rendered the invading hosts less fearsome, shook their aura of invincibility. The rare combination of Stuart's trained discipline and personal flair made him an embodiment of the Southern chivalric ideal of the *beau sabreur*.

Ladies garlanded the troopers' horses with roses and everybody wanted a look at the singing cavalier and his comrades in arms.

Stuart's staff was distinguished by its volunteer aides, and he had the only true "partisan" in the army in Farley, the South Carolinian who refused either rank or pay. Of a good though not fabled background, this University of Virginia graduate was that rarity, a scholarly huntsman, with interests equally divided between the chase and Shakespeare. Personally quiet and gentle, with a "bright, kindly smile," and the soul of courtesy, Farley was one of the intense revolutionaries who regarded the enemy as wolves coming to prey on his land. He had started his partisan career as an independent scout whose purpose was to stalk and kill as many enemies as possible. After Stuart outtalked the generals clamoring for the services of the twenty-seven-year-old partisan, Farley continued his solitary stalkings for the purpose of getting a horse, equipment, weapons, and clothes. He never bought or was issued an item for his fine wardrobe, personal arsenal, and fresh mounts.

Stuart had recently acquired another volunteer aide in the imposing person of a Prussian baron, Heros von Borcke, a giant who had run the blockade to volunteer with the Confederacy. Though his memoirs reveal a trace of Munchausen, the ferociously armed Baron von Borcke became a devoted Rebel, with deep personal attachment to Stuart, provided high splashes of color and, with his German accent, unconscious humor for that riotous group of young riding men. By all accounts, he wielded his outsize saber to the admiration of all. The huge Prussian was childishly pleased during the summer when he was commissioned major, with the meaningless staff title of "inspector general."

A rival of Von Borcke's as a gargantua was General Lee's son Rooney, not officially on the staff. Described as "too big for a man and not big enough to be a horse," W. H. F. Lee had been educated at Harvard, where Henry Adams disapproved of him as a prototype of the arrogantly imperious and backward aristocracy. Among his native kind, twenty-five-year-old Rooney was a high-spirited companion, a rough fighting man, and a good regimental commander.

Another of the boon comrades was John Pelham, also not formally on the staff but, as captain (really organizer) of Stuart's Horse Artillery, the twenty-three-year-old Alabamian was part of the group. Pelham's great-grandfather had been the organist for nearly fifty years in the famous Bruton Parish Church in Williamsburg. His grandfather had been a major in the Continental Army and his father, a country doctor and Alabama planter, was an opponent of secession who had six sons in the Confederate armies.

Resigned from West Point shortly before graduation at the outbreak of war, in his only experience in mature life the young Pelham demonstrated a rare gift for artillery warfare, a fighting heart and, like all of Stuart's favorites, a love of personal combat. He was a very good-looking boy, of an appealing personality that attracted men and women equally. He was the only officer below general rank to whose name Lee attached an adjective in an official report. "The gallant Pelham," Lee called him, and the gallant Pelham he was for the brief span of life remaining to him.

Of the five young men, all under thirty, only Rooney Lee was to continue to the end of the war, after recovering from a wound. Von Borcke was invalided out of the army with a serious throat injury from a bullet, and the other three were killed in action. Including the Prussian baron, all were aristocrats and, except for Von Borcke, all were of planter families, though Rooney Lee's father earned his living as a professional soldier. They even had their own minstrel, Sweeney, the sweet-natured banjo player. Except for his ability to make gay music while riding along with them, the renderer of "Kathleen Mavourneen" was otherwise useless. Of such a group the legends grow, and Jeb Stuart's army family personified the knighthood concept to which the Southern people were dedicated in their fight for independence.

Within Virginia, their status as a nation had already been tacitly accepted by Beast Butler. In accepting runaway slaves into his lines as "contrabands of war," Butler recognized the Confederacy as a foreign power to which the Fugitive Slave Law of the United States did not apply. Where the South was being invaded purportedly to return these states to the Union, where it served expediency, the new nation was recognized as outside the Union.

Southerners naturally accepted the viewpoint which recognized their independent status and grew in determination to perpetuate it. In their effort at perpetuation, and innocent of the continental destinies beyond their spans, the personal people needed personal heroes. In the hot and anxious June of 1862, Jeb Stuart came to join Stonewall Jackson. The people dared hope that their capital could turn McClellan away from its gates.

4

Though the people did not know it, maneuver in the Confederacy's defenses began with Robert E. Lee. He continued to be properly deferential with the President, as with whatever figurehead occupied the War Office, but from now on the larger strategy and tactics were his.

Knowing that mathematics (like the census returns) was on the side with the most of everything, Lee thought only of total defeat for the enemy, and that as quickly as possible. As long as he possessed even an outside chance, he tried for final victory and never to hold territory. His vast and realistic comprehension of the war in the East made his policy virtually at odds with the static-defense policy of the secessionist government.

On his first assignment as a field general—saving Richmond from McClellan—he never thought merely in terms of fending off the enemy. He thought of destroying McClellan's army, and through the anxious days of June he developed his complicated plan to that end.

As with all leaders on both sides, Lee had never previously commanded a large army, and the force he inherited from Retreatin' Joe was an assemblage of divisions without corps organization and with only limited experience in battle. Many of its division commanders were untried, and some of these were to prove unworthy. It was a collection of Rebel civilians trying to act like a traditional army.

Lee learned as he went, and on his first counteroffensive he had much to learn. One lesson was the proper use of his cavalry, though in the limited service placed upon Stuart's horsemen they served him well. Another lesson was in the selection of trustworthy men for crucial though small assignments.

Nothing would seem to be simpler to ask of a brigadier general than that he communicate to his division commander (A. P. Hill) the time and place of appearance of Stonewall Jackson's army. But General L. O'B. Branch, an educated North Carolina legislator, was a patriot without any military experience whatsoever. His name figures little in the weighty analyses of the Seven Days' Battle around Richmond, and yet Hill's almost anonymous brigadier was a key figure in the Confederacy's first effort at grand strategy in defeating the enemy.

The strategy of Lee was grand indeed. The Chickahominy River, with its expanding swampland, swings in an arc from due east to due north of Richmond. From the east, McClellan's main force was in front of the river; from the north, a wing was behind the river, placed there in expectation of juncture with McDowell.

For the Confederates, the vital element was that McClellan's army was divided by the nasty Chickahominy. Lee's strategy was to destroy the exposed wing and, then, on McClellan's flank, to force his main body into a retreat through the maze of dusty, brushy roads, where it would be destroyed. The audacious plan was sound enough, except that it depended on the human element.

Fitz-John Porter, in command of McClellan's wing to the northward, had the bridges across the Chickahominy guarded up to a point. At that point (Half-Sink), the Confederates' Branch was to cross with his brigade unmolested and be on the same side of the swampy river as Porter. At the same time Jackson, stealing down from the Valley, was to come in farther away from the river on Porter's side of it. Jackson's eastward swing would place him in the rear of the Union's strong defensive position back from the river at the sharp declivity of Beaver Dam Creek. When Jackson's then celebrated marchers appeared, Branch was to communicate with A. P. Hill. Hill's division, with two others, would then cross the bridges—which Jackson's presence would force Porter to uncover—and the whole force would unite in a counter-pincer movement on the Union pincer.

At the beginning, Stonewall Jackson was in a state of exhaustion. He never admitted it to anybody except his wife, but he wrote her at the end of the Seven Days that "during the past week I have not been well, have suffered from fever and debility. . . ."

It would have been a physical phenomenon if he had felt well. In the middle of his thirty-ninth year Jackson, for all his good care of himself, was never robust and needed as much sleep as the average man. On the four nights before he entered into his part of the battle he had only one full night's sleep. The night before the battle he had little if any, and on the first two nights he had none at all. On the first night, he rode fifty miles to a conference with Lee and his generals, and rode the fifty miles back the next night. He was simply not up to this kind of exertion with no sleep in forty-eight hours.

His army had marched badly in his absence. Not fully recovered from the strenuous Valley Campaign and physically depressed by the flat, hot, dusty country, the Valley men from generals to privates acted like school children taking advantage of the absence of the stern taskmaster. Jackson's force was late reaching Ashland, a little college town twenty miles north of Richmond, and the next morning they were six hours late in crossing the Virginia Central Railroad tracks for their crucial part in Lee's plan. At nine o'clock instead of 3 A.M., Old Jack, according to orders, communicated his presence to Hill's brigadier, L. O'B. Branch.

With General Branch, the pattern of errors began to unfold. What Branch did with Jackson's communication, nobody knows to this day. He vanished into the woods with his brigade while Jackson and Ewell, on separate roads, moved warily southward.

Ominously for their planned surprise, the troops were harassed by enemy cavalry and log obstructions. Though they were not slowed appreciably, the presence of the enemy in their front made the leaders move cautiously in the unfamiliar country. Around five in the afternoon, Jackson and Ewell converged at a crossroads called Hundley's Corner, barely fifteen miles southeast of Ashland, from where they had started. Bald Dick told Jackson that he had encountered Branch with his brigade ambling down a parallel road, and that Branch knew nothing about his division commander, A. P. Hill. The two veterans of the Valley stared at each other in consternation. Well they might. They could hear, less than five miles away, the sounds of a full-scale battle raging.

Jackson was where he was supposed to be according to the plan and, according to plan, the other divisions (A. P. Hill, D. H. Hill, Longstreet) should be near to move in echelon with his against Porter. Nobody was near except a small Yankee force observing Stonewall's Rebels with more curiosity than menace. Between Old Jack and the sounds of battle were obscuring woods in a country strange to them all. Jeb Stuart, partly familiar with the terrain, was following his orders by screening the infantry from any surprise to their left, and could not be used for reconnaissance. In the dilemma, Jackson followed the axiom which adjudged discretion to be the better part of valor, and discreetly did nothing.

As his strung-out troops and miles of wagon trains came up between five o'clock and dusk (the sun set at quarter past seven), he sent them into bivouac to the sounds of the nearby battle. Though Jackson has been endlessly criticized for this inaction, though endlessly defended too, it is difficult to see what he could have done. None of his men, according to their reports and memoirs, felt they were doing anything amiss when they made camp within earshot of some heavy firing.

On the following day, Lee showed that his trust in Old Jack was unshaken. By then Lee knew that his first battle had been a fiasco caused by the all too human elements of the leaders involved. The trouble began with the thirty-six-year-old Virginian, A. P. Hill, "Little Powell" to his troops. While Branch was wandering through the woods, keeping to himself the news of Jackson's movements, the high-strung Hill grew nervous at hearing nothing from the Valley forces and began to fear that the whole battle plan would be lost if the day were lost. Without consulting anybody, he impetuously threw his division across the Chickahominy above the little town of Mechanicsville. Since the bridge was not heavily guarded, Hill swept everything before him and pushed on through the town.

When the retreating Unions uncovered the other bridges, Longstreet and D. H. Hill, thinking the trap had been sprung, vigorously pushed forward their own divisions. Lee, observing from a nearby bluff, watched thunderstruck as A. P. Hill, caught up in the battle action, pursued the retreating Federals to their stronghold at Beaver Dam Creek, the impregnable position which Lee had planned for weeks to avoid attacking.

The patient gentleman was so deeply agitated that he even snapped at the President. As at the earlier battlefield of Seven Pines, Jefferson Davis, accompanied by an immense entourage, had come to general headquarters. He had already shown the way in which he regarded the army as personally his by ordering in a brigade of D. H. Hill's without consulting either Hill or Lee.

When Lee encountered the presidential force lurking around, he did not ride off to get away from them, as had Joe Johnston at Seven Pines. In his excited absorption, Lee in effect ordered them off the field. Davis reacted as if Rover had suddenly sprung at his throat. With a cold reply, he rode haughtily off. But the President never came on any more of Lee's fields and after the Battle of Mechanicsville (first of the Seven Days around Richmond), the general was not bothered with any consultations with the Commander in Chief about a battle.

5

Without repinings or reproaches, Lee picked up the pieces of his wrecked strategy and extemporized plans to catch the Union wing the following day. Though Porter had repulsed the Confederates with extremely heavy losses at Beaver Dam Creek, he knew then that Stonewall Jackson was potentially in his rear. During the night he moved eastward, beyond Jackson and near the bridges over which he could join McClellan's main army.

On the other side of the Chickahominy, McClellan possessed an open road to Richmond, since between him and the capital stood only the small force of Magruder. It was the great hazard Lee took, in which he depended solely on the stage effects of another of "Prince John's" demonstrations. The Great Demonstrator did not fail him, though Magruder got so beguiled by the illusion he created that he imposed on himself and rushed his troops forward in a disastrous charge. However, McClellan remained innocuously on his side of the river and Lee got his second crack at the wing under Fitz-John Porter.

The grand strategy worked no better the second day than it had on the first, and Porter selected another strong position at Gaines's Mill. However, all the Confederates converged that day, once in action Jackson's men fought up to their reputation, Lee kept throwing in men despite the heavy losses, and at dusk the position was carried. It was the first solid Confederate victory since the real war began, though the size of the victory would depend entirely on McClellan.

If he tried to recapture the initiative, he might hold Lee north of the Chickahominy by using his heavy armament to control the crossings, and run over Magruder in a drive at Richmond only seven miles away. Once gone, the initiative in anything is hard to recapture, especially under pressure, and McClellan thought about saving his army (and, perhaps, his reputation) instead of getting the Rebel capital. He began the long retreat through the fan of roads to his fleet-supplied and gunboat-protected base at Harrison's Landing on the James River.

Despite all the miscarriage in detail of Lee's plans, one objective had been achieved: he had pried loose McClellan's two pincers from the city and he had a retreating Union army caught in the maze of narrow roads winding through the woods and swamps to the river. Undaunted by the earlier failures in his plans, Lee again devised schemes for crushing the invading army. And again he was failed by the human element.

First off, while Joe Johnston occupied the territory, he had not mapped the country, and the invaders, under meticulous if poor-fighting McClellan, possessed more accurate maps than the natives. Some of the Confederate generals were no better than the maps.

Some wandered disconsolately along the wrong roads. Huger, the South

Carolinian who had commanded the Norfolk district, spent a day clearing a road the enemy had obstructed. Theophilus Holmes was so deaf that when his troops were scattering like quail from the shelling of Union gunboats on the river, the old man cupped his ear and said, "Don't I hear firing?"

Jackson, whose men had fought as fiercely as any on the field at Gaines's Mill, could not seem to get momentum in his part of the pursuit, and he became the key figure in the controversy over another trap that failed, Glendale and Frayser's Farm. That failure devolved more directly on Jackson, and entered more into the mysteries of human behavior.

At a crossroads, Longstreet and Hill had a large segment of McClellan's army in a tight situation and needed only Jackson coming in on the Union rear to win a victory of real size. Pursuing Franklin's rearguard corps, Jackson came upon another of those creeks (Whiteoak Swamp) at the bottom of a valley of steeply rising hills, and the bridge had been destroyed. Jackson quickly had firing room for guns hacked out of the woods and got twenty-eight pieces going. They were insufficient to silence Franklin's guns, and Franklin's artillery and sharpshooters kept Jackson's bridge builders from getting their work done. The men tried despite the fire; they just could not live through it.

Here Stonewall Jackson, with no indication of urgency, sat down on the ground and watched his losing artillery duel. Other leaders, frantic to get his troops in, suggested other means of getting across the creek and in striking position on Franklin. Jackson nodded, did nothing, and finally fell asleep. Clearly his exhaustion had caught up with him. Yet more than exhaustion must have been required to cause the fierce-fighting Stonewall Jackson to fall asleep on a battlefield.

The strange, complex, and lonely Presbyterian was one of those people who performed best only when the immediate situation was entirely in his control. While he did not have to be boss of everything, he had to be boss of the immediate job he was doing. Jackson continually demonstrated that he could execute any given assignment as long as he held complete control within his sphere. Ultimately self-reliant, never seeking advice (civil or military) in his life, during the Seven Days Jackson was placed in a situation outside of his control. He was part of a plan based on certain eventualities. When these failed to happen, his initiative seemed to fail too.

General Lee, in his kindly consideration of others, gave very loose orders for his first campaign, and even at his peak inclined toward discretionary orders which constantly caused confusion. Later, Jackson acted superbly under Lee's discretionary orders; but at the Seven Days Lee had not learned how to use him. The orders were not sufficiently discretionary: they were posited on a plan that failed in detail.

Also, as Jackson was a slow learner in everything, he had little intuitive feel for a terrain. He needed to study it. In the swampy, brushy labyrinth around Richmond—"this malarious region," as he called it—Old Jack was on strange and baffling ground. In all ways, he seemed baffled. His befuddlement would seem to have produced the same kind of apathy as boredom, and exhaustion literally overcame him at Whiteoak Swamp.

Poor Lee, still with never a reproach and struggling on to get at McClellan, finally brought his scattered troops together at the same time that McClellan, having escaped all traps, had his army in a powerful position. It was too late for any more maneuver then, really too late for anything. But Lee's fighting blood was up and he could not allow the enemy to escape without one more crack at him.

Even in that final test at Malvern Hill—of the old-fashioned straight-on charge against a fixed position—Lee was again failed in detail. Though Jackson's men, as at Gaines's Mill, again fought up to their reputation when the situation was certain, and individual units charged the steep hill in magnificent abandon, the co-ordination was faulty and the attack was repulsed with losses enough to demoralize an army. But under the Rebels' pressure, McClellan retreated again—all the way to his base.

Though McClellan's army had not been destroyed, the Southern people had not been privy to Lee's plan. They knew only that the siege of Richmond had been lifted and the Union's terrifying war machine had been driven eighteen miles from the city, down to the James River. There, under the sheltering wings of gunboats, McClellan started to throw up entrenchments against Lee!

To the barely subsisting Confederate services, the feast left by McClellan, in food and equipment, weapons and ammunition, was beyond their wildest dreams. For days bureau men and wagoners gleaned the fields where the gravediggers dug under the hot sun, and soldiers on the happy detail of collecting supplies marveled at the strange tastes of the invaders. Most puzzling of all to the country people were the little fishes in tin cans with which the Yankees burdened themselves, when they had been surrounded by creeks and rivers running with croakers and catfish and shad.

6

McClellan took up headquarters at Harrison's Landing, which had served as the private wharf of Berkeley, the plantation where President Harrison was born. There, where the broad shaded lawns sloped to the river, a young bugler passed the time by improvising notes which were to become a bugle call most prophetic for General McClellan and his effort to end the war by taking Richmond. It was Taps.

Taps blew also for the kind of war McClellan wanted to fight. In the battles which broke his siege of the city, there had still been on both sides a deep awareness that fellow citizens had become embroiled in a war. Officers from the Regular Army in particular were conscious of fighting old friends, old companions, in some cases, since college. When General Reynolds was captured after Gaines's Mill, he was brought to the headquarters of Harvey Hill, who had been his messmate and for a time his tentmate. Reynolds, in confusion and embarrassment, covered his face with his hands and said, "Hill, we ought not to be enemies."

Among the privates, there was the young Union prisoner who begged a friendly-looking young Rebel to stay with him, because he believed the South was overrun with guerrillas who would shoot him on sight. With the battle raging, the Southerner tried to persuade the prisoner that he would be safe in the rear, finally urging him, "Go on now, I've got to get in this line of skirmishers."

Porter said, in speaking of Confederates who had been his personal friends, "I learned to know them well and to respect their decision under conviction of duty, when, to my regret, they left the cause of the Union."

There was at that time an element of what the Southerners thought of as chivalry. Dick Taylor, the President's son and Jackson's brigadier, spoke of "the chivalric behavior" of McClellan. This began to pass as the nature of the conflict changed.

Once the horsemen of war were turned loose, unless they succeeded quickly, the time must come when the reason for success by arms was subordinated to success itself, when the ends would be determined by the means. That time came when the great Union Army, eight months in preparation after First Manassas, was pressed back from the Confederacy's citadel in the Seven Days' Battle around Richmond. From then on, the subjugation would be increasingly entrusted to leaders who did not question the future consequences of their acts in making an invasion successful.

The Confederates for the moment were suddenly spared looking into the future. From almost certain defeat, they had turned to win the greatest victory of their fight for independence. They had won in a way a personal people understand best of all—under a great leader.

To him the gathered knights—becoming soldiers since the time of elegant and lighthearted privilege in the first encampments—gave their allegiance. In him the foot soldiers found the patriarch who extended from their familiar parochial scene into the strange, new world of the army. For them all, caught up in a fight which they had never expected, he was *the* leader around whom would evolve an army—the famous Army of Northern Virginia.

Beyond the army, to all the people thirsting for a leader who could win, Lee began his emergence as a god of the new nation.

CHAPTER XII

The Three Cigars

HATE came into the struggle with the coming of Illinois's John Pope to Virginia. Lincoln unaccountably appointed this loudmouthed braggart to the command of all the scattered troops in northern Virginia who, under poor McDowell, had spent such fruitless months in chasing Stonewall Jackson and in standing ready to repel a Rebel attack on Washington.

With all the Confederates in Virginia consolidated against McClellan on the peninsula, all the peregrinating Unions in the north of the state, some 50,000-odd, were concentrated under Pope. A hero of the West, Pope with his pugnacity had won some success in the Confederacy's sad situation in the Mississippi Valley. He came east, snorting and pawing, and proclaiming that where he had come from "we have always seen the backs of our enemies." He told his soldiers he wanted them to get rid of such phrases as "lines of retreat" and "bases of supply," and announced that, as for him, headquarters would be in the saddle. Naturally his "headquarters in the saddle" came in for some ribald comment, the gentlest was that "Pope had put his headquarters where his hindquarters ought to be."

In addition to his boastful designs on the Confederate soldiers, Pope took the war to the civilians. He declared living off the country his policy. With this directive from headquarters, naturally some troops began the destruction of crops which they couldn't use and the plundering of houses; some families became angry in their protests and their homes were burned. Though Pope issued orders which decreed shooting for marauders among his own troops, when enraged civilians took to bushwhacking it was innocent people whom Pope arrested to hold as hostages.

Militarily Pope was supposed to make life uncomfortable in central Virginia, threatening or destroying the railroad from Richmond to the Valley, in order to draw off troops against McClellan.

After the Seven Days, Jackson immediately returned to his *idée fixe* of an invasion north down the Valley, as he feared a repetition of Manassas in gaining no fruits of victory. When Lee wanted time to consider, Old

Jack got his congressman to take the plan directly to Davis. No decision was made then, but Jackson and Ewell were sent northward to see what could be done about the fire-breathing Pope.

Lee was as invasion-minded as Jackson, and had not the least intention of sitting supinely on defense. But he had large reorganization to do with the collection of troops which for the first time had fought under him. First, units had to be reorganized after the staggering casualty lists of 20,000. (Unions lost 15,000—10,000 of whom were prisoners, wounded and unwounded.) Less than 1000 Confederates were listed missing, and as wounded were roughly at a ratio of five to one killed, roughly half of the 16,000 wounded could be expected back. That was about 10,000 gone for good, and there were few more like them.

Those were the volunteers, the flower of their section, the men who staked their lives on their civilization. They brought the traditions of personal independence, of honor and high courage: they brought a passionate personal identification with the land they fought for, and a deep sense of responsibility to it.

Those who had volunteered in the first headiness of heroics and had been turned away, to think better of their impulse, thought still better of it when the casualty lists reached them along with the stories of friends who had been invalided out of the army. Men who from the beginning had looked after their own hides (claiming exemptions and entering the spawning government bureaus) became fixed in their determination to avoid the army. There would be few replacements of the caliber of the men lost.

The loss was particularly felt among officers who fell, sword in hand, leading their men. The educated, intelligent, and natural leaders set the example in gallantry, but it was very wasteful of trained officer material. Other officers, such as Huger, deaf and inept Holmes, and "Prince John" Magruder, had failed to measure up and been transferred elsewhere. The gifted Demonstrator had grown so excited in command in actual combat that he suffered practically a nervous collapse on the field, and his personal magnificence was lost to the army in Virginia. D. H. Hill, who had stood up finely to the test, was transferred because of other considerations. His habit of carping criticism made him difficult to get along with and, as the outstanding North Carolina military leader, he went to take charge of the state's defenses. Their need was urgent since the Union landings in the coastal waterways during the late winter.

Before he left, Harvey Hill had to avoid a duel to which Bob Toombs challenged him. As a brigadier, the violent Georgian had not taken kindly to an upbraiding from his division commander, Hill, and he didn't hold with any West Pointer talking to him that way.

After that blew over, the other Hill (no relation) was more seriously involved with Longstreet. A. P. Hill, of the courteous smile, had served in the old army from his graduation from West Point until secession. "Little

Powell" was an intense, sensitive man, courtly and punctilious, and a Richmond social favorite.

On the other hand, Longstreet was a blunt, burly man, also from the old army, stolidly self-assured, opinionated and nursing a small core of jealousy which was slow to be revealed. His jealousy had been aroused when a temporary staff officer of Hill, without Hill's knowledge, wrote a glowing newspaper account of Hill's "Light" Division in the Seven Days. By implication, it reflected adversely on Longstreet who, in the loose organization of that time, was A. P. Hill's superior.

Longstreet had his A.A.G. write an anonymous letter to the paper denying the claims of Hill's supporter and building his own. But the anonymity was not kept from the army. When this A.A.G., Moxley Sorrel, later brought an order to Hill, he refused to accept it. When he refused a second message, Longstreet had him placed under arrest. From there the affair progressed rapidly toward a duel which would not have blown over.

Lee personally intervened, and sent Little Powell off to Jackson's command in northern Virginia. There A. P. Hill immediately got into further difficulties. He had known Jackson at the Point, though they had been too dissimilar ever to be intimates, and in the new command Hill had to undergo the common experience of adjusting himself to Jackson's secrecy and brusqueness. The underlying friction began to come to a head when Jackson's troops had a slow march, and he placed the blame on Powell Hill. The climax was reached when Jackson, dissatisfied with the straggling in Hill's division, gave an order directly to one of Hill's brigadiers.

The punctilious Hill turned to Jackson and, unbuckling his sword, told his commanding general that, since he was giving the orders, he had no need of him.

Without sending for a staff officer with sword and sash, Jackson said, "Consider yourself under arrest for neglect of duty."

A. P. Hill, remaining with his division but not in command of it, petitioned for charges to be preferred and have the case brought to court-martial. Jackson refused. He had a long record of arresting people, and Hill was an old story to him. Finally Hill was temporarily released to lead his division in action; Lee persuaded Hill to drop his demands for specific charges, and the temporary release became permanent. Though he never forgave Stonewall Jackson, Old Jack's respect for Little Powell's fighting qualities went so deep that it was Hill whom Stonewall called for in his dying delirium.

Longstreet also sent Sorrel with his sword and sash to another offender, Bob Toombs again. Longstreet had sent orders for two of Toombs's regiments to guard a ford. The order happened to come when Toombs was off visiting, and his second in command executed the order. When Toombs returned from the visit, apparently "feeling no pain," he came across his regiments out there in the night away from camp. Outraged that his neighbors from down home should be so treated, without even orders from him, he sent them back to camp.

Over that ford came Union cavalry who barely missed capturing Jeb Stuart and his whole staff. Hard riding on their part and bad shooting from their pursuers were all that saved them. As it was, Stuart's black leather haversack was captured, with orders which revealed Lee's plans against Pope. What hurt Stuart's feelings more, his plumed hat was captured too. At a distance safe from his pursuers, he suffered the indignity of watching a Union trooper ride off with the famous headpiece cocked on his noggin.

That was when Longstreet arrested Toombs. The old politician did not hold with these military regulations. He ran up to Longstreet, his gray hair waving in the breeze, and pleaded to be returned to his friends, the brigade. On seeing their patriarch, the troops sent up a yell, and Longstreet gave in.

This was the type of personality clash which Lee had to consider in reorganizing his depleted army before moving northward.

All the separate and unwieldy division commands, while still not placed in formalized corps, were collected into two wings which became the basis of the Army of Northern Virginia. Longstreet was assigned four large divisions and one small, and Jackson took three large divisions—A. P. Hill's, Bald Dick Ewell's, and the Stonewall Division under Charles Winder.

Winder was a thirty-two-year-old Marylander, West Point graduate, Regular Army captain, and one of the most promising of the young division commanders. In spite of rigid discipline with Jackson's veterans, Winder had won their respect and even affection by his courage and capabilities in action.

In Ewell's division, they missed proud Dick Taylor, who was invalided out of the army in Virginia with a mysterious and temporary partial paralysis. Rob Wheat, the widely liked soldier of fortune, had been killed at the Seven Days, and his Louisiana Tigers seemed to have become a little tamed. All in all, with other changes, the crack Louisiana brigade was not quite the same in color, though still tough.

Jeb Stuart was promoted to major general, and all the cavalry units finally organized into a three-brigade division. Wade Hampton, the South Carolina grandee who had brought up his own legion, and been twice wounded, was put in his proper slot as a cavalry brigade commander.

The artillery had been enriched by fifty-two of the Union's superior guns and the infantry by 30,000 rifles and muskets garnered from the Seven Days battlefields.

By the time this reorganization was completed, McClellan's men had begun to embark on ships at Harrison's Landing, while others started marching the long road back down the peninsula to Fortress Monroe.

They could be going only one place—to reinforce Pope. Leaving only two divisions and Hampton's new cavalry brigade to see off the departing masses of the once feared army, Lee joined Jackson to take on Pope before McClellan reinforced him.

2

The campaign against Pope represented the Confederacy's first aggressive maneuver. It was designed by Lee for the purpose of evicting the enemy from their territory entirely. For his offense against Pope, Lee faced a situation at once less complex and more mobile than against McClellan.

While Pope had half of Virginia to maneuver in, it was obvious that the Union design consisted chiefly of concentrating all the forces in the state where, with numerical supremacy, the single army could overwhelm the Confederates and return to Richmond by the direct, overland route. With the old Western commander, Halleck, then General in Chief, the Unions were extemporizing a piecemeal return to Lincoln's original preference for a quick victory.

Lee also wanted a quick victory, before mathematics worked against him. The Confederate commissioners abroad wrote that breaking the Richmond siege had exerted a profound impression in Europe, and Lee wanted to follow that favorable effect by taking the war to the enemy. Hopelessly outnumbered by the total Union forces in Virginia, he maneuvered to get at Pope before McClellan joined him.

With soaring morale in his reorganized army, Lee opened his offense in that pleasant rolling country called the Piedmont in Virginia. West of Tidewater and east of the Blue Ridge, it was plantation country without the éclat of the James River paradise but with very fine living. It was one of the sections destroyed almost beyond repair by the Union armies. Latter-day Northerners, with money and mercifully without motives to restore the Union, have settled in this fox-hunting country, and some of the world's finest steeplechases meet there. As of 1862, it was the fertile land on whose people Pope had turned loose his idea of war, and the country was in the transient stage between polite prosperity and desolation.

The Rapidan and the Rappahannock rivers flowing easterly and southeasterly, converge west of Fredericksburg (that midway city between Richmond and Washington). That was the area of Pope's first forays, before Lee and McClellan left the peninsula. An advance of his under "Commissary" Banks had run into Jackson in a rough engagement (Cedar Mountain). Though Banks, smarting under his rude treatment in the Valley, fought his troops as well as any troops fought in the war, Jackson had the superior numbers on hand and took the field. Jackson's forces suffered a heavy blow in the death of young Winder, the brilliant and promising commander of the Stonewall Division.

An unhappy experience befell a quartermaster captain in that fierce fight. Resplendent in store-bought finery, he stood out among the soldiers like a beacon to the eyes of Bald Dick Ewell, who immediately asked him who he was. When told, with considerable dignity, that he was Captain So-and-so of the quartermasters, Ewell threw up his hands.

"Great heavens! A quartermaster on the battlefield! Whoever heard of such a thing before? But since you are here, I will make you useful as well as ornamental."

He sent him with a message, requiring an answer, where the captain had to cross under heavy fire. The quartermaster surprised Bald Dick by performing the service handsomely. But he never performed any more, for that was the last time he was ever seen around Ewell.

After Commissary Banks had stood up so well to Jackson, Pope was inclined to come snorting after him. He was restrained by Washington, and ended up by waiting around for Jackson's next move. Nothing much had happened regarding Pope's general plans to disrupt communications, though he did draw off one or two clergymen from their parishes.

Whenever an Episcopal church came within occupied lines, the communicants were forbidden to read from the Prayer Book the prayer for "the President of the Confederate States." Frequently the church closed and the clergyman went off and attached himself to an outfit formed of soldiers from the section of his parish. Of 115 Virginia Episcopal clergymen, 29 became chaplains.

"Attached himself" is the proper description, since the Confederacy made no provision for its chaplains, beyond allowing them fifty dollars a month and the rations of a private soldier. The story goes that a congressman obstructed any other measures, as he held that a chaplain had nothing to do except preach once a week. If the congressman had ever been near troops, he would have known better.

Services were held daily; morning and evening prayer, baptisms and confirmations were continuous. In addition to spiritual work, most chaplains actively assisted the understaffed and undertrained Medical Corps, serving as anything from litter-bearers to holders of the anguished men suffering amputation without anesthesia.

With McClellan moving his army off the Virginia peninsula, in mid-August Lee joined Jackson to get at "The Man without a Rear" while McClellan was in transit. At first there was a lot of maneuvering, some sharp skirmishing, with Lee trying to set Pope up for the kill. Lee's first attempt was frustrated by the capture of his orders in Jeb Stuart's unhappy episode, along with the report of a spy. Then, with the help of rising waters, Pope succeeded in blocking all approaches across the Rappahannock.

While Pope stood guarding the Rappahannock, the Rebels suddenly struck between him and Washington—*and* on that "base of supplies" which Pope wished to be stricken from the lexicon of the Union armies. Lee had evolved the action which would bring Pope after him, where he could catch the Hero of the West with a counterpunch.

3

If ever "chickens came home to roost" for a braggart, they did for Pope in the hot August weather of northern Virginia. The first humiliation was largely personal, though it exerted vast effects on the coming campaign. This happened at Catlett's Station, far in the rear of the Union forces, where some of Stuart's cavalry fell upon those famous headquarters which Pope supposedly had in the saddle. Most of his staff was bagged, along with Pope's personal baggage and—most important to Jeb Stuart, lusting for revenge over the loss of his plume—the commanding general's dress coat. This was displayed in a store window in Richmond to the delight of all.

More important still to the army was the capture of Pope's papers. In a sort of turn-about-is-fair-play, as Pope had had Lee's, now Lee had his. He acted on them promptly.

All the doubts raised about Stonewall Jackson at the Seven Days were resolved and all the questions forgotten, when he made the march toward and then the fight at Second Manassas. He was acting with his own corps, with its artillery, and cavalry attached under his command. There was no confusion about where he should go, with whom he should co-ordinate, and what to do when he got there. His assignments were specific, he knew the terrain, and he was away from that "malarious region."

His troops were rested and eager. It was as if all of them unconsciously wanted to remove any blight they might have acquired in the Seven Days. They marched a half circle around the western flank of Pope's expanding army and well into his rear. They marched more than fifty miles in two days under the hot August sun.

At the end of the first day's march they were in such fettle that when a cavalry force passed them their jeers at the horsemen were, for once, good-natured. "You wouldn't have caught up with us," they yelled, "if our colonel's horse hadn't given out."

Close up, they must have been something to frighten children, or even adults. Their hair was shaggier, their skins darker, their clothes were beginning to come apart in tatters, with ragged edges where the pants flapped over broken shoes and bare feet. The frail of body and weak of spirit had been marched and fought out. These were hard men, with confidence in their hardness, and their wild independence forged into a single group spirit. They had the élan then. A Union observer, in signaling the passage

north of a body of Confederate troops, paid them what Old Jack would
have considered the ultimate compliment to his labors. "Well closed up,"
the observer signaled, "with colors flying."

Stuart's cavalry having taken care of Pope's headquarters, Jackson's
ravenous ragamuffins then fell on the general's base of supply on the railroad which connected the Unions with Washington. Jackson's three divisions, with some of Stuart's cavalry, struck the Orange and Alexandria
Railroad at Bristoe Station in the early evening and night of August 26.
They were eight miles down the track from Manassas Junction, the depot
for which they had fought a little over a year ago in the first battle of the
war, when their now famous Stonewall commanded a brigade. Now it
was the vast supply depot of the general who scorned "lines of supply."

Before they left Bristoe Station, a northbound train broke through
their first obstructions, but they captured the next two. On one of them
was a United States congressman, whose ankle had been broken in the
train crash. When he was informed that his captors were Jackson's men, he
asked to be raised up to have a look at the fabled Rebel. At that moment,
Stonewall happened to pass in his ill-fitting uniform, grown dingy since
spring, and the battered cadet cap pulled down over his plain, tired rustic
face. After one startled glance, the congressman cried, "Oh, my God, lay
me down again."

A fourth train approached and quickly backtracked, and unglamorous
Jackson knew that alarm would soon be given to Pope, as well as to Washington. Fortunately the Unions decided at first that it was another cavalry raid (as the engineer of the first escaped train reported being fired
upon by cavalry) but Jackson's men didn't know that.

Where they were headed for, Manassas Junction, was within twenty
miles of Washington to the northeast. McClellan's disembarking troops
were even nearer at Alexandria, and less than twenty miles away were
Pope's headquarters to the southwest, where his numbers were swelling
daily. Jackson and 20,000 men were in the center of the Union forces, with
Pope's army between him and Lee. Tired as the men were from the two
days' push, Old Jack sent them on that night down the tracks to Manassas
Junction.

Leaving a scattering of cavalry and three unhappy brigades of Ewell's
division to watch for the enemy, the rest of the Rebels pushed on for the
supply depot. They came in from midnight until about dawn, their wilted
bodies whipped on by the images of Yankee stores.

Whatever dreams their minds had conjured, as they stumbled through
the night, were inadequate to the reality. Jackson's men were never to forget to their dying day the supplies which, as a staff officer said, "were far
in excess of what any Confederate ever conceived to be in existence." It
would probably be true to say that the Union stores at Manassas Junction
far exceeded any army supplies that, until then, had ever been collected.

There was lavishly gathered the material might of a nation on its way to becoming the richest on earth.

Nothing could describe the awe with which the Southerners gazed upon streets of warehouses, two miles of bulging freight cars, food barrels scattered for acres across the fields, field ovens with bakery equipment of a size never before beheld by a man among them, rows of new ambulances, pyramids of artillery ammunition in an abundance that the whole Confederacy could scarcely turn out in a year. The vista was endless.

It might have demoralized the men who fought in rags, marched barefoot, and were served a little nibble of bacon, some corn meal, and the unsweetened coffee made, since the blockade tightened, from sweet potatoes or peanuts. However, accepting their lot, they regarded the prize wholly with incredulous pleasure. It boosted their morale to realize that *they* had gotten around an army accustomed to such splendor.

Since Jackson had no wagons beyond those in use for ordnance, medicine, and ambulances, he turned his soldiers loose to pack their own rations—after taking one precaution. Getting a picked guard from fellow teetotaler Jeb Stuart, and finding a captain who swore he "never used spirituous liquors," the general sent the troopers under the captain to guard the warehouse where the liquor barrels were stored while each barrel was punctured and drained. Old Jack said, "I expect you to execute this order at any cost, since I fear that liquor more than General Pope's army."

The order was executed, though they had to stand off a general and his staff. That warehouse did not hold all the spirituous liquors in Pope's stores. The great foragers from the Stonewall Brigade found brandy bottles in the medical stores, and the frantic men from the Medical Corps had to plead with them not to break the precious bottles of ether and chloroform in their haste to get at the brandy.

Like the liquor foragers, each man went after the things he held most dear. One barefoot fellow strung shoes around his neck, "like beads"; another bent under the weight of countless boxes of cigars, puffing on one the while; others burdened themselves entirely with coffee and those who had never seen canned goods before concentrated on potted ham and sardines. Bayonets were turned into holders of hams. Starved for sweets, all took molasses, filling their canteens with it, and their tin cups with sugar. They all ate as they ladened themselves, a few growing so gorged that they could not move on later.

As Jackson forbade them to appropriate blue uniforms, the rakish made an occasion of putting "sumptuous underclothing" on under their vermin-ridden tatters, and affected fancy manners by blowing sun-cracked noses on linen handkerchiefs.

The artillery, late to the feast, fared poorly. They had to content themselves with hardtack and pickled oysters, though their professional interest was aroused by two new three-inch guns they took along. These were a new-style Union weapon, of a "bronze-colored" metal, first used against the Southerners at Cedar Run, where the shells made "a singular noise . . . like the shrill note of a tree-frog on a big scale." Of course, they collected ample ammunition to go along with it. They also gathered for themselves two fully equipped and horsed batteries, which had been attached to the two regiments guarding the stores who had been captured or driven away. There was a little fighting, but the men never remembered that.

Late in the day, Ewell's three brigades, left at Bristoe Station under Jubal Early, after a sharp rear-guard action against Pope's advance forces under Hooker, neatly disengaged themselves (with Hooker character-istically claiming a victory), and came on to get the crumbs from the banquet. Praising Pope as a better commissary even than Banks, Jackson's men reluctantly ended the feast. Fires were put to the unused stores, and the men marched off to fight again.

They had a rendezvous with Pope, at Second Manassas, though the Hero of the West did not know it.

4

Jackson forced his bloated feasters to a night march north and a little east of Centreville, the old, the original line taken by the Confederates for the defense of Virginia. On the march Old Jack's secrecy confused his own men. One brigade disappeared in the darkness and, by the time Thomas was found, all of them had to do some countermarching. Jackson made their presence known at Centreville, right on the road to Washington, then vanished—literally, as far as Pope knew. Old Jack had gone west into heavy woods, and hidden there, with 70,000 Unions looking for his by then less than 20,000 thoroughly exhausted men.

When Pope came huffing and puffing after Stonewall Jackson, his tac-tics were based on the delusion that Jackson was fleeing. In his determi-nation to "bag" the quarry who had subjected him to further mortifica-tion, Pope spread out his troops exactly as if they were members of a posse trying to run down a fugitive. The widely dispersed divisions and corps, in their version of "Come out, come out, wherever you are," bore slight relation to an army in controlled movement. By then Pope knew that Lee, with Longstreet's wing, had moved from his front and was circling around to come in from the west to join Jackson. His whole pur-pose was to find Jackson before the juncture. However, except for Old Jack making his presence known, Pope would have missed him.

West of the old field of Manassas, near a place called Groveton, Jackson was nearly as tired as at the Seven Days. In the broiling sun, he lay sound asleep on the ground. As they had eschewed even headquarters wagons for speed on their march, Jackson and his staff were using saddles for pillows, with their few necessities in the saddlebags. An officer approached the sleeping general with a fresh order of Pope gleaned from a captured courier. The order told Jackson that Unions were moving north, past their hiding place.

The force was under McDowell who, still sinned against, had been reduced to a corps commander under Pope. By means of the tireless reconnaissance of Jeb Stuart, whose cavalry without glamorous heroics served the army throughout the Second Manassas campaign in a model of the functions of mounted troops, Jackson knew that McDowell's three divisions would complete Pope's gradual concentration at Centreville. Collected there, with McClellan's daily arriving divisions from the peninsula, Pope would have an overwhelming numerical superiority which would place his army beyond any possibility of Lee's attacking him. They would have returned to the situation of the early spring.

Jackson's assigned objective was to hold Pope in the open until Lee arrived for a flanking crusher. Where a rear-guard corps had immobilized Old Jack at Whiteoak Swamp, when he was acting on the details supplied by another, in the hot woods at Groveton, acting on his own initiative, he came fully awake and went into immediate action. He had to restrain McDowell from getting to Centreville, and to bring Pope after him, away from his concentration. To this end, he aroused his sleeping soldiers and sent two divisions with several guns to attack a 10,000-man division of McDowell's passing on the road to join Pope's main army.

That division, commanded by Rufus King, was one of those units of Westerners who did not run from noises, no matter how sudden. They turned on their attackers and there, in the falling dusk, was fought one of the most relentless, straight-on, stand-up battles of the Civil War.

Nobody won, though the Confederates suffered a heavy blow in the loss of Bald Dick Ewell. With Jackson distant from the fighting, Old Baldhead came up to indulge his passion for personal combat and some Georgians cheered him. King's men, apparently mistaking the cheer for a coming attack, poured it on. Dick Ewell was hit in the knee. When his men were temporarily driven back, he lay there bleeding in the darkness gathering over the countryside where he had played and hunted as a boy.

At night he was rescued, and carried off to have his leg amputated. Seeing his wan face, his men forgot his foolish furies and the brusqueness of his high-pitched voice, and were greatly saddened.

Jackson had achieved his purpose in the rough and costly action. Pope, with the fox viewed, came thundering after the quarry. He actually believed, according to his orders, that "McDowell has intercepted the retreat of the enemy . . . and I see no possibility of his escape."

Of these moves and countermoves, the tired soldiers with Old Jack only knew, as they prepared their night camp in the woods, that Pope's

whole army would be coming at them next morning. The jubilation at the
feast had faded by then, and they were sobered by the absence of comrades fallen in the twilight's fierce action and the passing from their midst
of Dick Ewell. They remembered his quaint ways, the uniqueness of his
character, and he seemed like a fatherly friend who had gone from them.
With young Winder killed at Cedar Run, they had lost both the division
commanders of their original little army, which had fought the Valley
campaign and come down to help lift the siege of Richmond.

A. P. Hill's division was new to the group, with only the more recent
bonds of sharing the great march to Manassas, but Little Powell's men
stretched out on the ground under the same sense of ominous apprehension. There were too few of them, and they knew it. They knew there
was no base to fall back on, no subsistence, and no nearby reinforcements. One of the South Carolinians in Maxcy Gregg's brigade wrote,
"God, Jackson, and our own hearts were our dependence."

Their dependence proved to be enough the next day, with nothing to
spare.

They withstood five separate waves of assault, led by bold men, like
Kearny and Hooker, and fought by brave men, who that day had a little
goad of hunger themselves. Every man with Jackson was used, some over
and over. Those broken units who staggered out in battle exhaustion were
rested briefly, refreshed with tepid water from canteens, re-formed, and
sent back in to meet a fresh wave surging at them. Ammunition ran out.
They threw rocks and met the close contact with bayonets. They fought
on, their ranks thinning, until the blue masses receded with the falling
light.

Old Jack forgot, for the moment, A. P. Hill's marching deficiencies in
the fierce fighting of the Light Division. Under Little Powell's intense
leadership, his troops did all and maybe more than could be asked of
them. Yet the soldier in Maxcy Gregg's brigade of Hill's division was right
about his premonition. In their five regiments all except two of the colonels
and lieutenant colonels fell, killed outright or wounded. The casualties
among officers all through the three divisions were the Seven Days all
over again.

You read of the "Stonewall Division," with its "Stonewall Brigade," the
most famous division in the army. Reports always stressed the name when
the enemy did well against the Stonewall Division. What was it except a
quickly won name, with survivors to sustain recruits in maintaining its
quickly created pride?

Of the three brigadiers who commanded at Kernstown, less than six
months before, not one fought at Second Manassas. When Winder was
killed at Cedar Run a few weeks before, the division had gone to Talia-
ferro. He was wounded in that long afternoon of Groveton when so many
fell, and the most famous division in the army was turned over to William

Starke, who only the day before had taken a brigade in action for the first time. This was a Louisiana brigade recently joined to the original Virginia brigades. All the brigades were commanded by colonels and the most promising of these, Baylor of the Stonewall Brigade, went down that afternoon even before he had a chance to win the promotion his performance deserved. Captains led regiments in the Stonewall Division, under flags which ladies had made little more than a year before.

When darkness fell on the shattered men with their sadly reduced forces —where young company officers were busily taking over their new and larger commands and the medical men under young Dr. McGuire worked on through the night—they had another day of it to look ahead to with the reassurance that Longstreet was there.

Longstreet had been there a long time, while Jackson's three divisions were dying, poised to deliver the counterstroke for which the whole plan had been designed. That was the first time he imposed his stubborn stolidity on the gentleness of Lee. The commanding general suggested three times that he should go in, but Longstreet made excuses, procrastinated, and the sun went down.

In the old army Longstreet had been a paymaster major, going nowhere particularly, but the new country gave him—as it gave politicians and speculators and all sorts of glory hunters—a sudden chance for the big fame. Second Manassas was that big chance. From a division commander at the Seven Days, he commanded a wing here, more than half the army. He wanted to be sure when he sent them in for the counterstroke that it would be a real crusher.

The next day, then, Longstreet thought the situation favorable. Pope waited until afternoon to come at Jackson again and Longstreet waited until the Unions were fully committed against Old Jack. When Longstreet sent his fresh men in on the exposed Union flank, to Lee it must have been one of those counterblows every general dreams of—right under the heart.

The Union men staggered back under the impact. There was nothing else they could do. The impetuosity of the Rebels' charge on the broken lines was, a Northern observer said, "like demons emerging from the earth . . . mad with excitement, rage, and the fearful desire for blood which all feel at such times. . . ." The boys in the University (of Mississippi) Greys, running ahead with Hood's new division, thought that was a little strong when they read it later, though they were somewhat impressed to think they had given the impression of demons.

The Union Army as a whole, however, was far from routed. Stabilized by George Sykes's Regular troops, divisions and batteries fought hard and skillfully in a retreat which checked the pursuit (with rare dramatic coincidence) on the Henry House Hill, where the old widow had been killed the year before while Jackson stemmed the Union tide. At night the

Unions moved on to Centreville, across the sluggish stream of Bull Run, almost like a rerun film from the year before. There Pope, who apparently never was sure of what had happened, formed to await an attack.

Frontal assault against that mass was not Lee's method, not when he was himself. He sent Jackson circling around again. Jackson's men were worn out. They moved on the last day of August over Virginia roads that, under the rain of two days, lived up to their reputation of being bottomless. On the first day of September, well covered by Stuart in a continuation of his flawless performance, Jackson's men reached a flanking position near an old mansion, called Chantilly. Every home with any claim to prominence in the white-column set had a name in the South, but Chantilly was only a name, since the house had suffered total destruction.

Near the desolate mansion in thick woods, about half of Jackson's men tangled with parts of two Union divisions in one of the weirdest engagements in the war. The men remembered the terrific thunder and lightning more than the fighting. Nothing decisive could be accomplished by either side, and Jackson's flanking movement came to an end there in the lightning-lit wet woods.

One of the Union division leaders, one-armed Phil Kearny, was shot as he rode through those woods with the reins in his teeth and a sword in his hand. On seeing the corpse, emotional A. P. Hill said, "Poor Kearny, he deserved a better death than this."

Jackson's action at Chantilly was not without effect. Pope took his army all the way back to the protecting guns of Alexandria and Washington. As with McClellan at Richmond, Lee had failed to destroy an army. But in the three months since he took command—with Confederates backed up in Richmond and Federals overrunning the state—he had virtually cleared Virginia of invaders. The war in Virginia was right back where it had started at Bull Run.

5

Lee had no intention of duplicating Bull Run beyond that, and so repeating the purposeless inaction of the summer before. Like his father in the Revolution, like Stonewall Jackson, and the soldiers who were beginning to call him "Uncle Robert," the aggressive-minded gentleman planned to *win* their independence. Coming into the fight in primal defense of his land, he planned to take the fight to the enemy—in his own land.

Pope had gone then, returned to the obscurity from which the setups in the West had briefly released him. As Pope said, where he had come from they were accustomed to seeing the backs of the enemy; in Virginia he saw their faces, coming at him where they weren't expected. Lincoln was forced to restore McClellan to command, where he was received with wild cheers by the army.

Lee also probably welcomed the return of his cautious friend. He would need an opponent he understood when he ventured into the enemy country, leaving his own state denuded of troops in the conviction that Lincoln would send all available Unions after him.

This bold decision was Lee's, though naturally the general cleared through the President. Lee's prestige was then immense, and the Southern papers expressed the people's desire that he strike back at the enemy. The people had had enough of merely defending against an enemy who proved to be bent on their destruction. Lee decided at the psychologically sound moment. All the signs and portents were right.

There were no political considerations with the Union to restrain him. With the issues of the war swallowed up in the war itself, it was becoming obvious, as stated in the Albany news organ of U. S. Secretary of State Seward, "that the contest between us and the Confederates is reduced to a question of pure brute force. . . ."

Since this was manifestly the case, a Confederate Army loose on United States soil, threatening the capital and other cities, would place the Richmond government in a position to advance a proposal for honorable peace. As Lee wrote the President, this "could in no way be regarded as suing for peace; but, being made when it is our power to inflict injury upon our adversary, would show conclusively to the world that our sole object is the establishment of our independence and the attainment of an honorable peace."

Showing *the world* was a bid for European recognition. This could in turn influence the United States in accepting a peace proposal, either directly through the government, or through the citizens in the fall elections. Thus Lee reasoned, in any case. On the European phase, he was entirely right.

Though some British textile manufacturers were still making fortunes out of the Confederacy's cotton embargo, the pinch of a cotton shortage was beginning to be felt, presaging the closing of mills and the suffering of thousands of unemployed workers. Along with this, powerful members of the aristocracy, sympathetic to the South, were urging the government to recognize the Confederacy in the brotherhood of world nations. The British government stood at the point of taking this decisive step, and France would definitely follow.

To influence Europe, as well as the United States, Lee's Virginia victories were supported by a great Confederate upsurge in the West, where the war was already being carried to the enemy. At the beginning of summer, the Confederates had been shoved down into the lower South, with only one weak force as far north as the hostile country of East Tennessee, only Vicksburg left on the Mississippi—and that under siege by the combined U.S. gunboat river fleets. Now two Confederate forces had cleared most of Tennessee of the enemy and moved farther north in Kentucky than the Rebels had ever been.

Of equal significance, the combined U.S. river fleets lost their undisturbed domination of the Mississippi. One of Naval Secretary Mallory's homemade contrivances of destruction, the *Arkansas*, took on the whole fleet and broke the river siege of Vicksburg. At the state capital of Baton Rouge, "Beast" Butler took alarm and retreated to the safety of New Orleans, where he had only civilians to fight. Thus, instead of Vicksburg holding out through a lonely siege, the Confederacy got back a three-hundred-mile stretch of their own river, and on the western side a new force was being raised in Arkansas.

The general impression could certainly suggest that the Southern states, after a naturally slow start against an organized nation, had collected their resources and were successfully driving the invader from the land. This was an illusion.

The Southern defenses in the West had collapsed early because of planlessness on the high level, poor matériel, and divided command on the local levels, plus the power of the U. S. Navy used against farmers. Then, when Halleck lost purpose after Corinth and scattered his might, Braxton Bragg surprised the Unions by seizing the initiative in the first offensive campaign conceived by a Southerner in the West.

By then, the South had had time to construct a floating fortress (the makeshift and unstable engines of the *Arkansas* would scarcely make "ship" the proper nomenclature) to dispute U.S. naval domination of the river, and in Butler the Union came in for some overdue vagaries of personal commanders. All that was a temporary situation, though it could be used for immediate advantage.

The same applied to the triumphant status of Lee's new Army of Northern Virginia. His troops were in hard case, even by Confederate standards. The marching and the fighting had worn out his men along with their shoes and clothes. Horses were breaking down and were scarcely adequate for cavalry, guns, and wagons. The poor old wagons had never been designed for such stress, and their wheels creaked and bodies groaned with every turn. To compensate for the 9000-plus casualties of the Second Manassas campaign, Richmond was stripped of the troops there, with D. H. Hill recalled from North Carolina to his old division. Even with this total concentration of troops, leaving the capital unprotected, Lee had little more than 50,000.

Against this McClellan could call on three times that number, with more coming in. Nothing could be gained by waiting for McClellan to bring the armies, reconcentrated under him, back into Virginia. Lee's decision to invade, then, had an element of necessity. The strike had to come then or never.

This necessity contained another aspect of immediate practical consideration. If Virginia could be freed of both armies, the farmers would have a chance to harvest crops, while the Confederates at the same time could victual themselves in the enemy's country—not by confiscation but by purchase.

Finally Lee, as did other Southerners, overestimated the Confederate sentiment in Maryland. He hoped to recruit for his army there. His hope never materialized. However, his Proclamation to the people of Maryland (September 8) did serve as a means of communicating to the world the peaceful intentions of the Confederate government, committed to the principle of "government by the consent of the governed," and opened the way for an honorable peace proposal to be submitted by Davis—if Jefferson Davis would have followed this suggestion of Lee.

Before any action was taken on the diplomatic level, the whole plan of invasion, with its high and far-reaching consequences, was wrecked by the three most famous cigars in history.

6

When the ragamuffins of Lee's army waded across the Potomac on September 5 and 6, they might not have been aware of the high destiny that marched with them, but the soldiers felt an elation such as would never quite come again to the Army of Northern Virginia. The bands played "My Maryland," the men cheered and sang, and the atmosphere was more of picnickers than of an invading army.

The soldiers did not regard themselves as invaders of Maryland. The Marylanders scattered through the army not only looked forward to seeing their families and friends but had prepared their comrades for a festive reception. The soldiers thought of themselves as liberators journeying among friends.

Their first stop was at Frederick in south-central Maryland, at the hub of main roads in all directions—due north to Pennsylvania and due south to the Potomac, east to Baltimore, southeast to Washington, northwest to Hagerstown, and southwest to Harper's Ferry. Tactically, the army was most favorably situated for movement and for the creation of uncertainty in their old friend McClellan. Materially, they were situated in a fertile country whose people were on the whole friendly.

Though there was no rush of recruiting, and no official welcoming committees of freedmen eager to have Southerners move "the despot's heel" from their shores, individual Southern sympathizers showered the men with attentions. There was white bread with butter, real coffee with sugar, fried chicken, spirituous liquors to fill the canteens of those indomitable whiskey-foragers, and many unaccustomed dainties, both homemade and store-bought from the confectioners. The men vastly enjoyed shopping in town, though not all the proprietors shared their pleasure. Hats were an especially coveted item, and Jackson's topographer bought his general a new hat. The famous cadet cap was finally discarded (to become at last a treasured item of the college where he had bored the students).

In the few days the army tarried at Frederick, the soldiers had time to cook apple dumplings in the camp kettles during the lazy afternoons, when they always received some "fair visitors." Young Douglas, Old Jack's aide, was visited by his mother and had the pleasure of introducing her to both General Lee and Jackson. At night there were dances, though these were chiefly for the benefit of the officers—particularly Stuart and his staff.

Sometimes women held their noses and waved Union flags when they passed the soldiers, who, a young Frederick boy said, "were the dirtiest men I ever saw, a most ragged, lean and hungry set of wolves. Yet there was a dash about them that the Northern men lacked. They rode like circus riders . . . were profane beyond belief and talked incessantly." The men swaggered a little more at horrified stares and grinned at the flag-waving ladies. Definitely *not* among those ladies was ninety-year-old Barbara Frietchie, at the time bedridden with her mortal illness. The abolition poet Whittier drew on his imagination about her defiance of Jackson, as he had for his heart-wringers of slave life.

In fact, Old Jack was ambulance-ridden himself most of the time, since he had been defied by a gift horse. His own horse, Fancy, called "Little Sorrel" by the troops, had been stolen. Before it was recovered, a Southern sympathizer presented the general with a powerful gray mare, "more suitable for artillery than the saddle," said Jackson's aide. The moment she felt the spur, the new mount reared straight up and kept going—backward, until horse and rider collapsed in a heap to the ground.

Longstreet continued to rival Old Jack in arresting his major generals —this time with the Texans' John B. Hood. When Hood was arrested, his troops protested to the point of mutiny, and Lee overruled Longstreet to assure the services of Hood in the coming campaign.

For the soldiers, the pleasant excursion ended all too soon, and it was to be the only pleasant memory they were to have of Maryland. Some unknown staff-officer of D. H. Hill must have enjoyed himself liberally in Frederick, too, since he left three cigars behind when the army moved out.

When Lee sent to his generals his secret order of detailed plans for the campaign, each general filed safely away or destroyed the vital information. As D. H. Hill was also a part of Jackson's command, Old Jack sent a duplicate to Hill, and the duplicate apparently reached Hill first. When the order from Lee's headquarters, signed by Colonel Chilton, came to

Hill's headquarters, evidently somebody decided that the matter had already been settled. This mysterious accomplice of fate used the paper as a wrapper for three cigars, and then lost the whole package. Needless to say, no one ever came forward to admit his guilt.

When the Unions moved in on the abandoned Confederate camp grounds outside the town, an Indiana volunteer pounced on the unexpected prize of cigars left by Rebels. It was in opening the package to get the cigars that Mitchell glanced at the writing, and then returned to it in one of history's epic second-takes. Special Order ✕191 was hurried rapidly to the top, from sergeant to captain to colonel to division commander to McClellan's headquarters. With astronomical odds against such a thing happening in the first place, to that was added a fantastic coincidence. One of McClellan's staff officers had been a peacetime friend of Lee's aide, and identified Colonel Chilton's handwriting. The Union general possessed the disposition of Confederate troops in probably the most dangerous dispersion ever deliberately undertaken in enemy territory.

7

Lee had made this reckless dispersal on his understanding of McClellan's caution and slowness to act. Certainly until the orders were delivered into his hands, McClellan had been absolutely supine. Though a composite of reports placed Lee's army at not more than 50,000—and all stressed its wretched condition, of bare feet and tatters, with men feeding on green corn—McClellan showed no disposition to molest the sojourning Rebels. Without the lost order, Lee would undoubtedly have completed his concentration near Pennsylvania. With it, McClellan moved to intercept the details of Lee's boldly scattered army.

Very roughly Frederick formed the apex of a triangle, leading northwest to Hagerstown and southwest to Harper's Ferry. The base, between Harper's Ferry and Hagerstown, ran forty miles by road and was crossed by the Potomac, where the river swung northwesterly in a series of loops. Lee's northern advance guard under Longstreet was at Hagerstown. Jackson's three divisions plus three others were forty miles to the south at Harper's Ferry, enclosing that Union garrison on three sides.

That was the major dispersal. But the two wings were again divided within themselves. Following Longstreet and the wagons as rear guard came D. H. Hill, some ten miles back. At Harper's Ferry the forces were divided by the Shenandoah and the Potomac, as troops took the commanding heights for the reduction of the Union garrison. That garrison was the reason for the dispersal. Lee could not wander around the North with 11,000 troops and seventy-three guns at his rear.

The garrison part of the plan worked well. The whole force surrendered, and the Confederates continued to supply their deficiencies of arms and matériel from the enemy—thirteen thousand rifles in addition to the seventy-three cannons, two hundred desperately needed wagons, and the customary quartermaster stores. All unaware of the fate enclosing them, Jackson's men ate heartily (thousands for the last time) and enjoyed fraternizing with the Unions.

The Federal soldiers were good-humored about the disreputable appearance of their captors and greatly interested in talking about Stonewall Jackson. A New York reporter damned Jackson for his seedy appearance, "in no respect to be distinguished from the mongrel, bare-footed crew who follow his fortunes." As for them, "Ireland in her worst straits could present no parallel, and yet they glory in their shame." But the Union soldiers took a different view.

"He isn't much for looks," one of them said, "but if we'd had him we wouldn't be caught in this trap."

Unbeknownst to friend and enemy, Old Jack was worrying about the trap that was suddenly being sprung on the Rebels. That is, it was sudden from their point. From the Union point, McClellan had delayed sixteen unrecoverable hours in starting his drive between the divided forces.

East of the Hagerstown–Harper's Ferry base line ran a rugged mountain range, which McClellan, moving ponderously out from Frederick, must cross to get at the Rebels. Stuart's cavalry, guarding the two gaps, was so severely pressed by infantry that he called for support. Then, by the spreading campfires at night, it became obvious to Stuart that McClellan was bringing his whole army, with unprecedented rapidity, to the vulnerable openings between Lee's wings. Later, when a Southern sympathizer reached Stuart with the startling news that McClellan had found an important order, the cavalryman understood McClellan's unwonted aggressiveness and certainty of movement. Continuing his magnificent performance in the northern extension of the Second Manassas campaign, Stuart hurried off the whole information to Lee.

On the following day D. H. Hill's division fought one of the bloodiest and greatest defensive fights of the war (South Mountain, September 14) in standing off five Union divisions at the pass over South Mountain. Hill's men had been driven back and were done beyond five minutes more of fight when night fell, but McClellan had been delayed a full day. Harvey Hill brought his battered men down the mountain at night.

At the pass farther south, Stuart with some infantry from Jackson had fallen back all the way to the foot, but the Unions were held there at dark, a temporary check before morning.

By morning all the Confederates were hurrying on sore and bloody feet to the point of concentration. This was at the little town of Sharpburg, practically midway between Hagerstown and Harper's Ferry. In their front was Antietam Creek, and low ridges of the pleasant rolling countryside formed some natural protection. At their back was a ford over the Potomac. Across that on the morning of September 16, two of Jackson's divisions waded after a night march from Harper's Ferry.

McClellan had then concentrated over 80,000 troops, with their awesome guns, on Lee's front: they'd come up the afternoon and early evening of the day before. Of Lee's scant 50,000 men in forty brigades, eighteen brigades were still at Harper's Ferry and the men of Jackson's recently arrived eight brigades were sleeping in exhaustion, while waiting for the attack.

Incredibly it never came that day. The brilliant and charming George McClellan, thirty-five years old and a darling of the gods, had been given a present by the gods such as few men ever receive. But the gods had compensated for their lavishness by putting in McClellan's character a fame-conscious need of having everything just so.

On the next day, the seventeenth, when McClellan turned his tremendous guns and powerful army loose on the hungry tatterdemalions, the eighteen Confederate brigades from Harper's Ferry had either arrived or came on during the day and the others had had twenty-four hours' rest.

When the battle was joined, the armies were all beyond strategy then. It was a slugging match, with the Confederates standing and reeling, standing again and reeling again, against the heavy blows of fresh lines driving at them. Sometimes they essayed local counterstrokes which stemmed the tide for a moment, giving shattered units time to re-form, giving troops from a less threatened point time to hurry over to the breach.

It was worse than Second Manassas. It was worse than anything. The Army of Northern Virginia would never be called on to endure such a day again. It couldn't have endured more than one.

The cavalry fought as infantry, young Pelham's horse-guns holding the extreme left flank. With McClellan's heavier armor concentrating on Confederate guns, it was murder for Lee's cannoneers. Crews were decimated and the guns knocked about. Staff officers righted the pieces and served them, Longstreet helping load one.

Young Starke, who had commanded the Stonewall Division at Second Manassas, inherited it again when the senior officer was wounded. Starke was killed horribly. A lieutenant colonel took command of the famous division. In its 2nd Brigade a lieutenant commanded the 21st Virginia Regiment.

The left was dented, the center splintered, and the dazed men fought on. Late came the thrust to the right, where Antietam Creek was crossed by a stone bridge—Burnside's Bridge, they called it, because he took his corps there. Burnside, the Regular Army man, A. P. Hill's classmate at West Point, was stood off during the afternoon by two brigades, one commanded by old Bob Toombs. The bluff Georgian fought with guns that day the way he used to fight with words in Washington. He was making his big play for the Confederate fame. It eluded him.

When finally his small force holding the bridge was pushed back, and the Unions swarmed across on Lee's flank and potential rear, their own flank was hit by the last arriving troops from Harper's Ferry. This was the division of Burnside's classmate, Powell Hill. Detained at Harper's Ferry to complete the details of surrender and temporarily released from his arrest in order to lead his troops, Little Powell, in a fireman's red hunting shirt, hustled his men the sixteen miles under the hot sun and threw the brigades in as they arrived. Toombs, who really served that day, was forgotten in the phrase that recorded Hill's arrival—"And then A. P. Hill came up."

Eight years later when Lee was dying he, like Jackson, still remembered the fighting of that great division commander. In his delirium he called, "Tell A. P. Hill he must come up!"

It was all over then.

At a cost of over 13,000 casualties (South Mountain and Sharpsburg), more than a fourth of his men, Lee kept his army from destruction. There had been no room for strategy. In handling troops in action against overwhelming odds, Lee, with Jackson, Longstreet, both Hills and Hood, with tough-bitten Jubal Early, who had risen to prominence after the wounding of Dick Ewell, had shown themselves masters of the profession most respected in the South.

The following day, the eighteenth, Lee kept a bold front to the enemy while his wagons were loaded with wounded. The Unions had been hard hit too. Counting the 11,000 gobbled up at Harper's Ferry, they suffered over 27,000 casualties. McClellan, with Lee apparently waiting for him to try again, risked no more.

That night Lee brought his limping men back to Virginia. The few bands tried to raise spirits by playing "Carry Me Back to Ole Vuhginny." Though nobody cheered on that crossing of the Potomac, they were undaunted. No one disagreed with the Southerner who said of those ragged valiants, "None but Heroes Were Left."

8

Politically, the war ended at Sharpsburg for the Confederacy. That was the last chance the Southern states had really to win independence.

By then, Lincoln's declared purposes of the armed invasion were meaningless. Yet, as the real purpose of the armed invasion was to return by force the eleven states of 5,500,000 white people who wanted to be free, it was not possible to proclaim that a whole section, formed into a nation, was to be subjugated by all-out war and *made* to consent to be governed.

That would admit the United States was not dealing with a combination of insurgents but with a people who, in asserting the rights of self-determination, had erected a legal form of government and successfully defended their borders. Once that was tacitly admitted the cry of "Union" might ring a little hollow, both in the United States and abroad.

But something had to be done. The "suppression" was well into the second year, at a cost of nearly 200,000 casualties, and the second Union army had been driven out of Virginia, with the Confederates having invaded the North. In the West things were no better. The Southerners were obviously going to fight for their independence until they were totally conquered. The war had to get a slogan, and Lincoln gave it: "To free the slaves."

When Lincoln (in repudiation of his own inaugural words) gave the Emancipation Proclamation as a war measure, he wrote Greeley, "If I could preserve the Union without freeing the Negro, I would do so."

That it was a war measure Lincoln made very clear by applying the Proclamation only to the states in rebellion, and not in all parts of those. Divided Missouri and Kentucky were excluded, as well as loyal Delaware and Maryland. The slaves were freed only where Lincoln had no authority at the time. He freed the slaves of the enemy.

In using the Negro and slavery as an expedient of war, Lincoln saddled the Southern people (not only slaveholders) with an onus of guilt for generations to come, gave the rest of the United States a false reason for moral superiority, and—as of 1862—immobilized the division between the sections, to which further bloodshed would add further bitterness and misunderstanding.

Ex-President Buchanan said that Lincoln's Administration had departed "from the principle of conducting the war for the restoration of the Union . . . [and] had resolved to conduct it for the subjugation of the Southern states and the destruction of slavery."

Despite the change of principles, the future effect on the South and the future confusion of Americans, the Emancipation Proclamation certainly put heart back into the war by supplying a slogan of more appeal than "preserving the Union." The old "moral" issue of the cold war gave the Union a crusade, as the Virginia legislator had predicted thirty years before, for waging a total war of conquest.

With the new slogan for the Union, all hope of foreign intervention went for the Confederacy. The British millworkers, though suffering unemployment for want of cotton, threw a fervid support behind the Union's fight for the freedom of man. The pro-Southern aristocrats could not then have forced recognition, which had become impractical with the failure of Lee's invasion.

When Lee brought his half-wrecked and exhausted army back to Virginia, the bold strokes for winning independence were left behind—

back with the 40,000 casualties his army had suffered in its whole summer campaign in the pre-slogan days. With the Confederacy outnumbered nearly four to one to begin with, the odds lengthened against them as they suffered equal and not proportionate losses with the Federals. For the future the only hope would be to outlast the enemy's will to conquer, as the long struggle entered its final phase of total war behind the new slogan.

There was still reason to hope to outlast the enemy. Lee, as aggressive-minded as ever, knew that when his veterans were rested, his sick well, his casualties returned, he had an army that could stand up to anything. In the four months since he had inherited the hodgepodge of unrelated divisions backed up against Richmond, he had created in the Army of Northern Virginia an army that would live in legends as long as tales were told about fighting men. Even in their battered state, McClellan—rebuilding his army to 130,000—showed no hostility toward them.

Other Union generals would try again in Virginia, and Lee would try again to catch an army where he could destroy it.

Meanwhile, as the invasion had accomplished the practical purpose of freeing the state of enemy troops, Uncle Robert could victual his starved men and horses in their fertile plain west of Harper's Ferry. The wheat harvest gave the men flour bread again, and fattened beef cattle provided vitally needed meat. The horses, who had been sharing the green-corn diet of the men, developed a new and unfamiliar sheen with hay and grains.

In October, Jeb Stuart took 1500 men on the famous Chambersburg raid. If accomplishing little from a practical turn besides replenishing their sorry stock of draft horses and wagons, the audacious raid into enemy country and the hairbreadth escape did kindle army morale and keep the people's spirits up.

Unmolested by the enemy in the bright, mellow autumn, Lee's soldiers began to take a philosophic attitude about their recent invasion. Though they knew nothing about the three cigars, the men felt that luck just hadn't been with them on the enemy's soil. But when it came to repelling an invader—particularly if they could get some shoes—they were more than eager for another crack at him on their own land.

Though their summer campaign had failed of the ultimate throw for independence, they had to regard it as a solid success in defense. They had only to compare their present situation with the tense hours before Richmond, and their confidence for defending forever grew as their emaciated bodies filled out, as tatters were exchanged for once discarded civilian clothes sent from home, and as their spirits were lifted by the boxes sent by ladies' auxiliaries with such luxury items as knitted socks and scarves for the coming cold. The soldiers went cheerfully about the camp routines, while Lee reorganized the units to replace officers and men, and sang the new song, "There's Life in the Old Land Yet."

They did not have many bands, but they were great singers. The more dignified Southerners frowned on the minstrel tune "Dixie," and tried hard to promote a national anthem out of such songs as "The Southern Cross," "God Save the South," and "The Bonnie Blue Flag," written shortly after South Carolina seceded. "Dixie" became their unofficial anthem by popular acclaim, and the soldiers sang some hilarious verses to it over a bottle of smuggled-in busthead in the fragrant fall nights of 1862.

Section Three

THE TOTAL WAR

CHAPTER XIII

The President Takes a Trip

IN SEPTEMBER of 1862, while Lee was still in Maryland, prospects looked bright in the Confederate West for the first time in the war. With the enemy driven out of Tennessee, except in the river area, people returned to their abandoned homes in little hamlets where the one hotel was boarded up, returned to their farms and set about repairing the ravages, hunting in the woods for cows and horses hidden months before, and hogs turned wild with their freedom. The young and old took to the woods with shotguns for rabbit and quail, with an eye out for any Yankee deserters lurking around.

In the cities, where everything must be bought, the pinch was not so bad and spirits rose at the news of their armies advancing toward the North. Their money held, even after Sharpsburg, at one to two against gold, and though food was high, only the imported coffee and scarce salt were really out of sight. The still-brewed bourbon was plentiful for use, as the British correspondent wrote, "as a prophylactic against the influence of the morning dews." For the first time since the invasion, the people in the Western Confederacy had something to drink to.

Their success came from the unlikeliest general in all their armies, rough-visaged Braxton Bragg, the martinet about whom the soldiers wrote those bitter and complaining letters. Bragg had literally been offered the opportunity when the Unions, apparently grown flatulent with success in the West, dispersed their forces in the evident expectation that the Confederates would remain permanently fixed in their scattered, defensive alignments. Bragg broke the fix.

Hated disciplinarian that he was, the migraine sufferer could train and condition troops for marching, and in their sudden and heady triumph marching had been all required of them—thanks to Bragg's bold and superbly executed plan.

Bragg had been down in Mississippi with the army he inherited from Albert Sidney Johnston via Beauregard, plus a fair-sized force from west of the river, when Halleck made his great dispersal. Grant was left with a force in northern Mississippi, while Buell led another force along the southern border of Tennessee toward Chattanooga, on the eastern tip. Chattanooga was the one railroad junction that linked the Mississippi with the Atlantic coast, and the way from Chattanooga led directly to Atlanta—in turn, a railroad-junction city between the coast and the lower South. There were no Confederate forces at Chattanooga and the nearest, north at Knoxville, was more than occupied with the Unionists in East Tennessee and another Federal force.

While Grant did nothing significant in Mississippi, Bragg observed that Buell was having a rough time moving his army overland across Tennessee and northern Alabama. The tenuous Southern railroad system (by which he was supplied from Nashville) was constantly interrupted by two alert and aggressive cavalry raiders, John Morgan and Bedford Forrest.

The ferocious Forrest of the legends, with his quotable and often misquoted "fust with the most" (*not* "fustest with the mostest"), was one of those few Rebels who fought with an innate understanding of the needs of their cause. Born, as Southerners say, "dirt-dog poor," of a pioneer family to the then new Southwest, he acquired wealth and power as a dealer in land, cotton and, to show his lack of social aspirations, slaves. At the age of forty he enlisted as a private when his state seceded, and by his native gift for warfare rose steadily despite the lack of enthusiasm with which he was regarded by some "regular" West Pointers.

He raised his own commands, supplied them from the enemy, and for wagoners used forty-two of his slaves (to whom he had willed freedom in the event of his death). His non-blasphemous swearing could sear the hide off man or mule; he feared nothing on earth and was belligerent almost beyond comprehension. Against Buell, like Jackson's forces in the Valley, Forrest's forces grew and armaments improved as his raids frustrated the Unions' lateral advance on Chattanooga.

The other raider, John Hunt Morgan, came of the more traditional Southern background and as a soldier was more in the romantic tradition of the partisan leader. Thirty-seven years old in 1862, of a well-to-do Lexington merchandising family (his sister was the wife of A. P. Hill), Morgan had experienced just sufficient military life, briefly in the Mexican War and with one of those semisocial militia companies, to become infatuated with the glamour of mounted troops.

He was a powerfully built man of imposing appearance, with a flashing smile beneath his mustachios, and was possessed of great personal magnetism. His troops were almost all Kentuckians fighting a most personal war, sometimes against their own brothers and frequently against neighbors and kinsmen. Such discipline as touched them came from St. Leger Grenfell, a sixty-year-old British soldier of fortune, though some of Morgan's highborn leaders developed a gift for military leadership. Essentially his devoted troops were "Morgan's Men," and he led their forays like the knights of old. Riding into their Kentucky homeland and wrecking the harassed Buell's lines, he published a proclamation which began:

Strike for the green graves of your sires!
Strike for your altars and your fires!
For God and your native land. . . .

With Buell's army scattered in protecting railroads against these active horsemen, in September Bragg made his own great swing. Using the Southern railroads as they had never been used before—seven and a steamboat—he had in late July moved along the two sides of a triangle from Mississippi, west of Buell, to Mobile far south, and back north to Chattanooga east of Buell. From there (August 28) his compact army struck north across Tennessee for Buell's supply lines and Kentucky. Bragg had left the Missouri forces in Mississippi to ward off Grant. As they kept him from serious mischief as well as occupied, there was nothing for it for Buell except to collect his scattered groups as hurriedly as possible and race Bragg for Louisville.

To heighten the Confederates' elation, the force at Knoxville, under Kirby Smith, was paralleling Bragg, knocking over its Union opponents on the way and heading for Cincinnati. Both forces were welcomed by Southern sympathizers along the way, everybody ate high on the hog, and thousands returning to the neighborhoods of their homes sang:

"I'se gwine to jine the Rebel band,
A-fightin' for my home. . . ."

2

At this hour of high destiny for the Confederacy, General Bragg needed what did not then exist in all America—a psychiatrist.

Like many another general on both sides, educated for war and experienced in combat as a line officer, at the ultimate test of committing an army to battle, with the lifetime's reputation hanging on the outcome, he shrank from the decision. If the decision was forced upon him by the enemy, his nerves collapsed under the strain and he lost the use of his intelligence, training, and experience. Once in Kentucky, confronting Buell, Bragg both avoided the decision and then collapsed when it was forced upon him.

In mid-September, Bragg had won the race for Louisville and stood squarely across Buell's path: indeed, he could have gone in himself. Instead, he turned aside, and allowed the relieved Federal to reach his goal in safety. As if to explain this aberration, Bragg went off with his staff for a week to attend the ceremonies of inaugurating a Confederate governor in Kentucky. After observing this strange behavior, Buell went on the offense, and Bragg anticlimaxed his dazzling march with a weird retrograde movement.

In central Kentucky, Bragg could avoid combat no longer. Though he had senselessly scattered his troops during his gyrations, and was outnumbered against Buell, those men in the Western armies thirsted for a victory. At Perryville (October 8) they demonstrated their quality as troops, attacking as if odds were of no consequence, and forced back parts of Buell's line. Elated at their partial success, the soldiers confidently expected to win a solid victory the next day.

That night, in his headquarters in a house near the field, Bragg suffered the near breakdown of his self-control. He was joined in the parlor by Bishop Polk, a corps commander, and William Hardee, another corps commander. Hardee, in his late forties, was an old army man who had authored a standard textbook on military tactics which was widely used in the Confederacy in the early days. A conscientious, unassertive, and deeply devoted Confederate, Hardee, with Bishop Polk, anxiously watched their general pace the floor, rubbing one hand with the other, his face revealing tormented thoughts that no one could imagine. Out of his bewildered anguish, the only decision Bragg could reach was to withdraw.

After their thousand-mile hegira, Bragg's troops started marching away from the enemy. Sore of foot and heavy of heart, they trudged day after day back to East Tennessee, with growing hate of their commanding general.

The army was accompanied by herds of sheep, hogs, and beef cattle, and four thousand new U.S. wagons loaded with supplies, ammunition, and guns—the best rifles that United States money could buy. Along with capturing those supplies, Bragg's marching army had accomplished a great deal for the Confederacy. He had completely frustrated the Union's first clumsy groping toward Chattanooga, the arrowhead pointed at the South's vitals; and in ejecting the invader, with the consequent morale lift to the people, he could provision his own army at the fat granary of Middle Tennessee.

But the psychotic warrior had not done what he should, even what he could. He knew it, and he knew that his officers and men knew it.

Once he was safely back in Tennessee, with his inner furies silent, he took a train for the roundabout ride to Richmond. He was going to make face with his friend and supporter in the White House.

3

An affinity existed between the forty-five-year-old North Carolinian and Jefferson Davis, nine years his senior. Both were very "regular" in their approach to the military, both lacked the gift for those spontaneous, intuitive actions that cannot be learned, and both suffered ailments of psychogenic origin when under stress.

Davis in the past year had gone from one suffering to another—dyspepsia, facial neuralgia, ophthalmic pains—and his face showed the strain that was beyond his equipment to support. The hollows looked chiseled out of his cheeks, his mouth was thin and hard, and unyielding will set the pale, gaunt face in sharp lines. With that will, in his conceit and the inflexibility of his type of "made" intelligence, Davis tried to do everything for the nation's defense himself, as if in fear of anything involving the military getting out of his hands.

Kean, in the Bureau of War, said that he wasted time on "trash that ought to be dispatched by clerks," and War Secretary Randolph said that Davis "does not discriminate between important and unimportant matters." Randolph also said that the President "has no practical knowledge of the workings of our military system in the field."

Davis considered that knowledge to be his genius. On this conviction he based his departmentalized defense system, with himself as the final authority on everything. In this way, with all the forms of a traditional government, in the practical sense there was never a commanding general of the Confederate armies who assumed responsibility for those armies and their military actions—as, for instance, Lee assumed responsibility for his army from its victualing to its strategy.

There was no one to relate the Army of Northern Virginia to another army in terms of total strategy. As Davis was committed to the static defense, total strategy did not exist in the Confederacy. Instead Davis, with his mind immobilized in bureaucratic habits, simulated an over-all command situation by means of the departments into which he arbitrarily divided the territory.

His unself-questioning sense of rightness in imposing his methods and opinions on men in the field—generals dealing every hour with the living details of their army and its condition, the enemy and the ground—suggested the egotism that hardened with power. In Davis' case, since he was incorruptible, it could be said that power did not corrupt but stupefied him.

While he never admitted, even to Mrs. Davis, any sense of inadequacy for the vast authority he assumed, the President did plead increasingly for help from Heaven. In the spring of that year, he was baptized at home and privately confirmed by Bishop Johns in St. Paul's Episcopal Church. A wag commented, "I think Mr. Davis is turning for help to a higher power than England or France."

With the help of whatever inner force sustained him, the President always took adversity like a man, as far as it was within his control. His color might fade a little and his lips involuntarily tighten, but he gave way to no lamentation.

When Braxton Bragg came with the tales of his troubles, in which he tried to shift the blame of his failure to others, Davis without reproaches offered full support to his regular friend and fellow dyspeptic.

Bragg entered some serious charges of defection against Bishop Polk, who immediately demanded a court-martial, for which Hardee offered to sustain him with evidence that would wreck Bragg. Davis quieted Polk and induced his old West Point friend to continue his loyalty to the man who tried to knife him. Kirby Smith had sent in complaints that Bragg, as commanding general, failed him in co-operation between their two forces in the Kentucky campaign, and Davis quieted Smith by transferring him to Texas—which Smith considered an exile.

Bragg was sent back, with the aura of his disaster around him, to take on the next Union assault into Tennessee aimed for Chattanooga. By then it was clear to the Confederates that, as Richmond was the Union objective in the East, Chattanooga was the objective in the center, and the Union forces along the Mississippi, somewhat aimless since Shiloh, were concentrating on the last river stronghold of Vicksburg. The war was growing big when three different Union armies undertook three separate objectives. For this large-scale warfare the Federals tried new generals.

McClellan was banished again, this time for good, to be replaced by Burnside (more famous for his whiskers than his generalship), and for Chattanooga Rosecrans replaced the long-suffering Buell. Both Burnside and Rosecrans came in with orders to strike heavily at the Rebels, as Lincoln was still trying for that knockout punch that would prevent the inconceivable dislocations of a long-drawn-out conflict.

For the blow against Vicksburg, Grant was kept on, though Lincoln was a little dubious about him. In his first overland attempt, Grant had exposed his supplies as recklessly as had Pope in Virginia, and a cavalry force under Van Dorn ruined his whole winter campaign with the destruction of his base at Holly Springs in northern Mississippi. Grant's right-hand man, Sherman, had tried a back-door attack on Vicksburg and the Rebels roughly drove him away.

But Grant was a busy general and his troops outnumbered the oddments of forces left in Mississippi when Bragg took off in the summer. To consolidate this heterogeneous collection, Davis sent out another regular, John Clifford Pemberton. This Pennsylvanian, whose sympathies went with the South through his marriage to a Norfolk girl, was a devoted Confederate and a trained soldier, but his sternness as a regulation general and the cold reserve of his social manner made him a very poor choice to lead those unruly Western troops—mostly products of the half-disciplined forces who fought the savage, personal wars in the wastelands of Arkansas and Missouri.

With untried Pemberton to defend Vicksburg and psychotic Bragg to defend Chattanooga, Davis then made his most revealing decision. Since he was manifestly unable to administer the details of the two separated

armies and unwilling to relinquish control of either, he formed the two
into a department under a co-ordinator responsible to him personally.
This general without authority was to supervise the transfer of troops,
under the President's orders, and act as something of an adjutant general's
officer on the scene. For this unrewarding assignment he selected the
second-ranking general in the Confederacy—ambitious, jealous, reputation-
conscious Joseph E. Johnston, recovered from his wound of early summer.

Now Joe Johnston's hatred of Davis amounted, Mrs. Chesnut said, "to
a religion with him." He had driven the President frantic by refusing to
communicate with him during the peninsula campaign and he detested
from the beginning his assignment in the West. Stating that his command
was only "nominal," he asked either to be given authority or relieved
from command. He rightly pointed out that Pemberton and Bragg were
not two wings of one army, but two armies with different objectives, in
different terrain, widely separated, and, in brief, no two armies could be
less designed for co-operation.

Davis dismissed Johnston's reasoning along with his feelings about the
matter. The President had worked out his chart of organization and in
the chart "Joe Johnston" did not symbolize a man—with all a mortal's
complexities and passions—but an item to be fitted into the department
as the chart maker designed.

Johnston relieved his disgust by writing friends letters critical of Davis
and spitefully jealous of Lee. One of his friends was fellow Virginian
George W. Randolph, Jefferson's grandson in the War Department. At
the time, the War Secretary was chafing under the indignities inflicted
by Davis' unconscious disregard of others' dignity and by being referred
to as "Davis' clerk." When Johnston, avoiding personal communication
with his enemy in the White House, called directly on the War Department for troops, Randolph decided to act directly and have a showdown
over his authority.

In the request for troops, Johnston was entirely sound. He wanted to
build up Pemberton's forces with idle troops from Arkansas. They were
accomplishing little in *their* grandiose Department of the Trans-Mississippi, horribly administered by old, deaf Holmes, transferred out of Lee's
army for ineptitude. But when Johnston bypassed the Commander in
Chief, only one result could be foreseen. Davis instantly countermanded
Randolph's order and sent him a stiff letter, from one block away, outlin-
ing the restricted functions of the War Secretary.

Randolph resigned, with his friends swelling the chorus of Davis' enemies. The former War Secretary then added a cynical note to the South's
struggle by selling his legal talents (and connections) to the defense of
conscript evaders. Pemberton was denied the needed troops; and Joe
Johnston was forced to swallow the gall of dealing directly with the
President if he hoped to accomplish anything for his country—let alone

for his reputation. He would have a chance to see the Commander in Chief personally.

Near the end of that year, 1862, Davis left Richmond for the first time during the war and made something of a personal inspection tour of his Western Department. He also had a secret mission, which must have seemed of extreme importance to him, for he left Richmond on the eve of a great battle for the Confederate capital.

4

The Battle of Fredericksburg was the result of each President's acting as his own Commander in Chief. Burnside, who had not sought the command of McClellan's army and probably did not want it, was goaded by Lincoln to get at Richmond right away by his favorite overland route, straight down from Washington. On the other side, Lee was forced by Davis to defend on ground not of his own choosing and which he and Jackson thought militarily unprofitable. Davis, in his obsession to hold ground defensively, arbitrarily decided on the Rappahannock River line and would not allow even Lee to retreat further in order to get maneuvering room for a counterblow on the Federals.

With the rival Presidents pushing the buttons, the two armies were forced to a stand-up fight at a city which was not important either to hold or to take. Fredericksburg—well situated for trade on the buff-colored Rappahannock, on the old Telegraph Road from Richmond to Washington, and on the new Richmond, Fredericksburg and Potomac Railroad—was one of the oldest and most charming cities in the country. From its founding in 1671, the community had enjoyed enriching and congenial trade with the planters and yeomanry of Piedmont Virginia, and was essentially a home city of well-to-do families with deep roots in the culture of Virginia. George Washington's mother had lived there (her house is still standing) and James Monroe had lived there and practiced law. In town, the lovely, red brick colonial houses sat flush on the streets, and in the environs plantation houses were enclosed in fine gardens. There was virtually no manufacturing in Fredericksburg—a couple of tanneries, a gristmill, and the like—and the life was as leisurely and mannerly and traditional as life on plantations.

From the beginning, the war had swirled around the city, devastating its countryside, and Fredericksburg had been occupied from April to August of 1862. Nothing worse had happened to it then than Pope's arrest of nineteen citizens, including the mayor, who were imprisoned in Old Capitol Jail in Washington. (Their offense had been that the Confederate authorities at Richmond removed a Unionist citizen from Fredericksburg to prevent his giving information to the enemy.) When Burnside's great army approached in late November, the Federals showed the effect of the new war that came into being with the crusade following on the Emancipation Proclamation.

The citizens were ordered to surrender the city or it would be shelled in sixteen hours—the time allotted for the evacuation of the old, the ill, and children. Lee replied that the city was non-combatant and he did not intend to defend it, but he advised the citizens to leave. Abandoning all their household goods, the families began to move out that night in a snowstorm. Some boarded the train to Richmond, others went in carriages and wagons to the homes of kinspeople and friends, and most bedded down in barns, cabins, and nearby country towns. The town was not then shelled, and Burnside devoted his energies for the next three weeks to getting at Lee.

The Federal commander had inherited an enormous army of somewhere around 125,000 of all services and, under Lincoln's prod to attack, he had moved with vigor and decision. A lot of excuses have been made for Burnside and extenuating circumstances offered. The fact remains that, with passable fords to the west of Fredericksburg, he threw his vast and finely trained army at the one impregnable defensive position on the Rappahannock River.

Though Lee had not wanted to fight there because, as Stonewall Jackson said, "we'll get no fruits of a victory," the general watched the Unions prepare to attack with the pleased interest of a spectator who knows everything is going to come out well. The city itself stretched back from the river on flat land, but outside the town the ground rose gently until it took the steep climb of Marye's Heights. Near the base of the hill a breast-high stone wall lined a sunken road, and there Lee placed most of the infantry. His guns went on the crest of the hill.

Two days before the battle opened, the Yankee cannoneers of 181 big guns held a daylong target practice on the houses in the partly deserted city. As some of the inhabitants had by then crept back from their barns and cabins, a number of families spent an unforgettable day of horror, huddling—with their children and old, slaves and families of freed Negroes—in candlelit cellars, with the masonry of their houses crashing above them. That night most of the civilians fled, but a few hung on and were still there when Burnside threw his pontoons across on the bitterly cold and foggy morning of December 13.

Though Lee did not contest the city, Barksdale's Mississippians gave the watching Confederates a fine show in delaying the pontoons by sharpshooting from cellars until cannon drove them out. Before they left, Barksdale was forced personally to see an importunate lady who had refused to abandon her home. Her cow had been killed by cannon fire and she wanted to be sure that the Confederates would butcher it for meat for themselves.

Then the blue masses had the town and the plains on either side, as the fog began to lift and reveal the panoramic action to the Rebels waiting on the hillside. From private to commanding general, there was no slightest touch of apprehension. With three months' rest, the army was in fine fettle. Except for some shortages in shoes and a serious lack of overcoats, the men were warmly (if variously) clothed. With no marching to do, the unshod bound their feet in sacks and rags to protect them from the solidly frozen ground.

It was a large army for the Confederacy: not including colored cooks and Negroes who served as teamsters, Lee had over 75,000 men, superbly organized and officered. It was the peak strength, in manpower and officer personnel, of the Army of Northern Virginia.

For the great Rebel gathering, Old Jack turned out in a handsome, new gold-braided dress coat, given him by his friend Jeb Stuart. As he rode along the lines, his men hollered and yoo-hooed at the sight of him.

"Come here, boys! Stonewall has drawed his bounty and has bought himself some new clothes."

When Jackson joined Lee and the other generals, their eyes widened at his finery, but they were more reserved than the men. Longstreet could not suppress his humor, though he turned it on something else. Seeing the Unions mass against Jackson's line, Longstreet asked him if he wasn't scared of all those Yankees.

Old Jack didn't joke on battlefields. Giving a straight answer, he said, "Wait till they come a little nearer, and they shall either scare me or I'll scare them."

Major Heros von Borcke, Stuart's Prussian aide-de-camp and a warm admirer of Jackson, grew nervous as his friend let the Federals come so close and ventured his opinion.

"Major," Jackson replied with conviction, "my men have sometimes failed to take a position, but to defend one, never! I am glad the Yankees are coming."

When the solid Union line unfolded in the rough ground on the Rebel right, in front of Jackson, they were unexpectedly greeted by artillery bursts in enfilade. John Pelham, Stuart's great young cannoneer, had run two of his horse-guns forward and was having the time of his life. Partly protected by a gully and partly obscured by the drifting fog, Pelham directed his two guns while he came gradually under the fire of five Union batteries. One of his guns was knocked out, most of the horses and most of the men of both guns went down. Helping serve the one gun himself, the beautiful blond boy kept firing until Stuart advised him the third time to get out while he was alive. The soldiers who watched him from the crest remembered "the gallant Pelham" more than they remembered the Yankees they fought.

The Union drive enjoyed some local success in the swampy underbrush in front of Jackson, before counterattacks drove them out, and they were badly cut up by Jackson's guns both in their attack and in their withdrawal. The heavy Union artillery got the range of those Jackson guns and punished his cannoneers severely. Jackson ordered two guns of another young man, Willie Poague of Lexington, to plague the Union artillery until their counterfire grew overwhelming.

John Pelham, resting from his own exertions, passed the time by watching Poague. After a while, he said, "You men stand killing better than any I ever saw."

That was before the Union advance shifted around noon from Jackson on the right to Longstreet directly above the town. Longstreet, who had been trying to divert some of the pressure from Jackson, could scarcely believe his eyes when the new Union line left the town. With cadenced cheering and bands playing, they started up the hill from four hundred yards away—straight for his protected riflemen and elevated guns.

The Union line melted away under the concentrated fire, and more came. All afternoon incredibly new lines kept coming, until from the foot of the hill to within a hundred yards of the sunken road the frozen ground was covered with blue-clad bodies, still and squirming. In an utterly hopeless and senseless waste of human life, new lines kept coming until dusk. A few individuals lay dead within twenty-five yards of the stone wall. None came any closer.

The battle was over then, though the Confederates didn't know it. They waited the next day for Burnside to try again. He had enough. That night a cold rain fell, driven by a wind from the South. Under cover of the storm, with the wind blowing away from the Rebels, Burnside withdrew his army back across the Rappahannock while the Confederate pickets were trying to get warm. He left his dead on the field. Confederates were glad to handle burial details in exchange for getting shoes and overcoats from the corpses.

The battle had been glorious during its action but, when it was over, Lee knew that nothing had been accomplished. The Unions could replace their losses; he could not, and he had lost some good officers—Howell Cobb's younger brother among them.

Militarily the battle had no effect on the war, though Lincoln's people were begloomed by the fight he forced on Burnside and Davis' people were jubilant at Lee's success in the defense forced upon him.

5

President Davis, then in Tennessee, was also pleased by the news of Fredericksburg. Holding ground in such a fruitless victory had satisfied him in his defense system since Bull Run. This satisfaction indicated no more than the fixed delusions of his limitations. In Tennessee, however, new delusions began to appear. These distortions expressed the inner frenzy behind the outward reserve—sometimes cold, sometimes gracious.

The President was at his gracious best as Christmas season approached in Murfreesboro. That was a red-hot Rebel town, where spirits ran high and gallantry was a fact, and dancing to "Lorena," no one considered the subjugation of their Southern land. Not only was Bragg's army there, but President Davis attended the very romantic marriage of thirty-seven-year-old John Morgan (whose first wife had died two years previously), to young Miss Martha Ready, a Tennessee congressman's daughter who had set her cap for the fabled raider before ever seeing him. The whole town did itself proud for the wedding and the army produced a bishop, Lieutenant General Polk, to perform the ceremony. (As well as having in Polk a churchman turned general, Bragg's army had in Dr. Quintard—of Connecticut—a physician turned clergyman, later bishop.)

All this was very heady for a regional hero who needed no further adulation. John Morgan was a flamboyant character. Though his raids are among the most cherished legends of the Western Confederacy, he needed at this time to be discouraged from his penchant for independent action. Morgan's cavalry was critically needed by Bragg in that December because Rosecrans, with a vast supply system organized, was making a most deliberate advance to battle for the way to Chattanooga.

Overriding Joe Johnston, Davis had already removed from Bragg two infantry divisions—which, proving Johnston's point about the impossibility of co-operation between the two Western armies, were uselessly employed. On top of that, Davis permitted Morgan to take off his 4000 hard-fighting troopers on a raid, while Bragg was preparing a defensive battle for the Confederate center.

There is reason to believe that Morgan's raid was involved with one of the perennial plots hatched by the secret societies of dissidents in the Midwest. These various orders, coming under the general name of Copperheads, played at being Southern sympathizers, though chiefly they were composed of cranks, malcontents, and conspiracy lovers, and the only real action most of them performed was giving each other secret grips and passwords. The Confederate government did communicate with some of the leaders, and Confederate soldiers were detached as "secret agents" in a bootless derring-do. It was the sort of thing that would appeal to John Morgan.

Late in 1862 very vocal anti-Lincoln sentiments were expressed among the Democrats in Ohio, Indiana, and Illinois. Primarily these Democrats were Unionists who opposed the war as a means of preserving the Union. At the same time a resurgence of Democratic votes all over the country gave the Republicans the barest majority in the House. New York, Pennsylvania, Indiana, Ohio, and Lincoln's home state of Illinois had all gone

Democratic in the fall elections. But the secret societies which developed among the more rabid anti-Administration Midwesterners were not remotely expressions of the Democratic opposition to the war.

It was in permitting Bragg's cavalry to go off on a junket associated with these play-acting conspirators, on the eve of a crucial battle, that Jefferson Davis made the turn from habitual delusions to a disordered grasping at wan hopes. Never depending on the Southern people to win their independence, with the hope of European intervention waning, the distracted man allowed an army's cavalry to be employed in some far-fetched plot involving supposed traitors within the United States.

Needless to say, no conspirators arose while Morgan's men rode through bitter weather on the fabled "Christmas raid," and accomplished nothing toward the defense of their country except some stories that grew in the telling. Coming back from the futile expedition, the tired men heard distantly the guns of the battle they had missed.

Outside of Murfreesboro, at the two days' fight of Stone River (New Year's Eve and New Year's Day, 1863), Bragg had a sound battle plan and his men as always, when given a chance, fought well. Though outnumbered by Rosecrans through Davis' dispositions, the Confederates fought the Unions to a standstill.

If Bragg could contain Rosecrans, it is not unreasonable to assume that he could have driven back the Union Army with the two infantry divisions sent away and Morgan's 4000 mounted troops. As it was, Bragg, his nerves already overtaxed by two days of combat, made another of his withdrawals, and his officers entered protests at his commanding.

This time Bragg asked for a vote of confidence. Instead, his generals gave him a vote of no confidence, and one of them sent a copy on to Davis. With that command situation, the Department of the West entered the New Year of 1863. This organization of Davis' charts had been sustained by Southerners with guns in their hands and by the mistakes of the enemy. Neither could be counted on indefinitely.

Men began to desert Bragg's army. To civilians the pall that gathered over the Western armies counterbalanced Lee's victory in Virginia. In the Deep South, Virginia was remote anyway: it was not a cotton state and had not even belonged to the original Confederacy. Events meant the most to a state-conscious and provincial people where things were happening. What the people in the West could see was all bad.

Over the whole South the effects of fielding and supplying armies were causing suffering, nibbling away at morale, developing what they call "croakers"—those faultfinders who moaned that all was lost.

For, with total war against them, it was not only the armed forces who must defend, but the people who must endure. When the armed forces had done no more than repel the invader at the end of 1862, heroic as that was, it was not enough for the people who had been left almost

entirely alone, in order that an armed defense might be made. By the
winter of 1862–63, the effects of their neglect began the insidious under-
mining of the armies.

6

The over thirty per cent absent without leave in the Confederate armies
at that time did not represent permanent desertions. Despite the discipli-
narians, and the morale brought by Lee, the organization of the country
and its armies was simply too new and too loose to restrain permanently
the individual assertion of the men. In joining state units to fight for the
defense of their homes, the men had not been transformed into cogs in
an operating machine.

Some wandered off out of tedium, some to go to town to see the sights,
some to steal a chicken or get a drink. Mostly they would come back.

The straight-away deserters, like the Union deserters, simply had
enough of fighting and the army. In the Confederate armies, this rejection
of the whole thing was heightened by the starvation diets, the poor clothing under which they suffered as winter came on, and in the West the
continued retreats and fights to no resolution. Most of these men were
gone, though warm weather would bring some back.

The middle group of absentees were largely men who had gone home
—some simply for Christmas, others because their families were in need
or in danger, with their neighborhood already overrun by invaders. Their
return depended as much on the morale of their families as on the men's
determination, deepened by loyalty to their fellows in the regiment. When
the family's need of a husband or son became stronger to the women
than their will to resist the enemy, that man was usually lost to the army.

By midwinter of 1862–63, that will was weakening in spots. The dollar
was dropping and prices were rising. Their money bought only one third
of what it had in the beginning, while the price of potatoes had doubled,
flour tripled and meat quadrupled. Sugar was up ten times and coffee out
of sight. To most that meant that sugar and coffee were gone from the
diet, meat was cut down to occasional bacon or sausage, and flour bread
became a rare feast.

Among the planters, the acute sufferers were those with plantations in
occupied country and in country adjacent to the invader's path. In the
occupied sections of Virginia, Tennessee, Louisiana, and northern Mississippi, most plantations had ceased to operate and the dispossessed people
crowded into cities.

Around Fredericksburg the devastation was complete. Hardly a house,
a building, or a fence stood. A Northern newspaper observer wrote of

seeing "tall chimneys standing, monuments of departed peace, in the midst of wastes that had been farms."

In areas adjacent to the occupation forces, raiding parties had run off slaves and stock, reducing planters and farmers to a bare subsistence, and robbing poor families of all sustenance. As the war coarsened men, wandering bands of hoodlums began stealing directly out of the homes, wrecking furniture and terrorizing women, and the vicious among Union deserters committed acts of wanton outrage. The well-connected families could move into towns or with distant kinfolk, but the poor suffered both privation and fear.

On the coastal plantations of South Carolina, in their feudal remoteness, families began to fear the Union bands who raided to steal their Negroes and incite them. Those who could transplanted entire plantations to the interior.

In the protected areas, no acute suffering was felt on the big plantations, though various dislocations began. It was not that slaves presented a problem as feared; they showed a surprising lack of unrest. It was King Cotton who gave the trouble. With the blockade causing bales to pile up on wharves, money grew scarce. Then, with the typical selfish individualism that marked the section's history, many planters refused to co-operate with the government's effort to have foodstuff grown instead of cash crops, even though they got no cash for the crop. Some traded with the enemy.

Where large food crops were attempted, the miserable work of the commissary and the intransigence of the railroad operators got little of it properly distributed. Then state governments, like Georgia and North Carolina, fought the Confederacy steadily to retain goods and foodstuffs as Georgia did with men. North Carolina gave handsomely to the Confederate armies in manpower, but the government never got the potential use of its textile factories, the best and largest in the South.

Where the actual suffering bore down was on the yeomanry, who ran farms without slaves. With the men away, the women tried to run the farms themselves and, where they had the help of young boys or gaffers, succeeded fairly well. Where a woman was alone, especially if she was not physically strong, farm production came virtually to a standstill. As the majority of men in the Southern armies were farmers, these cases grew sufficiently numerous to cause the states of South Carolina, Georgia, Florida, Alabama, Mississippi, Tennessee, and Arkansas to pass acts for the relief of families of soldiers.

The usual poor organization caused these measures to be largely ineffective. The distribution was unequal. Those nearest railroads and canals fared best; in the back country and in the cities (where trains were overloaded with war matériel and wounded) the people fared poorly indeed.

Nor was food the only shortage. Since the government made little effort to supply the formerly imported articles, there was a pinch in clothes and the barest necessities across all classes of people. For matches, the people hunted through attics and outbuildings for discarded flints and steel; soap was made from lye and kitchen fat; candles were made from mutton suet, lard, and beeswax, dipped on a cotton string, and gave, as a user said, "a flickering smoky flame that was very hard on the eyes." Lampblack mixed with chinaberries served for shoe polish; oak balls and all manner of berries were used for ink. Letter writers learned a new calligraphy, writing in tiny letters to cover every spot of the poor paper, and that fast disappearing. Sweet potatoes and peanuts became substitutes for mocha to a coffee-drinking people. Sassafras roots made tea, and sassafras bark, mixed with chalk, became tooth powder.

All these were ways of making do, as discarded old clothes were cut down for children and remade for soldiers. For shoes and new clothes there were no substitutes. In the Land of Cotton, calico goods, which had sold at twelve and a half cents before the war, went for two dollars and a quarter—and a soldier's pay, when he got it and could get it to his family, was eleven dollars a month. Naturally all privations bore hardest on the poor, and among these the situation became desperate in those isolated communities stripped of men.

This did not mean that all men were in the armies. Thousands moved to other states to avoid conscription, others holed up in the hills, and still others sought the safety of the bureaus. Where a woman was alone on a small farm in a deserted neighborhood, she could not even get wood for winter fuel. When a soldier went home to cut wood for the winter's fires, there was no way he could replace food and clothing. When small children were involved, his choice became very hard, unless the wife was strongly determined for him to fight. The women were the key.

In the cities and large towns, though physical want bore heavily on the poor, and nearly all suffered privations, the people's spirits were given more support by the group life, the presence of their troops and social diversions however modest; they were more likely to be literate and, with newspapers and magazines and discussions of the news, they could hold a larger view of the struggle.

On the isolated farms in the canebrakes and in the hills, it was different. The lonely night chilled the heart of the hungry and the cold and the frightened. Hate for the invader sustained some, but the instinct for preservation went deeper than an emotion in an ominously increasing number.

Hunger was gnawing at the structure of the Confederacy, while the people's leader brought home stacks of paper from the War Office and strained his one weak eye through the night hours, removed from the dark streets of the capital where thugs waited to garrote an unwary citizen and Winder's bully boys chased deserters through the alleys.

CHAPTER XIV

"We Are Betrayed from Within"

THE sword of war cut both ways. Though in the North the blade had more to cut through, the opening of 1863 found the Union far from a crusading unanimity. Increasingly, working groups opposed the competition of freed Negroes, and others resented the quick riches of war profiteers. The presence around the armies of the speculators in cotton and tobacco, trying to earn a fast dollar out of the enemy, contributed to the high desertions in the well-fed, well-clothed Union troops. Then, large segments of civilian population were simply growing tired of the war, whatever slogan of freedom it had. Not only the Copperheads but, for a different reason, powers in Lincoln's party opposed the Administration. The radicals wanted the war carried more ruthlessly and more successfully against the Southerners and blamed Lincoln for not doing it.

Burnside's heavy casualty list in the clumsy attack on Lee at Fredericksburg aroused bitter criticism of Lincoln's choice of generals as well as his operation of the war. There was even a cabinet revolution, designed to get rid of the less radical Seward. Lincoln's astute handling of this crisis, with his intuitive knowledge and use of the psychology of men, brought him out of the difficulties, and he rode the wave with disregard of Congress, the Supreme Court, and the Constitution.

All these happenings were discussed in the Exchange Bar in Richmond at the same hours they were talked about in the Willard Bar in Washington. Thoughtful Southerners, in and out of the armies, recognized that Lincoln was being pushed by the radicals, and Northern newspapers (which in the South had perforce supplanted British magazines in interest if not in appeal) reflected the attitude of a war of conquest against the Southern states. Clamoring for a "more vigorous prosecution of the war," those papers showed that the end of preserving the Union had been totally forgotten in the means of making the invasion successful.

From the time of the Emancipation Proclamation on, the men in the Union armies showed a new attitude too. They began to regard the citizens of the South as objects of their anti-slavery crusade whom, as had been predicted, it was "their right to despoil." Where thievery and personalized destruction had come before from individual hooligans and uninhibited animal spirits, the Northern armies became almost systematic in terrorism and despoliation. The little-recorded sack of Fredericksburg was only an outstanding illustration of organized hoodlumism released on an American community.

When the charming old city of homes was turned over to the vandals, its streets were lined with furniture taken from the homes of terrorized women, some of it lighting the winter nights with bonfires. Wrecked pianos served as horse troughs. Women's clothing draped the bodies of plug-uglies dancing in the streets on carpets dragged from parlors. The crash of chinaware was continuous, family portraits were slashed, silver carted away, and long-saved wine delivered to Union officers' messes. With few exceptions, officers either failed to restrain or actually encouraged the looting and the wanton destruction in the city and surrounding area. In fighting the Indians and the British, Southerners had never experienced such outrages as they did from the restorers of the Union.

Some of the soldiers felt ashamed of stealing the last food from the poor families. Some of the officers, appalled at this warfare on supposedly fellow citizens, felt that the base conduct of "low, ignorant ruffians" would only harden the Southerners in their desire for independence. Oliver Wendell Holmes, Jr., thought that "we are working vainly to effect what never happens—the subjugation (for that it is) of a great civilized nation. We shan't do it—at least the army can't."

The Northern army in Virginia could not, but that was not the only army, and the armies were not all of the war. In the hard core of all the Confederate armies and in the hard core of the country, the Hunlike behavior of some Union troops developed a hatred such as Americans have never felt for another people. It was as the French hate the Germans and the Poles the Russians: it was absolute and uncompromising.

This feeling was reflected in the foolish Confederate Congress when (assuming peace) the members were debating the repeal of the naturalization laws and, among the foreigners to be excluded from immigration, Yankees topped the list. One member even wanted a law to exile a Southerner who married a Yankee.

The feeling was observed by Europeans, and the *London Illustrated News* reported that "The South with no advantage except that of 'immortal hate' . . . has maintained the contest with a heroism that has carried men's hearts captive with admiration."

This was in the hard core. However, ultimately it was a people fighting a nation. Individuals, as always, had made mighty achievements—minor miracles for an agricultural people.

At the semiautonomous Tredegar Iron Works, everything was done from mining and smelting the ore to shipping it to the plant that turned it into guns; what amounted to an independent quartermaster corps of the Tredegar victualed and partially clothed its own workers, sparing them from paying speculators' prices for food and necessities.

A duplication of Tredegar's semi-independent sufficiency was made in medicine by thirty-nine-year-old Dr. McCaw, of Richmond. On the open plateau of Chimborazo Heights, at the end of the old part of the city, he constructed and operated the largest military hospital in world history. Using extremely advanced methods of physical and mental therapy—which gave Chimborazo Hospital the lowest mortality rates in the world until the sulfa drugs of World War II—Dr. McCaw's people raised their own vegetables and chickens, kept cows, a goatherd for milk and for "kid meat," and bartered with farmers for hog meat and mutton. In his great work in returning wounded and ill men to the armies, Dr. McCaw used for medicines largely the substitutes in which citizens all over the South showed a surprising resourcefulness. Opium poppies grew in Southern fields.

The huge hospital was officially an army post, with Dr. McCaw appointed commandant by the Secretary of War. Thus freed of the red tape and inefficiency of the government bureaus, the brilliant young surgeon demonstrated what could be done by initiative in *un*traditional methods.

To the horror of traditionalists, instead of constructing one big building, he constructed 150 small ones. Every patient had air, light, and space. In addition to the hospital buildings, there were barracks for guards (usually convalescents), storehouses, icehouses, a bathhouse, a brewery, and a bakery that turned out ten thousand loaves a day. Boilers from shutdown tobacco factories were used in five soup houses. Bedsteads, tables, and the like were made on the grounds from seasoned lumber designed for tobacco boxes. Incidentally, Sherman's famous quotation was anticipated at Chimborazo Hospital by Dr. Hubbell. After helplessly watching a young soldier die in agony from a lung wound, he wrote in his casebook, "*War is hell.*"

Other trained men of imagination and energy, topped by Josiah Gorgas (father of the doctor of yellow-fever fame), created a class of factory workers, mainly women, for the laboratories and arsenals spreading from the nucleus of the Virginia Armory. The big new plants in the lower South, especially at Augusta and Selma, also used former housewives to turn out heavy guns, powder, and matériel against overwhelming obstacles. With niter for explosives cut off by the blockade, rough crews worked in cellars and caves all over the Southern states, and finally urine carts went daily through the towns and back country to collect from chamber pots. What this detail was named, in Davis' departments, is not recorded.

Naval torpedoes and Secretary Mallory's inventive contraptions kept the U. S. Navy outside the harbors where blockade runners plied to Bermuda; and Wilmington, North Carolina, Charleston, and Mobile on the Gulf thrived as never before as ports.

In far-off Brownsville, Texas, across the Rio Grande from Matamoras, Juan Quintero, a Cuban-born and Spanish-speaking Texan, operated against U.S. agents, local Mexican governments, huge outlaw bands, and foreign agents of all descriptions, to get Texas cotton out and guns in for the forces of the grandly titled Trans-Mississippi Department. Kirby Smith, sent there to what he considered exile after disagreement with Bragg and virtually cut off from the Eastern Confederacy, developed a unique and virtually self-sufficient empire out of the simple use of cotton in exchange for imports.

With the government's cotton-withholding policy dying of inanition, practical-minded agents all over the South and in Europe were getting government cotton to European buyers for credit for war matériel. The government obtained the cotton through taxes in kind and the bond issue where the Confederate bonds were purchasable with produce.

Government-sponsored factories turned to the manufacture of clothes and shoes—exempting tanners from the armies—as government purchasing agents contracted for these items. To get the goods delivered to centrally established depots all over the South, another railroad supervisor was brought in—a former New Hampshire blacksmith who prospered in Georgia. Even this gigantic William Wadley, an experienced railroader as well as executive, with whom effective results were habitual, could bring no order to the railroads when the final authority was withheld from him.

Nothing the government tried worked as expected. When the government purchasers of food and clothing set ceiling prices for buying as their money fell, farmers and manufacturers evaded the government through speculators. The new class of working women—shut off from the government stores and shopping in the open market with the thirty-cent dollar they earned each day in the arsenals—could not meet the speculators' prices.

The money was doomed to depreciation when the Confederacy went on the gold standard with $25,000,000 in bullion in the whole region. The various loans were subscribed largely through states, which gave their certificates for Confederate bonds, and thus exchanged one set of papers for another. If money is on a standard of metal which practically doesn't exist in the country, that money must depreciate as faith in the future declines.

In defense, the armies were standing off the invader. It was the invader within, the specter of want, that gained on them. The government did nothing to protect its people from it. Instead the political leaders assumed a loyalty to the forms of a constitutional government and, while their bright new paper money fell in purchasing value, the people began to disintegrate as *a* people into their component parts as individuals.

Even their "cup that cheers" was denied them, or at least an attempt was made to do so. The evangelical Protestants in the South, long regarding the bottle as an instrument of Satan, took the occasion of war (as they did successfully in the whole United States in World War I) to pressure the government into exercising modified forms of prohibition. Alcohol-producing grains became subject to government control and stills were forbidden. Fortunately for the oppressed people, the government lacked there as everywhere else the machinery to enforce this method of bringing spiritual salvation, and native liquors simply became harder to get. The feelings of the people were not soothed by this intrusion on their personal liberties, especially when no leaders explained anything to them.

A year before, a Georgia editor had written that the people needed to be talked to. They still did; only they needed food too. In Richmond women rioted to get it. They formed in Capitol Square on a bright spring morning (April 2), with some boys and a few men, mostly transients. With the mob swelling, by some estimates, to a thousand, they marched past the War Offices on Ninth Street and down to the speculators' stores on Cary. They stormed in, emptying the shelves, and unloaded drays drawn up at the curb. They swung back to Main Street and by then, incited by their own violence, they began breaking in plate-glass windows and fighting for valuables.

Governor Letcher called out the City Battalion and threatened to fire on them. While they milled around uncertainly, President Davis came out of the Government Building, mounted a dray, and tried to quiet them. They threw bread at him. The mob temper then had burned out and the women sullenly dispersed.

The newspapers played down the "Bread Riot," as it was somewhat inaccurately called, but it made a deep and ugly impression on Richmond. Less-publicized riots of women government workers followed in Georgia.

While these symptoms of the people's temper went ignored by government leaders, Vice-President Alexander Stephens left the capital to go home to Georgia, in 1862, there the better to wage his anti-Administration campaign. Among a people ever susceptible to word-weaving, the diminutive egotist attacked conscription and Davis' suspension of the writ of habeas corpus as if Union armies did not exist. That Lincoln had gone further in both only determined Stephens to restrain his President from doing likewise. He said that he preferred losing the war to losing constitutionalities!

That he was losing both Stephens could not perceive. He had carried the Constitution as a sectional defense and his own absolutism into a monomania, in which he was used by those anti-Davis Georgians—like that shrewd red-neck, Governor Brown—who carried states' rights to the illogical extreme for local political power.

Old-line secessionist politicians occupied themselves with similar fantasies. It was only the non-secessionist military leaders who thought in terms of quick and sizable victory, and the military leaders who gave the Confederacy a history did not run the country. In fact, the greatest of them could not even run his own army as he saw fit.

2

In Lee's Army of Northern Virginia, the educated men perceived that the war must be won quickly or lost. The mathematics that Lee had feared were catching up. In the winter of 1862–63 these men could all see what the government was blind to: that the South was in a state of physical decline from the strain.

Quartered in a virtually untouched section of Virginia, their animals were gaunt from poor forage. Such beeves as they collected for the troops were too thin to be edible. The soldiers suffered with the civilians from lack of salt. (That commonplace item, which we take for granted, was a scarcity that incalculably increased the people's suffering.) Their guns were constantly improving in quality. In the long winter months, the arsenals could experiment in duplicating the superior cannons captured from the enemy. But for subsistence of men and horses, two of Longstreet's divisions had to be sent south of the James River to do commissary work for themselves.

What the soldiers could not see for themselves, letters from home told them. It was not that their morale was low *then*, despite drooping spirits from the tedium and the illness and the mud of winter camp. The morale needed to be turned to positive action: the men wanted to carry the war to a decision.

To sustain the morale of the soldiers and their confidence in a decision, the army had Lee. In his simple goodness was an understanding of the hearts of his fellow Southerners and, as an intelligent soldier, he understood the personal needs of Confederates as he understood the special needs of the Confederacy. He never expected the principles of "secessionists" (as his A.A.G. referred to the politicians) to have meaning to his men. Nor could the discipline of a regularly organized and supplied army apply to half-naked, underfed regionalists who elected their own officers and were often kept in company and regimental units on a basis of their home states rather than of efficiency.

To transmit their native loyalty to their land into disciplined action for a cause, a common bond was needed. Lee became that bond to his men, holding their loyalty as he controlled their discipline through their personal respect and affection.

European observers, accustomed to the pomp and formality of foreign armies, found that Lee's men regarded "Uncle Bob" more as sons regarded their fathers. He never set himself apart from them. The collection of a half dozen headquarters tents were not separated by sentries or handsomely caparisoned staff officers. The few battered wagons, with faded U.S. stamped on the canvas, were parked without any order in front of the tents, their horses browsing for forage around the wagons and tents. Negro servants strolled about among the seedy couriers, lounging on the ground while waiting for orders. A Negro served Lee's sparse meals on the metal dishes from the camp chest with no more nor less ceremony than he would serve the family at home.

For all his physical accessibility to the men, no liberties were taken with the general, any more than a son would intrude on his father's privacy. He was "Marse Robert," the personal idealization of the regional patriarch of their loveliest legends and finest realities.

Though Lee's name inspired the hopes of hundreds of thousands of Southerners who never saw him, his actual control was limited to the 70,000 men of the Army of Northern Virginia. His influence could have been so vast that probably he could have assumed dictatorial powers over the government. His inherent conservatism and ingrained respect for constituted authority restricted him to directing his own command *through* the President. This not only entailed time-consuming paper work which Lee detested, but the strain of his responsibility was intensified by the constant need of tactfully soliciting Davis on details in order to achieve his larger ends.

At fifty-six, the physically vigorous Lee was beginning his own physical decline as he prepared for the third time to contest a nation's invasion of his state. This accumulated power of destruction was to be hurled at a battered and half-starved people not from borders but from productive areas of their own land already occupied. With the naval attacks against cities, the land armies were to be preceded by far-ranging bodies of cavalry operating for direct destruction as bombing from the air now does.

The horsemen rode to join the specter of want already loose within the protected areas. Their intent was to destroy railroads and food supply, demoralize the population, crushing the will to resist as well as the support of the armies. Though their restriction to the ground prevented the cavalry's use against manufacturing centers, in an agricultural country they could bring hunger more thoroughly to the people by personalized attention to each farm—destroying the crops in the field and in the barn, destroying plows and hoes, stealing all livestock and running off slaves.

The cavalry raids opened on all three prongs of the Union advance in the South. In the middle, Streight raided down to Rome, Georgia, before his raiders were defeated and he was captured by Forrest. (As a captive in Libby Prison, Streight became a great army lawyer on the "rights" of belligerents.) On the Mississippi end, Grierson raided all the way down to Baton Rouge, and found the Confederacy "a shell." Stoneman raided in Virginia, doing some damage to railroads and bridges, and much more to private stables. He had a covetous eye for horses and mules.

Simultaneously, a new "On to Richmond" general flexed his muscles and prepared the finish of Lee. This Joe Hooker was no reluctant attacker, like honest Burnside. He had maneuvered and finagled for the job.

Charles Francis Adams said that Hooker's headquarters was a combination of barroom and brothel, and Southerners said that the word "hooker" for a prostitute derived from the train car of army whores they captured. Hooker may not have been an ideal person to represent a crusade, but he was a fighter, and he was as rough as Pope in his determination to beat the Rebels.

Lee had to plan a counter to this fierce fellow, with Longstreet and two divisions away. Longstreet had started out on his own primarily to victual his men and animals but, thirsting for independent command, he took the occasion to besiege Suffolk. This small city, separated from Norfolk by a river, is today virtually a suburb of the metropolitan Norfolk area. Then it was a pleasant small city south of the James River, in that region where Nat Turner's Southampton County rebellion had been staged thirty years before. The siege came to nothing and the Army of Northern Virginia was minus Hood's and Pickett's fine troops.

Permitting this foolish assertion on Longstreet's part was a weakness in Lee's gentleness of character, and it reflected a graver weakness in the whole military organization, which depended on personalities. When the Confederate defense experienced a personality failure there was no organization of command, no reserve of supply and manpower, to absorb the consequences of mistakes. The Union could afford its blunders. After total failure in Virginia, the Union armies could be resupplied, reinforced, with new commanders tried, and come on again with the situation unchanged.

In the West the Unions could make blunder upon blunder, and try it again another way. Indeed, because of their blunders, the Confederacy in the West had once escaped the consequences of its own mistakes. In the spring of 1863, when the time of decision was at hand, President Davis would precisely duplicate his earlier mistakes of personality alignment, and this time the consequences would catch up with the armies.

3

Before the roof fell in, conditions in the West outwardly looked favorable to the Confederate defense when spring brought, along with the flowers, the new total war against them. At Vicksburg, two gunboat attacks from the interior rivers had been driven off and a direct naval assault on Grand Gulf, south of Vicksburg on the Mississippi, had likewise been defeated. The Southern defenders had come a long way from Fort Henry and Fort Donelson. Over a year had passed since those disasters, and no more ripe apples had fallen to Grant's operations in concert with the navy.

But Grant, after more than a year of frustration and sufficient if limited presidential support, was ready for the bold move to which Davis' departments had invited him.

In an ABC of military logic, Grant perceived that the overland route southward to Vicksburg was too long, since his supply lines had proven vulnerable to Forrest and Van Dorn (lately dead from a jealous husband's bullet). Further, the fleet could neither reduce Vicksburg nor get in from the multiple rivers by which planters had once floated their cotton down to the Mississippi and on to New Orleans. The obvious choice was to get *south* of Vicksburg and march *north*.

To this end, he had the ever handy fleet transport his troops to the west bank of the Mississippi. From there the army first marched southward through unprotected country. The Confederate army in the Trans-Mississippi Department was off elsewhere as a consequence of the Confederates west of the river operating in a separate department unrelated to the forces east of the river. Then the navy took Grant's troops back across the Mississippi below Vicksburg. Once landed, he had to take an inland-river position (Port Gibson) and he had a major river fort south of him at Port Hudson. But Port Gibson was defended only by Bowen's few brigades, hurried inland from Grand Gulf, and the Unions had plenty of armies. "Commissary" Banks, shifted from his infertile fields in Virginia, was leading a force in the Red River country of Arkansas and headed for Port Hudson below Grant.

In early May, leaving the Port Hudson menace to Banks, Grant cut loose from the river and struck northeast for the Mississippi capital of Jackson, directly east from Vicksburg and militarily behind it. Grant was the first general in the Civil War to march his army across a Southern area with intent to subsist entirely off the people. His men grew weary of chicken and corn bread, but not as weary as the Mississippi poor grew of having their chicken and corn bread taken from them, along with all their animals. This was Grant's highly praised maneuver, in which his army was moving between the small force of Pemberton at Vicksburg and Joe Johnston's few hastily collected brigades at Jackson.

In the preceding fall, when Randolph resigned from the War Office, Davis had gotten his first good Secretary in four tries—James Seddon. This forty-seven-year-old Virginian was a successful lawyer and learned gentleman, cultured and charming. With his gay and literate wife one of the most popular of hostesses, their plantation home on the river west of

Richmond was a favorite center for young and old. Though in chronic ill-health, Seddon had served twice in the U. S. Congress, and in the Confederate Congress he was one of the pitifully few who might be called a statesman. He did think in terms of winning independence rather than of either politics or principles, and he thought realistically. He did not go into the War Office to be anybody's clerk and, with his graciousness and native tact, he had even Davis listening to his intelligently presented ideas.

Seddon did not essay any grand strategy which involved new plans for the war. Not a military man, he did not think in those spheres. As an intelligently observant patriot, he immediately perceived what was obvious to one and all.

As Joe Johnston said, the war was stalemated in Virginia; though, as Johnston did not say, the stalemate was maintained by Lee. Interfering with a working situation in Virginia was not the way to shift attention to the West. It was equally clear, however, that attention must be shifted to the West. Seddon rightly perceived that the problem was in command.

What Seddon suggested was simple: since Bragg had lost the confidence of his army, and since Johnston was dissatisfied with his anomalous position and was (according to the estimates of that day) a superior field general, let Johnston take personal command of Bragg's army. In his anxiety, Davis agreed to the removal of his dear friend Braxton Bragg.

At this point logical reasoning enters the unexplorable labyrinths of human behavior. Where Joe Johnston made out then and later a fine case for the unworkability of his anomalous assignment, once Seddon tried to give him an army, Johnston clung to his formerly hateful department as to his last friend. First he said, after inspection, nothing was wrong with Bragg's army; then he said it would wound his sensibilities to supersede a brother officer. When Seddon suggested that Johnston send Bragg on to Richmond, and they would look after him, Retreatin' Joe said that Mrs. Bragg was sick at the time and to intrude the unpleasant topic would further wound his sensibilities. Then, before Seddon could continue his graciously worded pleas, in which all understanding and support were offered, Johnston himself took to his bed. There he skulked in Chattanooga, absolutely refusing to do anything to change a situation which he had found abominable.

While this inconclusive action was taking place in the late winter and early spring of 1863, Pemberton on the river had been left completely alone with his hundred miles of river front to guard in a typical Davis arrangement of isolated garrisons. From Vicksburg to Grand Gulf, fifty miles by river, and on to Port Hudson, nearly another fifty, Pemberton had spread 28,000 troops plus the Port Hudson garrison and some irregular cavalry. They were very irregular indeed. These horsemen were not irregulars as Turner Ashby's had been, or John Morgan's were becoming: they were largely fugitives from the infantry, without a strong leader, and their thieving and carousing brought nothing but plaints from the countryside in which they operated.

With this force Pemberton was required to guard against (1) landings on the river, (2) direct assaults on Vicksburg, and (3) any move overland from the north. It was not a possible assignment, unless the commander was allowed to improvise as circumstances and conditions indicated. Pemberton was fixed, as in a vise, by the orders from Davis to hold Vicksburg and Port Hudson at all hazards, and to hold *all* places if possible. He was to do this with a hodgepodge assortment of troops which only technically could be called an army. Having arrived as separate units, their dispersal to points of defense prevented any opportunity for the forces to evolve into an army. Pemberton commanded an area rather than an army; he was, in turn, commanded by Joe Johnston, off sick in Chattanooga; and Johnston by Jefferson Davis, chronically suffering in Richmond.

Against this setup, Grant moved his heavily gunned 43,000 from the Mississippi south of Vicksburg northeastward toward Jackson, in the campaign on which his fame essentially rests.

4

Pemberton, at the Mississippi, and Johnston, his departmental superior, did not like each other; and Johnston, the department commander, and Davis, the Commander in Chief, did not like each other. In fact, Johnston seemed to like nobody except his inferiors, a not uncommon personality trait. In addition, Seddon had lost faith in Johnston and also patience. On May 10, Seddon simply ordered him to get from Chattanooga to Pemberton and assume active charge of his department.

Protecting his record by entering a formal statement that he was ill, Johnston went. To indicate the folly of East Tennessee troops co-operating with the Mississippi troops, Johnston personally had to go by way of the Atlanta, Mobile, Jackson triangle on a railroad journey for four days to reach the Pemberton area—though not Pemberton. They never met. Their later controversy is based on messages back and forth.

Once on the field, Johnston gave Pemberton a sound order: to throw all of his troops at Grant's flank and rear, while Johnston would strike from the other side with the few brigades which were hastily gathering from all over the lower South, some from as far away as Charleston.

What was Pemberton to do? Davis said, "Hold Vicksburg." Johnston said, "Leave Vicksburg and join me." Pemberton called a council of war and they decided to do neither. The trained soldier in Pemberton had been negated by the confusion in the mortal man, trying to follow conflicting orders neither of which equated with his own wishes. He tried to do all three, and did none. Keeping two divisions in Vicksburg, he pushed three toward Johnston.

Unbeknownst to Johnston and Pemberton, and vital to their plans, a spy had won the Confederates' trust and carried Johnston's order for convergence to Grant. *He that hath, to him it shall be given.* While Pemberton delayed with his council of war, Grant, knowing the Confederate troop disposition, struck at the collected brigades of Johnston. Totaling only about 11,000 and not assembled, they were driven out of Grant's path to the capital of Jackson.

When Johnston retreated northward with his few troops, Sherman was left with the task of destroying the railroad center and military potential of Jackson. He got his first practice in destroying property on Mississippi's capital, and this work seemed to enchant the man who had never before truly found himself. A fillip was added to the despoliation of the countryside when the soldiers found the home of the Confederate President. Among trophies such as books that were gleefully carried away went Davis' blooded horses. The soldiers were enraged at the Negroes, who gave their own odd turn to the war by refusing to leave their home.

Grant's main force then struck west for the three divisions which Pemberton had brought out from Vicksburg—really two and Bowen's stout Missouri and Arkansas fighters from Grand Gulf. Bowen and a division under Stevenson didn't do badly there at Champion's Hill, on the way toward the Big Black River and Vicksburg, and they might have done well except for the failure of co-operation from the division under Loring. He was that professional soldier who had given Lee and Jackson such a bad time in the early going.

(When Confederate generals failed in the East, they went West; when Union generals succeeded in the West, they came East. Thus, in the West to a large extent the upcoming Union generals were facing the Confederates' has-beens and never-weres.)

Pemberton had to put his two divisions in retreat. Loring, losing his wagons and guns, got around the Union Army to join the 10,000 under Johnston, then lurking futilely off to the north of the action. Then Pemberton tried his small force at a direct defense of the Big Black, the inland water barrier to Vicksburg. Their rout is one of the least discussed battles in the South. The heavily outnumbered Southern troops did not have it that day. Quick work in destroying a bridge and a transportation steamer were all that saved the remnants from being gobbled up. The men and guns made it into the works of Vicksburg, where the two unused divisions reinforced them for the defense of the city.

This was the "campaign" phase of Vicksburg. Then, after the dispersed defense structure on the Mississippi had collapsed, as it had the year before on the Kentucky-Tennessee frontier, troops were suddenly rushed to Johnston from all over the lower South. If they had come before Grant started his northern advance, and if one general had been in command with his own initiative, the Southern troops would have outnumbered Grant's original 43,000 and had him in a position for defeat.

As Johnston's 10,000 north of Vicksburg were increased by brigades, Grant was increased by divisions, going by various estimates from over 70,000 to nearly 100,000. By then there was nothing that Johnston could do to help bottled-up Pemberton, and Grant settled down to what is called the siege of Vicksburg.

He had already tried direct assault on the city and been decisively defeated. On the other side of Vicksburg, however, was the river and the U. S. Navy, completely shutting off the city from outside communication. With all supplies cut off from the soldiers and the civilians, the so-called siege of Vicksburg became in miniature a test in the starvation strangle hold being applied to the whole South.

From the river, the U.S. gunboats, unmolested by any Confederate navy, poured shells into the city until, with homes devastated, civilians dug caves for the women and children. On the land side, Grant's growing army, unable to carry the works in direct assault, formed a human vise to keep supplies out by land.

Though thus tightly beleaguered by water and land, the soldiers and the civilians in the Confederate river stronghold girded themselves for the trial by endurance with good spirits. Since Richmond had broken its siege the year before, and Charleston was continuously throwing back besiegers, a state of siege for a Southern city was not as alarming as it might appear.

Inside the city and out, the people expected Vicksburg to be relieved. The Confederacy had endured so many reverses in the Mississippi River country that they could not conceive that their real West (as opposed to Davis' artificial West) was about gone. They expected something like a Lee to rise up and smite the invader. But Lee was busy at the other end of the line, and he made his own fateful decision—which denied the West succor.

CHAPTER XV

"God's Will Be Done . . ."

ON MAY 18, when the investment of Vicksburg began, Lee stood in what was becoming the uncomfortably familiar position of having defeated an "On to Richmond" drive without crushing the invading army. His victim had been "Fighting Joe" Hooker, as vainglorious as Pope in his declarations of the ruin he would visit on Lee's Rebels, and possessor of what he modestly called "the finest army on the planet."

At that, he could have been right. Hooker had 130,000 trained, well-conditioned, and superbly equipped soldiers, including 10,000 cavalry and artillerists for over four hundred of the best cannons American technology could produce. He could have been right if someone else had been commanding the army.

Hooker came up with an original battle plan, finely executed by Northern troops as hungry for victory in the East as Confederates were in the West. Had Hooker led his mighty host in the West, against troops divided and generals transfixed by Davis' paper departments, Fighting Joe would have won the glorious victory he predicted. In Virginia, Lee was commander of his own army, and the historic division in the South did not apply.

With all the mistakes Lee ever made and those attributed to him, with all the military limitations of his gentle character and the limitations imposed by his innate conservatism, as a military leader at Chancellorsville his performance must rank him, if on that battle alone, with the great warriors of the ages.

In him, such genius as was inherent in the South's archaic civilization flowered in those first four days in May, in him and the self-educated mountain boy who assumed his own place among the immortals as Stonewall Jackson. As Vicksburg illustrated the weakness in the rulers of the South, Chancellorsville illustrated the strength in the people when unbetrayed by leaders.

The two armies were still in the desolated Fredericksburg area, with

Lee south and Hooker north of the Rappahannock. Ten miles west of Fredericksburg the Rapidan branches off from the Rappahannock and, after following roughly parallel courses for ten miles, the two rivers widely diverge.

After a demonstration to the east of the sacked city, which Lee disregarded, Hooker threw his main forces across the fords of the two rivers west of Fredericksburg and came on the same side of the Rappahannock as Lee. When he placed his army on the Confederate flank, Fighting Joe believed the game was in the bag.

He could do this with 90,000 men and still leave 24,000 under able Sedgwick directly across from Fredericksburg, threatening the main highway and what was left of the railroad to Richmond. Lee was in the position of fighting directly for Fredericksburg in his front and fighting an enormous host on his flank, or of retreating.

On that May 1—while Stoneman was wearing out Federal horses on bridge burning—Lee characteristically determined to attack Hooker, *though he had scarcely one half of Hooker's force.* Because of the inexperienced Seddon's lapse in detail and Longstreet's lust for independent command, the two powerful divisions of Hood and Pickett did not leave their commissary work and the futile siege of Suffolk until after the battle. This was the first direct instance of whole military units lost to defense through the failure of railroad distribution and quartermasters to provide food for men and horses.

In deciding to attack, with one fifth of his army away grubbing for sustenance, what Lee did was this:

With one division and one brigade, he faced Sedgwick's 24,000 across the river at Fredericksburg. With one division and three brigades, he resisted Hooker's advance along the road from the west toward Fredericksburg. They resisted the advance so fiercely, constantly inching forward themselves, that Hooker's advance withdrew back to the main body. Indeed, Hooker's well-conceived plan of attack gave way to defensiveness, and he declared that he would await Lee's attack and destroy him. By Lee's countering boldness, he had seized the initiative in the brushy, briary country surrounding Mr. Chancellor's square, red house. He was never to lose it.

Along with the initiative, Lee had won another vital advantage: the use of his cavalry. When Stoneman took nearly 7000 of the 10,000 Union troopers away to harry Lee's supply lines and people's stables, part of Hooker's plan was to draw Confederate cavalry off after them. Because of the bad winter of foraging, the Army of Northern Virginia was very low on cavalry present for duty at the time. Two thinned-out brigades of the Lee cousins, the general's son Rooney and nephew Fitz, totaled less than 3000. Lee sent Rooney's brigade after Stoneman to harass him—he could do no more—and prevent the Union horsemen from settling down too comfortably to their work. In the Chancellorsville area, Hooker still had more cavalry than Lee, but he didn't have Jeb Stuart. With Fitz Lee's one brigade, Stuart not only probed out Hooker's dispositions but screened Lee's audaciously ambitious movement.

With his army already divided between Fredericksburg and the Chancellorsville area, Lee redivided the larger portion within shouting distance of Hooker's main force. The details were worked out on that Friday night, May 1–2, between Lee and Jackson, the two of them sitting on Federal cracker boxes in the dim flickering light of campfires. Out of their low-voiced conversation came the flanking movement that crowned Jackson's one calendar year of fame.

In the May before, he had set out with his 6000 troops from the western foot of the Blue Ridge on the beginning of the Valley campaign which was to make possible the breaking of the siege of Richmond. On the May outside of Fredericksburg, he set out with three large divisions, the largest the Confederates were ever to have (one half of Lee's army), on the famous flanking movement which was to wreck Hooker. Fighting Joe was the fourth Union general Old Jack had fought with Lee in that one year, and the seventh Jackson had fought with Lee and alone. McClellan, Pope, Burnside, Banks, Fremont, and Shields as part of McDowell's army: they had all come with the great resources of the United States behind them and all gone, and Stonewall Jackson was just reaching his climax.

With Hooker facing the less than two divisions of Lee on the road to Fredericksburg, Stonewall Jackson marched his three divisions and guns on an arc which would place him on the other end of Hooker's army, against Howard's corps. The Germans were in there—Von Gilsa and Dachrodt, Von Amsberg and Buschbeck, Von Schluembach and Schimmelfennig—and the Rebels particularly hated these "bounty troops," as they called them, as preservers of the Union in Virginia.

Had Hooker attacked eastward while Jackson was detached, probably all would have been lost. But Hooker was waiting for Lee to attack him. Lee's seven brigades did a convincing job of demonstration—anyway, it convinced Hooker—while Jackson's men trudged in their fourteen-mile semicircle through the thick spring brush.

The winding roads were narrow and sandy, never straightaway. The entangled woods were bright green with new leaves, and dogwood blossoms brushed the shoulders of the marching men. Horsemen of Fitz Lee's brigade moved warily ahead of the column. On Fancy (or "Little Sorrel") Old Jack rode at the front of his men. He had caught a cold from sleeping on the ground, but he never gave heed to physical ailments. With his cadet cap discarded and the new resplendent gray uniform acquired for Fredericksburg, the stern, bearded Presbyterian really looked like a general as his weak eyes peered steadily ahead.

Old Jack did not have to say, "Close up, men," on that cool May Saturday. The once dazzling militia companies and the imperious volunteers were, with conscripts and latecomers, all soldiers then. They were tense, when every step took them further from their own people, placing Hooker's hosts between themselves and Lee. But no soldiers ever believed more implicitly in their leader than did they in Jackson. As the opposites of Pemberton's troops, these men felt victory in the air. They tasted it in the still and dusky woods. Nobody could beat them when they followed Stonewall Jackson.

After fourteen miles they came out of their green tunnel and formed astride the east-west turnpike toward Fredericksburg, actually behind Howard's corps. Two of Jackson's divisions rolled forward in waves, their red battle flags fluttering above them. Their throats opened in the historic yell and their hearts opened in confidence, and men who were to die and who were to survive rushed forward, firing, bayonets bright in the late afternoon, and the corps was never gathered who could have stopped them.

They weren't stopped by other soldiers but, with Howard's driven men in confusion, the dusk deepened and, in the shadowy woods, the two divisions Jackson had sent in became themselves confused. Old Jack called for his third division.

"Pass A. P. Hill to the front," he said.

Then with his staff he rode forward into the dusk for personal reconnaissance. Unions opened on the little party and they came riding back. By then A. P. Hill's North Carolina regiments were up. They heard rather than saw the horsemen galloping toward them and they fired.

Slugs knocked Jackson off the back of the little sorrel horse. He was shot in the chest and more seriously in the left arm, the heavy ball splintering the bone. A. P. Hill personally sent out litter-bearers, and awkwardly they gathered up the awkward frame. By then all the firing bothered the Yankee gunners and they began to throw shell back there into the darkness. The litter-bearers dropped the wounded general and dived for the roadside ditch. A. P. Hill sent out more, and then he was wounded by the shellfire. Somehow in all the bursting shell some men stumbled through the night woods with Tom Jackson. The only sound he made was a groan when the litter-bearers, falling, let his splintered bone strike the earth.

They carried him five miles back to the field hospital in a tent outside a tavern. Young Dr. McGuire hastily summoned other doctors from the army to the seriously wounded general. Jackson was covered with blood and, though obviously in great pain, his pale face was calm and he asked no questions. After the examination, Dr. McGuire asked Jackson, if they found amputation necessary, "should it be done at once?"

"Yes, certainly. Dr. McGuire, do for me whatever you think right."

Before the doctors administered the chloroform, devoted young Sandie Pendleton, Jackson's A.A.G., came with a question from Jeb Stuart. With A. P. Hill also wounded, Lee had turned over the command of Jackson's

three divisions to the thirty-year-old cavalryman, and Stuart wanted to
know his friend's plans and dispositions. Old Jack said:

"Go back to General Stuart and tell him to act upon his own judgment
and do what he thinks best; I have implicit confidence in him."

The confidence was not misplaced. On the next day, Sunday, the singing cavalier handled infantry for the first time in the war and he sent in
the twenty-odd-thousand men and their guns with the same impetuous
recklessness with which he led his horsemen. He didn't stop singing either.
He will always be remembered for that song as he drove against Hooker's
masses in the thick brush.

"Old Joe Hooker, won't you come out of the wilderness?"

Hooker's men fought stubbornly. They had built up works and they
dug in and they didn't drive. Maybe an infantry officer wouldn't have
sent the men in repeatedly the way Stuart did. But the men were confident and Stuart, fighting by the spirit, kindled their fervor.

"Remember Jackson," he called in his bugling voice. "Remember Jackson and charge."

It was their spirit, their invincible will, that carried the heavier Union
forces back into the Wilderness, back toward the river, jammed together
where their numbers were nullified and maneuver impossible. Then, to the
vast relief of all, Jackson's three divisions reunited with the other two divisions that day, and Lee was ready for the combined crusher on Hooker.

It could not be delivered.

Sedgwick, across the river from Fredericksburg, had come over and
stormed Marye's Heights, the grim ramparts of the December battle. Jubal
Early, Dick Ewell's successor, held the Heights with only one brigade more
than his own division, and against Sedgwick's 24,000 he could fight only
a rear-guard action. He fell back westward toward Lee, along the road
on which Hooker had started eastward. In effect, Lee was still between the
two forces. But his force was united and Hooker was beaten, already preparing to withdraw across the river.

However, Lee did have to move troops away from Hooker's position
and hurry a division and a brigade to help Early. The combined forces
drove Sedgwick back across the river at the small action of Salem Church,
on the road between Fredericksburg and the main battle. That action prevented Lee from striking Hooker with his united forces, and the Unions
withdrew to their side of the river.

For all the audacious brilliance of the battle, Lee had accomplished no
more than when he had halted Burnside's drive at the same river five
months before. At Chancellorsville, where he had the opportunity, he
lacked the men. Though Union casualties were higher, Confederate casualties reached nearly 13,000, almost a fourth of the men engaged, and
Stonewall Jackson lay dying.

2

Old Jack had come out of the anesthetic all right and seemed to suffer no shock, either mental or physical, at the loss of his left arm. He was moved from the field hospital to a private house near Guiney's Depot, a stop on the Richmond, Fredericksburg and Potomac Railroad, and Mrs. Jackson came to see him there, bringing their seven-month-old daughter.

Old Jack was cheerful, talking to his friends about the great battle, and he looked forward to a return to action. Then on Thursday, the day his family arrived, he took a sudden unexpected turn. His wounds were healing, but pneumonia had set in. The end came fast.

On another Sunday, a week after his amputation and after the day when Stuart had led his corps, Old Jack began to sink. His young A.A.G., V.M.I.'s Sandie Pendleton, visited the general and Jackson asked him who was preaching at headquarters.

Then his wife told him that he must prepare to meet his Maker. Tom Jackson asked Dr. McGuire if he were dying, and the doctor nodded.

"Very well," he said, and then used his favorite phrase, "it is all right."

He sent messages to his friends and said he wanted to be buried at Lexington, "in the Valley of Virginia." His mind seemed to turn to that land he loved and the little town where he and his Anna had been happy. Then he lost the clarity which he had held to that moment, and reverted to the hour in the dusky woods where he had been shot. He repeated his last order almost verbatim.

"Tell A. P. Hill to prepare for action," he said. "Pass the infantry to the front."

Even in his dying delirium, the wagon hunter thought of his soldiers. "Tell Major Hawks to send forward provisions to the men."

He was terribly agitated as he issued these orders and others indistinguishable. Suddenly the excitement passed. He grew very quiet. Just before his breath expired, he murmured the oft-quoted line, "Let us cross over the river and rest under the shade of the trees."

The warrior and the Presbyterian had become one as the soul passed over the big river to peace from the turmoil of wars and of life. He was thirty-nine years old.

3

Lee faced the painfully familiar dilemma of removing the Union forces from Virginia with an unfamiliar army. The Army of Northern Virginia which entered the Wilderness around Mr. Chancellor's house was not the

same that came out. It would never be the same without Stonewall Jackson.
In *The Song of the Rebel*, John Esten Cooke spoke for his soldiers:

> *In all the days of future years*
> *His name and fame shall shine—*
> *The stubborn, iron captain*
> *Of our old* Virginia Line!
> *And men shall tell their children,*
> *Though all other memories fade,*
> *That they fought with* Stonewall Jackson
> *In the old "Stonewall Brigade!"*

His officers induced Congress to pass a bill officially naming the 1st Brigade the "Stonewall Brigade."

In Richmond the largest crowd in wartime came to view his body, as he lay in state in the rotunda of the Capitol Thomas Jefferson designed. All over the South people mourned. They felt his death as the heaviest blow to their hopes. It was. Only the loss of Lee could have so affected the Confederate people, and Lee was perhaps affected most of all.

Yet it would be difficult to say whether Lee, in his personal sorrow, then realized the extent to which his army was weakened without Jackson. The combination of the patrician and the plebeian had been a strange union of minds—of intent, of the conceptions of achieving the intent, and of the techniques of the achievement. They were equally selfless and equally religious in their burning determination for the independence of their country, equally bold in concept and fierce in execution, always risking for the larger end, the total victory. The combination was broken and Lee had to go on alone.

Secretary of War Seddon approached Lee on his problem with Vicksburg. He wanted Lee to send two divisions (Hood's and Pickett's, those he had fought without at Chancellorsville) to Joe Johnston's aid in lifting the Vicksburg siege by attacking Grant's besiegers. Without the two divisions Lee's army, reduced by casualties to under 50,000, could not hope to pry Hooker out of Virginia. Lee would be forced to retreat to the works around Richmond, and have the chief cities on both fronts besieged.

Ultimately, as Lee said, it was a choice of the dubious situation on the Mississippi for the known situation in Virginia. He would not exchange his power of maneuver and withstand a siege for the possibility that the *existing* siege of Vicksburg *might* be lifted.

This decision of Lee has been written about as if the Mississippi front, at Vicksburg, had been a fluid and remediable situation. Vicksburg was lost when Pemberton took his troops within its works and the Union gunboats sealed him up in there.

Lee's so-called decision was really a rejection of the poor alternative of depriving his successful army for the support of a situation already lost. As it stood, Lee was straining his resources of tact and persuasion in order to avoid the stalemate which Joe Johnston found so simple (once he was away) and which Davis found so satisfactory. Aggressive Hooker, by no means immobilized by his defeat, was plotting ways of striking at Lee again. The Unions were still on their own side of the Rappahannock, and this was a line Lee had never liked. It could easily be flanked. Lee was held there while on defense because Davis would yield no further, even to the South's god, in abandoning another foot of Confederate soil.

To get off the defense—in considering the need of feeding his men and animals, of evicting the invader, of possibly striking a blow for peace—he chose another invasion north. He must break the stalemate which, as he was among the few to realize, was losing the war. More losses in barren defensive victories led only to the end. An army loose in the North could nullify in the Northern mind the siege at Vicksburg. Vital as was the Mississippi, the public mind—North, South, and abroad—was centered on Virginia and the East.

Once Lee decided that he could draw Hooker after him as he had Mc-Clellan before, he had to bargain with his President for troops for the big risk. He had to bargain and compromise. For instance, he wanted all of Pickett's troops back with the army. After long palaver, he got three of the four brigades. That one brigade, stationed uselessly somewhere, had meaning only in Davis' charts of organization.

Then, though he was essentially only commander of the Army of Northern Virginia, Lee wanted to interrelate his northward strike with a whole counteroffensive across all lines. Little attention has been given the details of the total plan Lee suggested, and they were of course ignored by Davis, since they meant disturbing the status quo.

Knowing he had to strip Virginia of troops, instead of leaving uselessly employed brigades around, Lee wanted a real force on the Rappahannock line. This could not only protect the state against raids but offer a threat to Washington which might divert some of the Union forces. For this he suggested that Beauregard bring his troops up from Charleston, where the fortifications had proven more than equal to the U.S. gunboats. Then Lee suggested that the troops out in southwestern Virginia, guarding the the South's only salt, move out against the enemy. At the center, where Bragg was waiting for Rosecrans to thrust his third Union prong, Lee suggested that Bragg move out against Rosecrans, or around him, threatening Kentucky again.

None of this was done. They were all inflexibly arranged departments.

Lee's strike for a decision, then, was not a united action of the Confederacy. It belonged strictly to the Army of Northern Virginia.

The hopes of the South for independence were, without the inward knowledge of the Southern people and without the understanding of the secessionist politicians, concentrated in the mind of Robert E. Lee and the confident hearts of the men from all over the South who followed him. The men in the ranks, and officers too, knew no more of the stakes than those timeservers in the Capitol, but they believed they could beat any army ever put together against them.

Lee counted on their confidence. And he would have been right so to do if he had had Stonewall Jackson. As Lee and Jackson believed in the will of the Almighty, so did the grandmothers of living Southerners. The grandmothers said, "God never intended the South to win, and that's why He took Jackson." Of course, we are more sophisticated today, but when Jackson went, so went the miracles that Lee could perform with his always outnumbered and outgunned army. The year before, the three cigars had ruined his invasion; in 1863 his invasion was ruined before it started when A. P. Hill's alert North Carolina troops fired into the darkness at a body of horsemen.

CHAPTER XVI

"With Pickett Leading Grandly Down . . ."

THERE was an amalgam of reasons why the battle fought at the Pennsylvania town of Gettysburg became dramatized as the crucial turning point of the war. The obvious reasons were that the South's great commander, regarded as virtually invincible, led the Confederacy's finest army on an invasion in the enemy's country at a time when the war on the surface seemed to be stalemated. This impression of the stalemate was illusory.

The turn of the war had come the previous September on the banks of Antietam Creek at the Maryland town of Sharpsburg. From then on, despite field victories, the South had resumed in 1862 the long rear-guard action it began in 1832.

If left to the secessionist leaders, there would have been no desperation counterinvasion. The war would have dwindled off, as it eventually did, without the high note of Gettysburg in American history. As Lee was not supported truly by his government in his effort to save it, so his own army of lost leaders was not equipped for success. The Unions had the might to destroy his army before it ever got out of Virginia. Only they did not have a Lee. And Lee did not have the army he believed he did. Its peak had been passed at Chancellorsville. It would never be the same again.

On leaving their own land, the Army of Northern Virginia was more of a legend than a reality.

This was not true among the soldiers. Possessing group unity and the élan resulting from a leadership the civilians lacked, the men of Lee's army had personally triumphed over all the lacks of borderline subsistence, inadequate medical attention, inferior equipment, poor clothes, and worse shoes. Having been failed completely on supply of uniforms, they did not even look like an army.

Mostly the officers wore the tailored gray cadet cloth of the photographs, though with little uniformity even among them. Few affected the dandyism of Powell Hill, with his brightly colored neckpieces. Some soldiers wore the government-issued butternut-colored homespun, though they rarely had complete uniforms of even this poor material. The majority wore unmatching coats and pants, whatever had been sent from home out of old trunks or could be salvaged from their dead companions. Shirts were the same, and these could be salvaged from the dead of both sides. Their most acute discomfort came from their miserable shoes: the home-made variety the men regarded as instruments of torture and on gleaning the battlefield it was hard to get a fair fit. The most acute pain to their egos was the lack of hats as, products of a country of hot sun, Southerners were vain of their headpieces.

Yet their successes under these circumstances created a pride in their ability to triumph over conditions, and certainly no troops were ever physically and morally equipped to march, fight, and endure on less. With their physical toughness and soaring morale, through experience the men had reached a peak of individual resourcefulness and group skill to mold their units into superb fighting bodies . . . as long as well led.

It was in command that the army was only a name, and even Lee was not aware of this.

His army had never been organized according to any charts of regulations. Before Jackson's death, Lee's two corps of four divisions illustrated how he adapted his material to his ends. Jackson's corps had been the mobile, striking force; Longstreet's corps was depended on for the more orthodox work, more closely under Lee's personal attention.

With Old Jack gone, since no other general possessed either his intuitive collaborative qualities or gifts in semi-independent command, the successful two-corps organization had to be broken up. Longstreet kept the bulk of his corps, Bald Dick Ewell inherited the bulk of Jackson's corps, and a third corps was formed for A. P. Hill. It was an untried organization, with generals untested in corps command, and with Lee *still conditioned* to operating through personal suggestions with Stonewall Jackson in the old system.

Though Dick Ewell and Powell Hill had been among the greatest division commanders in the Confederate armies, neither was fitted to operate as a corps commander with Lee's loose, discretionary orders. The intense Hill was too impetuous; devoted Ewell, accustomed to Jackson's strict orders, lacked initiative. Also, he was psychologically affected by the loss of his leg, and only desperation (and a sentimental leaning toward Old Baldhead) forced the Confederates to be the first army to use amputees.

The situation was worst where it was thought to be best. Of all qualities one could have associated with stolid Longstreet, dependability would come first. However, with Jackson gone and no rival on the scene, Longstreet returned to the army from his abortive attempts at independent command with a curious self-intoxication. He was the brains of the army. Far from the reliable Old Pete he was thought to be, the one experienced corps commander began to advise the commanding general on how the invasion should operate—essentially on the defensive—and actually believed that the kindly gentleman who extended him the courtesy of listening was under his influence. In effect, Lee had become a field commander under Longstreet, the chief of staff.

In this unhealthful situation, in an army of necessity built on personalities, worse was yet to come. This concerned the hitherto reliable if flashy Jeb Stuart, whose cavalry Lee had learned to use in one tumultuous year and on whom he had become completely dependent.

Stuart and his men had grown so accustomed to the inferiority of the Northern horsemen, as compared to themselves, that they ignored the effects of two years in the saddle on a numerous, determined, and very rich people. As Southern troopers still furnished their own mounts, there was no cavalry reserve and, with the government's failure to supply forage at the front, the horses were in progressively poorer condition. Conversely, the Union government bought horses from over a vast area and volunteers were induced with cash bounties, sometimes "$300.00 in gold paid down." Their equipment and weapons were of the best and forage always got up.

In numbers and materially, the toughening Union cavalry was superior to Stuart's by the spring of 1863. The Federals had fought in central Virginia so long, they knew the state as well as the natives. They lacked only the élan of those high-spirited cavaliers fighting for their land with confidence in their leader. As the Union cavalry grew sharp with experience, and skillful and energetic leaders began to emerge, the Rebel edge in spirit and leadership was no longer to be enough.

After Chancellorsville, with the Union horses rested from Stoneman's raid and commanded by Pleasonton (Stoneman had been relegated to raiding), Stuart encountered difficulty in working through a Yankee cavalry screen as stiff as his own usually was. Lee desperately needed information as to Hooker's intent with his own three corps separated in beginning their northward march. The information had to come from a partisan ranger, though the most famous one left in the East. This was John Mosby, the slight, wiry, sandy-haired and cold-eyed Virginian who, with a small and shifting force of irregulars, operated as an independent scout.

He and three followers lay in the June woods and watched the passage of Hooker's army, and at night the four men mingled with the troops, working their way to headquarters. When a major and two captains left headquarters with messages, Mosby's men followed. They overtook the Union staff officers at a house where they had paused for refreshments, took them and their message at pistol point, and Mosby rode through the Union Army, passing between their campfires, to deliver the messages to Stuart.

That was a desperate way for the great cavalry leader to be getting information of enemy troop movements. In combat, too, the Unions showed both new strength and aggression. Pleasonton's strong assertiveness showed in early June, when Stuart's cavalry had swelled to the peak strength it was ever to know, the final power of the South gathered in its mounted troops. With reconditioned troops returned and troops from other sectors, his division swelled to corps size, more than 9000 men and a full twenty-gun battalion of artillery.

As Lee's three corps, spread over fifty miles, began their march north-westward from Fredericksburg to the Valley, Stuart's assignment was to guard the fords and screen the infantry. Near the old happy grounds of Brandy Station, Stuart was surprised by Pleasonton's 11,000 Union troop-ers, through the failure of a new brigadier, Beverly Robertson. Before he realized what was happening, the Rebel cavalry leader was in serious trouble.

Fleetwood Heights was the largest battle ever fought on this continent between two cavalry forces, both fighting without infantry, fighting close up with sabers like individual fighters out of old wars, firing their horse pistols at point-blank range like gunfighters in Western pictures. Pleasonton's determined men were finally driven off, with no honors to the Confederates, except that the Unions failed to penetrate the cavalry screen and gain information as to Lee's movements.

The affair was very costly. While Pleasonton lost 936 of his nearly 11,000 men, almost 500 of whom were prisoners, Stuart lost 523, killed, wounded, and missing, and he lost some good ones. Rooney Lee went down wounded, gone from the cavalry. Farley, that gently smiling and ice-blooded South Carolina partisan ranger and Stuart's valued volunteer aide, was mortally wounded. One of Wade Hampton's sons, a promising lieu-tenant colonel, was killed outright in the personal fighting, and another son, on the staff, was wounded.

John Pelham, the beloved young cannoneer, had been killed earlier in the spring at a small action he was observing. That was personal sorrow to Stuart (he wept openly), as was the passing of Jackson. Stuart wrote his brother that "the great and good Jackson was the dearest friend I had. . . ."

With Stuart's grief went the goading knowledge that the veterans were going from his command, and of their like there were no more in the South. Then personally Brandy Station sat ill on Stuart. He felt defensive about the action. Though as devoted as Lee himself, or as Old Jack had been, Stuart's was a young and flamboyant ego, and he thirsted for new exploits which would straighten out his ruffled plume. On the road into Pennsylvania he found them, at fatal cost to Lee's invasion.

Across all commands, then, the one successful army of the Confederacy was not what it looked to be when Lee on his own began the last, doomed counterstrike.

2

On June 3, a month after Chancellorsville and with the Vicksburg defenders in the third week of their siege, Lee's first troops left Fredericksburg under Bald Dick Ewell. With three of the four divisions of Jackson's
old II Corps, he rode in as sprightly a fashion with his wooden leg as he
had in his dragoon days on the border.

Ewell's corps headed for the Valley, coming down from the Blue Ridge
at Front Royal, where with Jackson he had captured the Union garrison
a little more than a year before in the beginning of the Valley campaign.
In the '63 summer, the "old soldiers" remembered the Valley country
where they had first become Jackson's foot cavalry, and the men liked
Ewell as a successor. They liked the way he marched them, though some
observed that on the approach to Winchester Old Jack would not have
sent them into bivouac. He would have marched them on through the
night. They bagged Milroy in Winchester anyway, with four thousand
prisoners and the usual assortment of guns and victuals that kept the Confederates in the field.

The old Rockbridge Battery, originally composed of college students
and commanded by a Lexington preacher (General Pendleton, then Lee's
chief of reserve artillery), abandoned two blockade-run British Blakelys
for the superior Parrotts used by the Federals. For the first time in the war,
those boys had guns all of the same make, the best the United States put
out.

By then Longstreet had moved out to cover the mountain passes to the
Valley and A. P. Hill, finding that Hooker was following Lee, had moved
away from the Fredericksburg battle area. Again nothing stood between
Richmond and the enemy, except the name of Robert E. Lee.

In Vicksburg the people and the soldiers were starving (the undaunted
men concocting weird menus of mule meat), but the Army of Northern
Virginia knew little of this. They were given a bad turn when their
cavalry had that rough day with Pleasonton (June 9, Brandy Station).
However, with no harm done, the infantry kept moving northward in
three columns toward the Valley and the Potomac. For all their jeers
at the horse soldiers (such as pointing to spurs and calling, "How long does
it take you to grow them things outen your heels?"), they had implicit
confidence in Stuart's screening them.

It was in this phase of the Northern invasion that Lee gave the famous
orders to Jeb Stuart. You can read the orders and you can read Stuart's
reports and the comments of all manner of officers involved (such as
Colonel Marshall, who wrote the orders for Lee), and the orders *were*
discretionary.

Lee had no way of knowing that Stuart's discretion was influenced by his desire to silence the critics of his action at Brandy Station. Except for his youthful excesses in the "Ride around McClellan," which did act as a great morale lifter, Stuart had served the infantry as no army was consistently served in the Civil War. But the vainglorious young horseman was thinking of Stuart's legend in that summer of 1863. With all orders and reports and analyses, he was not discreet to abandon Lee when the army was attempting its second invasion, its big strike for the decision which the government would not strike for.

It was not that Lee lacked cavalry, but that he lacked Jeb Stuart. The general had come to depend on his former West Point student and not on new people, like Jenkins at the head of his column and Imboden to the west, both of whom were raiders and not experienced in reconnaissance. Lee also had the new brigades of Robertson and Jones guarding the mountain passes behind him as he moved northward, and he was not accustomed to dealing with cavalry brigadiers. He was accustomed to dealing with Jeb Stuart.

The one thing that Jeb Stuart's fame-hunting did, beyond all controversy, was to fail to provide reconnaissance for Lee's army moving into an alien land. That was the service of the cavalry and that Stuart, as the cavalry commander, was responsible for. Furthermore, he took with him the three experienced cavalry brigades of the Army of Northern Virginia —Fitz Lee's, Wade Hampton's, and Rooney Lee's under Chambliss—and left with the army those new people. Lee had never worked with any of them and, anyway, their assignments were not reconnaissance. Stuart's was reconnaissance and screening.

Instead he rode around Hooker's army back in Virginia, seeking another "Ride around McClellan." Then Stuart crossed the Potomac with *the Unions between Lee and the Confederate cavalry*. None of this was known to the commanding general.

It can be shown that Stuart also occupied the Union cavalry, that he occupied an infantry division in Pennsylvania, and that he captured and brought to the Confederate quartermasters 125 fully stocked, fine Union wagons. All that would have been glorious if he had not left Lee blind by so doing. Lee, depending on his usually reliable cavalryman, was forced to grope ahead north of the Potomac without *any* knowledge of the enemy or of his own cavalry.

Of Lee's deep concern as the army moved northward west of the Blue Ridge Mountains, the men knew nothing. When they crossed the Potomac on that trip, there was no singing of "My Maryland," except for a ribald version by the cavalry with them. The army bands played "Dixie." The soldiers were not seeking allies on this trip. Entering the foreign territory of their invaders, the men were seeking food.

In all the accounts by the men who walked north with Lee, you can search in vain for a discussion of the rights of secession, the defense of slavery, or even why they were marching into Pennsylvania. But the dietary habits of Pennsylvanians were described in details that were still glowingly fresh to the men in the long years afterward when they remembered.

Lee had issued strict orders, in another proclamation, for the protection of private property. Mindful of the fact that Northerners expected reprisals from the Rebels, also mindful of the hatred aroused in his soldiers by Union behavior in the South, the general wanted his troops to make a good impression on the enemy civilians. The Northern people would be more receptive to any peace movements when their feelings were not outraged by and hardened against the Confederates. Though this may have been naïveté in Lee's political thinking, he expressed his own deep convictions when he said:

"The commanding general considers that no greater disgrace could befall the army, and through it our whole people, than the perpetration of the barbarous outrages upon the unarmed and the defenseless and the wanton destruction of private property, that have marked the course of the enemy in our own country. . . . It must be remembered that we make war only upon armed men. . . ."

Lee's men accepted all the parts about no wanton destruction, no personal atrocities—"offending against Him to whom vengeance belongeth." But they did yearn for a diet of the victuals such as they had sampled from Yankee wagons and sutlers. They had trouble in satisfying this yearning because Lee meant what he said and his officers tried to enforce it.

On the roads the men marched in tight columns of fours, the old squad formation, with a mounted officer riding to the right of the first squad. Flung out on either side were flankers, men selected to discourage roving. In bivouac, pickets were placed around the camp and, if near towns, only a special permit could get a man in town. But Lee's men were experienced foragers, and hunger and change lent resourcefulness to their determination to avoid the restrictions.

Day and night individuals broke through the cordons to stroll toward some likely-looking farmhouse. The countryside was in full bloom and the men were awed at the richness in contrast to their ravaged land. A South Carolinian said that "in every direction yellow fields of grain extended themselves; on every farm were droves of the largest, fattest cattle; gardens thronged with inviting vegetables; orchards gave promise of a bounteous fruit-yield, and already extended to us an earnest in the most delicious cherries; full dairies, flocks of sheep, and poultry were almost monotonously frequent."

The men did not have to steal, though of course some did, especially the colored servants, mindful of the sparse messes of their masters. They regarded the whole trip as a frolic. Usually the soldiers asked for food and the citizens, in fear of the Rebels visiting on them the outrages their own people had suffered, freely offered up their meats and cheeses, pickles and preserves, in order to get rid of the invaders. Some of the people were friendly, and encouraged the Rebels to get to Washington and kill Lincoln to end the war. One young Virginian was served a breakfast which he still recalled into the twentieth century: "real coffee and sugar, light bread, biscuits with lard in them, butter, apple-butter, a fine dish of fried chicken and a quarter of roast lamb."

To provision the army, the quartermasters levied on communities and stores. They paid in Confederate money where it was accepted (probably in fear), and where not the people were given a duplicate of a full accounting to the penny of the requisitioning by the Confederate government. In one division, a wholesale grab was made for shoes. These were from the beautifully uniformed militia at York, Pennsylvania, who surrendered and were paroled to go back home. The Rebels found the dazzlingly uniformed militia looking very quaint without shoes.

Then, as the army passed through the streets of towns, the sidewalks were crowded with spectators, who wanted particularly to get a look at Lee. Even avowed enemies asked for his autograph. When the soldiers passed close to the sidewalk, the men could not be restrained from grabbing the hats off civilians' heads to cover their own unshorn locks.

The army did not look in such hard case as during the Maryland invasion the year before and, though patches were plentiful, rags were few. Still they were a motley-looking army to civilians accustomed to the Union blue. When a spectator jeered at their lack of fine raiment, the men answered with their line used in reply to so many jeers in so many places: "We don't wear our good clothes to go hog-killing."

The three corps were spread out west of the mountains in Pennsylvania, with Ewell heading for Harrisburg and a cutting of the railroad to Philadelphia. Except for the militia who quickly surrendered, the men hadn't seen a Union soldier since they crossed the Potomac. But Lee hadn't seen a Confederate cavalryman either, and he didn't know what was happening east of those mountains.

The weather had been rainy and stormy and, except for the good Pennsylvania roads, the troops would have been troubled by marching. As it was, the rain and the mist only deepened the mystery beyond the mountain passes, where Stuart's cavalry should have been and wasn't.

Then on a night, twenty-five days since the army's first troops moved out from Fredericksburg back in Virginia, a Confederate scout and spy was brought into Lee's tent. Desperate without Stuart and as Longstreet vouched for this Harrison, the general listened. The tired man told the dumfounded Lee that Hooker's army had crossed the Potomac and was moving toward the east passes of the mountains, which could place the Unions in the Confederates' rear. Furthermore, Hooker had been supplanted as commander by George Gordon Meade.

Meade was a different proposition from Fighting Joe. He was a high-minded gentleman of forty, who had graduated from West Point between the older men like Lee and the younger men like Grant, Sherman, and the Hills. To the Southerners Meade had shown his good taste by marrying a Virginia girl, the sister-in-law of Virginia's ante-bellum governor and eccentric political general, Henry Wise. Lee and his fellow officers always took more seriously the Meades than they did the braggarts, and those close to Lee knew that he was profoundly disturbed.

The next day, June 29, still rainy, Lee could not conceal his worry at the absence of the cavalry. Jones's and Robertson's two new brigades, which had been left to guard passes in his rear, remained on their original assignments after the danger was past. Imboden from the west had not put in any appearance. Jenkins' raiders, in advance of Ewell, were not deemed worthy of reconnaissance. Where *was* Stuart?

Records show that he was husbanding the 125 wagons captured near Washington across Maryland and Pennsylvania, after getting behind Hooker's army in a ride that would supposedly restore his plume. In Pennsylvania, Meade's army was between Stuart and Lee, instead of the other way around. Lee knew nothing of these vain exploits of Stuart. He only knew that, in an alien land without his cavalry, he'd better draw his corps together.

He gave the order for a leisurely concentration, since he had seen naught of the enemy, and the roads of the separated corps led roughly toward the town of Gettysburg. As A. P. Hill's center corps was nearest the appointed juncture, Pettigrew moved a brigade of Heth's division toward the unprotected town because he had heard shoes were there.

3

On the way toward Gettysburg, Pettigrew hit some of Pleasonton's cavalry. Heth was not particularly alarmed, not where shoes were concerned, and the next morning, July 1, he pushed his whole division ahead for the town. Heth was moving cautiously, his brigades deployed and his guns up, when his men struck Union infantry. Both sides began shooting.

Several miles away, Lee was startled to hear artillery thundering through the hills and galloped his gray horse toward the sound. Ewell, coming back from the north, was close, but Longstreet, the rear guard, coming up from the southwest, was some miles away. Only A. P. Hill's corps was actually on the scene. Lee sought the new corps leader. Nervous, high-strung "Little Powell" was sick that day, and he told the commanding general that he didn't know what was going on himself.

By the time that Lee rode close enough to catch the fighting outside the town in his field glasses, he saw, with whatever sinking of the heart, that Heth was too deeply engaged to break off, and another of Hill's divisions was ready to go in. Aside from the identifying blue uniforms assuring him that the other troops were Yankees, he had no notion whatsoever of who they were—a segment of Meade's army, an advance of Meade's whole army, or what. Furthermore, he knew nothing about the unfamiliar country.

However, as if Lee had planned most skillfully to catch those Unions in a pincer at Gettysburg, Ewell's advance division came hurrying from the north to the sound of the fighting. An opportunist, like any great leader in any field, Lee seized the situation as it developed and sent Ewell in on the flank of the Unions, whoever they were. They were Howard's corps (their old Deutsche friends from Chancellorsville) and Reynolds' corps, whose fine leader, captured at the Seven Days and exchanged, was killed as his men fell back through the town. The two Union corps, broken but undemoralized, retreated to a hill at the northern end of a ridge running north-south a little below the small town. The cemetery of Gettysburg was on that hill, Cemetery Hill, from which the whole ridge took its name of Cemetery Ridge.

Though Gettysburg is historically the climactic battle, like the thirty years' conflict and secession and the war itself, it was brought on by a series of individual blunders. Neither government nor commanding general decided to fight there. Meade, with his cavalry chasing Stuart, was groping as was Lee. Their advances collided and the men fought.

Late arrivals in the old Stonewall Brigade had heard some artillery firing and assumed that Jubal Early, the new division commander, "had found some of the Yankees someplace. We had no idea that the two armies were closing together, and the greatest battle ever fought on the American continent had commenced. . . . We marched on down the mountain . . . and just before sundown we reached the battle-ground, and saw some of the wounded and a great many prisoners." (There were 5000.)

They saw also that the opening of whatever battle it was had started well for them, and the high confidence which they had brought into Pennsylvania soared into an elated feeling of invincibility.

With Ewell's and Hill's troops crowding outside the town, and Longstreet hurrying toward it, the composite entity of those men was no longer the Army of Northern Virginia as the men knew it. The change showed first in Bald Dick Ewell.

Lee sent him an order to push on into the enemy, who were desperately gathering on Cemetery Hill, and to carry the position. Then he added the discretionary clause which he used to send Jackson, "if practicable." To the former great division commander of aggressive-minded Stonewall Jackson, and the lover of personal combat, anyone must have assumed that "if practicable" would mean "if humanly possible." Bald Dick never tried to discover whether the position was possible or not. The discretionary orders turned the skillful and energetic subordinate into a baffled and irresolute leader.

With the chance to take the end of the ridge, which would have removed the hills of Gettysburg from Meade as a defensive position, Ewell brooded, turned for advice to Jubal Early, did nothing. When Lee visited his camp later that night, he found a confused leader who, formerly reveling in stealing away from Jackson to get in some personal fighting, was paralyzed at assuming the responsibility for 20,000 men.

The first day's battle ended there, and with it Lee's chance for success, though such a thought never suggested itself as he worked through the night on plans for the next day for taking advantage of the situation which had developed.

4

All figures on the battle vary, but the consensus suggests that after the losses of the first day Lee had about 50,000 infantry and artillery, with most of its cavalry missing. The Unions had something less than 100,000 all arms, with heavy superiority in guns—in numbers and weight, accuracy and range. Lee was accustomed to such odds and he prepared to attack with a confidence which was false in basis.

For the second day of July, Lee ordered Ewell to attack that northern hill again, no discretion about it. But he *told* rather than ordered Longstreet (as was his habit with a familiar) to attack the southern knob of the ridge, Big Roundtop, the Union left flank. A. P. Hill was also to attack toward the Union left. By then Lee knew that Meade, like himself, had blundered into the battle, found a good defensive position, and was rushing his men through the night to occupy it. Lee's purpose was to seize the commanding ends of the ridge before Meade got up.

Ewell, not at himself and never having commanded a corps in action, committed the faults of unsureness and inexperience. He sent his divisions in piecemeal, and piecemeal they were thrown back by a stoutly manned defense of that strong position on the northern edge of the ridge.

At the opposite end, A. P. Hill did well in his attack straight ahead, but against the flank, around Devil's Den, Little and Big Roundtop, Longstreet's slowness to commit lost the whole movement.

Instead of getting out at daylight, Longstreet waited until afternoon, with Meade's men hurrying up all through the day. Lee is reputed to have said that Longstreet was slow to move; definitely, he wanted every detail arranged for his success when he struck. At Gettysburg, the longer he waited, the better became the chances of the growing enemy to repulse him. Accustomed to Longstreet's slowness to action, Lee did not realize that his subordinate was waiting because *he disapproved of the commanding General's plan.*

For the second day the army had failed, and Lee would not accept it. His belief in his men remained unshaken, as well it might have, and he brought no analyses, no judgments, to bear on his commanding officers. Even though Longstreet was sullen and openly opposed to Lee's plans, the general continued to act through the surly subordinate as though finally the man would behave like Jackson. Lee seemed to forget that Jackson had the temperament to command his mobile, striking force; Longstreet was conservative, and liked the enemy to come at him when he was ready, as at Fredericksburg. Lee assumed, perhaps because he had to, that in the final decision they would all perform as they must for the victory.

Of that final decision on the third day, no American action has been written about so much as the climax in Pickett's charge. Actually the final thrust, poorly organized and not well executed in command, was the anticlimax of the three days of blundering. Yet the magnificent performance of the Confederate soldiers, unforgettable to all who witnessed the awesome splendor of the charge—the men stopping to dress the line as artillery fire literally mowed down their ranks—caught in that hour's distillation the climax of the ante-bellum South in its archaic gallantry.

Whose charge it was would be difficult to say. Pickett's all-Virginia division spearheaded the assault and Pickett was the only general in the actual attack who essayed anything like central command. His three brigades were the only units to breach the Union lines under their commanders in anything approaching divisional unity, and the brigadiers got the poetry written about them by a Georgia volunteer who had enlisted at fifteen.

But there were ten brigades in that charge without a leader. Originally, Lee planned the assault for Longstreet's veteran corps, further to the Union left, where Hill had moved successfully the day before. Longstreet had other ideas. Two of his corps had been hard used on the second day against the Union left flank and, besides, he said, if they moved toward the left center, their own right flank would be exposed to the enemy. Longstreet was against the whole idea anyway. Instead of having prepared his troops for the assault, as ordered, the stubborn man had prepared new arguments to convince Lee to call off further attack and follow a plan of his own.

On many occasions, Lee had impressed his associates by the control of a temper which could rage with any man's if he indulged it. His staff had learned the warning signs—the stiffening neck turning red, the throb of suddenly protruding temple veins, the clouding of the usually calm face—and sometimes, not often, swift anger would lash out at some defection. At other times, when in control of the rage, his displeasure would be revealed in glacial tones. When Jeb Stuart had at last joined the army on the second day at Gettysburg, Lee greeted him in icy severity: "Ah, General Stuart, you are finally here."

As Lee listened to Longstreet's insubordinate harangue, he showed no indications at all of anger or displeasure. He showed only a tired patience in the effort to convince his one experienced corps leader that he should co-operate in the general's plan. Lee still clung to the conviction that Longstreet would fight well once he got him to move.

It was the judgment of desperation. It was brought on by prolonged responsibility and anxiety, by physical as well as mental strain to the fifty-six-year-old man, and by the cumulative strain of operating through personalities in an inadequate machinery—as with his persuasion of Longstreet. Without question, Lee was not thinking clearly. He was entrusting the climactic effort of the three-day battle, of the whole campaign, to an officer whose recalcitrance had already lost the second day.

Lee's custom with Longstreet and Jackson had always been to leave the fighting on the field to the corps commander and not interfere. If, for reasons of habit and tact, Lee could not personally assume command, he should have withheld the final attack. Meade manifested no intention of attacking. Lee could have withdrawn at night, with Meade's cavalry as tired as his, and moved to a more favorable position for receiving attack.

But Lee had come North for the big risk for the big victory. He had barely failed on the first two days. With confidence in his men and no aggression from the enemy, he simply had to make the supreme effort. He was right to believe in his troops: they did all that men have ever done in battle. His judgment failed him in believing that any troops could win with such leadership as demonstrated in the first two days.

5

In the first place, Lee compromised with Longstreet in order to win his reluctant and sullen agreement. He would not use Longstreet's two divisions facing the extreme Union left. He would shift his attack further toward the Union left center, and use only Pickett's division from Longstreet's corps.

The three brigades of Pickett's division were the only troops not used either at Chancellorsville or in the first two days at Gettysburg, and they were in top Confederate condition. The 4500 Virginians were fine troops, many from among the first volunteers and ante-bellum militia units, including the 1st Virginia Regiment whose history dated back to George Washington's militia force. George Pickett, thirty-eight-year-old Richmond-born West Pointer and Regular Army man, was a great favorite of Longstreet. With his perfumed, flowing locks, curving mustachios, and air of dash, the long-haired romantic was the infantry's answer to Jeb Stuart. He would be directly under Longstreet's orders.

The seven supporting brigades from A. P. Hill's corps would seem to have been nominally under Longstreet too, since he supposedly directed the attack. For some unexplainable reason those seven brigades were taken from all three of Hill's divisions. The only division that went in as a whole was the newest and poorest. Heth's makeshift unit was formed after Chancellorsville to fill out a three-division corps for Little Powell, and contained two weak brigades. Heth himself had been wounded, and recently appointed Brigadier Pettigrew took the division in, with colonels on brigades. Those four brigades came from Virginia, North Carolina, Tennessee, and Mississippi. In the Mississippi brigade were the two thirds left of the original company of University Greys.

From the division of young Pender (dying of a wound suffered the day before) came two fine brigades of North Carolinians. Finally, from Anderson's division, there was one five-regiment brigade of Alabamians.

This strange collection of brigades were the men who made the charge, about 15,000. Three fourths of the regiments, 36 of 47, came from Virginia and North Carolina, and 3 were from Tennessee—states which had not seceded to form the original Cotton Confederacy.

These troops gathered in the very hot noon behind the crest of their hill, which faced across the sloping farm country the stonewall-lined crest of Cemetery Ridge. The Confederates' less formidable hill was Seminary Ridge, named for a female seminary, and one of the young gunners in the Rockbridge Battery had received an invitation to attend commencement exercises there on July 3 at 8 P.M.

On July 3 the Confederate gunners were moving their pieces in front of the infantry, along the crest of their hill, in order to be close enough to silence the heavy Federal cannon. Most of the Confederate guns belonged to Longstreet's corps artillery, seventy-five of them under young Alexander, the wigwagger at Bull Run, who became the army's best cannoneer.

From the first, Longstreet shirked the responsibility which Lee delegated and tried to shift the attacking command to his artillerist. When Colonel Alexander demanded clarification, Longstreet sent an evasive message about "the intention is to advance the infantry if the artillery has the desired effect . . . when that moment arrives advise General Pickett. . . ." *The decision of the moment to attack at Gettysburg was thus thrust on an artillery colonel.*

When Alexander perceived that his artillery fire was not silencing the enemy guns, he wrote Pickett, "If you are to advance at all, you must come at once or we will not be able to support you as we ought." His ammunition was running low and the Reverend General Pendleton, chief of artillery reserve, was nowhere around with supplies.

In the grove of trees, which was to be the point of the Confederate attack, the eighteen Union guns there suddenly ceased fire. Then Alexander rushed off the decisive message to Pickett. "For God's sake come quick. The 18 guns have gone. Come quick or my ammunition will not let me support you properly." Alexander was a highly literate man and his urgency was reflected in his ungrammatical brevity.

Pickett, eager to go in, handed the message to Longstreet. Longstreet said nothing at all.

Pickett then asked, "General, shall I advance?"

Longstreet finally nodded. He never gave an order.

When the Confederate guns were silenced momentarily for the infantry to pass between them in going forward, Alexander told Longstreet that the ammunition was running low and Pendleton had moved the ordnance wagons to the rear.

Excitedly Longstreet ordered *Alexander* to go and stop Pickett, and then go back and get ammunition. There he revealed that in his opposition to Lee's battle he was unconsciously trying to erect every possible obstacle to its execution. When the artillerist explained why the order could not be obeyed, Longstreet said, "I do not want to make this charge," and walked away. He never gave another order in the attack—except near the end to restrain Anderson's division of A. P. Hill's corps from going in as support, as planned by Lee. He sat on a fence, from where he had a poor vision of the field, and never even advised Lee that the ammunition was about gone.

From the time George Pickett directed his own division down the hill ("with Pickett leading grandly down") it was *his* charge if anybody's. Wilcox's Alabama brigade came up on his right and the other six of Hill's brigades on his left. Union artillery fire opened in tremendous volume on the doomed men. Holes gaped in their ranks by the time the ten brigades crossed the road in the shallow valley between the hills. That's where they dressed their lines as their comrades fell around them. When the line swung up the slope to Cemetery Ridge, co-ordination became uncertain under the plunging fire of the Union guns and the obstacles to maneuver—stone fences, post-and-rail fences, double fences.

Closer to the crest, when Union muskets opened from behind a stone wall, order mostly became lost. The troops to the left fell away. Some veered off, some retreated, and others rushed ahead to the wall. That flank of Pickett was exposed. On the right Wilcox kept going straight. As Pickett's division had drifted slightly northward, the right flank then became exposed. Both flanks of Pickett's division were enfiladed by artillery, and the fronts of all ten brigades, or those still coming on, were decimated by direct artillery and musket fire.

That any kept going on was a triumph of spirit over flesh. Such was their sense of invincibility that the remnants rushing ahead expected to win.

They expected supports that never came. No one was in charge to send them. Close behind his own division, Pickett sent his four staff officers riding off through the lead storm in frantic efforts to bring order to the point of contact. It was useless.

In Pickett's three brigades, Kemper was down wounded ("A thousand fell where Kemper led"), Garnett was dead, his horse galloping wildly over the field ("A thousand died where Garnett bled"), Armistead, his horse killed under him, put his hat on his sword and, yelling, "Follow me," climbed the stone wall ("In blinding flame and strangling smoke, the remnants through the batteries broke, and crossed the works with Armistead"). Armistead fell, mortally wounded, with his hand on a Union cannon. Incredibly "the remnants" had driven the Union infantry from the stone fence and rushed on to fight for the Union guns. North Carolinians from Heth's division under Pettigrew (also fallen) got to the guns too, and some of the Tennesseans. In that ultimately climactic moment it was a battle of three border states who had tried to preserve the Union peaceably.

Then they were engulfed by the Federal reinforcements. More fell, others surrendered, the last few fought their way back down the hill strewn with their dead friends. The "thousand died" was almost literal. About 950 of Garnett's 1300 were casualties. It was the same with Kemper, Armistead, and Pettigrew, where a single staff officer brought out the survivors of a brigade.

Unpursued, the men helped the wounded. Other wounded dragged themselves along, with artillery fire beginning to break over them again.

One of the boys of the University Greys ('60) was among those brought back to die among his companions and not on the field. The young sergeant had strength enough left to scrawl a note:

My dear Mother, This is the last you may ever hear from me. I have time to tell you that I died like a man. Bear my loss the best you can. Remember that I am true to my country and that my greatest regret at dying is that she is not free and that you and my sisters are robbed of my worth whatever that may be. . . .

Young Jere Gage in dying knew their independence had not been won; he did not despair because a battle had been lost. That was characteristic of the army. Though the men were disappointed, their morale was unshaken. They knew they had done the best they could. If they had failed to carry the position, they had blunted the enemy's will to fight.

All the next day, July 4, they lay under a hot sun and, with virtually empty caissons, waited for a counterattack.

On that day Vicksburg surrendered, its people and defenders starved out after forty-seven days. No relief had ever come, and even the lowest rations gave out. Grant scornfully rejected Pemberton's request that his men might walk out under their flags to surrender, the honors of war. He was "Unconditional Surrender" Grant. South of Vicksburg, the Port Hudson garrison, after fighting off Banks's siege, surrendered when the defenders learned that Vicksburg was gone. The South's "Father of Waters" lay open to the enemy, and the Confederacy was at last cut in half.

Lee's troops knew nothing of that. They looked at the Old Man, and he had never in his career been more sublime than in the defeat at Gettysburg. To all, he said, "It's my fault." To emotional Pickett, distrait over his broken division, Lee said, "This has been my fight and upon my shoulders rests the blame. The men and officers of your command have written the name of Virginia as high as it has ever been written before."

A curious canard later arose about Pickett in the South. It originated with a South Carolinian who, for some reason disliking the Virginian, stated that on the retreat back from Cemetery Ridge Pickett was in a stone barn. That unsubstantiated story grew into the legend that he had huddled in the rear the whole time. Then—apparently because, later in the war and still affected by Gettysburg, Pickett did some heavy drinking—the story became embroidered to Pickett's being drunk and huddling in the rear. None of it was true. Pickett did not come back personally from Cemetery Ridge until he, with the scattered soldiers, was being enveloped by the enemy and his staff officers persuaded him that all was lost. As a matter of fact, Lee met Pickett after he came back down the hill from his futile effort to rally support for his men inside the Union lines.

Of such spites that grew later, and Gettysburg surpassed all other battles combined in the post-bellum controversies among the Confederates, there was no evidence when Lee prepared the long retreat. The men seemed anxious to comfort one another, units vying to present a solid front, and the exhausted men always managed to lift a cheer when they saw the careworn face of Lee with its mask of calm resolution.

6

Because of the climactic moment of Pickett's charge, almost nothing has been written about that retreat, an epic in horror which made a deeper impression on the soldiers than the battle. It rained again, most of the way, and the wagons of wounded were not following the main roads.

To keep Stuart with the army, once Lee had him again, only Imboden's raiding cavalry went along as an escort with the miles of the wounded. All they could hear, through the dripping rain, slosh of hoofs, and creak of wheels, were the groans and screams of agonized men. "Water, water, for Christ's sake, water. . . . Stop the wagon, and let me die. . . . For the love of God, let me die. . . ."

At Greencastle, where a staff officer had ridden alone through the crowded market streets on the way up, civilians ran out with hatchets and axes and cut the wheel spokes of the wagons holding the suffering men.

Finally, when the wagon trains reached the Potomac, the waters were up, the army was not there, and the Union cavalry was—in strength.

In one of the small, heroic actions of the war, the wagons with the wounded in them were formed in stockade fashion. Between the spokes wagoners fired with muskets which, even at Gettysburg, the thrifty Confederates had gleaned from the field.

They couldn't have held long, but two slim regiments got across the river from the Virginia side. Because of their weakness, they had been left at Winchester, on the way up, to deal with Milroy's prisoners and captured supplies. In one of them was the relic of Richmond's *corps d'élite*, Company F. Only eight men were left of the original unit of ante-bellum city grandees, and the company roster of fifty-two was made up of conscripts and paid substitutes for exempts.

Company F arrived first. With a veteran captain, the fifty-two infantrymen charged what turned out to be twelve Union cavalry regiments with twelve guns. One of the conscripts fainted when he saw the enemy and another caught an ache which forced him to lie on the ground, where they could hear him groaning. A few stragglers joined them and, in what Company F considered its finest fight, they held the enemy off half an hour until the rest of the regiment got up.

Then, before the combined forces could be overwhelmed, Jeb Stuart came.

The wounded were safe, but there was still the river to cross. As Lee's army arrived at the swollen waters, Meade's troops began to inch toward them from behind. That the men's morale was unimpaired is indicated by their confidence as they went into defensive alignment with none knowing of Lee's anxiety at their desperate plight. Finally, weird and unstable bridges were erected, and men, wagons of wounded, and guns crossed. A. P. Hill went last under heavy fire, crossing with coolness only minutes before his rear guard could be swallowed up.

They were back home safely again, and the enemy was out of Virginia again. Though Meade followed cautiously into Virginia, Lee had achieved vastly more than he would have by trying to fend off the invader from the ravaged Fredericksburg area. His men had fed well away, replenished broken-down horses, and brought back such odd items of necessity as stationery for the War Office and staffs. At home the Valley farmers were getting crops in. As for defense, the attempt at subjugation had been set back for the third time in Virginia.

When Lee heard of the criticisms of the failure of his invasion, he said that the people who had been elated when he won barren victories at Fredericksburg and Chancellorsville, with heavy losses there, now were downcast when he had actually accomplished more.

Even Meade did not claim a victory. He claimed only that he had prevented Lee from his objective of destroying the Union Army. At his end, Meade was criticized for not undertaking a more vigorous pursuit of Lee, though Meade's army had sustained 23,000 casualties at Gettysburg and his cavalry had been hard used. For the whole two months' campaign, from early June on the Rapidan until Lee returned to that desolated countryside in early August, the Unions had lost over 28,000 and the Confederates over 23,000—more men than were actually engaged on either side at First Manassas two years before.

For the defensive policy of the Confederacy, Lee had fought a summer defense in the enemy's country. Back where he began, he faced an enemy in no mood to launch an offensive on Richmond. And yet, in the civilian population, there was a deep sense of disappointment.

What did the Southern people expect? Why did the North regard the battle as the turning point? Militarily, Vicksburg was an incomparably more crucial loss, even though it only inescapably climaxed the series of Western disasters arranged by the department.

Of all the "ifs" of Gettysburg, what "if" Lee had won that battle? Did he possess the elements of a real success?

After all, Lee's army was cut to two thirds; he still had that long wagon train of wounded and those empty caissons, with no means of filling them. The shoes of the men were wearing out and bare feet were showing again.

Could his living off the Pennsylvania countryside with Meade retreating to the fortifications of Washington have induced the Union to call it quits *just when* Vicksburg surrendered, and Northern steamboats ran to the South's great city of New Orleans as a bitter symbol of the conquest of the Mississippi which split the Confederacy?

In the West there was Grant's victorious army of 100,000 virtually unemployed. Another Union army stood ready to move against Bragg in the center of the C.S.A.'s remaining half. On the east coast, though Charleston still held out from the sea, Fort Sumter was merely a defiant shell and the Southern land-hooks outside the bay were finally held by Union ground troops. To force the surrender of Fort Sumter and Fort Wagner, the Union commander threatened to shell the city; then with a long-range gun he threw thirty-five shells into the streets of Charleston before the gun burst. Even at Wilmington, the grip of the blockade was beginning to strangle and the United States was turning out naval gunboats faster than the Confederates were turning out guns. It seems most unlikely that a victory at Gettysburg would have ended the war.

Most certainly the Lincoln government would not have become receptive to any peace proposals because one hungry, battered Rebel army was loose in western Pennsylvania. Aside from Meade's large army, the Union could have concentrated scattered forces to form another whole army that would outnumber Lee.

Yet, with passing time, the legend has grown to give the impression that the Union was *saved* at Gettysburg. It provides the dramatic climax of the whole oversimplified story of "preserving the Union."

The summer invasion campaign which failed at Gettysburg was as complex in its reasons for failure as the reasons for the failure of the democratic processes which led to war as a solution. Pickett's foredoomed charge, in no way endangering the safety of the Union, merely dramatized the failures inherent in Lee's desperate throw toward a decision as opposed to a continuing and fatal stalemate.

If the invasion could have threatened the safety of the Union, then the Union owed its salvation to that fresh grave on the hillside outside of Lexington "in the Valley of Virginia." After the war, when Lee was able to do some detached thinking, he recognized that the Gettysburg campaign was lost when the combination was broken with the death of Stonewall Jackson.

While the Battle of Gettysburg could not have been the turning point of a war already lost, the drama of the Confederacy's only successful army being turned back on its one real invasion exerted a profound effect on the morale of both sides.

In the North this victory over the one force which had threatened them heartened the people in what had become, for those days, a very long war. In the South, the defeat of the only army in which they had confidence was psychologically a heavy blow. Coming simultaneously with the loss of Vicksburg and their river, and following on the death of Stonewall Jackson, Gettysburg accelerated the downward spiral of the spirits in the growing number of those worn out by the war and its privations.

Yet, even in morale, Gettysburg marked no distinct turning point in the Confederacy. The effect was revealed in the paper money, which reflected the faith of a people in its government.

In ratio to gold, the Confederate dollar had fallen very slowly in value, though steadily. In May, *after* the great victory at Chancellorsville, the money had taken its biggest single drop up to then, from 4.5 to 5.2. In June, while Lee was actually invading, the money took an even bigger drop from 5.2 to 7. In July, after Gettysburg, the dollar fell to 9, and in August, with the full effect in, the dollar dropped to 1 to 12 against gold.

From May through August 1863 the Confederate money fell more than it had in the first two years of the war. As its big fall began before the invasion, and continued through it, it is clear that Gettysburg only accelerated the falling faith in the Confederacy's future.

That faith, and the reasons for its loss, was outside the control of Lee and his army. Lee had done all that one man could do. With all considered, the Gettysburg campaign, aside from morale, made the Virginia situation for defense more favorable. If that defense was to continue until the North lost heart, the morale to support it was the concern of the people's leaders.

CHAPTER XVII

"Whom the Gods Would Destroy . . ."

THE people of the South had never been the concern of their leaders, and in Richmond the war leaders were surrounded by sycophants and die-hards. It was not among the die-hards, men and women all through the Confederacy, that morale was appreciably affected, however much their emotions were. It was in the middle groups, radiating out from the tough core, where patriotism thinned proportionately as it approached the rim of disaffection and open dissension.

These were the people who grew more susceptible to the growing numbers of "croakers." These were the people whose spirits faltered at the prospect of continued privations for a government dim and remote to them. When the long struggle threatened to drag out indefinitely, the spirit yielded to the demands of the flesh. "Even Yankees couldn't be any worse than this," about summed up the attitude of the hungry.

As their numbers grew, the influence of their resignation and disaffection spread like an infection. More tangibly, individual renunciations of the Confederacy and all its works undermined the soldiers who had grown tired of privations, danger, and absence from their families. Men who went home in the late summer of '63 to harvest a crop, cut wood for their families against the coming nights, and make moccasins out of cowhide for the children's bare feet were less likely to return to the armies.

New conscripts showed a stronger disinclination to adapt to their fate, and desertions among them were continuous. Deserters, captured, would leave again, some three and four times. This also influenced those soldiers whose will to fight was weakening.

Significantly, many deserters and conscript-evaders went from quitting the cause to turning against it. Since, despite the inefficiency of conscript machinery, their existence became semifugitive, these men took the next step to virtual and in some cases actual outlawry. In northern Alabama, the mountains of North Carolina, Virginia, and East Tennessee, bands of them collected with the Unionists and preyed upon loyalists. Open conflict appeared for the first time in South Carolina. In Mississippi, in the shadow land left by Union devastation, marauding groups formed of deserters from both armies roamed the countryside where no law existed.

The effect of deserters on both the Western armies and the civilians of Mississippi and Alabama was heightened by one of those obscure events in the annals of war that have more effect than some battles. When Vicksburg surrendered 31,600 men, because of the numbers and because Porter wanted to use his fleet for action and not for transporting prisoners, the troops were paroled instead of being sent to Northern prisons. As prisoner exchange between the two armies still went on, if erratically, at that period of the war, the government expected these parolees to be exchanged for Union prisoners actually held or paroled. Lee had captured or paroled approximately 10,000 in the Gettysburg campaign.

Instead of letting the paroled Confederates go home to wait, where they could make themselves useful and find a renewing relaxation with their loved ones, for the bureaucratic reason that he wanted their units kept together, the President had the men placed in a dreary camp at Demopolis, Alabama. More insidious than all the dramatic contingencies of battles was the confinement of those 30,000 men, already broken in health and morale from withstanding forty-seven days of starvation under the cramped strain of a siege by land and water.

They immediately demanded furloughs and, when refused, simply walked away. In its rapid disintegration at Demopolis, the force from Vicksburg spread disaffection individually through an area already depressed by the loss of their last river city. Some of those men joined the marauders, the new peace societies, and splinter secession movements, becoming active against the Confederacy as well as preying on its hardpressed loyal citizens.

These little-considered and peripheral aspects of the war worked physical and moral hardship on the poor and yeoman families whose loyalty had not faltered but soon might. Other factors, which would not normally come to mind, such as the uncertainty of mail, particularly from sons and husbands and sweethearts in the armies, worked against the people's will.

In the occupied borderland, where the invaders' cavalry ranged, it was virtually useless for long-suffering Reagan's postal service to operate. Even without the hazards of the enemy, most mail in the South went by horseback rather than train, and horses out of the army were in little better shape than those poor simulacra of steeds of war. With men either in the armies, or having taken to the hills or a bureau, mail carriers were boys with little sense of responsibility or those last dredged-up specimens who were deemed unworthy for any useful employment. Between the animals and the carriers, the postal-service motto could be paraphrased to "Rains and snows, hot and cold, moonshine and shady pools, will all deter the delivery of this mail."

A strange item of the Union contraband was Bibles. The lonely people deprived of their spiritual comfort were distressed and often went to great efforts to replace a Bible which might have gone off with a soldier or a marauder. The few printing presses in the South were mostly too busy with stamps, bonds, and paper money to make plates for Bibles. Like nearly everything else, Bibles had to come from outside.

As for the Episcopal prayer books, no facilities existed for changing "the President of the United States" to "the Confederate States." A Richmond bookseller and a Presbyterian minister combined to bring both Bibles and proper Confederate Books of Common Prayer in through the blockade. In England, the Reverend Dr. Hoge purchased his Bibles and a Mr. Stewart, acting for the bookseller, paid $1000 in scarce gold to have new prayer books printed.

Alas for Richmond Christians, Dr. Hoge's wife had befriended a Cincinnati lady, Mrs. Allan, who had married a Richmonder, and Mrs. Allan repaid the Hoges' hospitality by spying on their household and then informing the Unions of the blockader coming in. The good U.S.S. *Circassia* ran the blockade runner aground outside of Wilmington and jettisoned the whole cargo of books except for several hundred of the Prayer Books, Testaments, and Gospels. These were sold in a prize court in Boston. For the lost $1000, Mr. Randolph, the bookseller, immortalized his name in collectors' items of rare books.

The former Secretary of War, George W. Randolph, turned up here again, going from defending conscript-evaders to defending Mrs. Allan, the spy who caused it all. Throughout the South the sight of all too many well-placed persons, like Thomas Jefferson's grandson, openly putting their private interests before the country's caused a swelling of that refrain, "A Rich Man's War and a Poor Man's Fight." This made its contribution to defections.

Then, when state governors, like Joseph Brown of Georgia and Zebulon Vance of North Carolina, defied government conscript laws and the officers of enforcement, they gave support to all those of wavering allegiance.

Brown was the first of those Southern demagogues who won power by going to the masses. Howell Cobb, typical ante-bellum grandee, said he felt personally ashamed that the state of Georgia was disgraced by having the "miserable scratch" in the Capitol. An Augusta paper called him "Joseph the Governor of all the Georgias," and the Sandersville paper said that he suffered delusions in which he imagined himself "alternately the state of Georgia and the President of the Confederate States." He was a shrewd knave.

Vance was of different caliber. A sincere patriot who yearned for independence, his obsession with the interests of his own state blinded him to the defeat which his shortsightedness was bringing to North Carolina along with the rest of the states. As an example, for years there had been no railroad line between Danville, Virginia, practically on the border of Vance's state, and Greensboro, forty miles to the southwest in North Carolina. Davis had been in Richmond only a short time when he recognized the military need to fill that gap. At first Congress, intent on the political aspects of keeping railroads out of government control, would have nothing to do with it. Finally, steady demands won a charter in early 1862, and by May of that year plans were completed by which the Richmond and Danville Railroad would construct the line on a $1,000,000 (in bonds) government subsidy.

By August 1863, after the government was forced to seize unused rails from railroad companies which refused to sell them, after the government bought slaves in the open market because planters refused to hire out their own for the railroad construction, after the Confederate Engineering Bureau was brought in and after General Lee personally stressed the need of completing the line, Governor Vance still would not budge in his refusal to co-operate in any way. His reason was that the interests of North Carolina would not be served. In fact, the connection might divert commerce from the western counties to Virginia.

When, despite Zebulon Vance, the road was mostly laid by the end of the year, Vance's western constituents felt they had more reason to dislike a central government which had imposed its arbitrary will on them.

Everything the government did was arbitrary to somebody. Davis, because of his personal abrogation of authority, aloofness, and unremitting capacity for making enemies, was blamed as a despot for all the acts of the Confederate government designed to protect its citizens. By the late summer of 1863 the personal hatred of Jefferson Davis, spreading from a few early enemies into highly articulate segments, was having its own effect on the people.

Old Edmund Ruffin, Virginia's secession leader, in total disenchantment with Davis, called him "our tender conscienced and imbecile President." Nothing could be more harmful to Southern morale than to lose faith in their leader. Affection for Davis they'd never had, but always respect and at first great confidence. The confidence was shaken early, the respect was being supplanted by doubt, and the lack of affection was becoming a positive distaste.

2

As with most public figures, Davis was not only hated for many of the wrong reasons, but all manner of evils were attributed to him; and his failings, made with the best intentions, were given a sinister turn.

Anti-Administration newspapers hammered at him unmercifully, led not surprisingly by the Charleston *Mercury* of Rhett, the Father of Secession and perpetual revolutionary. The vituperative Pollard, in the Richmond *Examiner*, fought the Civil War entirely against the Davises, and he would always get that grain of truth to substantiate his wildest charges. Then, as now, some people believed all they read.

In Congress it was the same way. Davis on the whole got along well with that largely baffled and mostly undistinguished body (only one of his thirty-nine vetoes was overridden) and he had staunch supporters among able men, like Georgia's Ben Hill. But the vindictive attackers could always get the headlines. His most unrelenting enemy was Henry Stuart Foote, whose hatred dated back to Washington days when they were fellow senators from Mississippi. Since then Foote had transferred his constituency to Tennessee, but his loathing of Davis was so unchanged that it embraced all the President's cabinet members too.

That Foote got in fights with everybody did not minimize the effect of the venom he poured on Davis. As a matter of fact, in his few years in the Confederate capital, Foote was (1) attacked in the chambers by a man with a bowie knife; (2) had a fist fight with another man, pulling out his shirt bosom, and knocked Commissary General Northrop into a corner; (3) in his own rooms he hit over the head with an umbrella the second sent by John Mitchel, the Irish patriot, to challenge him to a duel. Word battles he held every day.

This should not imply that Foote was unique among his fellows; he only had the most fights. The journal clerk of the House shot it out with the chief clerk in Capitol Square and killed him. Before Yancey died, Ben Hill threw an inkwell at him and it broke upon his cheek. A woman invaded the chambers with a horsewhip and worked on the congressman from Missouri, and duel challenges went on as if they were all back in Washington arguing over the innocuous abstraction of territorial rights.

The Congress itself was not held in high esteem. The common complaint was that everything was held in secret session except "motions to adjourn, tinker the currency, or appoint days of fasting and prayer. . . ." One member said that "If the House would adjourn and not meet any more, it would benefit the country."

Yet, considering that they were politicians suffering the division between their states' rights instincts and national emergency, they were no worse than the average American congressional body. At least they never spent much time, as did Lincoln's Congress, appointing war committees to investigate events already past. As were all in the South, however, they were required to do more than their fellow Americans did. Failing that, along with the spectacles they sometimes made of themselves, they too were blamed for lacks inherent in the confederation of seceded states.

The people began for the first time in Southern history to resent their leaders. The reality of this resentment is indicated by the postwar rejection of the historic and conservative aristocratic leadership of the South, and the rise of the white-supremacy demagogue—that hater of the Negro as the symbol of his own former inferiority to the planter class. As an old woman in Montgomery, referring to the leaders, said to Mrs. Chesnut, "They got us into it; let them get us out."

"They," however, had gotten themselves into it and knew not how to get out. Their very real attachment to and belief in the state as a center—however politically confused with and made shrill by the principle of states' rights—had come immediately into conflict with the needs for centralized control. Since the ante-bellum leaders had been deluded into accepting abstractions for reality, for their leader they elected their leading abstractionist, and to that rootless man of ambition states' rights were *only* a principle.

On this basis, Davis and Congress worked with thoughtful attention on the political rights of states, while neglecting completely to bind the people's loyalty at the state level. Their states were the people's closest tie. The Confederate government never seemed to remember that the people had seceded as states, gone to war as states, and as state citizens largely carried the burden for a new and distant central government which ignored them.

That was not the fault of Davis or of Congress, nor was it so simple as the theory of states' rights. Nothing was simple about it. The complexities and contradictions of the regional consciousness made it impossible for a rational, unifying order to emerge under the impact of invasion, where the needs of war were antithetical to the people's individualistic nature and to the secessionists' basic position.

Given the opportunity to develop their nation in peace, with its customary aristocratic conservative leadership at state levels in a loose confederation, the Southern Confederacy would have defended itself out of an existing order and habit of government. As it was, they defended themselves as a people, which they never were, and not as the states which formed an alliance.

They remained relatively cohesive as a people as long as they did through love of their land, comparatively successful resistance, and the mounting hatred of the invader. Probably decent behavior and generous attitudes from the enemy might have softened the resistance which was hardened by brutality and despoliation. Always the cohesion was more apparent than real.

The appearances fell away when the people, losing faith in a future of independence, began to blame leaders personally for all the miseries they suffered to no purpose. Naturally their blame centered on the President, as Hoover was blamed for the depression—though in the case of the Confederacy the people were more justified. Also, as with any people, their apprehensive dissatisfactions with the way things were going, and their fear-inspired resentments, found objects in personalities. The chief object of all their protests in the fall of 1863 was Davis' favorite, Braxton Bragg, defender of Chattanooga. In this the people were wholly justified.

With Vicksburg gone, Chattanooga, formerly the center, became in effect the Confederate left. The Richmond–Chattanooga line is not normally thought of as the Northern defense border of the Confederacy, but such it had become during the summer of 1863. The breaking of the line there would be almost as vital a blow to their defense, though not sentimentally, as the fall of Richmond at the other end. Each was a doorway into the interior of the shrinking territory of the South. With the Mississippi Valley gone, the loss of the Chattanooga territory would mark the beginning of the end.

In centering their criticism of the Administration on Bragg as the commander of this crucial area, the people were demanding of the President that he change his ways in order to realize what they believed was their potential for a successful defense. Bragg represented a remediable situation. They demanded that the contumacious failure be removed.

Even the doormat Congress joined in the demand for Bragg's removal. Administration papers joined the anti-Administration papers in demanding a change before it was too late. It was the one subject on which all people were united, and Davis refused to heed the popular clamor.

Always stiffening against criticism, Jefferson Davis took the stand that completed his alienation from the people. He retained Bragg in a situation which Davis knew was deteriorating under Bragg's command.

The consequence of this despotism provided a public spectacle of personality clashes and collapses which, even at a distance, seem more like case histories of the damned than anything resembling a nation's struggle for survival.

3

In refusing to recognize the validity of the public's demand, Davis did recognize that something had to be done at Chattanooga. To this end, the President returned to his old adviser and comfort, General Lee. From his own troubles in rebuilding his diminished army with deserting conscripts, in making his never completed search for food and shoes (even the shortest marches were leaving again those trails of blood), the tired old soldier was called to Richmond for one of those old-time conferences at which his advice would be ignored.

In early September, when Lee came down to the lingering heat of Richmond, the western half of their country was being saved from total and imminent disaster only by Lincoln's continuing to essay military strategy. With Halleck at his side, the two of them repeated what they had done the year before after Shiloh when Halleck commanded in the West. The victorious army was dispersed.

The President had a plan for sending troops west to Texas, to plant the United States flag there for diplomatic reasons. Though under Secretary of State Seward's threats against any intervention, France was still friendly to the Confederacy; and its puppet emperors in Mexico, the ill-fated Carlotta and Maximilian, were regarded by Lincoln as potential troublemakers in international relations.

To further this plan, Lincoln dispatched part of Grant's army to Texas under Banks, where the pugnacious political general was to fare even worse than he had in the Valley of Virginia. Other Union units went to garrisons and others were sent off to Arkansas, where old fat Sterling Price was trying to do such damage as he could west of the Mississippi. Federal troops were also kept in Missouri by the raids of the tough-bitten volunteer cavalry of Jo Shelby.

Another of those in the archaic tradition of the partisan ranger, Shelby was a first-class cavalry leader when given the opportunity to operate with an army. He grew up on the same block with John Morgan in Lexington, Kentucky, but his fighting style had been formed in the Kansas border wars when he sought his fortunes in Missouri. As a Confederate, the independent-minded fighter wasted no efforts trying to get arms or equipment from the inefficient government and, except for some uniforms which his cavalry stole from a consignment intended for Pike's Indians, Shelby's men used the Federal army for their Quartermaster Department. Among the young men who were no less tough when with Shelby than when they earned their postwar notoriety were Cole Younger and Frank and Jesse James. On a small scale, Shelby's raiders were very troublesome people.

When Lincoln dissolved Grant's army, no reinforcements came to swell Rosecrans' army into what would have been an irresistible force at Chattanooga. Without departments, Lincoln had his ideas fixed on the always three separate objectives—Virginia, the Mississippi, the middle. The war started that way and so it continued. With no logical progression toward halving the remaining half of the Confederacy, slow-moving Rosecrans resumed his year-old task of getting Bragg out of eastern Tennessee.

Thanks to Lincoln, Chattanooga was the only danger spot in the Western Confederacy; thanks to Davis, that spot was in real danger. The two Presidents as military experts were still outfumbling each other. As a Confederate nurse quoted from Cowper:

> . . . *war's a game, which, were their subjects wise,*
> *Kings would not play at.*

To make things worse for Bragg, Davis removed from the migraine sufferer his able veteran, Hardee, the well-liked corps leader. He was sent on the task for which Bragg was fitted by nature and training: to re-recruit the disaffected in Mississippi and Alabama, to regroup and retrain them into a force. One of Bragg's two dependable generals was thus sent on the task of a recruiting sergeant and drillmaster, out where Joe Johnston was still lurking aimlessly around.

Johnston's Mississippi area had become, with the fall of Vicksburg, a periphery, as the former center of East Tennessee became the left of two fronts. This was not entirely a disadvantage to the Confederacy. The loss of the Mississippi was also the loss of a prolonged headache, even though brought on by Davis' departments and the government's neglect of the West. With Nashville and New Orleans lost early, the territory to defend was reduced to the Confederate centers of production—from Richmond, through cities in the Carolinas and Georgia, and southwest into Selma and Mobile in Alabama. With the borders contracted, the South was in a position for greater troop concentration and less fixed positions.

Also, with the formerly cumbersome Department of the West existing in name only, the Army of Tennessee and Lee's army were at last conceived of as units for co-operative action. Unfortunately for the efficacy of this joint action, the Confederates lost Cumberland Gap and the use of the connective Virginia-Tennessee Railroad, but roundabout ways existed for troop movements between the two armies.

When General Lee was summoned for discussion of the co-operation between the two armies, the object was to help Bragg. Davis' friend was in serious trouble again. Having practically flanked himself out of Kentucky the previous summer, and having been flanked out of middle Tennessee by Rosecrans, in the summer of 1863 Bragg was about to be flanked out of the fortified city of Chattanooga.

Under the joint goad of his own ambitions and his wife's for him, and with the fresh memory of his trail of failure, dyspeptic Bragg awaited attack in a state of what today would be called anxiety neurosis. Worrying about what the enemy would do, he fretted himself into total inanition. In this condition he was found by D. H. Hill, who had been sent out by Davis from North Carolina to assume command of Hardee's corps.

Harvey Hill himself was no charm boy, though an able and grimly fighting soldier, one of the heroes of Sharpsburg. He was an opinionated man with a highly articulate intelligence, and he could never refrain from criticizing others. He had been in and out of Lee's army twice and left no repining behind him.

However, Hill came out in good cheer, since he liked active fighting and remembered Bragg warmly from the days when he and George Thomas (then commanding a corps with Rosecrans) and John Reynolds (killed at Gettysburg) had been lieutenants in Bragg's fine battery. Also, when he wasn't criticizing others' defections, Hill had a sense of fairness, and he felt a loyal support to his old captain who was coming in for so much abuse.

Once on the scene, Hill was shocked at the change in his old companion. He found Bragg gloomy and nervous, greatly aged, and without any friendliness at all. With his initial loyalty repelled, Hill immediately reverted to his critical turn and, as many others did soon afterward, lamented the vast difference between Lee's and Bragg's armies. Around Bragg there was dissension, sullenness, none of the *esprit* of the Army of Northern Virginia. Worse, the commanding general was getting no information on the enemy and grew querulous as he worried about what Rosencrans was up to.

Even Lee would have been shaken at the cavalry situation. From the beginning, in the West much of the cavalry was addicted to raiding rather than to working in support of the infantry. The effective cavalry raids on the Union communication and supply lines in 1862 had started Morgan on his course of raiding for its own sake and from the raids his personal legend grew. Back in July, when Lee was at Gettysburg and Pemberton penned up in Vicksburg, while the then center army under Bragg remained uselessly quiescent, Morgan had taken his good fighters off on a raid almost incredible in its folly.

Apparently those melodramatic anti-Union conspirators in the Midwest had convinced the Confederate authorities that something tangible could be achieved in conjunction with a raid in force from the South. Of course the subversive societies found excuses for doing nothing, and Morgan's raid was a fiasco if any Copperhead uprising was related to its object.

In the cavalry, raiding had hardened the men never subjected to too much discipline, and in Ohio and Indiana Morgan's men behaved almost like Yankees in the South. They stole horses to replace their own exhausted mounts, stole food and forage, and they didn't bother to be nice about it. They rode on and on north, the farthest any Confederates ever went, doing no military damage, avoiding and fighting off the forces gathering to enclose them, until the men were riding in a daze of fatigue and the horses stumbled at a walk. Almost the whole of Morgan's famous command was captured and—with their prized mustachios and beards shaved off—placed as criminals in the state penitentiary of Ohio.

With Morgan's troopers permanently lost to him, Bragg made very poor use of the cavalry at hand. This was divided between Forrest's "critter company"—as the people called Old Bedford's command—and "Fighting Joe" Wheeler. This division was complete, since Forrest had vowed never to serve under Wheeler after one costly experience, and no two men could have been more antithetical.

Wheeler, then twenty-seven, and only two years out of the Point when the war began, was a short, slight, wiry man, serious-minded about fighting, humorless and very regular. His parents had come to Georgia from Connecticut and, after his father's business failure, Wheeler spent a good deal of time in the North, preparing for West Point at Cheshire. He never

seems to have considered anything except following Georgia, when the
state seceded, and was early associated with Bragg in troop training. The
commanding general showed a decided preference for this understandable type over the roughhewn and tumultuous Forrest, and the separated
commands went separately about assignments that were useless as far as
garnering information was concerned.

With no spy system, the Defender of Chattanooga could only complain
to D. H. Hill that the forbidding topography prevented his knowing what
Rosecrans was up to. The Chattanooga country was far removed from
the fabled land of plantations and Negroes. This was wild mountain country, with the small holdings of pioneer-stock farmers huddled in the valleys and coves, and with hamlets scattered along the few roads and the
one vital railroad from Chattanooga through Dalton, Georgia, on to Atlanta and eventually the coast. The country south of Chattanooga, on the
Tennessee border, was northern Georgia and northern Alabama. Western
North Carolina came near too, and geographically this was the center of
the South, though untypical of both the old seaboard South and the new
Cotton Kingdom.

The city of Chattanooga lies in the Tennessee River Valley, slicing
through the rough ranges, and from the city the river runs westward in
a series of large loops. The topography of the area is a specific study, for
every mountain has a separate name, each spur from it another name, and
all the valleys and coves have names left over from the first families who
settled in them. For Bragg's purposes, the north-south ranges ended on one
side of the river and began on the other. As he told D. H. Hill, "Mountains hide your foe from you, while they're full of gaps through which
he can pounce on you at any time. A mountain is like the wall of a house
full of ratholes. The rat lies hidden at his hole, ready to pop out when no
one is watching. Who can tell what lies hidden behind that wall?"

While Bragg stewed over what might be going on behind the holes,
Rosecrans crossed two corps of his army over the river well west of
Chattanooga apparently unobserved by cavalry, scouts, spies, anybody.
Then "Rosy," as the Rebels called him, started back eastward by climbing
the north-south mountains below Bragg.

Lookout Mountain, with its Lookout Point now familiar to tourists,
was the high and rugged peak nearest Chattanooga and slightly west. The
later famed Missionary Ridge was a spur of Lookout running to the east
of Chattanooga, with the valley between lying directly below the city.
East of Missionary Ridge, and other spurs of Lookout to the south, ran
the railroad to Dalton. This was Bragg's supply and communication line.
Rosecrans, with a third corps coming toward Chattanooga from the north,
was approaching Lookout Mountain and headed for Bragg's supply line.

The brilliant maneuver of Rosecrans had nullified the city's fortifications. Bragg, if cut off from his base, would be starved out by siege and

Vicksburg duplicated. There was nothing for it but to evacuate Chatta-nooga (September 9) and hurry to protect his lines, complaining pettishly the while that he didn't know what Rosecrans was doing on the other side of Lookout Mountain.

This was the plight of Bragg and the Confederacy when the President conferred with the South's great general over what measures to take.

4

Actually, Lee served only as a sounding board for Davis' voiced wor-ries. Nothing he said made any difference. There was no possibility of the President's doing anything except repeat his old mistakes of sending more troops to a bad command situation. In haranguing worn and half-sick Lee, Davis could not even concentrate on the crucial problem, but was dis-tracted by details concerning other fixed positions.

In late August and early September the Charleston harbor positions had taken a bad going-over. In grand waste of the country's prodigal wealth, the Union fleet stood off for five days and poured its full arsenal of shells into the ruin of Fort Sumter. Every rampart was destroyed, every wall crumbled, every gun silenced, and the fort was not taken. Those South Carolinians were serious about that symbolic mound in their harbor. Gar-risons huddled in bombproofs during the bombardments and then came out with rifles and bayonets to thrust off landing parties. It was never taken, and only surrendered at the end of the war when Charleston was captured from the land.

However, on September 7, Fort Wagner, on the southern land-hook, finally fell to overwhelming Union numbers. It did them no good. They were still there when Charleston surrendered nearly two years later. But Davis fretted over the threat to Charleston and transferred *two* of Lee's brigades, highly trained for warfare of maneuver in the open, to Beaure-gard's fixed garrison.

Then, for the major problem at Chattanooga, Davis detached Long-street personally with two of his divisions, leaving Pickett's decimated command at Richmond. Longstreet's ambition for independent command had long urged him toward those greener fields of the West, offering better opportunity for the display of his talents which could lead him to the command of an army. He took off in high fettle.

The movement of those two divisions and its artillery by the collapsing Southern railroads was a transportation epic which showed, like Bragg's movement in 1862, what could be done when concerted action was con-centrated on an objective without regard to traditional procedure and departments. Using sixteen separate railroads and traveling 835 miles, they went from north of Richmond to Wilmington on the coast, west to At-

lanta and north to Ringgold, on the edge of the battle area. The trip took
four days. Every kind of railroad car that still had wheels was used. A
South Carolina lady saw a line of flats going past, with the men lying down
wrapped in blankets and looking like mummies, and she said her heart bled
for those who were about to die in their youth.

Davis also rushed two divisions from Joe Johnston's useless force in
northeast Mississippi, and some other odd troops up from the lower South.
Bragg was to have approximately 45,000 men against only 60,000-odd,
which were practically odds to the Confederates. All that half measures
could do had been done. With cavalry, some 50,000 Southerners had been
concentrated at a point of betrayal by command.

Along with the size of his army, Bragg was given the greatest battle
opportunity of the war. Where the fatal three cigars had offered Mc-
Clellan Lee's army spread out over a forty-mile area, Rosecrans' overconfidence offered Bragg an enemy in three separate units spread over
sixty miles of the most formidable country. Bragg was closer to two of
Rosecrans' corps than any of the Unions were to one another. As to Mc-
Clellan for the Union side, such an opportunity came to the Rebels only
once in the war.

Evidently Rosecrans had become intoxicated by the ease with which he
outflanked anxious Bragg and acted as if no Confederates were present.
Even Bragg was not too self-tormented to perceive the exposed positions
of Rosecrans' separated corps. With his concentrated army he had only
to gobble up the Unions in detail.

That was Bragg's intention. Under pressure he gave confusing and con-
tradictory orders, and his resentful generals either grew confused themselves or, following the letter of a bad order, refused to assume any
initiative. The inevitable result was the aimless rushing around of Confederate divisions in the wild mountain country, while the frantic Federals rushed to a concentration of their scattered corps.

For the big battle for the Confederate left, the Union had a general
frightened by the consequences of his overconfidence (one of his men
saw Rosecrans, a devout Roman Catholic, crossing himself and knew they
were in trouble), and the Confederacy had a neurotic who was afraid that
he would miss the God-sent opportunity (Bragg, too, was a religious man).

The effect was that Bragg never hit Rosecrans in detail and Rosecrans
did concentrate. By then Longstreet's men were arriving, and in the cool,
autumn days the two armies had at it in the pitched battle of Chickamauga
(September 19–20, 1863). Neither commanding general had anything to
do with the two days' fighting between Chickamauga Creek and Missionary Ridge. The soldiers fought and the Confederates broke the Union
right.

Longstreet's vital thrust broke it completely, so that it ceased to exist
as a military unit. In striving to create a total rout, the Rebels were

checked by a fugitive Confederate, the doughty, massive, and deliberate Virginian, George Thomas.

He became "The Rock of Chickamauga" for the stand of his corps against the Confederate right, though not quite as the legends have it. It was not a one-man stand. He received timely aid from Granger's reserve corps, and he was forced to fall back to Chattanooga. He was not quite indomitable; with help, the Virginian checked what otherwise would have been a rout of the Northern troops.

The field was lost to the Unions. Dozens of guns and thousands of muskets were left. Rosecrans' brilliant maneuvering had ended in disaster.

It had also ended in disaster for Bragg. As always, the tax of the moment of commitment had proved too much for his nerves. Officers swore that they found the nervously prostrated commander asleep in his quarters when the whole Confederate Army was trying to make plans for the pursuit. Bragg couldn't believe that he had actually won a battle. He didn't believe it. He went back to sleep, while Southern women from the neighborhood searched the night field of dead and wounded for their own men.

That was Chickamauga, joining the melancholy role of battles won without any gain. It was the only big battle ever decisively won by the Confederates in the West—at very heavy cost in casualties—and nothing came of it. Rosecrans drew his breath in Chattanooga in the fortifications gratuitously provided by Bragg, and Bragg settled down in the overlooking mountains to starve him out. Rebels starving out Yankees!

So, as always in the West, Davis' generals had succeeded in outblundering Lincoln's generals.

Lincoln removed Rosecrans immediately. Lincoln picked some posturers and some phonies (of whom "Rosy" was neither), but he never retained a general with the aura of defeat on him.

Davis, however, came out personally to smooth things over, after receiving a document unique in the war. A group of general officers drafted a petition for the removal of Bragg and sent it directly to the President. Tracing the course of the lost fruits of Chickamauga, the generals stated that the army, "stricken with a paralysis, will in a few days time be thrown strictly on the defensive, and may deem itself fortunate if it escapes this position without disaster."

5

When Davis left Richmond, for the second time since the war began, he could scarcely be called rational in the sense of making decisions appropriate to a situation which had been intelligently appraised. Since he could not interfere with Lee's army, his mania for arranging military personnel and troop dispositions was concentrated on the demoralized force in the West. There the President revealed that his fixations had, under the strain, ceased to bear any relation to reality.

The Army of the West was obviously in a state of disintegration. As always after a failure, Bragg had fired generals right and left, including his two corps commanders, Bishop Polk and Harvey Hill. He had placed Forrest's troops—which Old Bedford had personally raised and equipped from the enemy—under Wheeler's command. As that was the second time Forrest's self-created command had been taken from him, he quit the army in a violent scene with Bragg, in which the enraged cavalryman called the commanding general "a damned scoundrel" and told him, "If you ever again try to interfere with me or cross my path it will be at the peril of your life."

In the ranks, men were deserting. A group of Texans, on the way back to the Trans-Mississippi Department from a Northern prison, had been shanghaied into Bragg's army before Chickamauga. Though wanting to be with their original unit back home, they felt the importance of the coming battle to their country and liked the enthusiasm of the troops. Before the battle one of the Texans wrote: "Cruel Cruel war and thrice cruel invaders that come to drench our sunny south in blood and drag us to worse than slavery. . . . Up southrons and strike for God and our native land may the God of right hover ore our Battle flag and may our independence be dated from the beginning of this pending contest. . . ."

After the battle, in deep disillusionment, the Texans petitioned seven times for the promised transfer to their state unit, and then simply walked away. All across the South the deserters were befriended and fed. Desertions from Bragg's army had become accepted as a matter of course. Those who remained, unswervingly devoted to the defense of their land, were half mutinous at trying to defend in the command of a general with whom all their sacrifices were wasted. Hating him personally, the troops, in that most personal and informal of armies, no longer believed that a battle could be won with Bragg as the leader.

Coming into this situation, Davis never considered removing Bragg— even after the officers who wrote the petition restated in Bragg's stonily embarrassed presence their conviction that the commanding general could better serve their cause elsewhere than in the Army of Tennessee. The President let D. H. Hill and lesser lights vanish from useful service. He promoted Forrest to major general and sent him off to Mississippi to raise another (his third) command. Then, for the corps of Bishop Polk he brought in the most unpopular general in the South, the Yankee Pemberton, who had surrendered Vicksburg on July 4 under the delusion that the date would arouse sentiment in Grant and cause the Union general to permit their surrender with the honors of war.

The soldiers would not have it. Polk, the dynamic clergyman, had served with the Western army since it was organized. While not among the great military minds in the war, he was a sincere patriot, a conscientious and energetic soldier, very brave; his men fought well, endured long, and they loved him. He baptized other generals—Hardee, Joe Johnston, and the like—during the campaigns, and his soldiers regarded the clerical phases of their general with affectionate good humor. They liked to tell about the time that Cheatham, Polk's division commander, sent them in with a "Give 'em hell, boys," and the bishop called encouragingly, "Do as General Cheatham says, boys."

Pemberton was needlessly humiliated by being told that the men would mutiny before they would serve under him in place of their old leader, Polk. Davis resolved that in a musical-chairs game by bringing Hardee back in from his recruiting service to command Polk's corps, and sending Polk out on the drillmaster's job.

With everybody dissatisfied, Longstreet then entered the controversy. After one battle with Bragg, the ambitious Dutchman completely lost his taste for service with the Army of Tennessee as it was. He thought "some such great mind as Lee" should be brought out; when convinced that Lee must stay where he was, Longstreet then suggested Joe Johnston as commanding general.

This proposed exhumation of the President's personal enemy (then buried with his small force in the Mississippi barrens) only aroused Davis' ire. Having gotten rid of Polk, Hill, Forrest, and others, in order to retain Bragg, Davis then got rid of Longstreet and his troops. Since Longstreet so lusted for independent command, Davis sent him off to besiege Knoxville. Burnside had been resurrected in the West and occupied that city in Unionist Tennessee. In trying to get Burnside out of Knoxville, Longstreet made such a grotesque failure of his second experiment in independent command that he longed to go home and serve again under "Marse Robert." He was kept on in virtual exile in the wilds of East Tennessee.

From depleting the army of its lieutenant generals and top cavalry leader, intensifying the dissension from command to ranks, Davis then propped up the wobbly Bragg with personal advice. His own military experience, he said, indicated that "cordial co-operation" was not necessary between officers for success.

Then, from his deranged support of Bragg, Davis turned to the soldiers with advice. Only a person speaking almost by rote what he had learned from rules could have so addressed men who had endured hunger, prolonged physical privations and dangers, anguish for their families, wounds and the death of their friends, in fighting again and again under a general who betrayed all their sacrifices and all their risks. After a flowery peroration on their deeds and valor, the President said, "Crown these with harmony, due subordination and cheerful support to lawful authority. . . ."

The soldiers said, "Send us something to eat, Massa Jeff. I'm hungry."

6

Leaving the castrated and headless Army of Tennessee still hungry, the President used his absence from Richmond to display his presence to civilians. Their reception, since he saw only the loyal townspeople, was most heartening. At Macon, Georgia, where he spoke from the balcony of the Lanier Hotel, the crowd was enthusiastic; in Savannah the emotional people held a riotous torchlight procession for him; and Charleston, always colorful in its exuberance, cheered him from the streets as he rode in an open carriage to the City Hall for a speech.

Back in Richmond, all looked well. Lee, even without Longstreet and with a corps gone from his depleted army, had used his tired old flanking routine to maneuver Meade away from the Fredericksburg line, and back toward the equally worn-out and familiar area of Manassas.

There was something sad in the soldiers' high morale, their belief in Lee, with their bleeding feet, their gaunt bodies, their new butternut "issue" and home clothes becoming rags again, and the new conscripts deserting all around them. Offense was no longer possible. The Old Man retired the willing skeletons back to their Rappahannock River country. Meade, later recognizing that Lee had imposed on him partly to prevent the Unions from sending out more troops to reinforce the army against Bragg, paid him the tribute of admitting that Lee had outmaneuvered him.

Though Lee had kept the invader off balance in Virginia, and prevented the possibility of another "On to Richmond" that year, none of the desperate moves of the physically declining general could help the army at Chattanooga, where the enemy occupied the Western key city. Had sane realism controlled the increasingly perilous situation, obviously the Federals would have been pried out of Chattanooga. A plan toward this end had been agreed upon, but Bragg continued his siege of the Unions. Though railroad and boat communications with Chattanooga were cut off, and Confederates in the same condition would have been in a fix, the very notion of the hungry Rebels starving out Yankees was the phantasm of a disordered mind.

The rich Unions brought in Grant and Sherman, thousands of new troops, and hacked supplies over the mountain passes, marked by the carcasses of a thousand dead mules. When the Union troops were large enough and fed enough, Johnny-on-the-bad-Confederate-spot Grant sent them out at the demoralized and leaderless men huddling in the rainy, autumn hills.

At Lookout Mountain and Missionary Ridge and sundry other places outside of Chattanooga, individual Confederates fought as always in the losing cause of Bragg, and many units fought well as units. But it was not an army. On the other hand, the Unions, smarting under their one defeat in the West, so exceeded their orders in climbing the mountain ranges that Grant angrily turned on Thomas to demand by whose orders those men were advancing. They were advancing by a group impulse against group dispersal, and modest Thomas' soldiers won Grant further honors as a military leader. The Confederate "siege" was broken, and Bragg's Army of Tennessee was driven out of the crucial area.

Beyond individual love of combat, or sheer oneriness, the Rebels wouldn't fight any more under Bragg. When he came to rally the dispirited men, calling, "Here's your commanding officer," the soldiers hooted back, "Here's your mule." On those November days (23–25) the people, as represented by the men in the army, quit the government as represented by the commanding general.

Bragg resigned then, after the invader had come into the doorway of the western end of the shrinking Confederate borders. The enemy stood poised for a thrust into the nation's vitals.

Still loyal to Bragg, Davis brought him into Richmond as "military adviser." Occupying the chair left vacant since the great Lee had left to command an army, Bragg took his desk job very seriously. By no means humbled by his failures, Bragg set out literally to "advise" his friend, the President. Davis must have felt an urgent if unadmitted need for someone with whom he could discuss military affairs, and he selected the greatest failure in the Confederate armies.

In completing his alienation from the Southern people, Jefferson Davis seemed personally to have become alienated from reason. There is certainly no rational explanation for his behavior with the case history who was Bragg.

CHAPTER XVIII

"When This Cruel War Is Over"

AFTER the disaster of the Chattanooga area, the people and the armies seemed curiously unaffected on the surface. It was as though they had become inured to losses, and no longer brooded over the consequences. Those who remained loyal were entering the phase where they continued their resistance because they knew nothing else to do.

To meet the immediate situation concerning the demoralized and disintegrating Army of Tennessee, Davis was forced to rescue Joe Johnston from his anonymous desuetude and put him in command. Even before Johnston arrived, the men had demonstrated what they would do without Bragg. Under the temporary command of Hardee at Ringgold, Georgia, the railroad town southeast from Chattanooga, the patched-together forces turned on Grant's overexuberant pursuers and showed there was still plenty of fight in them. Grant's people went back to Chattanooga, and the Confederates were given a chance for reorganization under Johnston.

Retreatin' Joe could do such things. The dapper little man, with the bright eyes and warm smile, had a way with all people who did not arouse his jealousy or threaten his fiercely guarded dignity. The soldiers saw only the pleasing aspects of a gracious personality, and more importantly they found behind his personal friendliness an effective interest in their behalf.

He got clothes for the half naked, shoes for the barefooted, blankets for the cold, and food for all. A thoughtful series of furloughs so the men could visit their homes checked desertions as it raised morale, and absentees and outright deserters returned to the army. It became an army again, small and poorly equipped and unready for offensive action, but the South had been spared another Vicksburg. There they lost the city *and* the army. As for the soldiers, though another fixed position had been lost, they had an army ready to fight again and, at last, under a general they believed in and liked.

The people accepted the loss of Chattanooga much as the army did. Another city in the West had been lost, and disaster had been avoided. It

was military minds and later historians, rather than the people, who perceived the significance of Chattanooga as the loss of the "vital center." Yet
the resignation with which the people accepted further defeat was indica-
tive of their own state of mind, and the tangible effect of the continued
losses showed in the further drop of their money.

While in the beginning of the year only three Confederate dollars were
needed to buy one in gold, by the end of 1863 it took twenty. Their
money had skidded to one fifth of its face value. For Christmas shopping,
it took ten dollars to buy a yard of calico, a pound of coffee, or a quart
of applejack. Food prices make even our high living costs seem like the
good old days in comparison.

Corn meal was $20 a bushel (government price, $5.00); bacon was
$3.50 a pound, pork $2.00, mutton $1.50, and chickens brought $6.00 to
$8.00 a pair. Irish potatoes were $5.00 a peck and sweet potatoes $4.00;
eggs were $2.00 a dozen and butter $4.00 a pound; salt was 50¢ a pound,
when it could be finagled away from the hoarders. Whiskey sold for $15
a quart. Wood for the bitter-cold winter of 1863–64 was around $20 for
half a cord and coal cost $31.50 a load. Seven hundred dollars would buy
a man's suit and $200 his boots.

Civilians on the streets of Richmond were beginning to look as ragged
as the soldiers. Men without gloves kept their blue hands in frayed pockets
and women were seen with worn pieces of carpet as shawls. Everybody
seemed to be carrying a package. The people were taking their household
goods and their prize possessions to the auction houses whose red flags
lined Main Street.

The auctioneers were strangers, speculators coming with gold to buy
up a people's personal treasures. When the auctioneers displayed silver
and china, brass candlesticks and pieces of silk, gilt picture frames and
hand-painted shaving mugs, few citizens could buy. The purchasers were
also strangers in town—other speculators, blockade runners, gamblers and
criminals and their women, and the cold-eyed natives who had turned
hoarders to build a personal future out of the misfortunes of their countrymen. The New South, of post-Reconstruction, was in the eyes of those
rapacious, conscienceless, and ambitious schemers.

As with all countries in all circumstances, there were people with cash.
Some of it had been come by legitimately: an officer of a planter family
or a planter might have part of the proceeds of a bale of cotton to squan-
der in the city. Some of the money was personal ante-bellum wealth, like
Judah P. Benjamin's, and was doled out over the months. Most of it was
unexplained and most of it was spent on a night life never equaled in a
Southern city before or since.

Gambling hells ranged from the hole-in-the-wall variety in the Tenderloin District to plush spots like Johnny Worsham's, across from Capitol
Square and from the War Offices. Benjamin would be found there, sam-

pling the lavish suppers served free to customers. Prostitutes almost rivaled the Yankee bullets in rendering soldiers unfit for combat, and in the cozy houses on Locust Alley, perfumed arms and painted lips helped officers forget the rigors of camp and the failure of their government.

Where closed blinds were not necessary for pleasures, the bars and restaurants were always crowded, and in the packed variety houses "the Songbird of the South" entertained the *hoi polloi* while the *haut monde* packed the new theater for drama on Broad Street. Those glamorous belles with their inventiveness in foods and clothes, decorations and games, still entertained in stripped and cold parlors that odd Southern cross section of high brass and privates with high social connections. And the unglamorous poor soldier on leave, getting drunk with a pint of bust-head, was still run down by Winder's plug-uglies.

All this night life made a sorry contrast with their own lot to the women huddling in icy rooms behind locked doors and blinds, scraping up kitchen grease as a base for soap and scraping off wallpaper on which to write a letter to some shivering man "on the Rappahannock line." Without carriages and Negro coachmen, those women would have been afraid to go on the night streets, and even the men who went alone went at their own risk. Nothing could be further from the ante-bellum South than the Confederate wartime capital.

In the winter when the suffering became unbearable, while the flesh-pots flourished like the green bay tree, the poor were further hurt by the worthlessness of their "shinplasters." Shinplasters are often thought of as being all Confederate money, though originally they were the paper money used for fractional currency in place of non-existent coins. In time, shinplasters became scrip, since they were issued by grocers and butchers, saloonkeepers and tobacconists, practically anybody who sold anything. By the time of the 1863–64 winter even the beggars on the streets refused them. Banks passed rules, eliminating shinplasters, that accounts must be kept in the round figure of $5.00—then worth $1.00. To the poor, who dealt in coppers and dimes, round figures were as meaningless as the national debt, theirs or ours. They had a paper which said "worth 25¢," and it was worth nothing.

To the well-to-do people, those who owned slaves as house servants, along with the pinch of feeding all the mouths arose the doubt of the use of it, and a new fear.

2

House servants for city people were not particular luxuries. With no central heat, plumbing, or lighting system, the servants made fires, emptied chamber pots, brought up hot water, trimmed candles and cleaned lamp-

shades and wicks—all as necessary as cooking and serving, cleaning and
laundering, which was done at home. Horses in the stable must be fed,
watered, groomed, and their stalls mucked out. For services accomplished
by pushing buttons today, servants were needed then, and in the South
a servant was bought outright—$1000, plus food, room, and care for the
rest of his life, beyond the serviceable period on to death.

It was never economical and Negroes were rarely good servants—
though they had gracious manners, beguiling charm, and sometimes deep
affection. But that was the system. In the terrible intimacy of master and
slave, the majority of the slaveowners, dealing humanely with the people
in the existing situation, had convinced themselves that the Negroes felt
security with and loyalty to them. Probably most of the house servants
did feel that while the world they lived in was static. When their world
was jarred by invasion and incitement to the joys of freedom, the Negroes
grew unsettled.

Their restlessness was caused largely by the field hands whom they normally wouldn't spit on. Among the field hands in areas near occupation
troops, thousands had seized the chance to escape to the Union lines in
direct action for personal freedom, and to others freedom meant taking
over the plantation themselves. It was the tales about these Negroes that
brought unrest to the city Negroes and apprehension to the whites.

Incited by Northern troops, the Negroes turned against the whites. In
suppressing the South's effort at independence, Northerners started an
insurrection of blacks against whites. Though Lincoln was gravely aware
of the problems created by emancipation and earnestly wished to spare
the Southern whites hardships (once they were back in the Union),
Lincoln was not in control of the soldiers. When the dogs of war were
turned loose as a solution, no one controlled the mob spirit of growing
hatred. Given right to add to their might by the crusade, Union soldiers,
under the brutalizing influence of war, saw Negro freedom as a means
of the blacks getting back at the lordly Southerners with their proud
chivalry.

What did the Negroes know about freedom except what their deliverers
told them? They had no conception of assuming the rights and duties of
citizenship. They had no knowledge of the world beyond the plantation.
Freedom to them frequently meant freedom from work, even freedom to
take what their whites had. The only law they knew was the will of the
white man—the master and his representative, the overseer.

With the master gone and other white men telling them they were
free, they locked up the overseer (as in the song, "The Year of Jubilee")
or drove him away, broke open the cider house and got drunk, invaded
the big house and moved the furniture to their cabins, sacked the pantries
and held banquets, and imitated the Union soldiers in destroying objects
for which they found no use—such as books and paintings and pianos.

"We drink Massa's cider," they yelled. "We sleep in Massa's bed. Maybe we get Massa's woman."

Some of the ladies escaped with the help of house people, most of whom remained loyal, though the fiercest urge to vengeance was in those who turned mean. Some ladies, with no chance to flee or no desire to, bravely faced down screaming, gesticulating, threatening mobs. Usually there were enough Negroes in the crowd without personal malice, probably remembering some kindnesses, to restrain personal violence. But the control of the ladies was lost, and they too were forced to abandon the plantations. These ladies, their children and old people, crowded into the cities, bringing their tales of horror.

After the Negroes had eaten all the food and run out of objects to destroy on the deserted plantations, they took to the roads and woods. Some of the men wandered into Union lines, where they became personal servants or soldiers. Some of the women sought out the occupied towns, where Union soldiers made a brisk demand for their favors, and paid for them with objects stolen from homes. Others roamed around, stealing food and becoming menaces to the small non-slaveholding families isolated on farms. By no means all the Negroes were vicious. Many of them, after the orgies were over and the mobs disbanded, huddled miserably around the abandoned plantations. Some worked plantations. But to the white women in the lonely countrysides, it seemed that a million Nat Turners were stalking the land.

With this dread realization of their long-dormant fears went a sense of the Negroes' treachery. Like many other white people before and since, the Southerners had deluded themselves into believing they understood their Negroes. At discovering the Negroes' real feelings about them, the whites felt betrayed. They felt for the first time a hatred for *the* Negro, and a distrust, which characterized the attitude of three succeeding generations.

The related experiences of the ladies refugeeing in cities all over the South brought suspicion of their own house people to city families. They lost a sense of security in their homes. People no longer went to bed with implicit faith in their "trusted darkies." Some of the house people vanished, taking valuables with them. A lady of fashion from Tennessee, wife of a congressman, lost all her jewelry and the bulk of her wardrobe when a body servant disappeared. People suspected a secret agency helped the Negroes escape.

In their pitting of servant against master, of race against race, the North had armed former slaves to fight against Southern whites. This too affected the house servant, and shook the master's whole concept of his world. In occupied Norfolk, when a white lieutenant directed a Negro company to arrest a local doctor, the doctor shot and killed the lieutenant for ordering colored servants to lay hands on him. The doctor was hanged, and by today's standard that was too good for him. It wasn't today, and the doctor knew that the lieutenant knew that he was insulting him. All that made for unrest among the Negroes, for uncertainty and fear among the whites.

Then, in the last arctic clutch of winter in late February and early March 1864, there came a new kind of fear to join all the known and all the vague apprehensions afflicting the people in the dislocated city which served as the capital of the Confederacy. Before this frightening thing happened to the citizens, they had been treated—mostly at a distance, to be sure—to the celebration for John Morgan after his escape from the Ohio State Penitentiary. (How the Kentucky raider escaped with a few men has never been known for a fact; maybe for once the Copperheads did some good for the cause they played at, with bribery and the like.) Morgan showed up in Richmond after the first of the year all ready for new worlds to conquer and without a command.

At the Ballard House, one of Richmond's three fashionable hotels, he was entertained by the famous of the Army of Northern Virginia, including his brother-in-law, A. P. Hill, and Virginia's own great cavalryman, Jeb Stuart. Across the years of their magic names, here were young men standing at a bar, laughing and joking, and probably not talking about the war that made their names immortal. All three were soon to die.

The President, in displeasure with Morgan, sent him and what troops could be gathered out to Saltville, Virginia, to guard *against* Union raids. To such low estate had fallen the magnetic raider of Kentucky, and unofficial Richmond soon forgot Morgan's visit in the raid against their city.

3

In proportion to all the preparations made for the raid of General Kilpatrick with Colonel Dahlgren, and to all the to-do afterward, the gaudy enterprise was a fiasco.

At that stage of the war, Confederate authorities still believed that any threat to their capital would come from Meade's army. As Lee was holding Meade on the Rappahannock, Richmond was virtually unguarded. The eastern approaches were guarded against any thrust by the Unions up the peninsula or landing parties from the gunboats. But to the north the breastworks were guarded by only a few hundred soldiers, mostly recuperating wounded, with a few guns of the sort abandoned by the artillery in favor of later Federal models. To the west were earthen emplacements for guns, but no troops were there at all. In the city there were the local defense troops, formed of old men and boys, department clerks and armory workers, who only gathered when the tocsin sounded the alarm from Capitol Square. All this was known in Washington. Neither side could keep anything from the other.

It was also known in Washington that Stuart's cavalry had seen its best days, and that for the second winter the horses were weak for want of forage. The horse artillery had to move west to Charlottesville to get grazing for the gaunt gun horses. The situation seemed ideal for a raid (from the north and west) into Richmond proper.

The purpose of this raid was to free the 5000 prisoners in Libby Prison and on Belle Island in the James River. What this would have accomplished is not very clear, but Kilpatrick had talked it over personally with Lincoln and Secretary of War Stanton, and they strongly supported it. Perhaps such a prison release would have acted as a tonic to the Northern population, with the war entering its fourth year in an election year.

There was great resentment in the North over the poor treatment Union prisoners received in the South. Since the sole object of the war had become victory, and an ingredient for success was hatred of the enemy, Union authorities naturally did not explain that the Southerners put the Union prisoners on the same sparse diet to which they themselves had been reduced. Every Union raid that destroyed food, stock, farm implements, and ran off the Negro farm hands, made that much less food to go around. Every railroad cut made that much less food to get to the cities for distribution. Thus the destruction by the Union armies caused their people who were caught in the South to suffer with the natives.

Needless to say, no point was made of the suffering of the Southerners in Northern prisons, where more died by count and by ratio than in the Southern prisons. Soldiers from the lower South placed in the damp and icy camps around the Great Lakes contracted respiratory diseases which left thousands, who survived the prisons, in permanent ill-health to become later fatalities.

Rebels were not supposed to have any rights anyway, and it was only the plight of their own prisoners (whom the Confederates were only too anxious to exchange) which agitated the North. Not all the agitation was directed at the Confederates, however, since there were citizens in the Union also who blamed the Administration for everything.

Orders were sent Meade, who thought little of the plan, to give it the full support of his large and well-fed army. Meade did all he could. First he sent Custer with 1500 troopers off to the west of Lee's line, combining feint with attack on the unhorsed artillery at Charlottesville. The Confederate gunners fought him off their pieces with rifles and pistols, and suffered no more harm than the loss of some personal luggage—a fairly severe loss at that, in those times. In the middle, two infantry corps shuttled back and forth with such activity that Stuart reported even "the sutlers and the women have been sent to the rear."

In the midst of all this motion, Kilpatrick with 3000 of his top-condi-
tioned cavalry, with artillery, swung east around Lee and headed south
for Richmond. They moved on down near the fringe of the area where the
Seven Days' Battle had been fought, where Jackson had made his slow
first day's march. Simultaneously, about 400 picked troopers under young
Colonel Ulric Dahlgren branched off and circled westward. Dahlgren
was to strike the city from the unprotected west while the main force
overrode the lightly held breastworks to the north.

The two forces destroyed sections of the railroads, damaged an aque-
duct, Dahlgren burned a gristmill, and allowed his troops to plunder houses
of silver and other valuables along the way. About twelve miles out of
Richmond, he stopped at the home of Secretary of War Seddon. Since
Mrs. Seddon was a friend of his father's, a U.S.N. rear admiral, young
Dahlgren let her off with a levy of wine and an interlude of his charm.

By then, the thieving of his command had aroused the farmers of the
pleasant countryside for miles around, and they were coming after him
with shotguns and squirrel rifles. These men were listed as Home Guards,
mustered in to give legality to any fighting they might do in such an
emergency. This was their first experience as soldiers, though not with
firearms. They began to snipe and bushwhack, and Dahlgren was forced
to abandon the more agreeable features of his expedition.

His original plan was to cross to the south bank of the James River,
nearest the prison camp on Belle Isle, but he couldn't find a ford. A Negro
boy he impressed as a guide took the cavalrymen to what he believed
was a ford, but the river was high from the winter rains, and they couldn't
cross. Dahlgren hanged the boy and decided to drive on straight into
Richmond. A few miles outside of town at dusk, he encountered a local
defense battalion, 300 overage men, underage boys, and workers from
the armory. They fired a rifle volley in the dim light, and Dahlgren veered
away. Giving up his part of the raid at one exchange, he circled back
north to fall in on Kilpatrick.

Kilpatrick was having troubles of his own, though mostly in his mind.
His lengthy report of the action reads as if he had encountered half of
Lee's army, fought them all to a standstill, and withdrawn only when his
assigned task developed insurmountable obstacles. Near Richmond he
had contended with only a few hundred infantrymen and some Home
Guards before he went into camp at night. At 1:00 A.M., in one of the
few night attacks of the war in the East, his camp was struck by the leading regiment of Wade Hampton's cavalry division, following down from
the north. This regiment consisted of 306 men and two guns, and Kilpatrick's 3000 scattered.

Hampton's horses were too puny to give much of a chase, but Kilpatrick's imagination did the rest. He rode on eastward fifty miles toward
Williamsburg, where he found safety with another of the Union armies

which practically infested the state. That one was under Beast Butler who, returned to Virginia, had inched up the unprotected peninsula from the base of Fortress Monroe. That was the end of Kilpatrick in the raid.

For Dahlgren, one company of the 9th Virginia Cavalry got on his rear and harassed him into a night ambush of more Home Guards. He was killed in the volley and his commandos scattered. That ended the action of the raid and began the repercussions.

When the cavalry company went chasing Dahlgren's scattered command in the darkness, and Home Guards hurried home, the young raider's body was left where it had fallen. Several days passed before authorities sent out a burial detail, when it was discovered that one of Dahlgren's fingers had been cut off by a thief after a gold ring. Also it allegedly discovered among his papers an order to his troops in which occurred the line, "exhorting the released prisoners to destroy and burn the hateful city; and do not allow the Rebel leader, Davis, and his traitorous crew to escape." When the orders were published in the Richmond newspapers, the citizens were aroused to a fury beyond any of their outrage at early atrocities.

Even Lee was sufficiently stirred to write Meade directly and ask if Dahlgren's orders had been authorized by the Federal Army and/or authorities. Meade answered graciously and assured Lee that neither he nor any authorities knew anything about the orders, and he personally repudiated such warfare. Kilpatrick grew indignant that such plans could even be associated with Dahlgren, and he wanted to avenge what he curiously called Dahlgren's "murder." Then all the furor took a macabre turn over Dahlgren's mutilated body.

There lived then in Richmond the spinster daughter of a Northerner who had prospered in the city and left Miss Van Lew a handsome home on a magnificent site. Betsy Van Lew was a devout abolitionist, and it pleased her somewhat eccentric vanity to flaunt her Unionism and play at spying and dark deeds. Her one recorded mission of espionage caused Beast Butler to try a sneak attack on Richmond from the east. Having been assured by Miss Van Lew that the city was unguarded in that direction too, the soldiers of that doughty warrior on civilians took a very bad going-over in a night trap at Bottom's Bridge. In the warped mind of this conspirator, who was locally called "Crazy Betsy," some purpose was served by stealthily removing Dahlgren's body from its grave and hiding it. As a result of her ghoulish prank, when Admiral Dahlgren asked for the return of his son's body, it was gone!

Recriminations then flew from the other side. No part of the story of the whole abortive raid was ever settled satisfactorily. Later investigators presented a convincing claim that the controversial line in Dahlgren's orders were inserted in a forgery, though neither Meade nor Kilpatrick said at the time that the photographed letters sent them by Lee were forgeries. If they were, the identities of the forger and the instigator will remain one of the unsolved mysteries of the war.

Naturally the Confederate authorities played the whole thing for all it was worth. In their wan and misguided hope that Europe might still be influenced, they offered this evidence of atrocities in an appeal to the sympathies of the civilized world—meaning England.

More practically, the incident did serve to arouse the adrenalin of that dwindling hard core of die-hard Confederates, who for the whole long winter had nothing to sustain their morale. These people still believed, sincerely, that they would outlast the enemy and win their independence.

The borderland of Confederates between the unyielding core and the disaffected was growing narrower, shrinking like their country's territory. The physical sufferings of the winter had further accelerated the defections whose percentage had increased in the summer after the morale blow of Gettysburg. There had been nothing since to check the downward arc.

Yet those remaining people of unshakable faith in their independence were not unreasonable in their hope. The sword of war was still cutting both ways, and many were the Northerners who wanted to give up the subjugation as a bad job. The peace societies were gaining members and a movement for peace was definitely growing. If the South held its defense lines until the fall elections, a peace party might come in.

The people had every reason to expect Lee to hold his end of the line. At the other end there was at last a general, Joe Johnston, uninhibited by anomalous departments, in whom they had confidence.

The winter ended with a smaller physical Confederacy, and with fewer Confederates within the region, but it happened that way in the Revolution too. They still stood on their land, with guns in their hands. They were ready for one more of those assaults which had begun so long ago, in the summer of 1861 . . . but only one more . . . and no mistakes could be made this time.

CHAPTER XIX

"If It Takes All Summer"

SPRING to the Confederacy always meant fresh invasions from the North. For the 1864 campaign against that surviving core of determined men and women, the enemy came up with a new alignment in the most powerful concentrations yet assembled. Lincoln had accepted his limitations as a military leader and abdicated (March 9, 1864) in favor of Grant, who was to assume personal command of the army against Lee.

With Grant in complete command, there would be no more of those dispersals of Union armies and cross-purposes between Washington and the field. The great numbers and resources of the Union would be concentrated, the purpose of the armies made clear and executed with aggressive and relentless determination. Familiar with Grant's habits and methods of pushing for a decision, the more thoughtful men in the armies felt, rightly, that the final test was approaching.

The heaviest thrust ever mounted was to come in Virginia, where the officers and men of Lee's army awaited the test with confidence. On their home ground, they still felt they could beat anybody. The government also had confidence in Lee—too much. They expected him to continue to produce miracles without support or supplies. There had been too much talk of that "stalemate" in Virginia. The government could not seem to conceive that the Virginia situation had been maintained by Lee's determined and successful efforts at counteroffensive. They remained deaf to his warnings that the loss of maneuver meant the loss of Virginia, and they left unheeded his increasingly urgent demands for the subsistence and manpower necessary to the ability to maneuver.

No changes were made in the inept Commissary and inadequate Quartermaster departments. Nothing was done to get farm produce to railroad centers, to keep the railroads repaired and running. No changes were made anywhere in government except to pass a conscript act enlarging the age range from seventeen to fifty and eliminating some of the exemption abuses.

More directly ominous, there was no change in the relations between Davis and the West, except if possible for the worse. At last general of an army again, Johnston was trying to be its commander, though entirely in his own way. Davis persisted in giving him the responsibility without the authority. In the final hour of its long defense, the South's inner divisions, as reflected in this personality clash, persisted while the war might of the Union massed for the decisive thrust.

The way we hear of Grant and Sherman in that last climactic year, it could be assumed that there there they were with their two armies hacking their way to Richmond and Atlanta against the two Rebel armies. It was not that way at all. East of the Mississippi, exclusive of occupation forces, of the besiegers of Charleston and other ports, of mounted raiding units and the U. S. Navy, there were seven Union *armies* in the early part of 1864 plus troops in the Washington area and forts. Three were in Virginia, one in North Carolina, and three in the West. The Confederates could only guess which army or combination of armies would strike, when and where and for what purpose.

Against these seven armies and the other Union forces, the South had essentially the two armies of Lee and Johnston, both of whose forces were at the time divided. If their armies had been fully united and the two forces combined, they would nearly have equaled Grant's main army in Virginia, which would still have outgunned them.

Before the Union pattern of attack evolved, the main force of Lee's veterans emerged from their bleak winter quarters north of Richmond, and soon forgot the sufferings of the cold months in the freshly green and flowering countryside. That section of the state had not been fought over to any extent. Though food was scarce, there was no large-scale devastation of property and the land held a familiar, reassuring look. The planter and yeoman families were friendly and outwardly cheerful; mail got delivered, and boxes from home—then smaller—were distributed in the warm, bright mornings.

In the Shenandoah Valley, where "the great and good" Stonewall had conceived his famous collaborative campaign two springs before, General Breckinridge, the bourbon-loving former U.S. Vice-President, commanded two brigades who could do little more than observe, and protect civilians from marauding deserters.

Longstreet, still pining away in the mountains of East Tennessee with his corps, after his blundering attack on Knoxville, was frantically writing everybody he could think of, suggesting some offensive which would include him.

In the southwest corner of Virginia, where the vital salt mines were located, the once glamorous John Morgan commanded a motley group of badly disciplined cavalry, mostly ex-raiders. Morgan, trying to recapture his touch and his lost fame, also beseeched the War Office for support in various gaudy schemes and further antagonized the Administration by attempting to lure convalescents away from Lee's infantry. He was burned out before forty. He neglected his command and some of the raffish troopers were a nuisance and sometimes a menace to the civilian families.

In that mountain country near Cumberland Gap, a hamlet boasted a distinguished Confederate officer not found in any records. A man no longer young, he had left home to volunteer in the early days and returned as a captain with his right arm in a sling. After he reported himself well, he went off again and returned as a major with his left arm in a sling. Again he went off and the autumn before had returned as a colonel with a bad limp. By the spring of 1864 he was still limping along the quiet streets, from home to the store gang, resplendent in gray frock coat with gold-braided *galons* on his sleeves. He had been near a Confederate army only once—for one awed look—never heard a bullet, and promoted himself on each trip by the simple expedient of buying a new *galon* for his coat in a Richmond auction house.

The South was getting a growing population of types similar to the colonel, and Georgia led all states with "militia" who were exempt from Regular Army service and near the ballot boxes.

The only other forces of any size in the East were about 12,000 scattered troops under Beauregard in South Carolina, and a division in North Carolina. Beauregard's troops were uselessly employed. Charleston's harbor defenses were still doing well, and they had to be cleared before invading troops could be landed on the mainland. With his other devices, Mallory's inventions had developed effective attacks from "spar torpedoes"—a torpedo attached to a thirty-foot pole on a small boat, which the crew would run out at night and, at almost total personal risk, ram against a Union ship. Throughout the South, thirty-one U. S. Navy ships were destroyed and nine injured by torpedoes of various kinds.

In North Carolina, with more of Mallory's waterborne contrivances of war, the infantry division had its hands full keeping Federal amphibious forces from the coast out of the country drained by rivers. At Wilmington and Mobile, garrisons of heavy artillery conducted their own private and ceaseless wars with the U. S. Navy.

Across the Mississippi and virtually unrelated to the main Confederate defense, a small force of Rebel die-hards like Jo Shelby were also fighting private and savage wars in the broad, wild country, and continuing to occupy Federal troops.

In Texas, completely isolated from the rest of the Confederacy, Kirby Smith, the first general exiled for complaint of Bragg, had erected truly a cotton kingdom of his own. This empire of the big plains was decorated by the magnificent Prince John Magruder, formerly Lee's "Great Demonstrator." Another exile, this Virginian contrived to live lavishly and in high style even in the dusty wastes of mesquite country, and his heroic

manners and grand affability were unchanged since his glorious days with
Lee's first army.

In the country of the long-betrayed Army of Tennessee, Joe Johnston
was rebuilding the inadequately equipped remnant of the main Western
army at Dalton, Georgia, on the way to Atlanta, and engaged in his usual
losing battle with the President over troop dispositions.

Farther west in the war-made barrens of the cotton country, Bishop
Polk was trying to make a force of the small collection of troops who
served as a command for fugitives from Bragg—though by title he commanded the imposingly named Department of Alabama, Mississippi and
East Louisiana. Forrest was out there too, upped to major general and
recruiting (often by force) his third self-raised cavalry.

The first fighting opened there. Before Grant became General in
Chief, he had always wanted to strike eastward from the Mississippi and
cut down through Alabama to Mobile. He sent Sherman on that project,
due east from Vicksburg toward the production center at Selma.

Sherman didn't do so well. The cavalry with whom he was to col-
laborate became diverted by Forrest and forsook Sherman for the plush
sanctuary which the Union government had made of Memphis. Though
Sherman still outnumbered Polk by at least two to one, instead of attacking this obstacle to his march, he developed his penchant for destroying
personal property. After he divested the civilians for miles around of their
slaves, animals, and vehicles, he put his men to the systematic destruction
of Meridian, Mississippi.

"I have no hesitation in pronouncing the work as well done," he reported. "Meridian . . . no longer exists."

From this "pleasant excursion," as he called it, Sherman and his people
were brought to Chattanooga to concentrate on the single drive on
Atlanta.

Polk with about 15,000 infantry and cavalry went on to join Johnston,
and his denuded department was inherited by Forrest's friend, Stephen D.
Lee.

The Union concentration toward a single goal in the West was actually
favorable for the Confederacy. With offense impossible, a concentration
of their scattered troops increased their chances under a defense-minded
general like "Retreatin' Joe" at the time in the war when defense was
more important than attack. All soldiers on both sides had become adept
at quickly throwing up breastworks and entrenchments and, unless an
army could be caught in motion, the going was very hard on attacking
troops. It would be safe to predict that the dapper Johnston would never
be caught in motion.

However, this favorable situation was immediately jeopardized when
Davis fell under the malign influence of Braxton Bragg, the chief of staff
without portfolio (a sort of assistant commander in chief). Psychotic

Bragg, scared of his shadow when he commanded in the West, became as aggressive as a wildcat in his Ninth Street War Office in Richmond. Under his promptings Davis suddenly broke his long fixation on defense, and was seized with an obsession for an immediate offensive. The two new attack-minded collaborators began to importune Retreatin' Joe to launch an offensive that would not only drive the enemy out of Chattanooga but thrust on and retake Middle Tennessee!

As Johnston could scarcely bring himself to communicate with the President, he sent a staff officer to Richmond with his needs for such an offense specifically listed in writing. He needed more troops, more wagons, more artillery horses. Ignoring his letter, Davis and Bragg, separately and together, in concert and in contradiction, continued to heckle Joe Johnston to do something he had never done in three years of war—open an offensive campaign. With their importunities, they sent out a new corps commander, John B. Hood, whom they briefed on their plans for an offensive.

Thirty-three-year-old Hood, one of Lee's better division commanders, was a Texas convert (native of Kentucky) who contributed to that state's legend as a fighting people. He was a magnificently built man, a handsome blond, whose courage and ambitious self-confidence were not equaled by his intelligence. A West Pointer, and Regular Army man for the eight years between his graduation and secession, Hood had lost his right leg at Chickamauga when he brought his division west with Longstreet. During the months when the stump from the amputation was healing, Hood had become a somewhat awkward darling of the Richmond parlors and devoted his afternoons to the cultivation of the President. As a reward for his proper deference, Hood was sent West to command a corps with Johnston and to act as an unofficial emissary for the Bragg-Davis combine.

One session with Retreatin' Joe convinced the aggressive-minded Texan that the commanding general had no intention of executing the authorities' plan for a counteroffensive, and he so reported to his Richmond friends.

By then the Federals, after shuffling around in the West and making preparations in Virginia, got down to business. Joe Johnston of necessity began to fight off Sherman where he was and regardless of the sudden offense mania which had seized Davis and Bragg.

In Richmond, in late April, Lee confronted his sixth Union opponent with an "On to Richmond" order in the stocky person of the new General in Chief, U. S. Grant.

2

For the main thrust in Virginia, the "On to Richmond" to end all "On to Richmonds," was not a test between Grant, the young and confident hero of the North, and Lee, the aging idol of the South. It was a showdown between the might of a nation, concentrated in Virginia, and one tired and disappointed old man.

Grant alone had his terrifyingly gunned hosts of 120,000 coming straight down at Richmond in Lincoln's favorite though luckless pathway. South of Richmond's James River, Beast Butler had an army which threatened both the capital and Petersburg, the city twenty miles south of Richmond which was its rail juncture with the south and west. Sigel, the poor-fighting German, had a force in the breadbasket of the Valley that was big enough to walk over Breckinridge's two brigades if it never even deployed for battle. There were Union cavalry units to hack at the railroads which supplied Lee's army, gunboats and transports to supply and move the various armies, and more supply bases than the Confederacy ever possessed. Lee was actually defending against an encirclement within his own state.

He was responsible not only for Grant but for the whole state of Virginia. He was responsible for his own supplies, and he was constantly forced to operate through Davis instead of moving the few forces in the state by his own needs and decisions. Also, though he stood at the peak of his mental powers as a general, he was declining physically along with his country. The length of the struggle had overtaxed the South's human resources.

Not only was the prolonged strain of the multiple responsibilities taking its toll of the fifty-seven-year-old man, but the rigors and exposures of camp life and the insufficient diet he shared with his men sapped his strength. During the winter he had been sick for the first time with the army. "Marse Robert" suffered from violent intestinal disturbances and probably a heart condition, accompanied by sciatica and what was diagnosed as rheumatic back pains intense enough to invalid him. His beard and hair were whitening, his face showed age, and he did not always move as well as formerly. But his spirits were good and he seemed really eager to take on Grant.

Against Grant's 120,000, Lee would have between 60,000 and 65,000, if he could ever get his scattered troops concentrated. His men were scattered partly for subsistence, as was his cavalry for forage, Longstreet was still sojourning unhappily in East Tennessee, and brigades were held in the Richmond area since the Kilpatrick-Dahlgren raid.

The veterans in the army were, like Lee, despite their physical condition, at the peak of their combat effectiveness. He and the men were old campaigners by then, old pros together. As he believed them well-nigh invincible, they *knew* he was unconquerable. They loved him as a leader is rarely loved.

When Longstreet's two divisions finally did get back from Tennessee, his men broke ranks to surround Uncle Robert, to touch his uniform, his horse, his stirrups, and for once Lee's famous self-control broke and tears streamed down his cheeks. The leader and the men were one indissoluble spirit: they formed the spirit of the Confederacy which Southerners like to remember.

By then, Lee's general command was failing along with the leader. Too many irreplaceables had gone. A. P. Hill, with all his devotion and fighting qualities, was no more than adequate as a corps commander. Bald Dick Ewell was clearly in over his head and not himself psychologically. Division commanders and brigade commanders were new and untried, and many simply lacked any qualifications except bravery and patriotism.

When A. P. Hill grew agitated over the failure of one of his generals, Lee said, "These men are not an army; they are citizens defending their country. General ——— is not a soldier; he's a lawyer. I cannot do many things that I could do with a trained army. The soldiers know their duties better than the general officers do, and they have fought magnificently. Sometimes I would like to mask troops and then deploy them, but if I were to give the proper order, the general officers would not understand it; so I make the best of what I have and lose much time in making dispositions."

He actually began to command the army at the battle line, like a brigadier moving regiments, and his exposure to danger worried his officers and men as the exertions, from 3 A.M. to 10 P.M. daily, continued to undermine his broken health. This was the Lee, with his gaunt tatterdemalions and broken-down cavalry, who was the hope of the Confederacy against the power accumulated by the Union in the fourth year of war.

Even at that, as Meade said, Grant was going to find the Army of Northern Virginia a different proposition from the West. He did. He hit with everything he had at nearly two-to-one manpower and immense gun superiority in range and weight, he flanked to his heart's content with his finely conditioned cavalry working ahead and his stout-legged animals pulling guns and wagons, and Lee was always in front of him. Grant said that he would "fight it out on this line if it takes all summer," and when summer was long past he was still fighting it out, losing about as many men as Lee had to begin with. He earned the name of Butcher, he fought his army and all its replacements out, he revolted the Northern population at his losses, and Lee's gray ghost of an army was still in front of him.

3

Grant started in his confident bulldog fashion in early May, at the same time that Butler made noises south of Richmond and Sherman opened on Retreatin' Joe south of Chattanooga. Lee was west of Fredericksburg in that old battle area, gathering about him his worn-out cavalry and the dispersed divisions of two corps; Longstreet was coming toward Lee from East Tennessee with his accustomed leisureliness.

Grant sent his people southward through the same Wilderness where Jackson had finished Hooker and met his own end. It was a little west of the Chancellorsville battleground and Lee, instead of being east of the Unions, was west of them. Both armies were south of the Rapidan on its single course before it joined the Rappahannock.

Lee was pleased that Grant took the course through the narrow roads of that tangle of woods and brush, where his superior armament would be nullified. He sent the two corps with him, under A. P. Hill and Dick Ewell, along parallel roads to head him off. When the advance troops of both armies collided, they began to fight, and that superbly trained army which Grant had inherited was full of fight.

The Confederates had a rough day, with that gap between Ewell and Hill. The large numbers of the Unions kept flanking to the right of Hill as well as to his left, where he had the opening toward Ewell on the other road. But the Confederates held off "those people" with nothing to spare, and Longstreet was coming up.

As it happened, Old Pete was so late out of his congenital slothfulness of movement that Grant's luck almost held. By the time Longstreet's first regiments reached a hard-pressed field the next day, Lee was excited to the point that he tried to lead the troops personally in a charge to save some guns. A marker is there in the Wilderness to commemorate the spot where the men grabbed their commanding general's bridle and the legend reads, " 'Lee to the rear,' cried the Texans." It was the first time the Old Man was goaded to take personal command of troops in action. In all of his grave calm, the Old Man was never more effective.

Fired by Uncle Robert's impetuous exposure to danger, Longstreet's late men turned the Union left flank and had them going there for a while. Then a Confederate bullet, at the angle where two Rebel lines met, knocked Longstreet out of the saddle as Jackson had been in the same dusky woods in the May the year before. (Truly, the grandmothers could say that "God never intended for the South to win.") Longstreet could not have done much more on that day; the drive was about spent. However, at a moment of opportunity Lee lost his only veteran corps leader in the first battle against the fearsome invasion campaign.

At the other end of the line on the same day, one-legged Dick Ewell, all his certainty in ferocity lost with high command (and affected by that wooden leg too), let another opportunity pass. He showed, by his depressed inanition, that he was really unfit to command a corps. As it was, Grant's losses were twice those of Lee.

Grant had the President's support as no other commanding general in Virginia ever had. He had confidence of past victory and that dogged determination to keep after it. He immediately tried flanking movements toward Richmond. He rushed his well-conditioned men and animals through the tangled woods and brush of that war-desolated countryside which, only as a geographical location, was still Spotsylvania County.

Lee had to race him to prevent being turned. The point of contact—near Spotsylvania Court House, south of Fredericksburg—was held for the Confederates by a great stand of Jeb Stuart until the infantry got up. It was the last large service the young cavalry leader was to perform for his country.

Again Lee had to take the ground as he found it, as in the Battle of the Wilderness. One projecting salient in his hastily formed lines, "Bloody Angle," proved a death trap for the defenders. It was as bad as Gettysburg in there, in casualties and loss in prisoners.

The heaviest losses in prisoners came in Stonewall Jackson's old division, then commanded by "Allegheny" Johnson, whose little force in western Virginia had been the first addition to Old Jack's division when he was building his Valley "army." With Johnson captured along with most of his men, the famed division built by Stonewall Jackson ceased to exist as a unit.

The 21st Regiment, with Richmond's Company F, escaped the debacle by being out as a skirmish line. In all the severe fighting and their deliverance from a Yankee prison, the deepest impression made on the Richmond company was by an Alabama sharpshooter. They found him alone, behind a tree, firing at an advancing force so heavy that the woods looked blue. As soon as he was joined by the 21st Regiment, the Alabamian stopped firing to open a captured knapsack stuffed with clothes. He stripped from skin out, putting on new underwear and socks, then pulled on his filthy rags over his clean finery, and went back to shooting.

The Unions were unable to exploit their local success in spite of rifle firepower that ripped heavy limbs from trees and severed the trunk of a tree fourteen inches in diameter. Their repulse was caused partly by the ferocity of the experienced Rebels and partly by the entrenchments which the men had become skillful and quick at throwing up. This digging was hard on men physically in poor condition, but the temporary breastworks greatly reduced the effect of firepower. The Union entrenched quickly too, with none of the men on either side aware that they were introducing modern warfare.

Ultimately Grant's masses were contained, by Lee personally handling the battlefield. Along the whole line he hurried a brigade here, a regiment there, pulling exhausted men out of one position as soon as the pressure was off and sending them stumbling to the next threatened point. For the second time within a week soldiers restrained him from personally leading a counterattack, promising they would take the position if he stayed back.

It was then the soldiers and *the* leader, really the stand of the knight-hood tradition against the machine of the new age. A. P. Hill was ill, getting the ambulance driver to bring him close to the lines to be near his men. Dick Ewell, suffering physically and mentally, had already shown that he would give no help. Anderson, taking over Longstreet's corps, had been selected more because he was personally acceptable as a replacement for Old Pete than for soldierly qualities.

Yet they held off Grant in another two-day battle (Spotsylvania Court House, May 11–12, 1864), the second in a week, though the fighting had taxed the army to the ultimate limits of its endurance. With Grant getting replacements to continue these sledge-hammer assaults, the long-dreaded test by mathematics would soon defeat them if Lee could not maneuver to get at Grant while the Unions were in motion. For his desperate need to strike at Grant, Lee suffered still another blow, one that gave Grant an advantage no other Union general enjoyed against Lee.

4

The beginning of the Confederate cavalry's end had been seen the year before against able Pleasonton, and to complete the end Grant brought along Phil Sheridan. The same class at West Point as John Hood, Sheridan was an undersized man (five feet three) with an oversized head, in all ways. He had been an infantry division commander in the West, and definitely anything except a Rock at Chickamauga. But Grant perceived in the man a quality he wanted in his all-out, no-holds-barred war of total conquest.

The Sheridans, Milroys, and Hunters had a different kind of arrogance from the neo-princelings of the Cotton South. They had the arrogance of unrestrained might. Without regard for rights—of belligerents or fellow citizens or even of the so-called "human rights," let alone of the Union— these bully boys had a lust for physical violence and wanton destruction.

Militarily Sheridan had the good fortune, like Grant, to come along at the right time. As Grant was in fact supreme commander, with no inter-ference from Washington, Sheridan in turn was completely supported by Grant. He had the military judgment to recognize that Stuart's cavalry was worn out and the confidence to apply his superior numbers, horses, and equipment in bold action against the tired men on tired horses—however legendary the name of their leader.

It was Sheridan's idea that he could defeat Stuart's cavalry in open battle, as Pleasonton had almost been able to do the year before. He took off for Richmond with his full force as the means of drawing Stuart toward him. The veteran Jeb Stuart at thirty-one was accustomed to Union raids and feints, and his job was to screen Lee and disclose Grant's intentions. He sent one of the lean brigades after the enemy cavalry to see what they were up to. They were up to going on into virtually undefended Richmond unless the Rebel cavalry stopped them.

Brigade by brigade the Confederate troopers were drawn off from the army, goading their gaunt horses into something like a gallop, with the partially fattened horses of the guns coming along. Drastic messages sent back brought the golden-voiced Stuart on personally.

He was the only one left of those laughing young men who had sung "Kathleen Mavourneen" as they rode around McClellan when their horses were sleek and their spirits high. The boy Pelham from Alabama had gone first, then soft-voiced, hard-bitten Farley from South Carolina, then big Rooney Lee, the general's son, wounded and dragged out of his mother's home and held prisoner against all offers of exchange while his wife died. Last the giant baron from Prussia, Von Borcke, was invalided out with a throat wound which kept his voice to a whisper.

Sheridan's solid squadrons were almost at Richmond by the time Stuart came up with enough of his men to give straight-on battle. The mounted thousands clashed near the present Route 1 to Washington, where the old Telegraph Road came down and the immediate area was known for a public place, Yellow Tavern. They fought back and forth across the road, over ripening fields and country gardens, the Union fellows always holding the initiative they started with.

Stuart personally rallied a break, galloping in with red-lined cape flowing, the wind in his long beard and plume, a gun in his hand, and his great voice bugling. The men rallied, closing in the break across the contested road. An unhorsed Union trooper, running back to his own people, heard the big Rebel thundering near, turned and fired, and ran on into anonymity.

Stuart held to his horse. He was a powerful man and superb rider. His stricken staff and younger officers flocked around, gazing in shock at their mortally wounded leader. He waved them off. "Go back," he shouted, in his weakening voice. "Go back and do your duty as I have done mine and our country will be saved."

They got him into the ambulance, fighting off the resurgent Unions to get him into Richmond. It was just a year since he had led the wounded Jackson's corps into the Wilderness, singing, "Old Joe Hooker, won't you come out of the Wilderness?"

In a private home on West Grace Street in Richmond, where the rambler roses were in bloom, he had them sing, "Rock of Ages, cleft for me." His wife came there to be with him. The President came. His old comrade Heros von Borcke went in to sit beside him.

It was a rainy dusk when the big Prussian came slowly out, and the anxiously waiting crowd gathered on the brick sidewalk knew it was all over when, in the yellow light, they saw the tears streaming out of Von Borcke's eyes.

Stonewall Jackson last spring and Jeb Stuart this (with Longstreet out wounded)—it was more than the people could bear. It was almost an anticlimax when the re-formed cavalry, with the local defense troops and two quickly rushed infantry brigades, drove Sheridan away from the breastworks and on down to his safety under the Union gunboats on the James River. Like Dahlgren, Sheridan had killed a guide he impressed (a white man), who gave him a wrong turn in the darkness. But the people were not thinking of the Dahlgrens and the Sheridans. They were thinking of their own. With Stuart above all, whatever was left in the Confederacy that was young and gay and bright was gone.

Though he had lost his former cadet, Lee had good cavalry leaders in his nephew, Fitz Lee, and in Wade Hampton, the massive South Carolina grandee, but he did not have Jeb Stuart. "He never brought me a piece of false information," Lee said.

With Grant massed in front of him, with feints and movements presaging more hammering somewhere, Lee could only say sadly to one of the fallen Jeb's officers, "Ah, Major, if I had my poor Stuart with me I should know all about what those people are doing."

5

"Those people" were up to flanking again to Lee's right, toward the southeast, always closer to Richmond, and closer already than any army had been since McClellan. They were flanking out of the old battleground of the Fredericksburg area toward the flat farm country and the two vital railroads from Richmond north to the army and west toward the Valley. Sheridan had ripped up stretches of both on his raid, though they were repaired again. Another cavalry raider, operating from the Suffolk occupation base south of the James River, had interrupted the lines south from Richmond into North Carolina and they were repaired too.

The cavalry raids seemed to be over for the moment, as even Union horses had to rest, and there had been two good turns for Lee against the general encirclement.

At the little Valley town of New Market, which had figured so often in Stonewall Jackson's dispatches, Breckinridge's small force was joined by the high-school-age battalion of cadets from Old Jack's V.M.I. "Little devils," to Sigel, the boys charged with a fine impetuosity and, in winning the only battle flag possessed by an American college, they sent Sigel flying out of the Valley. It was a pathetic reflection of the declining state of their defense when compared with Jackson's maneuvering two years before in May, in the strategy that was to break the Richmond siege. In 1864 the Confederates were grateful to have the Valley temporarily spared, and Breckinridge's two brigades could constitute "replacements" for Lee's losses.

Then, closer to home, Beast Butler had encountered his customary trouble with armed men, when he had a great opportunity at Drewry's Bluff. Across the James River from Richmond and southeastward, the river fort at Drewry's Bluff was held only by the artillerists on the stationary river guns. The loss of Drewry's Bluff would expose the city to gunboat attack from the river, as well as cut it off from supplies and manpower from the South through Petersburg.

For guarding the vital junction of Petersburg and all the way south to Weldon, North Carolina, George Pickett had what remained of his famous command. The division was then largely composed of new conscripts. The long-haired leader, never recovered from Gettysburg, was further distracted from his troops by attentions to a new, young bride. At the time of Butler's first huffings, Pickett reported himself "ill."

In Richmond proper, since the late winter raids, a number of odd units —regulars, militia, and local defense troops—had been formed into a so-called division. Below Richmond on the James River, high-school-age cadets of the Confederate Naval Academy were training on the good ship *Patrick Henry*.

When Butler's army first moved toward Drewry's Bluff it was those boys who, transferring themselves into marines on an hour's notice, acted as skirmishers against the 30,000 Union troops.

While the Confederate Naval Academy was winning a battle flag it would never get to display, the troops were hurried across the river from Richmond. Beauregard hurried on the brigades from North and South Carolina. They were formed into divisions as they arrived, and went in fighting as soon as they were formed. It was one of the most conglomerate forces used *up until then* to halt an army, and they did more than that. They attacked.

Beauregard, activated from his innocuous department in South Carolina, returned to duty in Virginia as if the war was still small and innocent, and victory certain. Messages flew from his headquarters. He wired Bragg, who had become a dynamo of telegraphic action himself; he wired Seddon, who had been pushed into a back seat since Bragg's ascent; he wired Davis, and Ransom, the city defense commander, and anybody apparently who came to mind. He was showing that Beauregard was alert and a soldier every minute. It was his first chance in two years and he wanted to make the most of it.

Old Bory did fine. Of course, he had help from the maladroit Butler. With the whole of southside Virginia to maneuver his army in, the Beast managed to get inside one of the large loops of the James River, a horse-shoe-shaped affair, where the open end was only four miles wide. Beauregard popped his own small force into the opening like, Grant said, a cork in a bottle, and there was the terror of New Orleans' ladies as helpless as a baby.

Though Beauregard's assembled force totaled less than 20,000, he did have plenty of artillery. When new guns came in through the blockade or the U. S. Ordnance Department, the enforcedly frugal Confederates did not discard their earlier models. They lacked horses to use the older guns in campaigning, but even the few plow-broken horses they impressed from the farmers would serve to pull guns up to fire from a stationary position, as impressed farm wagons would serve in those conditions for want of battery wagons.

That Beauregard had Butler was conceded by Grant when he began drawing off corps of Butler's as replacements for his own losses. Lee hoped to do the same from Beauregard, matching a new Confederate division for a new Union corps. Old Bory proved to be a hard man to get troops from. Still mindful of his own glory, Beauregard grasped at a department system which Davis had finally managed to erect in Virginia.

As commander of southside Virginia and North Carolina, Beauregard was, when he came to the Richmond front, separated from Lee only by the two hundred yards of the James River, crossed by several bridges. Regardless of the fact that Lee and Beauregard were defending the same city, and that Lee was responsible for its defense, Beauregard remained inviolate in his own department.

When Lee, with his trained system of scouts, knew what corps of Butler's had moved from Beauregard's front to join Grant against him, the Old Man was unable to order matching forces from Beauregard. Old Bory replied to Lee, in effect, that his information was wrong. Then Lee sent a positive order for the troops. Beauregard replied that such orders must go through the proper channels of the War Office and thence to his department.

At that the enraged general wired Davis without any of his customary forms of deference. He said simply that the result of delaying those reinforcing troops "will be disaster."

With those troops as replacements, Lee's cavalry was helped by two fine South Carolina regiments. When Beauregard left the Charleston area, these young horsemen had been finally relieved of their tedium and came on to Lee as full of fight and fire as those first splendidly uniformed Palmetto troops in the long-ago first spring of the war.

With at least some replacements for his heavy losses, along with the threat removed from his rear and to his Valley supplies, Lee could concentrate on Grant. He was the busiest general they had ever faced, and the Old Man was in the worst shape of his life.

6

Lee's decline was hastened by the nerve strain of constant self-control under exacerbations such as getting the troops from Beauregard. During Grant's flanking maneuverings along the northern banks of the south-easterly-flowing rivers, Lee's iron control began to break along with his health. Each river Grant crossed brought him closer to Richmond. At each crossing Lee wanted to get at him, to get off the defensive and seize the initiative.

When one chance failed, again in command, he turned angrily on A. P. Hill, himself half sick. Then, back in his tent on a cot, the Old Man cried out in desperation, "We must strike them a blow—we must never let them pass us again."

By then it was a one-man army, virtually back to the loose organization of divisions which Lee had inherited two years before. He still operated loosely through the three-corps system. He had to, since, in recovering from his intestinal attack, he was not strong enough to ride his gray horse. Lee was getting about in a carriage when Grant crossed the Pamunkey, the last river except the Chickahominy there was to cross if he was to strike at Richmond from the north.

But Grant's crablike movements, in moving his army to the east, had removed him as a threat to the life-line railroad to the Valley. Also his flankings had failed to place Lee in a vulnerable position. Grant was coming straight at Lee from northeast of Richmond, in the area of the old Seven Days' Battle. The Federals were north of the winding, marshy-banked Chickahominy, and part of Lee's troops formed on the ridge of the Gaines's Mill battlefield, where Fitz-John Porter's corps had stood two years before.

Against Porter, Lee's troops had been charging eastward to drive the Unions into a trap away from Richmond; now they faced eastward to await attack toward the city. That was the basic difference in the two years.

Grant, at a casualty loss which would have been unthinkable two years before, had reached almost to the point where McClellan came without a full battle. For strategy he had substituted aggressive tactics. Constantly crowding a weaker foe, he kept the initiative against an enemy unable to strike back, making use of the cover in the brushy flat country to screen his hurrying movements, and using his numerically superior cavalry not only to hold off Lee's prying troopers but for feints and bedevilment. On the "to him who hath it shall be given" basis, Sheridan's great numbers on strong horses had received an issue of the new breech-loading repeating carbines, to use against Rebel cavalrymen who considered themselves fortunate to own soundly working old-style single-shot muzzle-loaders. With their overwhelming numbers, Grant's cavalry got five-to-one odds in firepower.

Yet Lee's cavalry, while unable to penetrate the Union screen, kept pushing on their own and fought as if they didn't know the odds were against them and the tide running out. Sheridan thought the first time the fresh South Carolina regiments went in action that he had hit infantry. Occasionally the Rebel cavalry by sheer fury drove Sheridan back on his infantry supports and they gathered information that way. They covered Lee well on the whole too, though deserters and stragglers were giving information.

"Marse Robert" stubbornly refused to accept his army's loss of offensive power. His nature as a soldier rebelled against a defensive which his military intelligence warned could have only one end. He kept trying to get going even a limited offensive, anything that might develop into the big counterstroke he felt to be necessary. Every time he tried to catch an exposed Union segment, the attack was poorly co-ordinated by the division commanders and the Federals stood up strongly to slug it out. It was as if the Union soldiers and officers felt the physical weakening of the army opposing them, perceived the unsureness its generals caused in its movements, and did not expect to lose. Some Unions stated that the Army of Northern Virginia was no more than a shell of what it had been.

The veteran Confederates felt none of that. They hadn't lost a battle to this new fellow yet; that was as far as they thought. They were mighty close to Richmond, but he still had to overrun them to get there, and they just didn't believe he could do that.

Grant could not. With all the advantages of initiative, rapid and covered movement, manpower and firepower, supplies and reserves, all of his flanking and maneuvering had simply brought him to the point where if he wanted to take Richmond he had to attack Lee straight on.

Lee, with all his difficulties in getting information and screening his own movements, was prepared for the assault and his men were waiting *precisely* where it came. It was a six-mile front, with some good ground for defense and the men well dug in everywhere. The penultimate moment of the one month's fighting was an attack across the whole front almost as clumsy as Burnside's at Fredericksburg, when he had been goaded by Lincoln to attack.

Second Cold Harbor (June 3, 1864) was the easiest crucial battle ever won by the Army of Northern Virginia. At a total loss of between 1200 and 1500, they inflicted 13,000 casualties and were never in danger. Toward the end of the day, the Union troops tacitly refused to charge any more. The Confederates could hear their officers yelling for the attack and the men would spring forward, lie down, fire, and stay there.

After the gruesome defeat, Grant showed that he was indifferent to Unions as to Confederates where victory was concerned. He refused to concede defeat by asking a truce to gather his wounded and bury his dead. His wounded died, moaning for water in the damp heat. As the peninsula sun got at the corpses, the Rebels said, "My God, is he trying to stink us out now?"

7

The bulldog method had failed. Whatever weakening the Unions had felt in Lee's attacks was not evident in his defense. Some of the Yankees' high edge was blunted, and the confidence formed in beating off puny attacks began to wilt at carrying the attacks to the other fellows. There was a lot of skirmishing and vicious sharpshooter fire for the next days. Some of the lines (still there) were so close that you could throw a cigarette across. But there were not going to be any more attacks north of the Chicka-hominy.

On the other hand, Lee could do nothing to pry them out either. The Unions threw up works, and the Old Man knew he could achieve no more against those dug-in troops, with their heavy guns, than he could have two years before against McClellan. For maneuvering, he didn't have enough men or experienced general officers, and the toll among those continued to mount before they could gain any experience. Of the fifty-eight generals who started the campaign against Grant, twenty-two were already gone.

Even faithful Dick Ewell had to go. From suffering a psychological dislocation, the Old Dragoon developed intestinal disorders to a degree that General Lee was put to the painful chore of retiring Ewell from active duty. By then Old Dick had finally married his "Widow Brown," and she joined her husband in protests at the ignominy. Lee softened the blow by giving Jackson's great captain command of the newly organized Richmond defense forces, a conglomerate group of two regular brigades, militia, artillerists at the stationary guns, and the local defense troops. Its shifting numbers approximated 7000, if ever they were all assembled together.

The remnants of Jackson's old II Corps went to Jubal Early, veteran brigadier and division commander. Forty-seven years old and a West Point graduate, Jubal Early had been a successful lawyer in his home town, Lynchburg, and a rabid anti-secessionist. When his state was invaded, he became an equally rabid Rebel. Tobacco-chewing and awesomely profane, as a soldier Jubal Early was competent, aggressive, and a rough customer who believed in coddling nobody, friend or enemy.

In the corps he inherited, Early had two of the only four promising new division commanders in the army. Georgia's John B. Gordon, an untrained soldier of thirty-two who looked and acted like the ramrod type of old army man, was observant, intelligent, and very determined. Twenty-seven-year-old Dodson Ramseur of North Carolina, who had been out of West Point less than a year when the war came, wore a fierce beard to hide the youthful sensitivity of his face. Nothing could hide the fire in his eyes, and he possessed the skill and audacity of the trained and natural soldier.

Most of the rest related to the veterans much as an officer fresh from civilian life relates to an old army sergeant. Lee's soldiers took their new officers as they came, gave them nicknames, and went on, as they said, "about their hawg-killing." This meant anything from fighting the enemy to spearing some poor farmer's loose pig.

While they rested after the punishing campaign, waiting to see what Grant would do next, the emaciated fellows got a real treat in store-bought hog meat when some bacon came in through the blockade. For a few days, in unprecedented lavishness, the commissary issued half a pound of bacon a day per man and even some onions for the scurvy that was developing in the army for want of vegetables. When Lee, exercising on Traveller as he regained his strength, passed soldiers, some of them said:

"Marse Robert, we go' get so hawg-fat and lazy off all this food that we won't be able to fight."

Their spirits were never better. They hadn't believed Grant could beat them, and he hadn't. In Richmond, where the windowpanes had rattled during Grant's violent cannonade at sunrise on the day of the battle, even the people startled out of their sleep had believed that Lee could stop Grant, or anybody. That was the trouble. The people, along with the government, had begun to believe that Lee could do anything.

Whether the old lion admitted it or not, he had seen that he could not, though the obscure failures in counteroffensive were unknown to the people. They saw that Richmond had been saved again, from the greatest danger since 1862. They did not see that, if Lincoln continued to support Grant in this hammering without consequence of life, the capital stood in its gravest danger of the war.

Lee had always known that defense would not be enough against arithmetic, and it was finally coming to that. In the big test for their independence, the only hope of their main army had become what the government's had always been—to outlast, by a continuing defense, the enemy's will to conquer. Lee had never believed they could win their independence that way.

CHAPTER XX

"Like Grant Took Richmond"

WHILE Jefferson Davis had never conceived boldly, to his own commitment to defense he brought an unfaltering courage. The nearby guns hammering in his ears only hardened his resistance to any dealings with the enemy short of independence. Some Northern newspapers stated that only his iron will kept the rebellion going, and in the South some of the resigned claimed that only the President's uncompromising stand on independence prevented an honorable peace. Neither was right, though Davis' unyielding position did stand out in sharp contrast against the growing peace movements in North and South.

Most of the people engaged in peace activities, on both sides, were either unrealistic visionaries or crackpots. In the Confederacy, the most vocal of these bemused people was Vice-President Stephens, then openly attacking the President to whoever would listen to him in Georgia. Off in his private world of constitutionalities, Stephens believed that peace on terms of Georgia's sovereignty could be had for the asking. His ally, Governor Brown, carried his sovereignty rantings to such extremes that Georgia soldiers passed resolutions against his borderline treason.

In North Carolina a Raleigh editor was running for governor on a platform which meant the virtual secession of the state from the Confederacy and suing for a separate peace. At Richmond and other cities there were flurries of rumors about peace emissaries arriving and departing, and hope spread that an honorable peace might be in the making. Lincoln had the raiding troops in the early part of the year spread his proclamation of general amnesty to all who would "go over to the Union," and he offered to accept states back with full statehood—though without their slaves—where ten per cent of the 1860 vote would declare for the Union. Though the proclamations had no immediate effect, distortions of them grew with the rumors and conditioned people to accept as truth the deluded utterances of the likes of Stephens. In many war-weary citizens the dissemination of these false hopes weakened the will to further resistance. They regarded Davis as the obstacle to a peaceful ending to all their troubles. Having failed to personalize the Confederacy to them, by the summer of 1864 the President had become a remote symbol of their ills.

Even among the more knowing people, faith in the Confederacy as a country was seriously shaken by a belated and desperate measure of the government to tighten the loose currency. This hit the people in their pocketbooks. Though the saying in Richmond was, "I took my money in the market basket and brought home the purchases in my pocketbook," money was still the most personal symbol of the government. The new law amounted to repudiation.

The reason behind the law was sound. With nearly $1,000,000,000 in circulation, and hardly one hundredth of it supported by gold, Secretary of the Treasury Memminger believed a withdrawal of some of the paper would help stabilize the money. What Congress produced, with complications that would try a tax expert, was essentially a demand that all Confederate notes above $5.00 and under $100 be turned in for exchange at three old for two new. At $100 and over, the notes would be exchanged for tax-free bonds paying four per cent interest. Penalties for not exchanging the higher notes would be to tax them out of existence, and for the smaller notes presumably the old money would become worthless.

Southerners were never people to take kindly to such interference with their personal lives and, besides, machinery for this complex operation was sadly lacking. Some old money came in on this partial repudiation plan, more was continued in use through either defiance or ignorance, and the result of all the confusion was that methodical Memminger, the untypical Charlestonian, resigned as Secretary of the Treasury.

The bill, as it came out of the wringer of Congress, was not Memminger's idea. The sour German had never been able to get on with Congress and he was worn down by taking the blame for what they did with his measures. He could serve as a prototype for the able Southerner who failed all by failing of revolutionary concepts. His political epitaph, as written in a Richmond newspaper, would apply to all too many of his compatriots: "He has done his best, but he has been overtaken—that is all."

Then in its extremities the Confederacy finally appointed a man of finance to the Treasury. George Trenholm was also a Charlestonian, but one who had succeeded vastly as an international financier, a man of charm and presence, and passionately devoted. Unfortunately for the Confederacy, Trenholm came along when the country was bankrupt.

The early Produce Bond issue, which had received pledges of $34,000,-000 on the proceeds of planters' produce, had fallen short in collections by about one third. The invaders collected some of the produce before there were any proceeds, and some of the 1862 patriots had cooled off by the time their pledges were due to be redeemed. Even the cotton, which the government had slowly gotten around to accepting for bonds, had been either gobbled up by the invaders, destroyed to keep it out of their hands, or again the owners, apprehensive of the Confederacy's failure, clung to it as their one security in an uncertain future.

The country owed everybody—pay for the soldiers, rent for buildings used as hospitals, supply depots, and such—and their debts approached $500,000,000. That might seem small by today's standards; then there were no means of either paying it or getting further credit. A government draws on its people and the people were impoverished. Their economic system was disrupted through occupation, men in the army, workers (slaves) run off, such industry as they had concentrated in government work at government pay, and the one-fifth value of what money the people could get. Always the mercenary had hoarded their gold or sent it abroad; by the summer of 1864 the most loyal were holding on to what they had, *just in case*.

There was nothing that Trenholm could do. Nothing could be done anywhere through any apparatus of traditional government. The Confederate experiment was reduced to its two armies and their abilities to stand off the enemy in the type of static defense which, Lee said, made the end "only a question of time."

What the Old Man thought about the processes which had brought him to this pass can never be known. Not being reflective, he probably thought nothing. He had "done his duty to the full," which was his concept of a fruitful life. He would continue so to do, though definitely the general was aware (often bitterly) of the government failures which had made his duty so hard to perform with success. As Lee conceived success, militarily it was already past. In front of Richmond, waiting for Grant's next move, the initiative denied him, he could only do his duty from day to day . . . and hope.

That was all any still loyal Confederate could do any more, though this was not consciously articulated. The people who still hoped believed in the apparently unconquerable Lee.

As the lady said, "I've heard of God, I've *seen* General Lee."

2

The sick old man suffered the embarrassment of losing Grant for more than a day there in the hot, brushy countryside east of Richmond. The old phrase is literal: Grant stole a march on him.

With inferior cavalry, Lee could not ascertain Grant's movements except by feeling out with a weakened infantry. He needed to conserve those men *and* Lee did not have only Grant to worry about. His brief respite from pressures of the total encirclement was over, and he was again defending the whole state with his one army.

Aside from guarding against a thrust by Grant straight eastward toward Richmond, Butler was "bottled up" south of the city's river by only 6000 men under Beauregard. Grant could move across the river to reinforce the Beast as Butler had reinforced him, and the combined force break out of Beauregard's enclosure. Or Grant could cross the river below Butler and move directly at the rail juncture of Petersburg.

To occupy the Valley, the Federals had sent in new and larger forces to take up where Sigel had left off. With two cavalry units and infantry under Hunter, totaling about 20,000, they had broken a makeshift cavalry force, struck into the fertile central Valley, and for the first time in the war occupied Staunton—where the future President, Woodrow Wilson, had been born eight years before.

Lee could only hurry back the two brigades under Breckinridge, which had joined him for the one battle of Cold Harbor, to restrain Hunter as much as possible.

Then, when Lee learned that Sheridan had taken off a large part of the rested Union cavalry toward the Valley, the situation grew more ominous. Sheridan could not only destroy the railroad to the Valley, but Lee concluded (rightly, as Union reports indicate) that Sheridan would lead Hunter's force to Grant after Hunter had finished his work of destruction in the Valley.

Facing Grant straight on and Butler and possibly Grant to his southern flank, when a new threat came to his supply line to Virginia's west, Lee showed that neither Grant's hammering nor the encirclement had destroyed any of his boldness. If circumstances forced him to weaken his army in front of Grant, he would at least make a complete job of it.

Lee sent off the old II Corps under Jubal Early to destroy Hunter, permanently to remove that Federal menace from the Valley, and he sent two thirds of his cavalry under Wade Hampton to keep Sheridan away from Hunter. Remembering Yellow Tavern, where Jeb Stuart was killed, Lee did not send cavalry to try to divert or harass the Federals. Stripping the mounted force with him down to mere observation outposts, he sent the massive South Carolinian out prepared for cavalry battle.

Hampton, as physically durable as his fallen leader, drove his men and horses hard to head Sheridan off. Hampton caught him at Trevilian's Station on the Virginia Central Railroad, on June 11 and 12, and the Confederates were laying for Sheridan. They were less than 5000 to Sheridan's 9000, and in cavalry, too, command was such that details of the trap went wrong. The Rebel troopers had a hard fight on their hands the first day. However, Hampton fought his men dismounted, nullifying the poor condition of the horses, and got breastworks up to minimize the firepower of the Union's repeating carbines. On the second day, after sharp repulses, Sheridan showed no disposition to push for a decision, and drew off back to the Richmond line.

Though Sheridan refused to admit that he had encountered a very definite repulse, for his part of the plan with Hunter he had to settle for tearing up some stretches of the railroad on his way home to Grant.

For Hunter, who had been vandalizing personal property southward from Staunton, Breckinridge and Early combined in mid-June at Early's home town of Lynchburg. This pleasant hilly city was not in the Valley but on the eastern slope of the Blue Ridge, and its importance to the invaders lay in its railroads, to southwestern Virginia and to Richmond. Hunter, better at arson than at fighting, hurried away to the mountains of friendly West Virginia, pausing only at Lexington long enough to burn V.M.I.

With a second Union force dispersed from the Valley within a month, Jubal Early turned on the offensive to use the Valley as Stonewall Jackson had used it. From Lynchburg, the 8000-man remnant of Jackson's old corps started north again down the Valley, through the damaged country to Staunton . . . and on to Washington. It was late in the game to try that old threat again, but anything was better to Lee than keeping troops idle waiting on the enemy.

It was while one fourth of his infantry and two thirds of his cavalry were away that Lee lost Grant on June 13 and 14. The significance of Lee's losing Grant for a day was that the waning of his striking power, along with the enforced immobilization while guarding Richmond, removed the initiative from him and made uncertainty inevitable. The collapse of the whole, in relation to the cumulative might of the invaders, was reflected in Lee's army.

3

Holding the initiative, Grant had three possibilities for the attack to defeat Lee's army and capture Richmond. He could reverse his sidling and return northward, seeking to trap Lee into a vulnerable position; he could cross the Chickahominy, the last river between him and Richmond, and come at the capital from due east; or he could cross the Chickahominy and keep going, crossing the James River, and combine with Butler for an attack on Petersburg. This last would neither defeat Lee's army nor take Richmond, but it would isolate the city from the South and make certain its eventual abandonment.

Whichever way he moved, Grant had no worries about supplies. The bases in eastern Virginia made the Unions look like the defenders of their own land and Lee's lean people like the ones at a distance from home. The new big base was at City Point, where the James from Richmond joined the Appomattox close to Petersburg. With Butler already on the inside of the lopsided Richmond-Petersburg-City Point triangle, and near the pike and railroad connecting the two cities, action was to be expected from that danger point. Yet, as Lee's purpose was to thwart Grant's primary objective of taking Richmond, he had to leave the dangerous southside to Beauregard and a small cavalry force of observation, and keep his reduced army between Grant and the capital.

In studying the enemy's intention, Lee always thought of what he himself would do. As Grant had vastly superior manpower, Lee expected him to detach powerful segments toward the end of causing the Confederates further to disperse their weakened forces. Though Lee was attributing to a hammerer designs of which Grant was then innocent, a surprise small attack on Petersburg (June 9) tended to strengthen the Old Man's conclusions.

As it was, the Confederate forces were spread so thinly that in the thrust on Petersburg the Unions were stopped from taking the city only by themselves.

The only soldiers there, on guard, were a brigade under General Wise, the imperious ex-governor who was one of the few of his ilk to settle down and become a competent leader. He had his men in breastworks, along with a collection of those overage and semimobile guns the Confederates used on such fixed positions.

Against this brigade came two Union infantry divisions from the City Point base. Farther southward from the Norfolk base came a cavalry force of between 1500 and 2000, with guns, under Kautz.

The Union infantry commander, apparently surprised to encounter Wise's resolute fire from breastworks, paused in indecision. At the same time Kautz's veteran raiders, with repeating carbines, struck to the south of the city against what the tablet in Blandford Church calls ". . . the Citizen Soldiers of Petersburg, the gray haired sires and beardless youth, who . . . laid down their lives near this venerable church in successful defense of our Altars and Firesides. . . ."

These few hundred old men and boys formed one of those local defense units, without uniforms and armed only with old flintlock muskets remade for percussion. They were commanded by a volunteer veteran of the Mexican War. Some had been in camp for several weeks, ever since Butler moved south of the James, while others went about civilian duties and came only when the tocsin sounded. The principal of the academy did not hear the alarm bell over the children's voices and was summoned in the classroom with the dread words, "The Yankees are coming!"

As the men ran through the streets, they were joined by the sick and wounded from the hospitals and the prisoners from the jail, thus giving to the action the name of "The Battle of the Patients and the Penitents." The whole force was well placed in a gully that ran on both sides of the road by Brigadier General Colston, formerly of the Army of Northern Vir-

ginia and on detached duty in the neighborhood. They overturned a
wagon in the road to block it.

They held their ground steadfastly under punishing fire from Kautz's
well-armed veterans, with four guns, and did not break until they were
literally overrun. Even then only a few were gobbled up as prisoners,
though the total list of prisoners included a Union man who had come to
watch in a buggy and protested at having his horse and buggy taken from
him, and an aged free Negro who had long been a hotel chef and refused
to sign the oath of allegiance.

Kautz had been held up long enough so that, by the time his cavalry
started into the city, one regular battery had gotten there. Those four
guns were commanded by Captain Graham, son of a British army officer,
who had been on guard at the railroad. The guns went through town at
a full gallop and, the old-timers said, the dust was just settling when the
four guns opened with fine accuracy on the approaching cavalry.

That was all for Kautz. Hearing nothing from his collaborative infantry
and not knowing who was supporting Graham's battery (actually nobody), he withdrew his men back to their base when Dearing's small cavalry brigade hurried to the scene to speed the parting of the unwelcome
guests. Though it was a near thing, Lee was not to be distracted by diversions.

With that state of mind he (along with his equally bewildered soldiers)
was given quite a turn to wake up one morning (June 13) and find the
Federal trenches outside Richmond empty.

He was embarrassed by want of cavalry with Hampton away, and his
1200 troopers under his son Rooney—recently recovered and returned to
the army—were scattered on either flank to watch for Grant's turning
movements. Lee could only send his popeyed infantry cautiously through
the woods beyond the abandoned Union breastworks at Cold Harbor.
After two miles without seeing a blue uniform, they only established the
fact that Grant was moving in his old southeasterly arc. This time he was
on the opposite shore of the Chickahominy, the last river between him and
Richmond, unless he was heading for the James River and the southside.

Lee did not expect Grant to give up his direct assault on Richmond. In
chasing the vanished enemy, he kept always between the city and the
Federals' crabwise movements, and could not follow directly. First he
crossed the Chickahominy, to be on the Richmond side of the river, then
pushed his men through the dusty heat where the narrow roads fanned
out in the region of McClellan's retreat. Uncle Robert's somewhat baffled
veterans kept between Grant and all approaches to Richmond and stayed
near their own pontoon bridge across the river in case the southside was
Grant's objective. Then, late in the day, A. P. Hill's men pushed back
stubbornly fighting Union cavalry in their front.

If Lee did not know where Grant's main army was going, by the next day he at least knew the way it had gone. Far east of Richmond, Grant had crossed the Chickahominy and was on the same side of the river as Lee. All indications pointed toward the Unions moving on southward to cross the James River. But in the absence of positive information, and fearful of uncovering the capital, Lee felt obliged to prepare for all contingencies.

With the troop shortage caused by Early's absence, the anxious old gentleman detached one division and placed it at the pontoon bridge crossing to the south at Drewry's Bluff, ready to reinforce Beauregard or rejoin the main force. He pulled his main army back closer to Richmond, to guard against attack there, and closer to the pontoon bridge if Grant was moving his whole army to the back door of Richmond at Petersburg. To this desperate defensiveness, the South's greatest general had been reduced, and in the extremity for information he must depend on volatile Beauregard.

4

Neither Lee nor Old Bory knew that the President, in an unprecedented release of bureaucracy, had suspended Beauregard's department and placed the joint forces under Lee. Ever proper, and full of alarms, Beauregard sent a flurry of telegrams to Richmond—only the wires had to go to Bragg, as military adviser to the President, instead of to Seddon, the Secretary of War. In this new division of authority, Lee got only some of the wires, and no information at all on what troops were alarming the Creole.

Along with Beauregard's rash of telegrams, Bragg *and* Seddon were receiving, separately and together, the usual desperate calls for reinforcements elsewhere, along with other routine petitions of various kinds. Lee and Beauregard, twenty miles apart, had to conduct their urgent communications through this bureaucratic maze. This must have exacerbated the nerves of both men and was certainly no balm to Uncle Robert's temper, which had been growing shorter as the failures in his army showed up.

The confusion in the War Office was, in turn, heightened by the well-intentioned patriots who constantly announced it was obvious to one and all that Grant had crossed the James and it must be his troops who were massing before Beauregard.

Then, on June 15, Lee and everybody in Richmond learned that two Union corps, 35,000 men, had appeared in front of Beauregard's breastworks—though whether Grant's or Butler's or some stranger's, Old Bory kept to himself. In any event, *one* certainty was that an attack was coming at Richmond's supply junction with the South.

Petersburg is on the south bank of the Appomattox, and the Union troops were on the same side of the river, which served the Confederates as their northern flank. Their breastworks were in a loose arc facing east. While not good works compared with those the armies were then building, they gave adequate protection to riflemen, and the so-called lunettes placed at intervals were fairly strong placements for the guns. With their older guns supported by half a dozen mobile batteries, the artillery fire had some weight if little range. Since the Kautz-infantry raid the week before, Wise's brigades had been strengthened by oddments to bring the Confederate infantry up to 2200—against 35,000 or more.

The hard fighting from the Wilderness to Cold Harbor, and Cold Harbor in particular, had taken its toll of the Union troops. The attack of the two corps accomplished little against the 2200 men, coolly and capably handled by Wise. General Meade, in the anomalous position of "second in command" to Grant, implied that the Union troops, on finding Confederates in breastworks again, had little heart for the business. The Unions effected some lodgments and the Confederates pulled back to an inner, shorter arc of lines.

There had been no punch in the Union assault, but there were an awful lot of them, more coming, and that night Beauregard sent a desperate message direct to Lee. He had abandoned his lines facing Butler between Drewry's Bluff and Petersburg, leaving only a skirmish line for the night, and concentrated all his troops in the city breastworks. Who he was fighting he did not say.

Lee had already sent a division across the pontoon bridge and on southward to Petersburg, followed by a regular brigade from the Richmond city defense force. With the division withdrawn from Butler's front, Beauregard would have about 15,000 men plus more guns. But Beauregard's withdrawal of the troops containing Butler, without forewarning Lee, threatened to break the defense line in the center and separate Lee and Beauregard.

The country between Richmond and Petersburg is flat and open, with no natural obstacles to check an enemy rolling westward toward the turnpike and railroad connecting the two cities. The area was covered with good farms and small plantations which, until Butler came in May, had been steady food producers. East of the railroad most of the houses had been abandoned since the Drewry's Bluff fighting, when the homes were shelled after the Union soldiers ran off the people's stock. Women with children and their old people were still moving about the county trying to find places of shelter, when Beauregard's excitable withdrawal of troops allowed Beast Butler to break out in the early morning of June 16.

His troops rolled unopposed to the railroad connecting Lee and Beauregard, driving frightened civilian groups ahead of them, and the blue soldiers were busily engaged in tearing up the tracks when the first of two divisions rushed by Lee came up. The leading division was commanded by

Pickett. In what was to be his last recapture of his Gettysburg glory, the long-haired beau charged as if his old great division were behind him. He drove the Beast not only off the railroad but all the way back to what had become his reservation.

Unaware of these desperate goings-on that kept the lines open and with no time for heroics, at the Petersburg entrenchments Beauregard fought his best battle of the war. A third Union corps had come up, bringing a total of over 50,000 men against him. They could accomplish nothing decisive. Though breaches were made, portions of the six-mile line temporarily taken, the attacks were not co-ordinated, the pressure was not kept on, and for the second day the Union troops showed none of the confident drive of the beginning of the campaign.

Once he was saved, even momentarily, Beauregard reverted to wiring plans of grand counterattacks, which he alternated with dire forebodings that unless he was reinforced "the city will fall." Still he didn't say who he was fighting.

By then there was little reasonable doubt that most of Grant's army was at Petersburg. However, without the final certainty, Lee prepared two more divisions to leave the next day, and brought A. P. Hill's corps near the northern entrance of the pontoon bridge across the James. Those 12,000 infantry were the last defense of the city against even a strong raid, except for Bald Dick Ewell's conglomerate city defense force, then about 5000.

At Petersburg on the third day (June 17) Beauregard was confronted with still another Union corps, bringing the attacking force to 70,000 before casualties. On his 15,000 infantry, before casualties, the attacks of the Union army corps bore very heavily that day, however poorly managed the assaults. Even so, the Confederates suffered only one serious breakthrough. By one of those happy coincidences which never seemed to happen against Grant in the West, that break occurred when the brigade left as a skirmish line against Butler arrived at the precise moment of danger. Breaking into a run as they deployed from close order, Gracie's brigade charged and closed the gap through which the Unions could have rolled up the Confederate line.

It was the end of the day then. The men were fought out and fresh Unions kept coming after dark. There was nothing for the exhausted men to do except lie down behind their earthworks between rushes, then lean on the top to fire, and bend down to load again. They were practically shooting in their sleep. Any well-organized concerted attack must have overrun them. None came. Toward midnight the firing died down all along the line.

After that, Beauregard finally wired Lee that prisoners reported that Grant was on the field with his whole army. Grant had abandoned the effort to take Richmond directly and the effort to defeat Lee's army. He was trying the back door to the capital through which, if successful, he would open in effect a siege.

For the fourth day of the Battle of Petersburg, Grant gathered some 90,000 Unions, before casualties. Old Bory, for all his wild and conflicting messages, stood undaunted, though the disaster he had long prophesied was at least a fearful reality.

On that night of the seventeenth Beauregard moved his sleepwalking men out of their breastworks, back closer to the city to a line drawn by his brilliant engineer. There, with no rest, the men were put to digging new breastworks with shovels, axes, bayonets, knives, any tool or utensil at hand. In the early morning hours they fell out, were aroused with water, and went back to digging. They did not stop until daylight.

When the Union masses moved forward in the morning, the abandoned works seemed to confuse them. The Federals re-formed slowly under the Confederate cannonade. The spent Confederates, waiting behind the new earthworks, saw coming toward them the bright rifles and shining bayonets above sweat-dampened rags, which could mean only Rebels. The exhausted men, forgetful of snipers, jumped up and waved and cheered and burst out crying at the relief. It was only one division, with another on the way behind, but they were enough.

On the afternoon before, Rooney Lee's few troopers, drawn in from the flanks, had finally discovered that only Union cavalry remained north of the James. One of his two brigades, 500 men, was coming on to join Dearing's little brigade, giving the Petersburg line something to pass for cavalry. And two of A. P. Hill's divisions had crossed the pontoon and were walking through the choking dust of that hot day on the Petersburg Pike, passing their own stragglers and the debris of the fight with Butler. They were in fine spirits and their eyes were keen for ripe apples and stray chickens.

The spirit of the whole combined force was as high as it had ever soared in the Army of Northern Virginia. All the men were fought out and tired and hungry again, there was a lot of sickness from the marching of the physically weak men in the heat, but they hadn't believed that new fellow Grant could beat them and he hadn't . . . even by trying the back door. He was farther from Richmond than before he started all this sidling to the southside, and his own army was fought out too. Nobody could beat General Lee. Richmond was saved again.

5

Nobody could beat Lee, as the soldiers understood the war within the limits of their experiences. It was not their responsibility that the supply base on the James River at City Point would grow into a Union war village, that Union engineers would construct a railroad from the river to their army more easily than the Confederates would repair the half mile destroyed from Richmond to Petersburg, that the overwhelming strength of the Union cavalry would hack at their own railroads until, as with air bombing, they were destroyed beyond repair.

The soldiers knew nothing about fighting a nation; they only fought other men, and those other men didn't have good leaders. It was as simple as that to them, when they settled down in mid-June unknowingly to withstand a siege.

With everybody dug in and attack possible only in movement, Lee was too weak to move and Grant had nowhere to go. It was beyond the soldiers' comprehension that this siege was a loose and large-scale version of the investment of Vicksburg. Digging new entrenchments, they did not read the portents in the first heavy raid against their railroads.

With Sheridan resting from his abortive Valley enterprise, Kautz joined with still another mounted force, under Wilson, and they broke all three railroads from Petersburg—to Weldon and thence to Wilmington and Charleston, to Danville and the new line into western North Carolina, and the east-west line to Lynchburg. The heavy raiding force was barely stopped from destroying a vital bridge, irreplaceable in wartime, by another of those collections of farmers, shooting through notches they made of tree limbs, and paying no attention to Yankee artillery.

What the soldiers knew was that Wade Hampton and Fitz Lee, just returning from driving away Sheridan, took after Wilson and got him in a box which he had to cut his way out of, leaving guns and wagons and 1000 prisoners. The Rebels were very interested in the stolen silver which weighted down the prisoners, including a chalice from a church. That made the Yankees no better than burglars, and the Rebels thought contemptuously of the personal enemy facing them and not of the miles of track torn up behind them.

That was the way the pattern of the siege began. Psychologically, the Virginia front was as sound as ever. The hero of the North had failed, like all his predecessors, to take Richmond, and his casualty lists sickened his own countrymen.

The will of the North might not last as long as the siege, if other fronts held up as the Virginia front was doing.

CHAPTER XXI

The Military Defeat

IN THE WEST, where Grant's drive for a decision was to be duplicated by Sherman, the Federal commander was curiously cautious against Joe Johnston.

In Virginia, though Lincoln's "On to Richmond" fixation made that city the objective of the Union armies, most of the Union generals and certainly Grant tried to get Lee's army first.

In the West, Joe Johnston's army was reasonably the primary objective, since Sherman had no way of knowing that Retreatin' Joe was about to spin his retrograde masterpiece of one hundred miles to Atlanta. They didn't even know it in Richmond. If they had, Old Joe's second chance at brightening his reputation would have lasted briefly indeed. Sherman did know, however, that Johnston was an orthodox, defensive fighter, whom he outnumbered clearly two to one, with heavier guns and far superior supplies, and his timidity is difficult to explain.

In any event, he made no effort to bring Johnston to battle, which, it must be admitted, took some doing. Sherman would dig in a part of his army and, while confronting a strong position of Johnston with something like equal force, he would move a corps or more around to outflank Johnston. While Grant's sidling had been for the purpose of getting at Lee advantageously, Sherman seemed content to flank Old Joe out of his fixed positions. Sherman had the strength and the initiative, and Johnston was obviously more concerned with avoiding a flank attack than with any bold action that might catch Sherman in movement.

The skirmishing was constant and heavy. On several occasions Sherman struck out at one of Johnston's well-chosen positions where the Rebels were snugly entrenched. As Sherman was invariably repulsed, he made no effort to try for a decision on the field. Always the Federals swung wide, wider than Johnston could stretch his thin forces, and in effect won the field without a fight. In this way Johnston's army constantly escaped to remain always in front of Sherman. Having in three years learned the difference between the United States and Confederate quartermaster corps, Johnston no longer left guns strewn behind him or burned supplies. Yet, however skillfully he avoided Sherman, or however strongly his men fought from their entrenched positions, he was repeating his retreat pattern of 1862. But he was wholly sound in perceiving that Sherman's line of communications was dangerously exposed and in expecting Davis, as the Commander in Chief, to have the Union supply line wrecked. Indeed, Sherman's supply line became the vital issue concerning everybody involved on both sides.

His supplies started from Nashville, in north-central Tennessee, and through Chattanooga reached him on the one railroad which he had to follow as he followed Johnston. Even before Sherman left Chattanooga, he arranged to have the railroad protected. As it could not be guarded for its entire length, he planned to guard it indirectly. He would send attacking parties into Mississippi and Alabama to give "employment" to the Confederates, particularly to Forrest.

Since that ferocious man of violence had gone on his own in the preceding fall, from the nucleus of remnants of his old command he had raised a well-gunned cavalry force of 5000. In "raising" this force, Forrest showed himself to be a highly effective one-man conscription bureau: he grabbed up infantry deserters, conscript evaders, and likely-looking citizens who should be conscripted. With this mounted force, in raiding and in fighting, Forrest became the greatest mobile striking power in the South, and the one most feared by Sherman.

At the time when Forrest was preparing to go into Middle Tennessee after Sherman's railroad, Sherman ordered out from Memphis a veteran cavalry force double Forrest's size, with the new breech-loading carbines and twenty-two guns. In one of the small masterpieces of the war (Brice's Crossroads, June 10, 1864) Forrest routed this enemy, which included the Grierson who had enjoyed finding the Confederacy "a shell" when he raided through Mississippi unopposed the year before.

With rest, Forrest could still have gone on to Middle Tennessee after the Union life line. When Sherman immediately organized another and larger force to take out after him, with the admonition to "kill Forrest," it was obvious that the Union general felt his campaign against Johnston depended on keeping the Rebel cavalry leader out of Middle Tennessee.

As Sherman showed his hand (and apprehension) so plainly, it was equally obvious to Johnston and other Confederates that of all things Forrest *must* go into Middle Tennessee and break Sherman's supply line. In Forrest's absence, Union raiders could do local damage; as Sherman said, they could "bring ruin and misery" to a segment of the civilian population. The individual suffering would have to be accepted in exchange for thwarting Sherman's main purpose, which would bring large-scale ruin and misery as well as military defeat.

If Forrest could disrupt the vital supply line, Joe Johnston would be justified in his long retreat, which was bringing him constantly nearer his own supply base at Atlanta. In turn, Sherman would be forced to a long retreat of his own and would look very foolish for not having brought Johnston to battle.

This cause-and-effect principle of military reasoning foundered on the rocks of the Johnston-Davis personal relations. Retreatin' Joe knew that Davis expected him to assume the offensive and knew that he had no intention of doing this. It was necessary that Johnston explain to Davis that he was too weak to attack Sherman and their only hope lay in a disruption of Sherman's lines which would force the Unions to retreat or to attack at a disadvantage.

Johnston had reason to believe that he could defeat Sherman if attacked. In addition to repulsing the forays and limited assaults, on June 27 at Kennesaw Mountain, very close to Atlanta then, the much-put-upon Army of Tennessee decisively threw the Unions back in the one pitched battle which Sherman attempted. But Johnston would not confide in the President. Though he hoped to have the supply lines disrupted, he hardly more than suggested that Forrest be sent against them.

As Johnston continued to fall back without explanations, Davis grew increasingly peremptory and began to catechize Johnston (as he once had Beauregard) on his failings. He wrote like a pompous taskmaster dealing with some stupid and willful employee. While the exchanges only drove the two stiff-necked men of touchy pride further apart, Davis was immobilized in his thinking by his departmental fixation.

With Johnston falling back to Atlanta, physically close to Alabama and connected with Montgomery by railroad, Davis retained a separate department under Stephen Lee for Alabama, Mississippi, and East Louisiana. There is no question that Sherman sent troops into this Department for the sole purpose of keeping Forrest off his supply lines. His orders read: to "keep employed the forces of the enemy that might be mischievous in my rear." But the commander of the Department of Alabama, thinking about his own threatened area, ordered Forrest to stay where he was and not go into Middle Tennessee. In this the President supported him.

By holding defensive troops there, Davis did precisely what Sherman was trying to get the Rebels to do.

Johnston was supported by others who urged that Forrest be sent on Sherman's communications. Among the petitioners was Georgia's Governor Brown, the demagogue who had spent the war thwarting and tormenting the Administration.

From his Washington days, Jefferson Davis had never operated as a cause-and-effect thinker—as he revealed in his Douglas involvement—and this especially applied to dealing with people. It satisfied his conscience to act according to his beliefs in his rightness. He was not going to be told what to do by the likes of Joe Brown, nor would he consider some plan which Joe Johnston offered as an alternative to attack.

As he considered the unlettered Forrest to be suited only for rough mounted action, certainly that ex-slave dealer could give Jefferson Davis no lessons in strategy. After all, Stephen Lee, the department commander, was "Regular," and had graduated from West Point when Robert E. Lee was commandant and he, Davis, U. S. Secretary of War. Finally, as whenever the public clamored for a course of action, his resistance stiffened against it, particularly where it interfered with his defensive troop dispositions.

Grant wrote that Jefferson Davis often gave them help with his "genius" (Grant's quotation marks). At Atlanta it would look as if all of Davis' delusions were concentrated and rigidified to the point where, as applied to the realities of the Atlanta defense, he suffered actual derangement.

Refusing to heed anyone on the ground, he gave ear to Bragg's sinister promptings for that belated and untimely offense. As the newspaper editor said in Memminger's political epitaph, "He has been overtaken—that is all." The strain was exposing the weaknesses in Davis' limitations and few of his strengths. Without humility or deep self-analysis, listening to the sycophants who told him what he wished to hear, the tailor-made gentleman never considered that *he* could be wrong.

Though he did recognize that the whole situation at Atlanta was wrong, Davis thought that only he could cure it. He revealed it all in an anguished cry to his wife, when he said, "If only Lee could take one wing of our armies, and I the other . . ."

As he could not personally take "the wing," the President directed the operations from his paper-piled office, and forbade the one action feared by the enemy. Davis would not permit a strike at Sherman's only weakness. Instead, he fought his own general.

2

In the hot, narrow middle room on the second floor of the White House in Richmond, a tight-lipped Davis faced the alarmed members of the Cabinet. On the Fourth of July (again) Joe Johnston had backed into the outer works of Atlanta. To Davis the whole reason for Sherman's presence at the key city lay in Johnston's failure to attack. The cabinet members were not military men and all they knew was that Johnston had a habit of retreating and refusing to confide his plans to the President. For all they knew, he might retreat right on through Atlanta. After several conferences, the decision was made to send down Braxton Bragg to discover Old Joe's intentions.

When Bragg went to Atlanta, he never asked Retreatin' Joe outright to explain his intentions. Instead he wired that Johnston "has not sought my advice, and it has not been volunteered. I cannot learn that he has any more plan for the future than he has had in the past." He did add, "It is expected here that he will await the enemy on a line some three miles from here, and the impression prevails that he is now more inclined to fight. The enemy is very cautious, and . . . his force, like our own, is greatly reduced by the hard campaign. . . . The morale of our army is still reported good."

In Richmond the next day, July 16, Davis apparently absorbed only the line about the absence of plans. Immediately he wired Johnston: "I wish to hear from you as to present situation, and your plan of operations so specifically as will enable me to anticipate events."

In answer, the same day, Johnston finally admitted what had been his purpose all along: "As the enemy has double our number, we must be on the defensive. My plan of operations must, therefore, depend upon the enemy. It is mainly to watch for an opportunity to fight to advantage. . . ."

Though this could scarcely be called so specific as to enable Davis "to anticipate events," it was all Johnston could truthfully say—or could have said from the beginning. He should have said it then, instead of allowing the Administration to expect a course of action he had no intention of following. The misunderstanding between them had reached a point where for Davis it could be resolved only by Johnston's dismissal.

Then Davis, with the unanimous support of his Cabinet, made the decision which was the death blow to the Confederate West. On the surface, the supplanting of Joe Johnston with John Hood certainly seems the blunder to crown the sad series of blunders in the West.

The move was not approved by Lee, whose advice was asked and of course disregarded. Having commanded Hood, Lee said that he "was doubtful of other qualities" besides his aggressiveness in fighting. He thought it "a bad time to change" and said, "Why not Hardee?"

In the long retreat, Bishop Polk had been killed by a sniping Union cannon, which sent a shell through the body of the old clergyman and removed from the Army of Tennessee their best-loved and oldest commander. Next in affection and long in service was Hardee, who had earlier refused the command in favor of Johnston. Giving the army to Hood was something else. The adopted Texan was not only a newcomer to the army but far junior to Hardee as a lieutenant general. Hardee was enraged at being passed over and refused to serve under Hood. Though he was talked into it, the relations between them were strained and militarily unprofitable.

Hood himself, supported by Hardee and Cheatham (who had succeeded Bishop Polk), wired Davis requesting that the order be rescinded at least until Johnston had a chance to fight his battle for Atlanta. Davis would never rescind an order.

Seddon, the then neglected Secretary of War, though he had entirely lost faith in Johnston, sent Hood an encouraging wire which showed his own misgivings at the change. "You are charged with a great trust. . . . Be wary no less than bold. . . . God be with you."

Every soldier who commented on the change damned it. One thought, when the three generals petitioned Davis to keep Johnston, that the command was acting as though the change might not go through in order to hold down desertions. Everybody agreed in disapproving the dismissal of Johnston and the elevation of Hood. The final expeditions of Hood certainly would justify all the criticisms of his fitness and the bemoanings over the passing of Old Joe.

Yet what would Johnston have done? Sherman was not going to attack the Confederates' fixed position. He would have done against Johnston what he did against Hood, what Grant was trying against Lee: he would have cut the railroads supplying Atlanta, and placed the city in a state of siege. His whole movement to Atlanta was a siege movement. He crept along behind mobile entrenchments at the rate of one and two thirds miles a day. Nor was it likely that Johnston would have found the advantage he considered sufficient to warrant attacking Sherman.

Withstanding a siege and trying to protect the railroads as well as possible was probably all that could be achieved by then. The great question of the war at Atlanta would have been the effect a prolonged defense would exert on the United States fall elections.

Davis was beyond thinking of such considerations as the effect of Atlanta on the U.S. fall elections. In the collapse of his powers, he could think only of his belated obsession with the offensive by the outnumbered army, and Hood was placed in command for the purpose of attacking Sherman. The fatal element in the change of commanders lay not so much in the choice of generals as in the reason for the change, and in the details of the change.

For Davis, even with his sudden offensive mania, still clung to his fixation of dispersal. Far from concentrating troops for a grand assault under Hood, Forrest's attacking force was broken up to send units to *guard* areas in Alabama. Then John Morgan, little more than an adventurer desperately seeking to recapture fame, wasted his new command on purposeless raids in East Tennessee. During the same period some tough remnants of his former command, no longer with Morgan, were being prepared to waste more precious manpower and cavalry on another of those "uprisings" of the disloyalists in the Middle West.

This was the old familiar pattern of dispersal without co-ordination, only then rendered more immediately dangerous to the Confederacy by the simultaneous order for a worn army to leave strong entrenchments and attack a numerically and materially superior foe.

Ortega y Gasset once wrote that "our firmest convictions are apt to be the most suspect, they mark our limitations and our bounds. . . . Obstinately to insist on carrying on within the same familiar horizon betrays weakness and a decline of vital energies."

In Davis' decline, the appointment of Hood was not in itself the fatal blunder. It dramatized the long disintegration of the Confederate President, which went from a demented support of Braxton Bragg in the field to giving Bragg the power of advising about an army he had failed. Hood, for all his ambitions, was the victim: he was the executioner of the President's collapse in command.

3

As for the recently one-legged Hood, assigned to attack, he demonstrated that openings existed if Johnston had been alert for them. In concept, he was bold and skillful. He had not fought with the Army of Northern Virginia without learning the techniques of audacity. Hood also demonstrated that he lacked the capacity, as Lee had hinted, for controlling a whole army in assault.

He made his first attack (the Battle of Peach Tree Creek) two days after he was placed in command. Hood caught Thomas' army group of three corps crossing the creek north of the city and separated several miles from the other two army groups. Because of the usual confusions when command is not running smoothly, the attack was made too late, was faulty in detail and execution, and Thomas' corps (which in size about equaled Johnston's army) were very good and confident fighters.

Two days later Hood found another opening on the northeast (Battle of Atlanta, July 22) against McPherson's three corps. The flank was in the air. Out of his Virginia experience, he tried one of the flanking movements made famous by Stonewall Jackson. His execution was better in that, but he encountered the imponderables. Two Union divisions had come up during the night and, by accident, assumed a position where Hardee attacked on the assumption that the space was empty. It was a hard-fought all-day battle, with casualties heavy on both, and the Confederate soldiers never fought better. Then, neither did the Federals, and there were more of them. At the end Hood was repulsed again.

The Unions were pretty well where they would have been had Hood not attacked, except that casualties were less serious to them than to the Confederates. Sherman was able to hold entrenched positions to the east and swing in an arc around the city to the southwest. There he began on the railroads, the one to Montgomery.

Still undaunted, Hood charged out again and that day (Ezra Church, July 28) he neither conceived well nor executed well. It was a desperate throw of an unthoughtful and aggressive man who, placed in command for the purpose of attacking, attacked at all hazards. It was the third, and worst, repulse in eight days.

No more assaults were left in the army. They were to withstand the siege anyway. The only effect of their fighting was that it slowed down Sherman. His movements ceased and he entered a formal state of siege. Assuming that Atlanta was doomed once Johnston backed into its fortifications, the Confederate position was no worse than before Hood attacked.

To the people of the country, the situation appeared to have definitely improved. They had been depressed, as the Cabinet was alarmed, by Johnston's steady retreat, and they took Sherman's inaction to mean that he had been halted at Atlanta as Grant had before Richmond. Hope began to return again. Maybe they could hold out, after all, until the fall elections. Peace sentiment, growing in the North, had been stimulated by the heavy casualties Grant suffered only to end up with a fought-out army facing Lee across trenches twenty miles and two rivers from Richmond. With Sherman (apparently) similarly halted at Atlanta, they only needed to hold their defense line, and the war-weary North might elect a peace party. Then, at last, independence would be theirs.

4

Through the rest of July and August, Sherman, aside from shelling the civilians in the city, did nothing at Atlanta except send out two abortive cavalry raids on the railroads. They were commanded by exiles from the Virginia front, Kilpatrick and Stoneman. Kilpatrick was no more effective at wrecking railroads than he was at freeing the prisoners in Richmond, and Stoneman, encountering some of Georgia's old men and boys, suffered a failure so complete as to be personally captured. Like Kautz and Wilson in Virginia, the Federal mounted raiders were pretty well fighting over-age and underage civilians by this time, but *at* this time there was still fight in the people who were loyal.

Everywhere everything tended to feed the hopes of the loyal people. Charleston and Wilmington still held out on the east coast, with blockade-runners regularly bringing in supplies and taking out cotton. Mobile was holding out on the Gulf and the threats to Alabama had come to nothing. From Forrest came a real fillip.

With his self-raised force depleted by army inspectors, who removed from the ranks the infantry deserters Forrest had corraled, Old Bedford faced yet another assault on him out of Memphis. This was bigger and more heavily armed than any Sherman had sent before. By his determination to "kill" Forrest and "punish the poeple" in whose territory he operated, Sherman began to reveal the conqueror's resentment of anyone's asserting personal rights against him.

When unknown persons (soldiers or civilians) fired on the supply trains which supported Sherman, he wired a brigadier in the neighborhood to "burn 10 or 12 houses of known secessionists, kill a few at random and let them know it will be repeated every time a train is fired upon. . . ."

He was approaching the stage where all secessionists, and particularly Forrest, fell into his category of asserters who must be punished. He offered a brigadier a major-generalship if he could kill Forrest.

When the new force marched out against Forrest's government-diminished troops, they might well have bagged him if he had fought along regular lines. Without consulting anybody, he fought most irregularly. Leaving a small force to demonstrate against Smith's hordes, Forrest took 1500 troopers through the night on a Sunday dawn raid into Memphis.

The Union department commanders, who fled from their bedrooms in nightclothes, claimed that his raid accomplished nothing, but they failed to attribute to Forrest's raid the fact that Sherman's great cavalry expedition was recalled to Memphis. Infected by Sherman's lust for spreading desolation, the expedition which missed Forrest turned its energies to burning the university town of Oxford, including its courthouse and public building, and the home among others of Jacob Thompson, Secretary of the Interior under Buchanan.

While Forrest actually defeated that grandest of all expeditions by raiding their base, to the men in his command the satisfaction was purely personal. Memphis was the home of many. Forrest had lived and made his success there before the war, and the river town was about the most splendid of all the oases the Union kept for its people in the South. For men starving in their own desolated countryside, and reading of the lavish goings-on of the occupiers of their home town, it must have been a satisfaction to send the invaders scuttling through the familiar streets. It gave one boy the chance to ride by his own house and wave to his mother and sisters at the window.

It was the sort of personal triumph that heartened all the remaining loyal Confederates and sustained their hopes that the end was not yet.

Close to the Confederate capital, all was well. Jubal Early had cleared the Valley of the enemy and for more than a week in early July threatened Washington.

Early, with a total of some 13,000 men, could accomplish nothing against the Washington forts. Manifestly it was too late for a small force, the size of Union raiding parties through the South, to cause alarm in the capital as Stonewall Jackson had done two years before. Yet troops were pulled off from Grant to give Lincoln reassurance and, in a Tinker-to-Evers-to-Chance, Union troops at New Orleans, scheduled for Alabama, were moved to Grant. Thus Sherman's infantry threat in Alabama was checked in Virginia by a parlay the Confederate President would never understand.

Lee was the only general with the power, won through tact and success, to play his own game of cause and effect, though even he had not conceived of the effect Early would have on Alabama. All the other generals were forced by the Commander in Chief to play the Federals' game. That is essentially why Grant never looked good in Virginia. In the West he had fought Davis; in the East he fought Lee.

Having sent off troops to save Washington, Grant then sent off Sheridan to get Early out of the Valley. It worked the other way around. For the second time against an enemy alerted for him, Sheridan failed. He was driven out of the Valley, all the way across the protecting Potomac. With Jackson's old II Corps (at least in name) controlling the Valley, and Lee making Grant look bad at Petersburg, any still hopeful Confederate would feel that this was 1862 all over again, with elections coming up in a nation grown weary of trying to subjugate the Southern people.

Grant had looked at his worst in the Battle of the Crater (July 30, 1864). Unable to defeat Lee straight on, the dogged soldier tried to beat him from underground. He had his men dig a shaft under a salient in Lee's lines, and fill it with high explosives.

To make sure that Lee's powers of recuperation from the blast would be sufficiently reduced to permit a Union breakthrough, Grant used the protection of the United States Navy to send troops back across the James River to attack Richmond from the east at the same time. This attacking force was impeded by stationary artillerists and local defense troops (the elderly fathers of families falling along with the youngest born) until Lee could hurry back over the dusty Petersburg Pike to Richmond some of his hungry ragamuffins.

With Lee's army reduced by Early in the Valley and the divisions in front of Richmond, Grant exploded his mine under a line of South Carolina troops. They were mostly killed and their mangled bodies fell into the five-hundred-foot hole made by the explosion. Through that segment the Union troops could have poured and ended the war. But Grant was a bad psychologist in Virginia. He sent in Negro troops, to add insult to injury.

This setting of race against race clearly indicated that the Union leaders had become interested only in destroying the Southern whites and not in preserving the Union in which Negroes would be free citizens. Also it was setting the worker against the master, adding class conflict to race conflict in a confusion which had yet to be clarified.

At the Crater, the Southerners reacted in immediate violence. A division of A. P. Hill's corps by sheer fury drove the Unions, white and black, back into the crater which they had created. Thousands of Federals swarmed on the slippery banks of loose earth, while the Confederates ran up new mortars to pour shell into the squirming masses. The trap set for the Confederates became a death trap for 3000 more of the lives that Grant threw away in his attempt to repeat against Lee his Western triumphs.

Southerners have never hated Grant, as they do Sherman and Sheridan. Nor have they held him in the contempt they do the house-burners, like Milroy and Hunter in the Valley, like the horse thieves later under Stoneman in North Carolina, like the shooters of civilians under Grierson in Mississippi.

But Grant left a bad taste at the Crater. With a two-to-one army, with troops all over the state and support from the navy, it seemed low and mean that he should blow people up. The Confederates used land mines as early as 1862, in Johnston's retreat up the peninsula, and discarded them under McClellan's protest at this "barbarous warfare." They agreed with McClellan. Part of the post-bellum alienation of the South was dug at the Crater.

5

The people were spared the knowledge of their government's foolish adventures in plots with the Northwest (Midwest) conspirators. After all the failures of these secret societies to act for the Confederacy, three distinguished Southern gentlemen and an assortment of young hotbloods went to Canada and the Chicago area to supervise the most grandiose plot of them all. During the Democratic National Convention in Chicago, the Confederate agents with the help of their underground allies were to spring the thousands of Rebel prisoners in the region.

Fifteen thousand men added to Hood's and/or Lee's then could have made a decisive difference. Grant had halted the prisoner exchange, because the Confederates always returned to the armies. Even if the Unions returned in equal numbers, which they did not, the ratio of odds in favor of the Union forces was reduced. To release their prisoners was certainly a sound idea for prolonging the war, but the scheme for the Chicago area was a venture in cloak-and-dagger farce.

The three distinguished agents were James P. Holcombe, Confederate congressman from Virginia; Clement C. Clay, Jr., Alabama's prewar U.S. senator and among the lesser lights of the secession movement; and Jacob Thompson, the powerful secessionist in Buchanan's Cabinet whose home had just been burned in Oxford, Mississippi. With some of Morgan's former raiders, they were to operate with the grip-giving and counter-sign-passing conspirators who would in some fashion influence the Democratic convention to serve as a blind for the desperate doings.

Needless to say, nothing happened. What the planted Union spies did not learn of the schemes, betrayers in the secret societies divulged, and none of the play-acting disloyalists had any intention of action anyway. The remnants of Morgan's men, not under him, who were to demonstrate with a raid at the same time, demonstrated into a trap and even the remnants of the once fearsome raiders ceased to exist.

Then Benjamin in Richmond, apparently seeking activity for the restless mind which got little employment in the State Department and advising Davis, sent the agents in Canada some suggestions for retaliatory action on the North.

Though Jefferson Davis had been deeply and personally outraged at Union atrocities, both his conscience and his desire to present an "honorable" appearance to the world rejected retaliatory measures. Lee personally disbelieved in carrying war to civilians, no matter who did it. Individuals in Lee's army, however, had to be restrained from retaliation. When Jubal Early took his force across the Potomac, away from Lee's control, he allowed his men to vent their long-smoldering resentments against at least the property of civilians. This had always been against the Confederate policy.

In Benjamin's case the schemes which would have enraged the North would seem to have been working at cross-purposes to the election of peace-minded Democrats. Maybe Benjamin held no illusions about the fall election. Maybe he felt the ship was sinking and wanted to get in a few licks of his own before it went down. While not a brooder over past events, he never ceased resenting, for the rest of his life, the burning of his law library in New Orleans by the Union occupiers.

In any event, the schemes involved wrecking trains in New York State, setting fires in the city of New York, and robbing a bank in St. Albans, Vermont, near the Canadian border. A few small fires in New York accomplished nothing except to arouse a mob against the arsonists, who were lucky to escape with their lives with the help of some real New York conspirators. The young train wrecker was caught and hanged. The two dozen young men in St. Albans did make way with over $200,000 in cash and escape across the border, but the money never made its way back South. It is still unaccounted for.

But more than $200,000 in gold was accounted for in scarce cash spent by the hard-pressed Confederacy on the various plots, including thousands that vanished into the pockets of "conspirators."

Fortunately for the lingering faith of the die-hard Confederates, nothing was known of all this foolish waste of money, manpower, and energy. The people looked at the arc of their defense line and prayed that it would hold. They literally prayed as, during 1864, the Confederacy was swept with another religious revival. While the believers were sincere, many of the conversions doubtless came from what today is called "crisis religion," and to some extent reflected the shift of the people's hopes to powers outside their control.

Though Davis from the beginning had depended on outside intervention, the loyal people as a whole had depended on themselves until the summer of 1864. After the hammering of the gigantic spring campaigns, with growing might threatening to overwhelm their own declining powers, even to the most optimistic loyalists it became evident that their only hope depended on sustaining the line of their defense arc until the Northern voters granted their independence.

Nor were their prayerful hopes without justification. Lincoln personally feared a Democratic victory, which he admitted could bring peace to the embattled South. There was a lot of the Confederacy to conquer and all its areas of vital defense production were still protected by the foreshortened Richmond–Atlanta line and its extension through Alabama to Mobile.

Along that whole line, as long as Lee held Grant at Richmond, Atlanta was the keystone. The Confederate border had contracted to its final inner line. With Atlanta gone there would be no more defense line left. In terms of the issue of victory, the war would be over.

But Atlanta was holding. In addition to its strategic position, the city was a producer and storehouse of war matériel. Its rolling mill had turned out the well-nigh impregnable plates of the new ram, *Tennessee*. Long in production, this latest contrivance of Mallory's Navy Department was to be the Confederate's answer to the U. S. Navy in Mobile Bay. (Mallory always believed, as with the *Merrimac*, in one ship which would nullify the U. S. Navy.)

On the surface, the total situation sustained the people's hopes in the season when they felt the best anyway. Summer was their time. Then they were not depressed by the problem of getting fuel. There were no bleakly cold rooms to pinch the souls of sun-loving people and shrivel the spirits of the staunchest. In summer their homes were filled with the sweet warm air and the scent of flowers, and in the long blue nights with the stars close the soul of man could soar in unarticulated prayer.

By August 1864, with all its lost territory and greater losses in personal defections, the Confederacy was still a nation. In the fourth year of its existence, it stood a chance—a good chance, it seemed—of entering at last into the race of nations.

6

The first ominous signs were little noted in the people's concentration on Atlanta. The bad steering gear and typical Confederate engine in the mighty *Tennessee* caused this potential savior of Mobile Bay to flounder among Farragut's superbly served ships and surrender after a brief day in the sun. In the U. S. Navy, courtesies were still exchanged as in the Sumter era. Commodore Johnston was received by his conquerors as a welcome guest, and Southern-born Farragut among other Union officers complimented the defeated Rebel on the courage with which he had defended his ship and the honor he had brought to his flag. These amenities, however they mitigated the sting to individuals, could not soften the blow of Farragut's fleet storming into Mobile Bay ("Damn the torpedoes! Go ahead!"), taking the forts, and closing the port to the Gulf.

Far less noted in the ominous signs than Farragut's entrance into Mobile Bay was the cavalry raid of Joe Wheeler on Sherman's line of supplies. When Joe Johnston and others had petitioned Davis and Bragg to send Forrest on Sherman's lines, Davis had suggested that Retreatin' Joe use his own cavalry for that purpose. Johnston was too soundly trained to denude himself of cavalry while retiring before a superior force. Wheeler's cavalry had been able to make solid contributions to Johnston's "clean" retreats by the less than good use which Sherman made of his own mounted troops. That was an odd thing about Joe Wheeler, the diminutive Connecticut-Georgian: his one talent as a cavalry leader was in covering retreat. As a raider, Wheeler was demonstrably poor.

For the final act of the Western tragedy, Jefferson Davis gave the final proof of his dementia. Having restrained Forrest, the only good railroad-raiding outfit in the West, while Sherman's lines were lightly defended, when they became heavily defended, with blockhouses and minor forts, the President approved of Hood's sending Wheeler, the able operator with infantry, on the raiding job.

The West Point-trained and orthodox Wheeler accomplished little or nothing against the railroads. Then he divided his force for side expeditions, which likewise came to nothing, and took his main body on a wild-goose chase toward Nashville which demoralized the survivors of this futile junket and brought Wheeler to the point of resignation.

While Wheeler's tired and discouraged men galloped across Tennessee, Hood, blind without cavalry, was caught way behind by Sherman. The quiescent Sherman suddenly swung in a great arc to the south of Atlanta on the railroad to Macon and the coast. About twenty miles south of Atlanta at Jonesboro (in the same relation of Petersburg to Richmond), part of Hood's army belatedly made contact. There, in a poorly organized at-

tack, the Confederates were thrown back from the Union's entrenchments.

As an indication of the failure of the offensive in 1864 against the
newly developed works the soldiers dug, the next day at the same place,
with the same troops fighting, the Federals were equally repulsed.

However, since Hood was placed in command to attack, the unreflec-
tive Texan attacked himself right out of Atlanta. While Hood and Sherman were physically fighting to a draw twenty-odd miles south of the
city, entrenched Union troops whom Sherman had left to the northeast
walked in.

Of all the decisive campaigns of the Civil War, not since the Tennessee
river forts fell in the early days had a Confederate stronghold fallen in
such an anticlimax. On the second of September Sherman achieved his
great triumph and entered the city whose defense had been literally vital
to the Confederacy's life.

Hood was no more than a supernumerary villain, the dupe who carries
out the action of the tragedy designed by others. As of his own time,
to the long-suffering soldiers of the Army of Tennessee, the big blond
was a very personal villain. To the people of the South nobody cared
who the villain was. The deed was done. Atlanta was gone. The last line
of defense was broken, and the last support of hope knocked away.

As a grim foreboding of things to come, Sherman's treatment of the
Atlanta civilians sent a shiver through the lower coastal South. The old
men, the women and children, emerging from the dugouts in which they
had endured his shelling, were ordered to pack their personal belongings
and leave the city. The excuse for the military necessity of this civilian
exodus was that the houses were needed to quarter his troops. The troops
were quartered fine while the sick and the old, the mothers with babies,
all deprived of their horses and vehicles, trudged the countryside to find
such refuge as was offered.

As if the fall of Atlanta was a signal, the last, tenaciously held prospect
for independence suddenly collapsed in a series of disasters.

As a personal anticlimax, the formerly glamorous and feared John
Morgan was killed in East Tennessee. While a year before his command
had, however foolishly, ridden "the furthest North" in Ohio and Indiana,
this victim of his own wild ventures had his life ended in a small and
pointless affair south of his home grounds. Even the final action was surrounded by melodramatic charges of "a woman's betrayal."

West of the Mississippi the last flare-up of those hard-bitten Rebels
ended in rout when the Unions finally put their minds to stopping those
periodic excursions once and for all.

In Virginia, Grant, knowing that he was safe against attacks from Lee's
haggard veterans, organized a heavily gunned army of 40,000 under
Sheridan to clear the Shenandoah Valley of Rebels. By then Union num-

bers were such that a general could simply *decide* to eliminate a Confederate force.

Against this new army, Early offered such resistance as he could. At the outside, counting the cavalry from Lee's army which had been sent him, he could not have had 15,000 men of all arms. Sheridan was at his boastful best in driving this small force south along the Valley. At that, Old Jube kept from Grant a full Union army corps, alone larger than Early's total force, a division of cavalry under Sheridan, and two heavy forces of raiding cavalry which otherwise could have been operating against the railroads.

But such countermeasures of Lee by then amounted to no more than techniques of his generalship. The power against him, like the sweep of destiny it represented, amounted to a force of nature. The South of the individual in its doomed struggle against the machine was symbolized by Lee and his survivors, as the encirclement began to close in toward the last small center.

When in late September Sheridan felt that Early's little force was sufficiently shattered to be ignored, he turned to the most widespread and systematic desolation of civilian life that had yet occurred in the war. Among largely non-slaveholding people, the self-reliant frontier democrats who farmed their own land, Sheridan put his soldiers to the burning of houses, barns, farm implements, the haystacks in the fields and the corn in the cribs, while running off every animal that lived. He took it very personally if anybody shot at his soldiers. Those he caught he hanged.

By then *the* Union was composed of the states fighting against the Southern states. The Confederacy was only something to conquer, and all the latent and actual antagonisms between the sections and the cultures were given vent to by the invaders. The Valley conquerors got a poem on the brilliance of Sheridan at the battle when the Confederate soldiers interrupted his harvest of destitution.

Sick with hunger and discouragement, from marching and fighting when in no condition for either, the troops with the proud regimental battle flags could still revive for one more crack at the enemy, when they got the smallest help. It came when Lee, convinced that Grant would not attack him straight on, sent to the Valley Kershaw's division, then under 3000, a cavalry brigade of 600, and a few pieces of artillery. Even this little was enough to cheer the men, and they willingly took after Sheridan.

With courageous Kershaw, John B. Gordon, and young Ramseur, Early had three of the four best division commanders left in the army. Though all new, each possessed the quality and the fire that had slowly faded from command since the great days. Their combined force, less than half of Sheridan's, caught the Federals when they were relaxed and fat from plunder. They caught them where Stonewall Jackson had written his annals of warfare at the northern base of the Massanuttens, outside the little town of Strasburg where Cedar Creek crossed the Valley Pike.

Sheridan was off in Winchester ("twenty miles away") on some business of his own, when the Rebels, after a night of mountain march, fell on his surprised and flatulent troops. They gave Sheridan's fellows a thoroughly bad going-over and had a heartening victory within their grasps, with captured guns and wagons, when two elements in the imponderables of attrition took over.

Jubal Early, the fine commander under Lee, was a good commander on his own up to that crucial moment of pushing a battle to its final decision. Where so many other men on both sides had hung before, Old Jube paused at the decision to deliver the finishing blow. As his able and spirited young division commanders watched in disbelief and then horror, Early hesitated, wavered, let the initiative pass. Unions rallied, reorganized, and prepared for the counterattack while Early did nothing. That was attrition in command.

In the army, it showed in the effect of the Yankee wagons on the ravenous men. The troops gorged themselves, frequently without interference from new young line officers, and experimented with strange dainties as order fled from the troops at the moment of victory.

The Unions, outnumbering the Confederates over two to one, only needed the chance to reorganize. Early and the starved Confederates gave them their chance. When the Unions counterattacked they caught the Rebels in about as disorganized a position as any army ever fielded in Virginia. Despite the religious revivals and the ravenous condition of the soldiers, some men were still susceptible to the alcohol they found in the wagons. Some got so drunk that they were run over as dead, and only came to days later.

The Confederates suffered few casualties in killed and wounded. Their losses were in prisoners, in exhausted men too stuffed to have the impulse or the energy for rapid movements.

For the rest, the men ran. Their flagging spirits could be rallied for a night march and surprise morning attack with a chance of victory. When those blue masses covered the horizon for the second time on the same day, it was too much. By afternoon, the men simply had enough of fighting against odds without hope of victory. They quit the field.

The hard losses in killed came among officers trying to rally the disorganized men. One was twenty-four-year-old Sandie Pendleton, who had been the much-loved A.A.G. of Stonewall Jackson, and then was serving brilliantly as Early's chief of staff. This V.M.I. graduate was the son of Lee's chief of artillery, General Pendleton; as a rector in Lexington, Sandie's father raised the Rockbridge Battery and, instead of numbering the guns, named them Matthew, Mark, Luke, and John. Young

Pendleton's loss was felt personally throughout the army, and especially among the survivors of the II Corps.

The other death was that of the promising new division commander, Dodson Ramseur. To a handsome home, one of the few to survive Sheridan, the twenty-seven-year-old Ramseur was taken with a mortal wound by a Union classmate from West Point. The young North Carolinian talked of wanting to see his newly born daughter, while his life's blood stained the wide panels of the polished floor.

The rout of Early's bacchanalian troops (with heavy losses in guns) closed the Shenandoah Valley as a source of supply to the Army of Northern Virginia. It no longer mattered whether or not the Union cavalry wrecked the Virginia Central Railroad, which had figured so prominently in both armies' plans for three and a half years. What Grant called "the covered way" to Washington was gone. Its food was gone. That section of Virginia was gone. The region where Lee and Jackson had circumvented Davis and Joe Johnston to save Richmond and give the Confederacy a real chance at victory was no more.

Less significant to the whole South than Atlanta, but more poignant, the field of the first great operations had fallen (October 19) along with the keystone city in Georgia. It was all over then.

7

Lincoln of course was elected. The war would be prosecuted to the finish. Only, the finish was already there.

Money, that bloodless barometer of the people's spirits, showed the effect. Since its fall in December 1863, the Confederate currency had been virtually stabilized at around twenty to one. As late as August 1864, only twenty-two Confederate dollars were needed for one in gold. That was still money. By November, after Lincoln's election, it fell to thirty to one, the next month thirty-eight to one, and the bottom had dropped out by the first of the year.

From the Unions' spring campaign in early May until Lincoln's election in early November, the Southern states had lost their attempt at independence. Militarily the Confederacy had no future, even in strict defensiveness, mere holding on. The original Confederacy of the first seven states was falling around the only stable front, maintained since Jackson and Lee turned back the invasion in the spring of 1862; but in the late fall of 1864 the holding out of the Virginia front was no longer enough at best, and its collapse was only a matter of time.

The last despairing and prayerful hope had been for intervention from the North. That was gone. By then Lee had become the single desperate symbol of the Confederacy to the dwindling core of die-hards. He was only a symbol of a dying civilization which the Union, then forming without the South, had to destroy. Chivalry was archaic, traditions made people backward and look to the past. The new Union was in a hurry to get the job done and get to its future; people had to get on in the world.

When peace was not made with the Confederate military defeat at the end of 1864, the period of annihilation began.

Section Four

"STRIKE THE TENT"

CHAPTER XXII

The Winter of Despair

BANDS still played "Dixie," though the bands were fewer. People still read books and magazines, and a publishing business had blossomed in the South—though the old *Southern Literary Messenger* (where Poe's drunkenness had tried the owner's patience) folded in 1864, along with the new *Southern Fields and Firesides*. Sheet music was published for family and group singing in the cold parlors and even plays produced in the South were published and sold—such as the Richmond show of that year, *Great Expectations; or, Getting Promoted*. In Augusta they had been treated to a musical, *King Linkum the First*, produced by its composer, John H. Hewitt—a versatile New Yorker turned Georgian who composed and taught music, worked as journalist and producer.

With all the heavy hearts over loved ones lost and fears for the survivors, people still fell in love. Mr. Davis' private secretary, Burton Harrison, was courting one of the Cary belles, those "refugees" from Baltimore who were Richmond's most indefatigable and ingenious entertainers with parlor amateur theatricals. Wherever they lived, in moving about the overcrowded city, their parlor was the center for the younger social favorites of the Confederacy.

Jeb Stuart had danced there, Von Borcke and Fitz Lee, and John Morgan had gone there on his last trip to Richmond. Regulars were "Uncle Robert's" sons, Custis and Rooney, Roger Pryor, the duelist, and "splendid" Breckinridge; the good-looking Marylander, Henry Kyd Douglas, who survived to describe staff life with Stonewall Jackson; and John Esten Cooke (cousin of Jeb Stuart's wife), who later moved the Southern heart with his stories and memoirs of the Army of Northern Virginia. The three colonels of the President's staff came with their friend Harrison: Lubbock, the ex-governor of Texas, Albert Sidney Johnston's son, with his father's sword, and John Taylor Wood, the U.S. President's grandson and the C.S.A. President's nephew. Literate and high-humored Wood doubled

as an "irregular" raider on Union supplies and was proscribed as an outlaw by the Federals.

Hettie Cary, the beauty of the belles, topped the makeshift social season
by a fashionable wedding to young General John Pegram at St. Paul's
Church, across from Capitol Square. The Davises worshiped there and the
Lees (when the general got to town), and the large church was packed to
the galleries by what they described as "the belles, beaux and brains of
the Confederacy."

Three weeks later, to the day, John Pegram's coffin was placed at the
chancel where he had stood to be married, and the beautiful Hettie Cary
had changed from a wedding gown to widow's crepe.

By then the people had begun to question the purpose of this loss of life.
The war of subjugation was moving toward its inexorable end and, with
all hope of intervention gone, the hope of independence grew dimmer
and dimmer. The educated could no longer apply reason to their situation.
Their taut hope was sustained only by pride and desperation—and prayer.
The uneducated—who were not simply giving up—remained loyal through
primal attachment to their piece of land and their own kind who were defending it. As one soldier wrote his father, after fraternizing with the
enemy, "I just didn't feel right no how."

In the armies, veterans stayed on out of the same primal loyalty. In
front of Atlanta, a soldier wrote, "I have ever thought that Sherman was
a poor general not to have captured Hood and his whole army at the time
. . . we had everything against us. The soldiers distrusted everything.
They were broken down . . . almost dead with hunger and fatigue.
Everyone was taking his own course, and wishing and praying to be captured. . . . They were willing to ring down the curtain, put out the foot-
lights and go home. There was no hope in the future for them."

In Lee's army the desertion of veterans reflected the same collapse of
hope in the future. The men were going home to look after their own,
since no one else did. Those who stayed were thinking of peace.

One soldier had a conversation about peace with a Yankee picket, and
said, "We talked the matter over, and could have settled the war in 30
minutes had it been left to us."

It was not left to anybody except Jefferson Davis. He refused to consider any peace short of total independence. As all the means of achieving
independence had passed, and the unified enemy was using irresistible
might to complete the subjugation of an already devastated region, the
Confederate leader could no longer be considered a responsible person.

Davis never conceived that the support of the dwindling Confederacy
was maintained by Lee. The President believed that it was maintained by
his paper work, and by the abstract rights which he so clearly outlined.

The duality between the civil leaders and the fighters, which had been apparent after Bull Run, was continuing when the military leaders could no longer strive to introduce bold strategy. Like Hood, they had all become executives of the President's deranged concepts.

With Lincoln making unofficial tentative peace feelers, and individuals from both countries spouting proposals for peace, Davis worked on with his details in undisturbed conviction of his rightness, while the people were exposed to the final horrors and the army outside the capital was collapsing within earshot.

2

Only on the surface was Lee continuing that "stalemate" in Virginia, against Grant. In practical terms of a fight for independence, even a successful stalemate would avail nothing with the rest of the country falling around them. But, as Lee pointed out with increasing firmness, the continuation of the stalemate was not possible without change.

As far back as August, before Atlanta fell, Grant had begun a grim whipsawing at both ends of the line which could lead only to the arithmetical disappearance of Lee's army. He attacked to the north at Richmond with one group of soldiers, then he attacked the railroads to the south with another, and kept a main body always pounding away at the center of Petersburg. From the stinking, hot Petersburg trenches, Lee detached part of his force to hurry to Richmond, then detached another part to hurry south of Petersburg to protect the railroads. Each time Grant lost more men than Lee. Each time Grant brought up replacements; each time Lee had that many fewer. To Seddon he wrote, "Unless some measure can be devised to replace our losses, the consequences may be disastrous."

Then, hating to write military letters as he did, the Old Man offered the War Office some plans of his own for getting men. Having long protested against the policy of permitting able-bodied men to act in bureaus, he suggested that, since conscription was bringing in no new men, the conscript officers come into the army. Even a few thousand more men, if second-line troops, could help the most powerful sections of his entrenchments and give his veterans a chance to strike. He ended by saying, "Without some increase in strength, I cannot see how we are to escape the natural military consequences of the enemy's numerical superiority."

Nothing was done. No new men came—even after Richmond had a narrow squeak in late September. Atlanta had fallen then, when Richmond came closer to being captured than at any time in the war.

Instead of sending a force north and then a force south, Grant had sent simultaneous forces at the railroads south of Petersburg and at Richmond north of the river. On the flat farmland to the east, Richmond was defended by a chain of connected earthen forts which swung in an arc from the river to cover that maze of roads leading to the city. Except for the forts on the river, Fort Harrison was the most formidable in construction.

It was lightly manned, mostly by the artillerists of stationary guns. Those fellows had had it comparatively easy during the long ordeal of summer. Above the river, they enjoyed a breeze that never touched the men sweltering in the trenches, and they also enjoyed sufficient idleness to cultivate vegetable gardens. Things had been too easy. They were surprised and the fort was lost with hardly a shot fired.

Suddenly the long-guarded road to Richmond was open. The triumphant Union troops had to pass only Fort Gilmer on an inner line. This was no more than a huge and nearly empty earthen breastwork with a ditch in front and emplacements for guns inside the high banks.

Here, against two corps of Butler's army, citizens and a few soldiers made another of those little-recorded stands which loom so large to a people in their history. On the road leading from Fort Harrison to Fort Gilmer, the defending skirmish line consisted of Richmond's local defense troops—the old men and boys, clerks and armory workers. Actually they formed the only line until several batteries arrived with two thin brigades of regulars, Texans and Tennesseans.

Butler's attack was poorly co-ordinated. The Tennessee and Texas men fought one assault on one side of the road and then ran across and met the other. In the road, gunners were fighting off Yankees with pistols in order to keep firing their pieces. It was a wild and confused and fierce affair, and one of the best battles ever fought by Bald Dick Ewell.

The small but crucial action gave Old Baldhead his chance to get back to fighting, and Fort Gilmer was a size field he understood. Remaining cool during all the confusion and hairbreadth repulses of the enemy, Ewell fought like what he was—an old border dragoon. Wherever the new assaults came, there he had his panting men. Finally, when fresh troops swung wide to come straight at Fort Gilmer, Ewell had men and guns there too, one minute ahead of the enemy.

Butler sent in Negro troops there and they were good fighters. Again it was bad psychology. Between the accurate shooting of the gunners and the high earthen wall above the ditch, the fury of the infantrymen was enough to save the fort.

Gilmer was saved, and the way into Richmond, but Harrison occupied a strategic position in the whole line of defense. From Petersburg troops were rushed out of the trenches in front of Grant's army to hurry over and fight Butler's.

In the attacks to retake Fort Harrison, September 30 and a week later, October 7, it was there clear for all to see that this shell of the Army of Northern Virginia could no longer mount successful attacks even on a local scale. The tired men were still willing, but the failure in divisional command sent them in piecemeal and unco-ordinated.

Lee had crossed the river to take personal command. As he watched the bungling in detail and the useless valor of his poor scarecrows, he must have known then that it was all over for his army. The replacements were not coming. The morale and health of his men were going, and command was practically gone. It was then that he wrote Seddon another warning: Richmond might fall.

This warning might well have served as a feeler for the abandonment of Richmond. In the early days of the war, before defense industries had been developed in the South and before Virginia had been destroyed as a food producer, Lee had conceived of the defense of Richmond as essential.

In the slow change of things since then Richmond, though still a productive center, was placing on Lee's army a burden it could no longer carry in protecting railroads which brought to the city food supplies for its workers. At best those food supplies had been inadequate for the city and the army. Always Lee had been forced to depend on Virginia farmers and his own commissary work. Twice in order to get the crops in and fill out the borderline-subsistence diet, he had been forced to Northern invasions.

With Virginia lost as a food producer and invasions out of the question, he was sacrificing his army to protect railroads to ensure poor subsistence for the workers and submarginal subsistence for his soldiers. Men were deserting in hunger; thousands were ill from malnutrition and exhaustion. As long as they were chained to Richmond, protecting the railroads and the city by losing men, this could only worsen.

On the other side Grant, supplied by the U. S. Navy, had nothing whatsoever to guard. In fact he grew so careless that Wade Hampton ran off nearly three thousand of his beef cattle in a "commissary raid." Though the meat propped up Lee's army for a few days, the loss meant nothing to the Unions. Grant could continue to direct his might at two ends of the line, confident of his own protection and of the grinding arithmetic.

October 27, a month after the joint attack on Richmond and the railroads, Grant did it again. Butler did not surprise them north of the river that time. The city was in no danger, though more irreplaceable lives were lost to Lee and more replaceable lives to Grant. It was that simple. At the other end, on the railroad, A. P. Hill and Hampton's cavalry combined again to contain the enemy at Burgess Mill, lose another stretch of railroad, and among the casualties Wade Hampton saw one of his sons wounded while administering to his dying brother.

To abandon Richmond and try for the final throw in the field was the only possible escape from the consequences of the "exceeding small" grinding of the wheels of the Union. That is not to imply that a breakout of Lee into the open would have been successful. It was merely the only alternative to having his army wither away in actions which promised nothing and which must have galled the soul of the aggressive fighter "Uncle Robert" still was.

None of this was borne in upon the President. Officially Lee's army stood in front of Richmond; Richmond was the capital of the Confederacy, and the Confederacy was still in existence. The structure existed only in the unmalleable mind of the man who, with all that he taught himself, could never learn that armies and cities and nations were composed of people.

That was not Davis' tragedy. It was the tragedy of the people who were yet to be killed, whose homes were yet to be burned, their possessions stolen, their cities yet to be razed.

In this final phase of annihilation, the people were to have no more voice than in the first phase of Calhoun's abstractions. They were to be sacrificed while Davis carried the actual physical fighting into the same realm of fantasies that had overtaken Calhoun during his own dying hours. The general who was to lead this final flight into unreality was not Lee, or any of the great ones. It was one-legged John Hood, born in the year that Calhoun made his Nullification fight.

3

Typically, after Atlanta had fallen and the urgency for joint action between the Georgia and Alabama areas had passed, Davis appointed Beauregard as the single commander of what became a new (and the last) department. With relative simplicity, this became the Military Division of the West.

Old Bory was happy enough to leave Virginia, where there was really no place for him since the troops of his earlier "department" had fallen under Lee's command. There was not much Lee could offer a lieutenant general who'd never forgotten that he was the Confederacy's first hero. Pemberton, for instance, though excoriated by the people of his adopted country, was still sufficiently devoted to the cause to serve as artillery colonel in the Richmond defenses. That was scarcely the way of the gorgeous Creole. For him, a belatedly created department provided a position befitting his rank and renown, though Beauregard must have known (from the experience of his predecessors as department commanders) that little could be accomplished.

By the time Beauregard went, the game was already up in the air. Old Bory, probably like most of the others knowing the end was coming, conscientiously went through the duties of what amounted to department "adviser." Under this last stand of department commanders, Hood took off on the flight which removed him from the Alabama and even the Atlanta areas more completely than any of the Confederate armies had ever been separated from one another in any of the departments.

Hood personally was caught up in the fantasia which the death throes of the Confederacy had become. After Sherman entered Atlanta, Hood still had his army. It was by no means impossible militarily that a single bold stroke with everything concentrated could still have broken Sherman's communications and forced him to fight (assuming Hood received reinforcements) in a position disadvantageous to attacking troops. Again, this is not to imply that even a defeat of Sherman would have won the South its independence. It was simply the rational course open. However, the Confederates seemed to rush to their doom as their arrogant ante-bellum leaders had rushed them to this Götterdämmerung.

What Hood decided to do was sound enough in its original concept. Since cavalry could no longer raid Sherman's communications, he would put his whole army on the railroad and force Sherman to break off the luxury of occupying Atlanta and come out and attack him. Hood had seen enough to know what breastworks could do. Beauregard and President Davis all agreed that this offered the soundest plan for forcing the reluctant Sherman to fight an offensive battle where the Confederates would hold the advantage.

The President journeyed personally to Georgia where, along with getting in a few speeches designed to keep heart in the people, he could investigate the rumors of dissension about Hood. Davis found even loyal Hardee, who had suffered everything patiently until Hood's promotion over him, to be openly hostile. Either Hardee or Beauregard, if he wanted field command any more, would have served the morale of the army and the agreed-upon plan better than Hood.

For Davis to change any commander (except Johnston) was to admit a mistake, and this would shake his belief in his own infallibility. As customarily in dealing with the West, he removed Hardee from the army (sending him to Charleston's defenses) and left Hood's army without a single corps commander of long service in that capacity.

After fixing the command situation, by getting rid of Hardee and appointing Old Bory as something of a monitor over Hood, the President worked on army morale as he had the preceding fall. He made a speech to the soldiers. He brought out other speechmakers in Howell Cobb and Bob Toombs, the great secession leaders who were then serving the cause with the Georgia militia—and personally demonstrating the remoteness of ante-bellum leaders from the struggle of the country they helped bring into being. The unleashed forensic powers of this trio fell on irreverent ears.

On hearing the flowery praise of their own armed might, the Tennessee soldier said that it sounded as if all of them had gathered there "for the purpose of receiving the capitulation of and to make terms with our conquered foe." They thought violent old Toombs was the funniest man they had ever heard when he described how they were going to whip the Yankees. Prophesying the aftermath of one of Davis' exhortations, they had their own headline:

JEFF DAVIS MAKES SPEECH
Sinner, come view the ground
Where you shall shortly lie.

Before the war, the people had believed their politicians because they had no experience beyond their counties. After four years of fighting the enemy *and* listening to speeches, the people in the army knew that the politicians were humbugs. If they weren't trying to delude the soldiers, they certainly were deluding themselves. The soldiers wrote that home or, better, went home and told what they had learned.

Those apparently unconquerable ones who went on were still good fighting soldiers, those few who were left. Even without faith in their leaders or in their general, they'd still fight hard and well when their experience told them they had a chance.

Hood, sensing the disrespect of those men and not close to them, never believed in them. Or perhaps, after the failures of his fierce sorties around Atlanta, he lost belief in himself and tried to shift the blame to others. Before he was through, he blamed more people than Bragg had.

Lincoln was right to get rid of defeated generals fast. Their psychology grew warped. They pressed or drew back. Hood did both.

After the speechmaking was over, the men returned to their more familiar and homey conversations with Yankee pickets. Suddenly Hood swung out in an arc which placed him on the famous railroad just about where Sherman had been three months before. Actually he had reversed the siege of Atlanta, by cutting off the one railroad supplying the Union occupation.

Sherman, in the mellow, bright weather of October (the second), found a contretemps indeed. The whole campaign was turned around. Then he and Hood entered into the weirdest campaign, if such it can be called, of the whole war.

Hood cut the railroad all right and Sherman had to come after him, all according to plan. But Hood, after successive battle disasters, was for the moment gunshy. When Sherman advanced, Hood retreated *up* the railroad. When Hood retreated, Sherman advanced—but only so far as Hood retreated. He made no effort to attack him.

General in Chief Grant, himself showing reluctance to attack Lee straight on, goaded Sherman to attack Hood's army. After all, that was the purpose of the whole Western campaign. Sherman swore he would do this thing, but he complained that Hood was not behaving the way anybody could understand. He wanted Retreatin' Joe back, he said.

In this grotesque parody of a military campaign, Hood and Sherman marched all the way back to the Chattanooga area in ten days, when it had taken Sherman three months to go in the other direction. Except for the fact that depopulated Atlanta was occupied by one of Sherman's corps, the two armies were back precisely where they had started in May. As an "if" of the war, suppose Hood had stood still for Sherman to attack and had decisively defeated the cautious Attila? *That* would have given a new turn to the dying conflict.

That was an impossible supposition, since Hood was already personally defeated. He could not go any farther northward, tearing up the railroad. The only alternative was to sidle westward across northern Alabama, and then strike (where Forrest had been restrained) into Middle Tennessee. That would really finish Sherman's supplies. For this newly conceived plan, Hood even gained the consent to employ Forrest in cavalry support.

Beauregard seemed somewhat unenthusiastic about this shift but, even less enthusiastic about assuming responsibility, he gave his approval.

The folly of Hood's northern "invasion," which even included a possibility of taking Nashville, lay in the condition of his troops. With winter coming on, they were poorly clothed and shod. They lacked sustenance and the wagons to haul it if they foraged for it on the way. The army was not in condition for the northern march, even if the idea had been practicable.

The whole plan had been extemporized from day to day, and from day to day it was thwarted. The Tennessee River, which they had to cross, was high. Supplies they had counted on were not obtainable. Forrest could not join them at another crossing. They shifted on westward, from mile to mile, further and further into unreality.

Finally they met Forrest, crossed the river and, hungry and barefoot, the men shivered northward in a sleet storm. By then, Sherman had long since ceased chasing Hood. By concentrating the Union troops in Tennessee, by removing a corps from his own army and a corps from somewhere else, Sherman could raise another whole army of 70,000 without even calling for reinforcements. He directed this new army to take care of Hood in Tennessee.

A factor in the Union manpower—aside from the fact that it was four to one, that its draft system was incomparably more efficient, and, as the war progressed, its armies suffered fewer desertions—was their use of Negro troops. The 180,000 Negroes in the Union armies in late 1864 were more than all Confederates under arms at the time. As the bulk of these colored troops were former slaves, this figure reads well as a statistic of the freedom which was a by-product of the war. However, there is also the statistic of the $200,000,000 personal loss this meant to Southerners.

This was to have its own disastrous effect in the future of the freed people in a destroyed society, which they had helped to destroy.

Unmindful of the future beyond getting a meal and getting warm, the largely non-slaveholding army of Hood was pushed ahead to catch the two main columns of the concentrating Union forces before they converged into one army. In this Hood was successful. He caught Schofield's force, about equal to his own. Then, in the collapse of command throughout the Confederacy, Schofield was allowed to escape from one of the tightest traps any general devised on either side. For the third time Hood had demonstrated that he conceived brilliantly. But conception was no longer enough.

Then, goaded, he had at Schofield head on at Franklin, Tennessee (November 30), where his perhaps 30,000 survivors of all the travails put upon them charged breastworks as though life was no more worth living. Even then they couldn't carry fixed works. They did induce Schofield to hurry on to his concentration with Thomas, though that was not the point. The point was to destroy Schofield before he joined Thomas, and in this Hood failed with extremely costly casualties.

From there on it was a fast downward spiral for the hard-fighting and ambitious adopted Texan, promoted beyond his capacities and warped by reverses and the mad assignment he gave himself. He moved on to Nashville, the most heavily fortified city in the South, and entrenched himself outside of the combined armies under Thomas. Now, with his infantry down to less than 25,000, and Forrest away, Hood at last invited attack. There was nothing else to do.

Though ponderously deliberate Thomas moved so slowly that Grant grew frantic for action, when the Virginian struck he had everything ready. He had far too many men and too many guns against the hungry, demoralized remnants of what once had been an army. They fought for two days (December 15-16) and then the Confederates broke. They broke like Early's men at Cedar Creek, as Confederate armies never did in the first years.

Their retreat, barefoot across the icy roads a hundred miles to the Tennessee River, was another of those futile epics of heroism. With an army routed, its men starving and dying of cold, there were still individuals who fought enough to contain the pursuit of Thomas—to his own admiration of their gallantry and courage in a hopeless cause. Forrest joined them and fought off Wilson, sent out by Grant to reorganize and command Thomas' 10,000 cavalry.

That the remnants still fought savagely and skillfully was a tragically fitting finale to the personally unconquerable men of the Army of Tennessee. Except for an anticlimactic and humiliating burial ceremony of their survivors, that was the end of the army of the West. Even then, they had a song.

In romantic moods during the war the Southerners liked to sing:

> *You may talk about your dearest maids,*
> *And sing of Rosalie,*
> *But the Yellow Rose of Texas*
> *Beats the belles of Tennessee. . . .*

Hood's survivors did it this way:

> *You may talk about your Beauregard,*
> *And tell of General Lee,*
> *But the gallant Hood of Texas*
> *Played hell in Tennessee. . . .*

4

With the disappearance of an army in the West, Sherman showed an unwonted boldness in the "campaign" on which his fame rests. He got a song too, "Marching through Georgia," though the soldiers didn't sing it then: it was written after the war. Sherman also freed a lot of slaves—armies of them followed him—though he had said, "I would not abolish slavery if I could." No more an abolitionist than Lee was a slaveholder (Lee had freed his), Sherman said, "All the Congresses on earth can't make the Negro anything else but what he is; he must be subject to the white man, or he must amalgamate or be destroyed."

No crusader for freedom, Sherman made his vastly praised contribution to preserving the Union largely against defenseless civilians. When he gave up the chase of Hood, whom he never seemed too anxious to catch, he turned to the method of warfare that had grown increasingly appealing to him and executed a scheme he had been cherishing for some while. Instead of chasing Hood in order to protect his railroad, since the Confederate army had removed itself from Georgia, he would abandon the railroad and subsist directly off the people.

He wrote Grant: "It will be a physical impossibility to protect the roads now that Hood, Forrest, and Wheeler, and the whole batch of devils, are turned loose without home or habitation." He proposed to break up the railroad south from Chattanooga and, with wagons which would be filled from people's meat houses, kitchens, and livestock yards, to strike from Atlanta to the coast. He said that he could "make Georgia howl."

He left no doubt about what he meant by making the state howl. "I am going into the bowels of the Confederacy and propose to leave a trail that will be recognized 50 years hence. . . . I am perfecting arrangements . . . to make desolation everywhere."

After the war, Sherman denied that he brought needless "ruin and misery" to the Southern people out of any spirit of vengeance. There are his own official orders and the trail he did leave, through three states, which stood into the twentieth century like the blight of a plague.

In his effect on the history of the South as a self-conscious region, Sherman looms as large as many Southern leaders. He occupies a place in the actual war period analogous to that of the more extreme abolitionists at the beginning of the cold war. He was the executioner of the sentence which the sitters-in-judgment wished to have carried out against the Southern people. He destroyed a civilization. To the South he remains a symbol of the wanton and ruthless brutality of a might which denied all human rights to its victims.

Once the United States Government released its powers of destruction on the subjugation of a people, the policy inevitably bred the type of man who was affected by unrestrained power as were the barbarous rulers of old. In Sherman's case, the power of destruction fed on itself as any power feeds. By his own gloating descriptions of the "desolation" he left in his wake, Sherman all too clearly revealed the hold that his own power of terror had on him.

In his soldiers, violence likewise was self-feeding, and they regarded Southern families as no more than helpless victims. "Rebels have no rights," was said to a thousand defenseless women who protested at having their personal belongings stripped from them.

The Union soldiers not only had the rights of conquest, they had the righteous slogan "Free the slaves." Every slave whom they freed under the law of their own government, including those they freed forcibly, gave justice and glory to the release of all the instincts of greed, rapacity, brutish power over others and the sheer hooliganism of uncivilized bullies turned loose in the homes of cultured people.

All through the reign of terror, the coarsest of the Union soldiers displayed the lust to degrade and desecrate the symbols of a civilization superior to anything they had personally experienced. Class hatred had been focalized into hatred of a section which represented the pride of the aristocrat. That pride they wanted to humble and, by humbling, establish their own superiority to it.

As regarded either restoring the Union or "freeing the slaves," Sherman's glorified march set back the real cause of union by at least the fifty years he mentioned. No purpose of uniting a people, white and colored, in one common country, could be served by making the soldiers who represented this goal objects of loathing and bitter contempt, and the name of their commander a dirty epithet forever. And as for resolving the inherent duality within the nation, Sherman struck the heaviest and most lasting blow for continuing division.

He started his "trail" at Atlanta. On leaving the city in early November, he looked back with pride on the work of his accomplished arsonists. He saw behind him the city "smouldering and in ruins, the black smoke rising high in the air, and hanging like a pall over the ruined city."

With this ghoulish paean, Sherman started toward the sea and the hundreds of plantations and thousands of farms between Atlanta and Savannah. All hitherto outside even the reach of raiding parties, they would offer fat living for his troops.

Southerners did not believe the claims of military "necessity," based on the grounds that Sherman was depriving the Confederate armies of food support and destroying the will of the people to resist. At the time, there were virtually no armies to support, and Sherman had been given every opportunity from the first of May until middle November to get at the one army of the West directly.

The Johnston-Hood army was his military necessity. Defeating the Army of Tennessee would have brought the war to the quickest end, and the end designed best to heal the wounds of internecine war. Sherman took war to the people instead of to the people's army. Along with breaking their immediate will to resist, he created a deeper resistance to the thing he represented.

There is a personal example of how Sherman as a restorer of the Union appeared to a lady from Maine who, as a resident of Georgia, happened to live in the path of his hordes. Mrs. Burge had been born Dolly Sumner Lunt, in Maine, and was a kinswoman of the abolitionist, Charles Sumner. She had come as a schoolteacher to Georgia, and there married a planter. He had died before the war and, when Sherman came through, the Maine lady was a widow with a nine-year-old daughter and a hundred inherited slaves.

The grounds around her home were lovely in a typical regional style, though in no sense spectacular. The low white house was set in a grove of large oaks, beyond which were cherokee roses, wild honeysuckle, pink and white dogwood, and azaleas. From her front window, the forty-seven-year-old widow could, in one direction, see the cotton fields, and from the other, past the garden and white well house, the road.

It was down the road from the direction of Atlanta that she saw the wagons, carriages, and horseback riders fleeing before the scourge. A judge rode into her yard and called, "Mrs. Burge, the Yankees are coming! Hide your mules and carriages and whatever valuables you have."

The little girl cried, "Oh, Mamma, what shall we do?"

Silver and china were buried in the ground, clothes were spread through the slave quarters, the meat was placed in a lard tin and put in a hole. The barrel of irreplaceable salt, which had cost $200 in a bargain buy, was set in a vegetable garden of the slaves and covered with leached ashes. Even the homemade soap was hidden, under bricks.

The frantic household had scarcely finished when a young Negress cried, "Mistress, they are coming! They are riding in the lot. . . ."

There were only two of them, riding with silk dresses under their saddles, who came to the front door and broke it down. Then, asking to know why it was locked, they demanded breakfast. While Mrs. Burge had her servants bring food to appease the invaders, they told her that they were Rebel cavalry.

She said, "You look like Yankees to me."

"Yes, we are Yankees," they said. "Did you ever see one before?"

"Not for a long time," said the lady from Maine, "and none such as you."

When the hoodlums left, taking three mules, Mrs. Burge and her house people realized that those two had been only stragglers from Sherman's army, and they still had to face the main body.

They got the advance troops on November 19. At their horrifying approach, Mrs. Burge asked, "Is this the way to make us love the Union?"

Then they came. She said: ". . . like demons they rush in! My yards are full. To my smokehouse, dairy, pantry, kitchen and cellar, like famished wolves they come, breaking locks and whatever is in their way. . . ." Meat, flour, lard, butter, eggs, all "gone in a twinkling. . . ." Turkeys and chickens and young pigs "shot down in my yard and hunted as if they were Rebels themselves. . . ." The buggy horse, the brood mare, her colt, were driven off.

Then the slaves were driven off at bayonet point. "Jack hid under the bed," but they dragged him out. The Yankees yelled at her that they were taking the slaves, capturing those trying to escape, because the Negroes wanted to fight with the Union.

"It is strange," she said, "that the all-powerful Yankee nation, with the whole world to back them, their ports open . . . should at last take the poor Negro to help them out against this little Confederacy. . . . They are not friends to the slaves. . . ."

They stole the Negroes' belongings and the money of those who had saved from the sale of their own crops.

The oven, skillets, coffee mills, and coffeepots—all were taken.

An Illinois captain, who had known Mrs. Burge's brother in Chicago, saved the little girl's doll, and asked that the house be spared. He could do no more. Cotton rolls in the carriage house were set on fire and thrown in the carriage. By chance, the eight cotton bales stored there only burned over, and the fire simmered out.

Then came the main army of Sherman, cutting across her lot, tearing down the fences and garden rails, driving stolen stock across the fields. "Such a day, if I live to the age of Methuselah, may God spare me from ever seeing again!"

With nothing to eat, Mrs. Burge kept her house people huddled in the living room. The Negro women were afraid to go out, for they "could not step out of the door without an insult from the Yankee soldiers."

As the main army passed, a humane officer left two guards there to protect the house from fire. They turned out to be Dutchmen who could not speak English, and they "came into my room and laid themselves by my fire for the night."

Mrs. Burge spent the night at the window, looking at the glares of other homes burning in the distance.

This one New England lady, who got off lightly (she was only impoverished) because an officer happened to know her brother in Chicago, represented one of the sweeter episodes of Sherman's unopposed "March to the Sea."

The only armed men available served merely as supernumeraries to provide an illusion of warfare, to give the spurious impression of a contesting force falling back before a victorious army.

These miserable stooges of history were the "army" of Governor Brown's voters, the militia he had held from the Confederate forces in order to protect Georgia. Estimated in the tens of thousands at the ballot boxes and on the roster rolls of Georgia defense troops, less than 5000 of all arms showed up to play their part in the tragi-farce of Joe Brown's states' rights put to the test of invasion.

Among them was the former Unionist turned secession leader, Bob Toombs, at the end of his road as an obstructionist. The end of Toombs's long training in opposition led the wild-haired old-looking man in flight through the neighborhood of his boyhood, of his family and friends, of his young triumphs as a lawyer and his later triumphs in politics. The Confederacy's first Secretary of State, and later brigadier in a great stand against Burnside at Sharpsburg, stumbled along the winter roads with the home-guard rabble which observed in horror, rather than resisted, the systematic devastation of their lands.

Generals arrived in plenty. Misused and faithful Hardee was hurried down from Charleston. Beauregard, having waved farewell to Hood on his flight into fantasia, came along with the other general from his department—Dick Taylor, the Confederate President's brother-in-law, and the young brigadier who in the good days of 1862 had brought his tough Louisianians to Stonewall Jackson. Taylor, the learned planter-soldier, came along to see what if anything could be done. Nothing could.

Then Joe Wheeler, partly recovered from his fiasco of a raid, brought the remnants of his cavalry. They were worse than useless. Their discipline gone along with morale and numbers, the men apparently decided that as Sherman was robbing the people they might as well get some food themselves as have it go to the Yankees. The feeling of the Georgia people against Wheeler was so intense that, before he came back from Tennessee, Toombs voiced a passionate hope that the Georgia trooper would stay there.

Wheeler's men got some blame for crimes they did not commit. With

THE LAND THEY FOUGHT FOR

all law and order gone in the areas devastated by Sherman's "bummers," deserters from both armies preyed on the people and passed themselves off as "Wheeler's men." Many of these war-hardened characters, with loyalty to no one, drifted into the condition of bandits and they committed crimes against persons as well as against property.

For Sherman's excursion, the end of the line was Georgia's port city of Savannah. Though its fort was defended only by a couple of hundred garrison troops, it sounded like the true glory when Sherman could wire Lincoln, "I beg to present you as a Christmas gift the city of Savannah, with 150 heavy guns and plenty of ammunition, and also about 25,000 bales of cotton."

Sherman's extemporized march revealed that the South, for whatever amalgam of reasons (including the self-destruction of the Western army), could no longer offer even a token defense except with Lee's diminishing army. Unopposed, Sherman stood steady to thrust upward through the body of the older, coastal South to join Grant at Richmond. There was nothing to prevent this, nothing to hope for.

The decision to allow the annihilation to continue was left to a leader who had retreated into the sanctuary of his last "principle"—the abstract concept of independence. Isolated in his lonely house in the gathering ruin, the proud and pallid man, his nerves twitching with ophthalmic pains, stared with his one good eye at the historic judgment of his defense of rights and saw not the people dying, suffering physical and psychic impairment for the future, and the loss of all means of supporting themselves in that bleak future.

5

The normally docile Congress, without analyses of the reasons for Davis' failure, kicked over the traces after the fall of Atlanta. By the time that Sherman was marching through Georgia, they had repudiated the President and all his works.

They began to talk of peace and a resolution was introduced for the formation of a committee of thirteen (one from each state) to negotiate with the North. When that came to nothing, Foote, Davis' abiding enemy, started for Washington in December to make a personal peace. He was arrested and returned, adding his scurrility to the confusion. Then he escaped and made it to Washington, only to discover that the United States was not interested. Following that adventure, he went to Europe, from where he appealed to his Tennessee constituents to secede from the Confederacy and negotiate for a separate peace.

Foote was only the most extreme. Judge Campbell, the Assistant Secretary of War and Alabama's former Supreme Court justice who had been used in the Fort Sumter negotiations, began writing his old friends on the bench with a purpose to opening peace parleys. From Washington old man Blair, who could not believe that his family did not decide the destinies of the nation, wrote Davis on some scheme of his, of which Lincoln was aware. Peace was in the air. Southerners wanted peace, as Congress reflected.

However, as Davis did not represent the Southern people and he did not want peace, New Year's Day opened 1865 as another year of war. In Richmond, it was a cold Sunday, with snow on the ground from a snowfall during the night. The President wore a knitted woolen cap when he attended services at St. Paul's, where Dr. Minnegerode directed his sermon against the "croakers" who had lost heart.

Among the croakers on that New Year's Day were loyalists who could no longer deny the inescapable facts of their defeat. They saw the absence of and the disaffection among the leaders of 1860, "the patriots who contributed most in the work of preparing the minds of the people for resistance to Northern domination." They saw that Davis had failed in his one-man show, that "consternation and despair are expanding among the people," and, that though "nearly all desire to see General Lee at the head of affairs . . . the President is resolved to yield the position to no man."

One of the staunchest and most intelligent of the women Rebels in Richmond said on that New Year's, "If there was no foreboding of the coming wreck of our coveted independence, we could at best only look forward to an indefinite continuation of the dire evils which had shrouded our land in misery and sorrow. Day by day our wants and privations increased . . . in the cheerless season to which we had looked forward with dread."

"In the cheerless season" of winter, wood and coal for the icy homes cost $100 a load, corn meal was $75 a bushel, and flour $500 a barrel and skyrocketing. Where was the money coming from? Their dollar, down to one to fifty-three in gold, was worth about two cents.

Mrs. Pryor, the wife of one of the fiercest fire-eating secessionists, and herself a friend of A. P. Hill, said, "Our famine grew sterner every day." Even from a house in Richmond she saw that "the common soldier perceived the cause was lost. He could read its doom in the famine around him, in the faces of his officers. . . ."

Though the nightly dances went on in the besieged capital and the pious frowned on the revelry, one of the beaux of the day said, "The short spasm of gaiety, after all, was only the fitful and feverish symptom of the deadly weakness of the body politic. It was merely superficial; under it was a fixed and impenetrable gloom."

Even the devout Mrs. McGuire, whose religious faith protected her from anticipating defeat, admitted that, "while we do not believe one word of the croaking, it makes us feel restless and unhappy."

By then the people could no longer be called croakers. The most passionately enduring simply accepted the inevitable. In the middle of January came the capitulation of Fort Fisher, which protected the one open port of Wilmington. The people knew that Wilmington must soon follow, and the last Confederate port would be closed. Blockade-run supplies had been indispensable in even their starvation diet. The Confederacy was cut off from the world.

As a soldier in Lee's army said, on his way home to look after his family, "The Confederacy's done gone up the spout."

In that month of severe cold and sleet, when the physical suffering and the mental suffering collaborated to make the soul long for an end to the war, the peace commissioners arrived from Washington to visit the Confederate President. With nothing secret, the result of the peace negotiations were awaited with an anxiety equaling that at the Battle of First Manassas.

Yet from the beginning the negotiations that led to a peace conference with Lincoln were not on the Confederate side related to peace at all. Davis used the negotiations (and unwittingly the people's hopes) to defeat his political enemy, Vice-President Stephens.

With a belief in his infallibility as impervious as Davis' and a dogmatism in his own abstractions, the puny pedant had returned to Richmond ostensibly to preside over the Senate. Actually he led the chorus swelling against the beleaguered President. With Davis repudiated by Congress, Stephens saw the opportunity to prove that he had been right all along in opposing the President.

First off, Stephens cast the deciding vote to restore habeas corpus. Then he proclaimed that if the country would likewise expunge from the books Davis' evil laws of food impressment and conscription, constitutional liberty would return to their land and victorious peace would follow as the night the day. This lunatic victim of his obsession with constitutionalities believed that peace would be theirs for the asking anyway, if the procedure could only be conducted along constitutional lines.

As his vaporings filled the air at a time when the wolf pack was after Davis—demanding that he abdicate as Commander in Chief and some even wanting him to resign as President—the peace negotiations gave Davis a chance to silence Stephens along with all the fuzzy thinkers who believed peace could be had on desirable terms.

Davis was never deluded into hoping that Lincoln would grant peace on any save his own stated terms of reunion and emancipation. Nor was he remotely taken in by the grotesque proposition presented by the elder Blair and his son, who had been Lincoln's first Postmaster General. Having experienced the Fort Sumter negotiations with Lincoln, Davis was well aware that Lincoln's "unofficial" representatives acted wholly without authority and were used as feelers by the Union President.

What the Blairs proposed to the Confederate President, an old friend of the senior Blair, was that the two armies declare a truce for the purpose of uniting under the Monroe Doctrine to drive Napoleon's Maximilian out of Mexico. After a truce, during which the two countries had acted in concert, their difficulties could doubtless be ironed out. Foolish as this proposal was, Davis, for reasons of his own, agreed to send representatives to confer with Union officials on peace in general on the basis of the Blairs' truce.

For his commissioners Davis tagged Stephens, who had been talking about peace, and Judge Campbell, who had been writing about it. For the third, the President selected Virginia's Hunter, that portly and quietly operating aspirant for presidential honors.

More of a Davis supporter than otherwise, though not an Administration man, Hunter had brought to the Senate (over which he presided in Stephens' frequent absences) dignity, intelligence, and industry without taking a strong position. At fifty-five, he stood to lose the fruits of a careful, frugal life devoted to study and work. More crushing at his age than the wiping out of his political hopes would be the loss of his investment in slaves and the land that depended on them. Obviously fearing that the end was at hand, Hunter, his plump cheeks grown flabby with worry, could be counted on to grasp the cold realities of the conference which Stephens and Campbell might miss. Also, his report would be respected.

The report was precisely what Davis had expected. Lincoln personally, accompanied by Seward, had met the three commissioners in the saloon of a steamer in Hampton Roads (Hampton Roads Conference, February 3, 1865). There he patiently explained that he had meant what he said: the only bases for peace were a return of the seceded states to the Union and with slavery abolished. Both he and Seward offered generous terms of compensation to the slaveowners, at least in so far as they could guarantee compensation, and that must have held some meaning to anxious Hunter.

As for any truce, however, such as the Blairs had suggested, Lincoln dismissed that and said that peace would come when the Confederates laid down their arms and not before. To the Confederate survivors and their government, peace only meant "unconditional surrender." Lincoln had gone on record for total subjugation, as Davis had known he would.

In his maneuver, Davis had gotten shut of Stephens, who staggered off to Georgia with his house of cards around his head, never to be seen in Richmond again.

But in maneuvering Lincoln into going on record with his terms of absolute surrender, Davis revealed that his own private world was almost as removed from the real situation as Stephens'. Three days after the conference, Davis addressed a Richmond crowd on the basis of Lincoln's demands for a people with arms in their hands to surrender their liberties. It was the most impassioned and most human speech the Confederate President made in the whole war. It came the nearest of all his words to stirring the heart. Even Stephens, tarrying in Richmond long enough to hear Davis, found his speech brilliant.

However, he said, "I looked upon it as little short of dementation."

Though Stephens was scarcely a judge of sanity, he happened to hit close to the truth on that one. *Davis actually believed that his airing of Lincoln's demands was all the people needed to put the heart back into them.*

So the President and Vice-President of the C.S.A. were engaged at the end in questioning each other's sanity.

6

Hunter might have been swayed by that talk of compensation (for his slaves), but he came up with a sound, statesmanlike idea. He suggested that they accept Lincoln's reunion with emancipation, since that was inevitable, and strive for a less harsh settlement than unconditional surrender. He knew the course was run and he was only concerned about capitulating with more dignity than was offered.

Davis wouldn't hear of it. The crowd had responded wildly to his speech and his few faithful followers had carried his words into the remaining segments of the Confederacy. He honestly believed that by showing Lincoln's terms he had revived the movement.

Nothing had changed. The people were not interested in terms. They were interested in eating, getting warm, in saving their farms from Sherman (who had started northward from Savannah), in holding what little they possessed against the future, in having their loved ones home or going home to families.

There was so little of the Confederacy left that the government largely represented occupied territory. Omitting Kirby Smith's separate cotton empire in isolated Texas, except for some threatened areas of production in Alabama and some sparsely settled non-productive areas in Florida, for practical purposes the Confederacy consisted of the seventy miles of Virginia south of Richmond minus its coast, North Carolina with its disaffected western areas and its whole coast about gone, and South Carolina with its ports closed and Sherman slicing up against virtually no opposition from the southward. That was two and one third states, cut off from their own west and their coasts, with one of the states undergoing unopposed invasion.

In that February of severe cold, Davis had been told that Lee's army was in a critical position, and its only desperate hope for survival lay in abandoning Richmond and *attempting* to escape. With the wretched condition of the starved and sick men and horses, the broken-down wagons and gun carriages, it was problematical if they could even escape. They certainly couldn't try until spring thawed the slushy roads and warmed the stiff bones of the soldiers. While they were waiting for spring, Grant was waiting too and building up another spring campaign, mightier than ever, to throw against the ghost of Lee's army. Davis listened to all this, and would hear nothing that so much as hinted at surrender.

With this stand, as of February 6, Jefferson Davis condemned the un-defended Southern people to the ultimate ravages of the conquerors, con-demned the proud Confederate symbol of Lee's army to a hopeless and humiliating flight, and removed the government of Confederate citizens from the dignified position of an honorable nation honorably admitting its defeat by arms.

The final phases of the annihilation were no longer war, because the remaining Confederate forces were no longer armies. Except for the empty forms of government and a few endangered production centers, there was no nation behind them. The remnants of armed men entered the last stages as fugitive groups.

CHAPTER XXIII

"Stand to Your Glasses Steady"

IN THE LAST dark days of the survivors, enough pressure was finally brought to appoint Lee General in Chief of all the armies (February 6). This was one full year after the position could serve any useful purpose. Congress had passed the law and Davis swallowed the bitter pill, but the new appointment made no significant change.

At the same time Seddon resigned as Secretary of War in despair at the future, and Breckinridge was brought in from the field. The hearty Kentuckian had no interest in the detail work of an office which could only record the futilities of a dying cause. He suggested bold measures that were based on insufficient knowledge of the condition of the few troops in the field, and there was no one around to advise him. Braxton Bragg had gone to North Carolina to help with the defenses, though his own fellow statesmen refused to rally around a soldier whom disaster followed like a shadow. Most of the work which Bragg and Seddon had done devolved on Adjutant General Cooper, the sickly Hudson River gentleman who went on conscientiously about his paper chores as if he were still signing orders for the innocent times of Fort Sumter.

The effect of the changes was essentially that the War Office ceased to be Davis' toy, and Lee personally—though still clearing through the President and the War Office—assumed a supervisory responsibility for the forces defending the remaining Southern coastal strip between the armies of Grant and Sherman.

In continuing to clear through the President, Lee was motivated largely by his habits of kindness. Then, the final problems of defense were narrowed to the point where all action was interrelated in any single military decision. Since the Confederacy, with one exception, was only the shrinking coastal area, bounded by mountains, the sea in control of the enemy, and Grant and Sherman moving toward one another, the few forces within the closing vise of necessity operated toward a common end and, through Lee, under a single head.

The exception was the almost defunct Military District of the West, far beyond the reaches of Lee's supervision, even had he been minded to extend it. The West then consisted of the closed port of Mobile, the production center of Selma in Alabama, some small cities not yet razed or occupied, some railroads not yet wrecked, some plantations standing in Alabama, and some untouched farms scattered through the wasteland left by raiders and armies in Mississippi. All these oversights were being attended to by fresh Union raiders and new armies striking east from Memphis, Vicksburg, and Baton Rouge, west from Pensacola and, for the coup de grâce, the most awesome mounted force ever assembled on the continent was readying to strike due south from Tennessee.

These 22,000 troops, thousands of whom were armed with the Spencer repeating carbines, were commanded by young Wilson, whom Grant had sent out to Nashville and who had been treated so roughly by Forrest when Wilson tried to cut up Hood's retreat. Wilson didn't need the new orders from Sherman in Savannah, "to hunt down Forrest and kill him," to put heart in his work. Like Sheridan, he had come along late when the enemy was weak, and he didn't cotton to the idea of being roughly handled. Forrest was his meat and Selma his goal.

Forrest by then was only a reputation. His remnants on broken-down horses were fought out and starved out. All too many of the forcibly inducted recruits came from the undisciplined, semilawless elements who had roamed the war-made barrens and preyed on the people. No morale was possible.

Dick Taylor, with his own plantation among those wrecked, with the destruction of his fine collection of books, commanded the last ghost department east of the Mississippi—Alabama, Mississippi, and East Louisiana. His few troops, plus the garrison at Mobile under Dabney Maury, even combined with Forrest's cavalry, were insufficient for Wilson alone. They all could only fight a rear-guard action until overwhelmed. There was no military future for them. It would take about two months of their futile sacrifice of life for the last survivors to be engulfed.

Though the Union forces hunting them down were as hot for glory and as bent on devastation as their fellows in the East, the heart of the Cotton Kingdom in the death throes became militarily a periphery to the war in Virginia and North Carolina.

South Carolina was eliminated by Sherman's march upward from Savannah. His "bummers" reached Charleston on the coast and Columbia, the capital, in the center of the state, before more than a token force could be organized. Charleston, the aristocratic city-state where it had all begun, was entered on February 17 with none of the ceremonies which had characterized the surrender of Fort Sumter nearly four years before.

On the evening of the same day Columbia was burned. The resultant horror that befell the state capital was so great that even Sherman and

some of his officers sought to throw the blame for the fire on the Confederates. They claimed that the city had been ignited by cotton the Rebels
burned. But Sherman's hosts had it in for South Carolina, the seat of secession. One of his officers said, "On every side, the head, center and rear of
our column might be traced by the columns of smoke by day, and the
glare of fires by night. . . . Over a region forty miles in width . . . agriculture and commerce . . . can not be fully revived in our day."

A newspaper correspondent with Sherman reported, "I hazard nothing
in saying that three-fifths (in value) of the personal property of the
counties we passed through were taken by Sherman's army." That meant
rings, watches, bracelets, earrings, silver, linen, personal possessions in addition to food, animals, vehicles, and even trinkets. The correspondent
went on, "As for wholesale burnings, pillage and devastation . . . magnify
. . . Georgia's some fifty-fold, and then throw in an occasional murder,
'jist to bring an old hard-fisted cuss to his senses.' "

Sherman personally said that "the whole army is burning with an insatiable desire to wreck vengeance upon South Carolina. I almost tremble
at her fate, but . . . feel she deserves all that is in store for her."

Against this personal god of vengeance, Lee used his new powers to
establish such order as possible in the oddments of forces collecting in
North Carolina, the last Confederate state without occupiers or invaders
in its interior. For the third time he resurrected Joe Johnston to command.

For all of Retreatin' Joe's spiteful jealousy of Lee, "Uncle Robert" was
always thoughtful of Johnston and gracious. Here at the end (February
22) the two old soldiers were to work together for the common good.
The bulk of Johnston's new force, probably around 10,000, were the survivors of the Army of Tennessee, brought East to serve for the last time
under the only commanding general they had ever liked.

In January, Hood had resigned. At the end, haggard and haunted, the
luckless general rose above the faultfinding and backbiting which defeats
had brought out and joined the noble tradition of accepting all blame personally. The nobility of their ill-fated leader at his resignation meant nothing to the tattered remnants who returned to their old friend, Joe Johnston.
Like the officers, these war-wise veterans knew the war was over, the
cause lost, and only a sense of personal honor kept them under arms until
death or the inevitable end should release them from what one Rebel
called "the long agony."

Now that it was all over, the survivors of the Army of Tennessee had
all their old commanders together at the end. Beauregard, with his short-
lived department reduced to the expiring forces of Forrest and Dick
Taylor, returned as second in command as he had begun at First Manassas.
Faithful and long-suffering Hardee brought the garrison troops, then in
the hundreds, from the abandoned towns. Bragg was with them again and
also the corps commander of Chickamauga, D. H. Hill. Hill was near the

home of his wife's family, the in-laws of Stonewall Jackson who had his "Little Sorrel" out to pasture.

Lee had also sent down his own cavalry commander, Wade Hampton, to take over the demoralized forces of Joe Wheeler. With the cavalry and all the generals included, Joe Johnston could count on something like 15,000 men, who in nowise composed an army. His paper force doubled that, but the majority were undependable troops of state militia, home guards, and the like, most of whom would not keep up beyond their own neighborhoods.

With this force, forming as it fell back from Sherman and Schofield (a recent new Union army thrown into North Carolina from the coast), Lee was trying to evolve a joint defense against Grant at the northern end of the millstone and Sherman grinding up from below Johnston. The combined forces of Sherman and Schofield, Grant and Ord (who had replaced Butler as commander north of the James River) would approximate close to a quarter of a million men. The combined forces of Johnston and Lee would approximate one fourth of that, assuming that the men and horses would be in condition to move. Yet some combination of the two forces was the only remote hope for admittedly desperate measures.

After planning and counterplanning through February and into March, the only outside chance seemed to be in abandoning Richmond, with Lee stealing away from Grant to join Johnston, when their combined forces would take on Sherman and Schofield. If victorious, while those Unions retreated southward without supplies over the ravaged country, they would turn and face Grant, who would be following Lee from Richmond into North Carolina. That this farfetched enterprise was even considered, with the dilapidated condition of their enfeebled troops against the experienced might of the Unions, showed that even Lee and Joe Johnston were driven by the mad prolongation of the hopeless struggle to think as desperate gamblers and not as trained soldiers.

For General Lee, of all men in and out of the armies, knew that the cause was hopeless. He had only to glance at the relic of his once proud army, knowing it to be the only force in the Confederacy which was even a simulacrum of an army, to realize that surrender was inevitable—indeed, desirable.

2

The Army of Northern Virginia even in organization was an extemporized makeshift designed to hold points of a line nearly forty miles long and the railroads extending from that. With the soldiers too weak to run back and forth any more north and south of Petersburg, the Old Man had erected through the months such a powerful system of entrenchments around that city that a relatively small force could hold the lines. The survivors of the Valley debacle of Jackson's once famed II Corps were commanded by Georgia's young John B. Gordon, the untrained soldier who looked like a ramrod-style martinet. With all his courage, intelligence, and initiative, Gordon's limitations in experience were to show up in the desperate measures.

Longstreet, returned to duty with a partially paralyzed arm, commanded a force located permanently in the works east of Richmond. Realistically recognizing the end, Old Pete had established friendly relations with the Union's General Ord (Butler's replacement) and was trying to promote peace measures.

One of A. P. Hill's divisions protected the railroad and turnpike connecting the two cities. Richmond and Petersburg and the twenty miles between were defended by about 20,000 infantry.

To the south and west of Petersburg, against Grant's monotonous flankings, the railroads were protected by the rest of Hill's corps plus an assortment of brigades, totaling about 14,000. Since Little Powell's men could no longer keep marching out and back, as they had through the fall and early winter, they dug high works behind which the thin lines were stretched thinner. By then the Army of Northern Virginia was strictly under a siege, which could have only one end—and they knew it.

A. P. Hill revealed the effects of the strain on his high-strung nature, and was often invalided during the winter in the nearby house which his wife had taken to be close to him. George Pickett was completely through. He commanded a force called a "reserve division," composed of a few demoralized survivors of the Gettysburg era and unwilling, last-dregs conscripts.

Jubal Early, after his small observation force remaining in the middle Valley had been gobbled up, had gone home to Lynchburg to await the inevitable end. Bald Dick Ewell's Richmond local defense unit had been placed under pacifist-minded Longstreet, and under Old Baldhead was General Kemper, the only one of Pickett's three brigadiers who survived the wounds of Cemetery Ridge. Kemper had the old men and the boys and the invalided soldiers, who guarded bridges, warehouses, and served on the sentry-box in front of the White House. All this was known to the other side.

Grant said, "They're now robbing the cradle and the grave."

It was known, too, that the forty miles of works were defended by barely 40,000 infantry—of all kinds—shivering and starving and, in the darkness, stealing off to go home. Those without homes "went over" to the enemy, sometimes a whole platoon together, for food and warmth.

The loyalty of the most faithful was taxed by the interminable digging of those new works, to contain Grant's interminable extensions on the lines. This tired the men more than fighting, but Marse Robert could no longer afford to risk lives in fighting.

Among these ditchdiggers were the South Carolinians who as magnificent militia had formed at Charleston four years before and had been among the first troops from the South to parade down East Franklin Street in Richmond when Virginia joined the Confederacy. Now these young bloods dug in the frozen earth to make a ditch six feet deep and eight feet wide. The earth was thrown back to form an embankment six feet high, twelve feet at the base, and four feet across the top. This was not the kind of war that Rhett and Yancey had talked about in the antebellum days, and that they had welcomed with flaring torches and group singing on the Charleston Battery.

"This was hard work," one South Carolinian wrote, "for we had to walk at least two miles over ground almost always either shoe-deep in mud or frozen hard and rough, and we had to dig up earth frequently frozen to the depth of a foot, and at other times running streams of water. It was at this work that I had the strongest evidence of the exhaustion of the troops. Some men dug and shovelled well; but the majority, even of those who looked strong and healthy, would pant and grow faint under the labor of half an hour. This was most strikingly the case when our meat ration failed. A pint of corn-meal could hardly keep men hearty in the winter."

Along with the digging went night picket duty. Rifle pits were five hundred yards in front of the breastworks and sometimes as close as fifty yards to the enemy's picket line. It was bitter cold at all times, with the wind slashing over the open stretches, and almost unendurable to men in flimsy overcoats and broken shoes when it rained, sleeted, or snowed. Even the warmly clad and well-fed Yankees suffered in that weather, and firing between the lines was tacitly forbidden.

Fraternizing had been forbidden since the days when their bands vied in music "contests" and pickets played poker with coffee and tobacco stakes. But if no officers were around, the men still talked though rarely visited with one another.

After freezing on the picket line every third or fourth night, it was hard for the men to get warm again. All the firewood in the area had been cut, and the teams were too weak to haul wood from a distance. There were no meats, no proteins, no sweets, to give energy or inner warmth. The spirit chilled too at morning roll call to learn that even some of the bravest had deserted during the night. Human flesh could stand no more when hope was gone and the letters from home grew more piteous. The realistic women, seeing no purpose to the suffering of their children, frankly begged the men to come home.

Those who stayed, knowing the fight was lost, were sustained only by a sense of duty to an inherited tradition. There was nothing else. Their commanding general was sustained by no more. He wrote Mrs. Lee at their home in Richmond, near the War Office, "I shall . . . endeavor to do my duty and fight to the last."

The general was in no better case than the soldiers. He was sick again, this time from exhaustion. Marse Robert had deeply upset his colored mess steward in midwinter, when he allowed the soldiers to have a saddle of mutton his family had sent the general. Lee's young son Robert, artillery captain, had been saddened to see the suffering and age in his father's "careworn face." They were dying together, the Old Man and the troops, in sustaining the code of honor that was almost the last thing left them in the land they loved.

3

The only practical course Lee could have pursued as General in Chief would have been to surrender his army, and he wanted peace. As early as February he talked to his friend Hunter about peace negotiations. That depressed commissioner to the Hampton Roads Conference said that Davis had spread the word that he was a croaker when he wanted to bargain on Lincoln's terms and he would have no more to do with the President. Hunter urged Lee to advance negotiations himself.

"Uncle Robert" gave a reluctant no. He said that for him personally to advance peace negotiations "would be almost equivalent to surrender." Apparently, as with the others, the only concern of the Old Man was to get the best terms possible which would avoid total surrender. The two men talked on through the night and Hunter suggested that Lee tell the President he believed their chances were gone. Lee seemed unwilling to go that far, though he left Hunter with the impression that he thought it was all over.

Then Longstreet told Lee that he and the Union General Ord believed that Lee might make a good peace with Grant. Immediately the Old Man wrote Grant (on March 2). Two days later, on Lincoln's second inaugural, he received Grant's flat reply that any such conference was outside his authority. "Such authority is vested in the President of the United States alone."

Yes, and in the President of the Confederate States alone. As a soldier, Lee could deal with another soldier only for the surrender of his army. As a soldier and a traditionalist, he could not presume to advise his President. Then he conferred with Gordon, the general nearest his headquarters, and the young Georgian thought that the best terms of peace should be made at once. On both sides, then, the armies facing each other knew that the end had come. But no one would tell Mr. Davis.

The most Lee could bring himself to do was to visit Davis in the little study of the White House and mention the necessity of abandoning Richmond. While Mrs. Davis served them tea, the President told the general that if he thought the abandonment was necessary he should "anticipate the necessity" and move at once.

To this deranged man, who had exercised supreme command for four years, patient Lee was put to the necessity of explaining again that his army was not in condition to move. He explained in detail that the animals were too weak to move guns and wagons over the winter roads, the men too weak to walk through the mud. He explained that, with Virginia stripped of food supply, his men could no longer do their own commissary work. They must be supplied. What he wanted was food and forage to condition his army for movement when the roads dried.

Davis never heard a word he said. Later he attributed Lee's remaining at Petersburg to the general's "reluctance to retreat." For his own part, he took no step either to meet the requirements stressed by Lee or in any way to prepare the city for evacuation.

Lee returned to the house which served as his headquarters, back of the heavily shelled city of Petersburg, knowing that the sole responsibility for the "escape" to Johnston devolved on him. It is not likely that he believed it possible. It was the only alternative to slow death where he was, and his code demanded that, however he had been failed, he dutifully make the attempt. While he was brooding over the techniques of a course in which he had no heart, he was offered what he would normally have considered a wild scheme by young Gordon and Joe Johnston.

Instead of evacuating Richmond and joining Johnston, Retreatin' Joe suggested that Lee leave "part of his force" to hold the lines against Grant and bring the rest to him for a joint move against Sherman. Once he personally was out of Virginia, Joe Johnston had always believed that the Unions could be easily held. However, for the Virginia end, devoted Gordon came up with an idea that just *might* contain Grant at Petersburg for a while.

Gordon had discovered a salient in his front that could be taken by surprise. Its three rear forts could be occupied and Grant would have to shorten his lines to launch counterattacks against the occupied forts in his rear. With Grant's lines shortened, the interminable stretching momentarily over, Lee could then dispatch a part of his force to Johnston.

The Old Man was tired. He had been fighting too many people too long. He agreed to this harebrained gamble within the hopeless gamble he was already undertaking.

Within his limits, Gordon had become a good soldier. The attack on Fort Stedman was the first Confederate assault delivered in the nine months of Grant's siege where everything worked right. The Union picket lines were muffled without an outcry, the inner lines were taken in the last

Confederate attack of the war delivered in the great tradition, and 300 picked Confederates rushed to the rear to capture the forts.

That was where Gordon's limitations showed. There weren't any forts.

While the picked men rushed about looking for something conjured up by Gordon's lack of engineering knowledge, and while the other Confederates waited to go into the forts, the Unions reformed in overwhelming numbers and gobbled them all up. Over 1000 could have chanced the gantlet back to their own lines. But they were too weak to run twice on the same morning and too hopeless to offer a walking target of their backs. They surrendered inside the Union lines.

With a loss of several thousand survivors of Jackson's II Corps, Gordon's young man's dream showed the general that he could not leave part of his army to hold Grant and move with the rest to Johnston. There was nothing for it but the evacuation of Richmond. Even then no plans were made by the government.

With the war reduced to Lee, in a single sector, and Davis, with no departments, it became clear—as former War Secretary Randolph had said long before—that the President had no practical knowledge of the armies in the field. It was clear too that, unknowingly and unacknowledgeably, Davis and his charts of organization (carried over from his great Washington days) had been dependent upon Lee's defense.

Lee then was the name of a sick old gentleman, the patriarch of a shivering, exhausted band of provincials who remained with him only because he did not tell them to go home. Davis understood none of this. He could not attend when Lee tried to tell him. Lost in his abstract concepts, the iron-willed and self-righteous doctrinaire was removed to a sphere where he could not be reached by the details of the minutiae of life in the South's last army.

Nor did the President have any meaning to those soldiers who "waited for spring" with simple trust in "Uncle Robert." Whatever happened, *he* would do what was right. In their own pride—in themselves, in their fragments of regiments and their army, in their native land—it devolved on them, as on their leader, to drink the cup like men.

> *So stand to your glasses steady,*
> *'Tis all we have left to prize;*
> *Give a toast to the dead already,*
> *And hurrah for the last man who dies. . . .*

CHAPTER XXIV

The Fugitives

IN THE MIDDLE of March 1865 the last Confederate Congress adjourned, forever. There had been five sessions of the provisional Congress of one assembly, four sessions of the first permanent Congress of two houses, and two sessions of the second (1864) permanent Congress. Before the ineffectual democratic political body adjourned the eleventh and last session (March 18), they finally passed a law offering freedom to slaves who would fight. Though the government was too late in getting around to such measures, the whole slave-Negro question was extremely tricky in the Confederacy.

If slaves were freed, in order to fight, this emancipation wedge would nullify the reason for the secession of the planter powers. Then, not only would planters lose their property, but communities would be confronted with the long-dreaded problem of the freed Negro in a white society. With these traditional practical considerations went the threat to the order on which the region's total society was built.

Against that, of course, was the outside threat to the society itself, the nation.

Faced with this dilemma, the Confederate leaders had adhered to their historic position of choosing the "principle" over the practicality, of acting for the immediate issue as opposed to the possible eventuality. But by March of 1865 the eventuality of destruction was no longer a possibility; it was a certainty; and freeing the slaves who would fight was only a technicality.

All during the war the slaves were divided, along with the rest of the people in America. There are no statistics on how many slaves fled plantations at the approach of the Federal armies. On the basis of the 200,000 plus who were used in the Union's armed forces, the number must have been very large. Then there were the thousands who, not going over to the invading armies, took over their own plantations or wandered through their own countryside. To the majority, the "freedom road" was not a very clear course.

Individuals had the human impulse to escape bondage. What the act entailed beyond the immediacy of escape was extremely hazy to most. Certainly those who went into the Union lines, joining Sherman's bummers as camp followers, expected something from their deliverers which manifestly was not in the Federals' minds.

Many who remained with their families were not necessarily, as the Southerner thought, "faithful." They illustrated that old war joke about one Negro asking another if he'd ever seen the bone, itself, fight when two dogs were fighting over it. They were waiting to go with the winning side.

It is likely that those who went over to the Federals, those who took over at home, and those who waited to see who won, formed in composite a vast majority of the nearly 4,000,000 slaves in the South. The many true stories of the loyalty of individual Negroes to their people almost always concerned house servants. Affection through association and shared lifetimes gave them an attachment stronger than any other consideration. Years after they were legally free and slavery long abolished, these individuals remained close to those they knew and loved and felt safe with. General conclusions can no more be drawn from them than from the 200,000 Negroes who fought with the Union forces.

The one group who were totally undivided were the personal servants in the armies. Probably the Confederate armies would have dissolved sooner if it had not been for the morale given officers by the devotion, the humor, and the philosophy of the corps of colored men who, serving faithfully unto death with the Southerners, further confused the causes of the war. Years before the bill, many of these could have been considered at least part-time soldiers. In their implacable hatred of the enemy, they would become sufficiently enraged to take up rifles themselves for a few shots. Related to their morale building was the food they supplied, for not even the Texans or the Stonewall Brigade surpassed them as foragers.

Contrary to the legend, there could have been Confederate volunteer Negro troops if practicality had been the only consideration. As practicality was seldom considered in the South, the Negroes, despite the desperation measure of March 1865, remained in the Southern myth as a a servant class. They came down historically to Southerners as the people who caused the trouble. This was a particularly bitter thing to those ninety per cent of non-slaveholders who fought against colored Union troops. To a man fighting for his land, the Negro fighting him was simply on the enemy's side—and stayed there.

2

Ths Negroes had a song about the "Year of Jubilee" and, as March wore out, they did not have long to wait to sing it on the streets of Southern cities. In North Carolina, about which the last, fevered plans had been made, it was manifestly all over. At Bentonville, while Congress was adjourning, Johnston's patchwork army caught the overconfident advance troops of Sherman and laid into them. This was purely personal for the survivors of the Army of Tennessee. The last star on their battle flag would be a victory.

It was a meaningless victory, since they were only fighting the same number of men as themselves. Sherman had three times more than that to bring up, with the oppressive power of big guns and cavalry so vast that Stoneman, with another complete unit, could strike in unopposed from the West at the same time. In Stoneman's run over North Carolina civilians, he finally achieved in the third state in which he tried it a curious ambition to rob people's stables. In the Tarheel State, as long as men lived who were then children, the Yankees under Stoneman were remembered as horse thieves.

With Stoneman and his men turned loose like a bandit horde on the people, Joe Johnston admitted that he could be "only an annoyance" to Sherman. After Bentonville, Sherman and Schofield united in a force far larger and more powerful than Lee's and Johnston's forces combined would have been. With this power, on March 23, Sherman reached Goldsboro, North Carolina. There he was the same distance as was Lee from Greensboro, a main surviving supply depot on which Lee's army could draw. By then, uniting the two "armies" of Lee and Johnston was only a tortured vision.

Before even this impossible dream could be attempted, Grant struck. With the winter muds drying, the Federal commander swung in the same old pattern of flanking, and Lee knew exactly where he was coming. Indeed, if Lee had still had the men to continue to contain the flankings, Grant would have completed a circle and flanked all the way back to Spotsylvania County, outside of Fredericksburg, where he had started the spring before. But Lee no longer had the men. He had stretched his thin line to the limit.

Grant's nine months of sidling for advantage had extended his army from the east in front of Petersburg to the south and then westward below the city. Since there was nowhere else to go, the new movement at the end of March must swing northwest, to the point where Grant would be behind the city. This would form a half-circle from east to west which, with the Appomattox River bordering Petersburg above, would complete the iron embrace on the defenders. That upthrusting claw would also sever the last railroad out of Petersburg and block Lee's escape route to the west.

For this climactic move Grant sent over 50,000 men, infantry, artillery, and cavalry—about as many as Lee had of all arms for his total defense. The Federals swung so far to the west that they struck northward beyond the last works Lee's survivors had thrown up.

To meet the thrust Lee sent the only force that comprised a "reserve," the 5000 dubious troops of Pickett's division, along with cavalry under Fitz Lee which virtually denuded Richmond's defense force of mounted troops. Since this combined force of roughly 10,000 was separated from the furthermost extension of the breastworks, Lee filled the gap with a light brigade of cavalry which would serve as liaison between the Petersburg defense lines and the isolated unit. The Old Man had planned as carefully with what he had as if the war were still at issue.

His commanders did not. The Old Man's twenty-nine-year-old nephew, Fitz Lee, who had graduated from West Point five years before the war, was a gourmet and bon vivant. Later, this grandson of Washington's cavalry leader, Lighthorse Harry Lee, was to be governor of Virginia, Spanish-American War general ("Charge those Yankees"), and international good fellow. In the business at hand, General Lee showed that he had displayed good judgment in appointing the untrained Wade Hampton over his nephew after Jeb Stuart was killed. With Hampton now gone, good old fun-loving Fitz was in charge of the cavalry in collaboration with washed-up Pickett for the infantry.

This pair was invited by one of Fitz Lee's cavalry generals to a shad bake. This was a very special thing to Virginians. These delicately white and guilefully boned fish had just begun to run up the rivers in late March, and to men starved on a diet of corn bread and occasional bacon, a shad bake was not the trivial event it would be to well-fed troops. While the future governor and the past hero of Gettysburg were enjoying their repast, Unions struck the indifferently laid Confederate lines in the overwhelming numerical superiority of five to one.

Had George Pickett and Fitz Lee been present, alert and energetic, they could not have contained this tide. They might, however, have prevented the action from becoming the rout it was. This so-called Battle of Five Forks, on a Saturday, the first day of April, marked the beginning of the military disintegration of the Army of Northern Virginia. For the first time a segment of Lee's army had been driven from the field. With them went the flank. All left to the army was escape.

3

The defenders behind the earthen walls, which had hospitalized the men who dug them, realized that the grand assault was finally coming. The soldiers had fought Grant so long, they were as familiar with his habits as Lee himself. The grizzled veterans had also fought in the war long enough to appraise accurately their own army and the Unions. After nine months of shilly-shallying and line-stretching, Grant, under his over-powering artillery, must feel confident at last that he could attack along the whole of the thinned line. Then they would be engulfed by the weight of numbers.

That Saturday night the sparse line grew sparser as troops were moved out to support the cavalry which had escaped from Five Forks and still protected the last railroad out of Petersburg. That night Longstreet came over personally from the Richmond line, in advance of a division which would help hold back the tide until Lee could get his men out of the works and escape to the open. That left in front of the capital only one small division, the local defense troops and a cavalry "brigade" of something over 300 troopers. Longstreet's coming personally with troops meant that Richmond at last was being abandoned, whatever the President had not done to prepare for the evacuation.

The soldiers knew the sense of all that, if they were not concerned with the details. They knew the time had come on that Saturday night which ushered in the fifth April of the war.

With full darkness, the night grew nervous with picket fire and restless movements within the dark earthen walls. Troops were shuffled about to change positions. The army was still operating on orderly plans, though the tense soldiers knew nothing about plans. They saw stretches of works so thinly manned that they seemed deserted in the blackness, and their nervousness increased. Some were so apprehensive that they could not lie down to rest; others were so worn that they fell asleep leaning against the works.

Around midnight the heaviest cannonade of the war began. The dark sky was lit by the shellbursts, flashes of mortars and rockets, and the earth shook for miles under the swelling roar. As the volume rose toward a crescendo, musket fire cracked in fast and concentrated volleys, the violent bursts which presaged attack. All along the lines the pale men turned toward one another and, "although they said little, seemed to feel that the end was drawing near."

Before daylight on Sunday morning the built-up infantry waves rolled over the Confederate lines. The overwhelming assault did not embrace the whole line from end to end. Massive spearheads struck earthen works

where the line turned westward, thrusting up from below and to the west
of the city. The division-sized II Corps of Gordon remained unharmed
in the heaviest works directly in front of the city to the east, and a few
thin brigades at the westernmost end of the works were bypassed by the
avalanche.

Those within its paths, chiefly the remnants of two of A. P. Hill's divisions, were engulfed. Some were killed, some caught up in the rushing
masses to become prisoners, and some fell back northward without order
or purpose beyond escaping.

The whole breakthrough, from the assault to the wreckage, happened
so quickly that the Unions within the lines became as confused as the
Confederates. Except for the stable line in the old works in front of
Petersburg, where Gordon's men held fast, at daylight of Sunday morning the brushy and marshy country below the city was filled with fragments of both armies wandering through the woods, along country roads,
and across farms.

A. P. Hill broke short a sick leave at his wife's house and returned to
duty, pale and gaunt, to take personal charge of his wrecked corps. With
Sergeant Tucker, the staff courier who had attached himself to Little
Powell as more or less a personal attendant, the general rode down toward
a wooded swamp to seek any body of his troops which could be re-
formed for a nucleus. The deeply courteous Virginian, a favorite of his
troops, did not look the dandy as he rode his big iron-gray horse down
the slope. His eyes were fevered, and his slight figure huddled inside a
black cape. Sergeant Tucker took the liberty of warning the general that
they were in dangerous territory. Hill said he had to find his men.

Then they saw two blue uniforms, lurking behind a tree. Hill, anxious
to get on with his search, called to the Union soldiers to surrender.
"You're in our lines," he said.

The two men muttered a quick exchange, then quickly leveled their
rifles and fired. Little Powell rocked back in the saddle and pitched forward to the ground. The black cape billowed out and spread over the
still, wasted body. A. P. Hill, thirty-nine years old, was dead when the
sergeant reached him. Tucker caught the general's big gray and rode fast
to Lee's headquarters.

The Old Man's eyes filled with tears when he heard the news. Then
he said, "He is at rest now, and we who are left are the ones to suffer."

A year before, the defiant old lion would not have expressed such a
thought. More than anything else, his spontaneous and unguarded words
revealed the hopeless despair with which he and most of the others were
going about their duties in the senseless prolongation of the conflict. Certainly a part of the suffering of those who were left was caused by the
useless deaths of their friends, men of long and warm and admiring associa-

tion in the armies, the leaders of proven character and loyalty who could have helped rebuild the South.

The day before A. P. Hill was killed, his twenty-three-year-old artillerist, Willie Pegram, had been killed at Five Forks. A brilliant and greatly loved artillery colonel, the bespectacled and gentle patriot followed by weeks the death of his brother, the General John Pegram who shortly before had married the glamorous Hettie Cary in the last fashionable wedding in wartime Richmond.

Though hearts were heavy, there was no time for grief. Somehow the fragments of command must be collected, and the way held open for escape.

The Unions, as if spent themselves in the morning attack, did not exploit the breakthrough, beyond consolidating their gains within the bend of the works, where the north-south line turned west. There they were impeded and no more by several heroic stands, notably by a few hundred men from Hill's shattered corps who gathered in Fort Gregg.

Those Federals far to the west beyond the entrenchments, in the Five Forks region, pushed on in great force toward the Southside Railroad to cut the rail line of retreat. At Sutherland Station they were met by some Confederates who, for the first time in the war in Virginia, formed into groups by personal initiative and fought as individuals. After four years of formal war, Southerners were reduced to fighting as Rebel bands.

Skirmish lines, with "the skirmishers as far apart as telegraph poles," were formed of a staff officer without a general, an artillerist without a gun, a courier without a horse. Picking up rifles from the dead, they fired and fell back to the railroad, giving time for a regular line to be formed behind the embankment. The men behind the embankment were mostly from those brigades of A. P. Hill who had been west of the Union morning attack and east of the Five Forks attack the day before. Cut off from the rest of the army and suffering heavily from stragglers, the men had walked to the point where the threat came.

The Union force was not long in appraising the thin lines. In a small version of the breakthrough south of Petersburg, they swarmed over the embankment and crushed the defenders. The men who broke out did not know where to turn next. Some surrendered. A few, in effect, committed suicide. They stood and fired at solid masses until they were killed. Others stumbled away as individuals. Guided by experience, they moved westward away from the enemy in the only way their own army could come —if it ever got there.

The railroad west was lost. The Union troops at Sutherland Station, like the majority in the big breakthrough, seemed to feel they had done their stint for the day. Time was still allowed the Rebels to abandon their main works and begin their flight as fugitives.

With the direct way west closed, Lee planned to cross his troops over the Appomattox and move west along the north bank of the river. The troops between Petersburg and Richmond, already on the north bank, could converge farther west. The troops north of Richmond would cross the James at Richmond and converge with the other columns still farther west. Westward too they would pick up the remnants of the escapees from Sutherland Station, who kept walking in that direction away from the enemy.

Because Grant withheld the assault on the main lines in front of Petersburg, Lee had all day Sunday to prepare troop movements for that night. The Southside Railroad was lost, but there was still the Richmond and Danville. The army could try to reach this railroad at Danville, to the southwest. From there Lee could still try to effect a junction with Joe Johnston.

By then, with all hopes of victory gone, Congress in one of its last acts had fired the wretched Northrop and appointed a new and able commissary general. St. John had collected supplies for Lee's fragments at Danville. Lee directed other supplies, the last from the Richmond warehouses, to be sent to Amelia Court House. This was a station on the Richmond and Danville Railroad, which the army would reach in its westward flight thirty-six miles from Petersburg. As he had told his wife he would, the Old Man had done his "duty to the full."

While making plans for the escape of the remnants of his army, he sent the War Office the long-dreaded wire. It was received at twenty minutes to eleven, Sunday, April 2, 1865. "I see no prospect of doing more than hold our position here till night. I am not certain I can do that." Then, explaining his plans of escape toward Danville, Lee sealed the doom of the capital he had defended for four years with the undramatic line: "I advise that all preparation for leaving Richmond be made tonight."

4

In Richmond, a copy of the message was delivered to Jefferson Davis in his pew at St. Paul's Church. Leaving the church without a word, the President went first to the War Office, down the hill from the church about a block. From there he wired Lee that "to move tonight will involve the loss of many valuables, both for want of time and of transportation. [However] arrangements are progressing, and unless you otherwise advise the start will be made."

Despite Lee's detailed warnings and the evidence of supplies being sent by the new commissary general to lines of retreat, Davis had made no plans for the evacuation of the capital.

Now that the moment was on him, Davis reacted as an individual—as the *representative* of a cause and not as the leader of a people. The identification of the abstraction of the Confederacy with his personal self had become complete. He acted to present personally a brave front to the world while he planned, like the heroes of old, to seek refuge from the enemy where the heart and head of the cause would continue to direct the fight for freedom.

Meticulously dressed in gray, he walked in his erect, military carriage through the shaded paths of Capitol Square, for the last time on the way to the White House on the hill. Davis' family had already gone south, and in the big empty house of bitter memories he met the three colonels of his personal staff—those charming young men who decorated the soirees of the Cary girls. With the help of some clerks, who had rushed away from their Sunday dinners, the silent group worked until eight that night packing the President's personal belongings and the papers and records he considered most valuable. All during the gloomy hours the President displayed only a calm though grim resolution. No one talked of the calamity or expressed concern, not even at dusk when the rumble of mobs gathering in the streets rolled in through the open windows.

That Sunday was a warm, balmy day; spring had suddenly blossomed after a cruelly cold and rainy March. Ladies going to church had worn new homemade bonnets and garden bouquets, and everywhere there was a new brightness in the wan faces, a look in the eyes of hope returning with the spring.

Then around noon, as congregations were leaving the churches, the people had first grown apprehensive at the unwonted scurryings about the streets of a Sunday. They were accustomed to the dead wagons rolling through toward the cemeteries, the ambulances of the wounded and the creaking wagons hauling ordnance and supply. But every imaginable kind of vehicle crowded the streets and for the first time in years the gaunt horses were rushing along under the whips of frantic drivers.

Clerks with frightened and worried faces hurried toward the Government Building, packing more records. The battalion of C.S.A. naval cadets marched sternly behind their commandant, Captain Parker, late U.S.N. Those boys took charge of the nation's wealth—less than half a million in bullion—which they hastily packed in boxes, crates, shot pouches, anything at hand.

Orders had been given by a few officials to specific groups for specific assignments, but no general orders had been given and no authority assumed responsibility for the whole operation. Even in the War Office, the clerks didn't know what was going on and denounced the government for abandoning its people. Men from the war plants and men on special services, all varieties of citizens, crowded into the Government Building, seeking information and assignments. A commander of the local defense units, General Kemper—the invalid hero of Gettysburg and first post-Reconstruction Virginia governor—wandered about in search of someone with orders. Between the frenzy of those on assigned tasks and the angry bewilderment of others, the rumors spread from the centers of government operations throughout the city.

The citizens heard only the wild rumors and saw only the rush of government workers beginning their exodus from Richmond. The people could learn nothing definite. Some believed this was only another of the alarms that shook the city. Others believed that Yankees were already at the gates. Some went home, locked doors and window shutters, and prepared to wait for whatever happened. Others hastily packed personal belongings, grabbed up treasured possessions, and prepared to get out of the doomed city. Those who possessed any sort of vehicle joined the frantic jams in the streets; others swelled the crowd growing around the depot of the railroad to Danville.

At full night the President's party pushed their way through the crowd outside the depot and, followed by the wails of the stranded, left on what they believed was the last train out of Richmond.

Then the mobs took over the abandoned capital. Colored and white, deserters from both armies, criminals and whores, the war-debased poor and the riffraff accumulated through four years of siege, all came out of their dens and hiding places and formed in a lawless army in the center of the city.

The last order passed from the capital when Bald Dick Ewell brought the motley remnants of the city's local defenders down Main Street and south out of Richmond over the one remaining bridge, which they burned behind them. Before they left, they fired the tobacco warehouses and government stores. Through someone's mistake, these last food supplies had *not* been sent out on the Danville railroad for Lee's army at Amelia.

The mob did not intend that food and alcohol should go to the flames. They burst in the buildings, fighting among themselves for the loot. By the time they had emptied the burning buildings, the fires from the tobacco warehouses had spread and the flames were enveloping the old heart of the city. The hysterical mob marched ahead of the fires and broke in private stores and warehouses. Hungry harridans fought over ostrich-feather fans and china bowls in the auction houses. Emaciated ruffians shot one another over cavalry officers' boots and red sashes.

When the buildings were gutted, the fire swept on to private homes and the boardinghouses crowded with refugees. Throughout the night, the old took the children to the one downtown place safe from the flames —the green hills of Capitol Square. There, as the night winds blew, they crouched on the grass, wrapped in shawls and pieces of carpet. Some had brought settees, and groups huddled together on the faded cushions, their faces stained with the reflected fire, while hoodlums rushed and whooped past them.

During this fiery end of the Confederate capital—when all the state and government arsenals burned with the rest—the President was taking his Cabinet to Danville to set up a new seat of government. In that friendly city of homes, in agricultural country on the banks of the Dan River, the President intended to prosecute the war to a successful conclusion.

5

Lee was supposed to come to Danville, on his way to join Joe Johnston. He never had a chance of getting there. When the converging remnants of his army reached Amelia Court House and found the ordered supplies had not reached there, the men lost a day sending out wagons to beg from the farmers of a lean countryside. They got few victuals, and in that lost day Sheridan, supported by infantry, got on the line of the railroad to Danville. That was the line of their retreat.

Holding to the vague purpose of the flight, to join Joe Johnston, Lee turned the army westward, back toward the Southside Railroad. Though broken from the east, outside Petersburg, the railroad still functioned from the west at Lynchburg. The belatedly efficient Commissary Department had stored supplies at Lynchburg too. These could be hurried east on the Southside Railroad, victualing the physically weak and hungry men sufficiently for them to turn southward farther west.

Of these desperate extemporizings the Confederate President was ignorant. Neither he nor Lee realized that history was focused almost entirely on the flight of the Army of Northern Virginia and not on the government. In the hospitable city of Danville, Davis established himself and his Cabinet. Nearly all of them knew the jig was up and wanted the President told. Like Lee, no one wanted to be the villain to burst the bubble of their leader's dream.

While the depressed cabinet members protected Davis in his delusions, the glory that had been the Army of Northern Virginia was dragged into the dust and mud of the men's staggering flight westward away from the enemy, vaguely toward supplies, and very vaguely toward a junction with Johnston. Those left were only going on blindly, sleepwalking in hunger and fatigue and despair, as an alternative to quitting their fellows in the old units. Their red battle flags were the only symbols left of what their land had stood for.

Yet stumbling along, day and night, through the wooded farm country, pausing to fight off the infantry pressing from behind or cavalry harassing their flank, the men completed all of Lee's planned convergences. A couple of survivors from a company would join squads from other companies, with a sergeant from still another, and form their regiment around a captain or even a lieutenant. Then several regiments would reform the brigade, some of which were as small as 200 officers and men.

The soldiers were all very gentle with one another. Nobody came up with his old ribald, earthy humor, and there was no joking, little talking of any kind. Mainly their minds were on food. Foragers drifted out constantly from the army, begging of the farmers.

Most of the country families had no food to spare. Some, reading the end in the wreckage of Lee's army, looked to the futures of their own people and kept meat houses and chicken houses locked. The families in the few big houses fed the generals, who had no more than the men.

The soldiers began to take the ears of green corn from the horses' forage and, though the hard kernels gave them toothaches, life was sustained. Then the horses began to break down, and at every halting place another gun or a wagon was abandoned.

Of what would pass for infantry, there were perhaps 30,000 men, including naval units formed into a brigade, stationary artillerists with rifles, and fragments of Richmond's local defense troops who went on with Dick Ewell after the city was left to the fire and the mob. It fell to the lot of the sailors to become engulfed with poor, one-legged Dick Ewell in the final catastrophe in action which befell the fugitive army.

In a declivity called Sayler's Creek, for the little stream which meandered through it, one part of the rear guard was cut off from the rest through the faulty liaison that had dogged the army in the past year. Surrounded, they were destroyed as a unit. Because of the absolute hopelessness of their position, most surrendered. For Bald Dick, the schoolma'am's son, the end of his defense of his land came as he stood on his wooden leg beside a turned-down flag and silently awaited his captors.

As an example of a unit in the Army of Northern Virginia, there were the University Greys from Mississippi. Demolished in the breakthrough at Petersburg, its survivors had been advised to shift for themselves. The color-bearer tore up the flag the ladies from home had presented, tied the fragments to the staff, and threw it in Hatcher's Run. Of the men who escaped by swimming the creek at Hatcher's Run, one made it into Richmond, to find the Yankees already there, and one was caught with Ewell at Sayler's Creek. The first sergeant, who at twenty-two had four years of military service in the C.S.A., was left to go on alone to the end.

The end was made mercifully brief by the fine condition of the enemy. With the war degenerated into a chase, General Henry Wise took it upon himself to offer the Old Man some advice. In becoming a useful subordinate, the former politico had lost none of his sense of personal privilege. Bearding his commanding officer, the arrogant eccentric told Lee that the time had come for him to consider a higher duty than that to constituted authority. That was a duty to the lives of his men. He alone, Wise said, was responsible for further bloodshed, since the men were following only *him*.

With all of his humility, Lee could not fail to recognize that. It must have been in his mind when on April 7, the sixth day of the flight, he received a very decent note from Grant. It said that "the results of the last week must convince you of the hopelessness of further resistance. . . . I feel that it is so, and regard it as my duty to shift from myself the responsibility of any further effusion of blood, by asking of you the surrender of . . . the Army of Northern Virginia."

There it was, the long-postponed inevitability.

As the enemy was commanded by "Unconditional Surrender" Grant, Lee shied away from the act of surrender. He answered immediately and, while denying that their cause was hopeless, asked the terms of surrender.

The "Unconditional Surrender" Grant of the early days, when he was driving his way upward from obscurity, had mellowed as personal achievements and his country's purposes were accomplished. While Grant had fought a hard war in the East, on his own people as well as on the Confederates, while he had been merciless toward the Valley in the ultimate extension of military necessity, he had never made war on civilians as had Sherman, never conceived of himself as a God of Vengeance or directed his army toward purposeless destruction of personal property. In the end, as a conqueror, he seemed motivated by humane considerations and personal civility.

In replying to Lee, he said, ". . . peace being my great desire, there is but one condition I would insist upon, viz., that the men and officers surrendered shall be disqualified from taking up arms again against the Government of the United States until properly exchanged." Grant added that he or designated officers would meet with Confederate officers to arrange "definitely the terms."

Softened and spelled differently, the answer still added up to "unconditional surrender" in effect. Lee still shied away from the finality. The next day, April 8, he replied. Again denying that surrender was necessary, he suggested a meeting the following day to discuss Grant's proposal with an end toward desired peace.

As when Lee had written Grant during the winter, the Union general again refused to meet for the purpose of discussing peace. He repeated that "the terms upon which peace can be had are well understood. By the South laying down their arms they will hasten that most desirable event, save thousands of human lives, and hundreds of millions of property not yet destroyed."

That note reached Lee on Sunday, April 9, outside the court-house town of Appomattox County. Nearby was the railroad where the army was to be victualed by the supplies sent on from Lynchburg. The enemy, actually in front of Lee, had already gotten those supplies, though the Old Man didn't know that. He did know that the Federals in strength were across the line of march of Gordon's advance corps, and pressing heavily on the rear guard under Longstreet. There was no middle, except the remaining wagons and the remaining hangers-on who had followed the army from Richmond. In the week since his flight from Petersburg, the army had dissolved. It had been physically too weak even to escape.

It was at this point that Lee, who had never assumed more than the command of his army, admitted that his decisions in regard to that army affected the whole South. To a question of Longstreet's, he answered that further sacrifice of blood in his army would contribute nothing to the Southern cause of independence. He was very late in getting around to that question and its answer. Once he faced it as his personal decision, Lee alone assumed the full responsibility.

Yet before he put on his dress uniform with sash and sword to go to the meeting with Grant at the McLean house, the human feelings overcame the general who had become the symbol of his cause. Looking out at the Union lines, he said, "How easily I could be rid of this, and be at rest. I have only to ride along the line and all will be over."

He knew others had taken that way out. Others swore they would never surrender. Indifferent to the shadow government represented by a handful of fugitives, they wanted to cut through and make their way as individuals to the West. As a personal people, those personally refused to accept defeat.

Both ways were closed to Lee. Without his seeking it, the leadership of the Southern people had fallen on him, the political innocent. Like his model, Washington, the simple man of dedication thought only of those people.

"But it is our duty to live," he said. "What will become of the women and children of the South if we are not here to protect them?"

On this great soul was placed the burden of surrender of all left that had meaning to the secessionists' empire and the people's self-determination.

In tribute to him and to the men who followed him to the end, the Union troops who received the surrender of the army came smartly to the marching salute of "carry arms" when the first Confederates, fully accoutered for battle, approached them. The first to surrender were the first who had saved the new nation at the first big battle—the Stonewall Brigade.

Four years before in April, as county militia and state volunteers, they had gathered at Harper's Ferry under the grim rustic who looked like an overseer and made a business, not a holiday, of war. Most of the men who had met Old Jack on the Potomac had gone from the command—dead, captured, invalided out or, at the end, deserted. Conscripts had come and some of those gone. Other decimated units had been added, and they too had been lost again. Under an immortal name and a red flag, 210 officers and men surrendered as the Stonewall *Brigade*. As if on parade, they stacked arms in front of the silent Yankees, threw their cartridge boxes over the top, and then the regimental flags were furled and laid upon the guns.

The men had done their weeping before, on the Sunday when Lee came back from meeting with Grant and they knew it was all over. They had wept with and for their general, crowding around to touch him, his horse, his stirrups, to assure him of their love and loyalty. They had wept at his last, short General Order.

"With an unceasing admiration of your constancy and devotion to your Country, and grateful remembrance of your kind and generous consideration of myself, I bid you all an affectionate farewell. . . . You will take with you the satisfaction that proceeds from the consciousness of duty faithfully performed; and I earnestly pray that a Merciful God will extend to you His blessings and protection. . . ."

All their tears were gone. The survivors of the Army of Northern Virginia went through their last stacking of arms, before the enemy, with stony faces and set gazes. They would not look at one another, or at the respectful lines of Unions, and at that moment they certainly could not have looked back to their past. Like the gray-bearded nobleman who was their chief, they tried to do their duty and maintain the dignity which the generous Federal soldiers offered them.

Even after the ignominious flight which their government had placed upon them, the Southern people, who had formed the Confederate core in the Army of Northern Virginia, reached their end with dignity in themselves and were accepted in dignity by their enemies.

Their end at Appomattox is historically regarded as the end of the Civil War, though it was the surrender of only one army which had never fought outside of one state, except for its invasions of the North.

But it was the army that made the suppression of the rebellion a long war: it was the army of the men who were defending their land, and it was a distillation of the best in the ante-bellum South. It had been so recognized by the enemy and it is right, if not accurate, to regard "Lee at Appomattox" as the formal end of the South's attempt at independence.

6

When the news of Lee's surrender reached the President at Danville, he still tried to carry on the fight for independence. Between Stoneman's cavalry, swarming in from the west, and Sherman's army to the southeast, Davis led his entourage on the southward flight that robbed the Confederacy of the opportunity to terminate its career with the dignity which Lee had salvaged for his own army.

This last mad act of a nation's executive gave a character of illegality to the whole movement. Davis had gone from condemning the armies to behaving in effect as fugitives to behaving personally like a criminal on the run. He gave to the world the appearance of seeking to escape the consequences of his acts, with the implication of guilt.

Practically he left the Southern people in a nether world, in which they were not citizens of the United States nor was there any Confederacy of which they could be citizens. All the machinery of government had collapsed by the time Davis began his flight through the western sections of the Carolinas. Law and order were provided only in the cities occupied by Union troops, and this was martial law. In Richmond the citizens were denied access to any news of the rest of the South, of the armies or the fugitive President. The only people with any legal status were the surrendered soldiers. Paroled prisoners of the United States, they were placed under the custody of the Federal government. Never, since the secession of the states, had the people stood in more urgent need of a leader.

Never, since he made his first Washington speeches on the principles learned from Calhoun, had Jefferson Davis more clearly demonstrated his detachment from people. As he fled, the mentally ill man actually believed that the Southern people could be rallied to continue the war. He believed that a "show of continued resistance . . . would have overcome the depression that was spreading like a starless night over the country. . . ." He never understood that the depression was caused by hunger, misery, and the fear that were spreading over the country along with the enemies.

He wanted the people to rally to Joe Johnston's army. This "show of resistance" would bring out the fainthearted and return deserters. The gathering force would march southwestward away from Sherman, make juncture with Forrest and Dick Taylor, and "fight on forever."

As Davis suffered this last fantasy of a man who could never project outside himself, Selma, Mobile, and Montgomery had all been captured and Wilson's mounted might was ravaging the countryside like a Tartar horde. In Georgia, Wilson's cavalry hunted down cotton bales, which impoverished families had saved for the future, and made bonfires of the cotton.

Close to Davis in North Carolina, Johnston's fragment of an army was melting away by the hour. The men, along with Johnston, recognized that the last desperate hope was lost when Lee's army surrendered. They were leaving for their homes to look after their families. When Sherman approached Johnston on the subject of surrender, Retreatin' Joe immediately agreed that any further fighting would be not war but "murder."

When Johnston and Sherman met, their purpose was to arrange a surrender of all the Confederate armies and end the useless bloodshed and further destruction of personal property. For such a portentous decision, the new Secretary of War, Breckinridge, came along to represent the

Cabinet. Though Sherman refused to deal with him as a government representative, he cheerfully received Breckinridge in his capacity as Confederate general, and personally welcomed the great bourbon fancier with a nip from his brandy flask. As the men talked, Sherman absent-mindedly toyed with the top of the flask, while Breckinridge stared longingly at the brandy. Finally when Sherman, with his mind on the conversation, slipped the flask back in his bag, he was the only one who missed Breckinridge's stricken look.

Despite the big Kentuckian's heartbreak, the soldiers evolved a sound plan for ending the needless horrors of the Southern people. If Davis could be induced to proclaim a formal cessation of hostilities, Sherman would, unauthorized, offer a general amnesty to the people, with their constitutional rights recognized and their state governments received back into the Union. As soldiers, they thought that was what the war was about.

Davis didn't like it, but he gave his Cabinet a chance to vote. This was their first opportunity to speak their minds, and they unanimously and passionately urged the President to accept. Faithful Reagan drew up the ABCs of the situation, pointing out the impossibility of making war without production centers for matériel and without ports through which to get matériel, let alone without armies in the field.

After Davis reluctantly signed, the final calamity befell the South. Lincoln was assassinated. Lincoln was aware of the problems of dislocation created for the South, bore no vindictiveness toward the Southern people, and was sincerely committed to *Union* in the practical and the mystic sense.

With him gone, the spoilsmen and the haters seized control behind Andrew Johnson, the Unionist Tennessean and wartime governor. As a former tailor, Johnson cherished his own personal hatred of the planter class. He instantly repudiated Sherman's terms. Joe Johnston must simply surrender his army, as had Lee. Men would be paroled prisoners, officers could keep their side arms and cavalry their mounts—since their horses were personal property.

Davis was given the chance to say, in effect, "You see, they won't *let* the Confederacy surrender."

With this warranty for his dream of independence, he wrote Joe Johnston not to surrender his army. Instead he was to mount "the pick of his infantry" on draft horses and, with cavalry and light guns, escape to the West to join Dick Taylor, and fight on to Texas.

Johnston, who had always operated on the maxim of "a good general knows when to retreat," also knew when it was time to quit. He simply ignored the order of his ancient enemy and on his own authority surrendered his army (April 26) two and a half weeks after Lee.

Enraged at this perfidy, Davis, deep in western South Carolina (the region of Calhoun's youth), then called on the forlorn band of 2000 poorly mounted cavalry of ex-raiders, serving as escort for him and the Confederate treasure. With them, the President would cut through to the West. The young leaders listened in astonishment as he likened them to Jeb Stuart and Stonewall Jackson, stirring up the fires of dead bivouacs.

Then, in deep embarrassment, the young soldiers told Davis their men were through with fighting, and had no equipment for fighting if they wanted to. The officers personally opposed continued fighting which could only deteriorate into guerrilla warfare. This would deprive the men of the dignity of surrendering as units, and expose the impoverished and terrorized population to personal retaliations.

Still the realities of fellow human beings could not penetrate Davis' personal abstract concept. If these soldiers refused to emulate their revolutionary forebears, then he and his loyal followers would cut through to the West and join Dick Taylor, and go on to Texas.

But Dick Taylor, learning of Johnston's surrender, also surrendered the few forces of the last "department" in the East on his own authority. Davis denounced his former brother-in-law for ignoring the "established channels" of communications, and decided to keep going even without an armed force in the East.

Then, one by one, the personal followers dropped off—Attorney General Davis in North Carolina, Secretary of the Treasury Trenholm in South Carolina, Navy Secretary Mallory in Georgia. They all went home to await their capture. Benjamin left at the Savannah River, making it alone through the Confederate underground to Florida, in an open boat to Cuba, and on to England. Breckinridge was the last to leave, when the cavalry disbanded and were paid off out of the treasure they had guarded and which they threatened to take. Breckinridge followed Benjamin's course and, after turning pirate off the Florida coast, finally made it abroad.

The Confederacy had been reduced to its individual components, and still Davis fled on, through the pine barrens of Georgia. By then only Reagan of the Cabinet was with him, his three personal aides, and about two dozen scouts, teamsters, and quartermasters. The party joined forces in the thickets with Mrs. Davis and the children—who had been fleeing ahead—to protect them from the marauding bands hunting the Confederate gold, hunting horses, guns, and food.

The camp of the Davis family and the few followers was overrun at first light of a morning in early May by a segment of Wilson's cavalry. They ripped open Mrs. Davis' luggage in search of the Rebel gold. Of that, there was none. It had been disbursed along the way to almost anybody who asked for it, until only $25,000 remained to be divided among the eight quartermasters who had escorted the last wagon into Florida.

While the Confederate President was chained like a dangerous felon in Virginia's Fortress Monroe, Kirby Smith surrendered the last organized Confederate force in his isolated Texas empire.

Die-hards led by Jo Shelby refused to surrender, and made their way across Texas into Mexico. On this last hegira went magnificent "Prince John" Magruder, who thought the transplanted European court of Carlotta and Maximilian would better suit his elegant tastes than life as an ex-U.S.A. officer in his desolated Virginia.

All over the South thousands of others refused to surrender personally. Bands went to Brazil and Canada. The Reverent R. L. Dabney, Stonewall Jackson's first A.A.G., wanted to form a colony of expatriates. Individuals made their way into the wilds of Texas and the cattle West, where ex-cavalry officers (with memories of plantations) used their war experience as a means of earning a livelihood as cow hands.

Mostly from the armies, the prisons, and the hospitals, the men took the long walk home, stripped of their Rebel buttons and any Confederate insignia by Union officers along the way. As the conquering armies prepared to leave the South, occupation forces were formed, and the whole land that had composed the Confederacy existed under martial law.

The Confederacy in this manner never came to a formal end. It slowly ceased to exist as an entity as its armed forces disintegrated one by one.

It owned no property. Its records were taken off to Washington by Federal soldiers and officials. Its leaders were fugitives or under arrest. Its President, in solitary confinement in prison while under indictment for treason, was at last free to act by his personal convictions in a situation which affected only him personally.

Under brutally harsh treatment, the fifty-seven-year-old prisoner displayed the courage which was native to him as well as part of his self-conscious code. Relieved of the responsibilities which had overtaxed his mind and temporarily wrecked his health, he seemed more cheerful than in years and his dignity shed its cold stiffness. With all lost, the tormented man of ambition was able to live as an individual in the great tradition of the Southern planter—which he had never been.

Finally freed, without having been brought to trial, he wandered about with Mrs. Davis for twenty-two years—finishing as he had started as a representative of the plantation South. During this time he wrote a two-volume book on the war and, with the long years of contemplation, revealed that he had learned no more about his limitations than during the ordeal. Dying in his eighty-second year, Jefferson Davis still believed he had been right in everything.

CHAPTER XXV

"Virginia's Son"

> *A gallant foeman in the fight,*
> *A brother when the fight was o'er . . .*
>
> *And so, thy soldier grave beside,*
> *We honor thee, Virginia's son.*
>
> JULIA WARD HOWE, *on Robert E. Lee*

IN THE CONFUSED, troubled, and sorrowing time after the conquest
was completed, it was to their greatest Southerner that the people turned.
Broken and ill, General Lee came to the red brick house in Richmond,
one half block from the bell tower in Capitol Square, from where the
tocsin had sounded so often to call the citizens to the defense of their city.
Showing the world only the grandeur of his self-containment, "Uncle
Robert" suffered the ordeal of living as a public spectacle when his heart
cried for solitude.

The gutted city, under the law of occupation troops, was overrun with
sight-seers, speculators and adventurers, reporters and illustrators, and the
advance guard of the Reconstruction government who came to batten off
the defeated people and exalt the Negroes. Nearly 50,000 freed Negroes,
more than the total population of ante-bellum Richmond, flocked into the
ruins. Union soldiers, in addition to the occupiers, constantly passed
through. The Grand Army of the Potomac paraded through the streets of
the city with its bands playing.

It seemed as if everybody wanted to see Lee.

His son Custis and other young kinsmen served as screeners to eliminate
pure curiosity seekers, except among high Union officers. The flow was
continuous. Many veterans of his army on their sad journeys home wanted
to see him for the last time. One Texan was arguing with Custis for a look
at the general when the old man walked into the room. With one look at
the aged face and whitening beard, the soldier burst out crying and ran
from the house.

In the aristocratic republic of Virginia, the families of many private soldiers were friends of the Lees, and in his role of patriarch Uncle Robert saw those young men. To all he gave the same advice: "Go home . . . and help build up the shattered fortunes of our old State."

To those who suggested that he leave and go among his own, he said, "You would not have your General run away and hide. He must stay and meet his fate."

His fate was shown him by kindly General Meade, his opponent at Gettysburg, and an old friend from years before. Meade suggested that Lee set an example to the people by taking the oath of allegiance. Lee hesitated before committing himself in order to discover the course of the Federal government under the Radicals.

On May 29, after all arms had been laid down and the Confederacy existed only as a ghost in the minds of people, Andrew Johnson delivered a proclamation. All former Confederates would be afforded amnesty upon signing the oath of allegiance—*except* for certain specified groups. Lee was included in those excepted groups. Amnesty would not be extended him unless the Old Man asked for a personal pardon.

This was a greater ordeal for Lee than riding to the McLean house at Appomattox to meet Grant. To ask a pardon admitted a wrong. He had no consciousness of wrong. At the same time many Southerners, like Bob Toombs, bitterly repudiated the very notion of taking oaths which implied they could have been wrong. They determined to suffer anything in preference to giving allegiance to the conquerors who were trying to force them to accept "Reconstruction." Refusing to admit that force of arms affected their nationality, these formed the nucleus of the "un-Reconstructed Rebels," who regarded the denial of their Rebel status as a denial of their birthright and honor. In Virginia former Governor and General Henry Wise vehemently opposed Lee's applying for an amnesty, which Wise called "Damnasty."

But Lee, the generic aristocratic patriarch, by nature and by training felt a responsibility deeper than his personal preference. He accepted the accomplished fact of arbitration by the sword and, though disliking much in the nation that reclaimed them, believed the Southern people would serve their region better by submitting with good grace and going along with the conquerors for the sake of their own future. Grant and others joined Meade in supporting Uncle Robert in that belief, and urged him to set the example for the Southern people.

It was for them that the Old Man forced himself to this last public act and asked Andrew Johnson for the pardon under which he could take the oath of allegiance.

It was not granted, ever. Robert E. Lee never became a citizen of the United States again.

This was not known to the hundreds of thousands who believed that, following his request for a pardon, Lee had actually taken the oath of allegiance. The people, following what they believed was his example, took their personal oaths of allegiance. This, they also believed, would admit them to citizenship in the United States.

In their spiritual loyalty to their own land and their own kind—stronger and more unifying than the actual Confederacy had been except to the bravest and most long-suffering—the people turned to Lee, as the symbol of their unofficial nation.

It was not to be that simple, because the causes of the war and the change of its nature during the conflict were not simple. The people were to become disfranchised inhabitants of a conquered province, used in vindictiveness of spirit for the purposes of economic exploitation. As the Confederacy had never formally ended, in this bitter aftermath its people extended its life from the brief existence as a nation into a secret existence in their hearts. This extension was stronger and more unifying than the actual Confederacy had ever been; and, in this loyalty to and identification with their own land and their own kind, the people turned to Lee—the symbol of their unofficial nation.

This final call to duty was not sought. Remote from politics, and convinced that all would come out right if each individual did his duty to the full, "Uncle Robert" left Richmond in the summer of 1865 to seek a usefulness in quietude for his few remaining years. Though only fifty-eight, his tide was obviously running out. Removal of the responsibilities did not restore his health; that was permanently broken, and the people would not let him forget his spiritual leadership.

He went to "Fool Tom" Jackson's town of Lexington, "in the Valley of Virginia," as president of the college endowed by and named for his father's friend, George Washington. His office was only a short walk across adjoining campuses to the V.M.I. barracks, rebuilding after Hunter's fire, where his war friend had lectured so short a time before as an eccentric professor. For exercise on his aging horse, who still held a good canter, the former general could ride to the hill where Stonewall Jackson lay buried near his young adjutant, Sandie Pendleton.

Everywhere he rode or walked, Lee encountered ghosts and relics from the country he loved. Sometimes old friends would get him to talk about the war, and occasionally to write letters relating to it with his rapidly waning energies. The controversies between Confederate generals were beginning, and the Old Man was regarded as the final arbiter—the ultimate patriarch. He offered advice and comfort to the families trying to rebuild a life out of the wreckage and despair, in military districts governed by bayonets.

Lincoln had said in his moving Gettysburg Address that "government of the people, by the people, for the people, shall not perish from the earth." The Confederacy never imperiled democratic forms of government. It was in revolt so that a government based on the consent of the people might be allowed to survive. And it was when they were defeated that democracy perished from the earth, at least their share of it.

During the twelve years of "Reconstruction"—the longest military occupation in modern history—"the Southerner" was born, of necessity and legend, under the godparentship of Lee. In him the people perceived the distillation of the best in their land. In their years of oppression, the legends grew to attribute the best to all.

The personal defections and group failures of the Confederacy were forgotten, and each partook of the heroism of Lee. The statistics of the few who were actually plantation masters were also forgotten, along with the assertive newness of the late-arriving bourbons. The slumbrous, isolated baronies of a time in thrall belonged to them all, and each was touched with the aura of a lost enchantment.

For the new Confederacy of the spirit there was a new generation. Children born before the war in areas early occupied had no memory of life on their land except under the martial law of the enemy; by the time Reconstruction ended in 1877, the generation under twenty experienced for the first time freedom from occupation forces on their own land. By then they were unchangeably molded. They were molded on the symbol and the model of Robert E. Lee.

Even before he died, an old man at sixty-three, "Uncle Robert" had passed into legend.

When death came to the cotton-bearded college president, for all his efforts to turn his countrymen's minds to peace, his own mind (like Jackson's) returned to the hours of the mortal conflict. Also like Jackson, he called for A. P. Hill, the long-dead Little Powell. "Tell A. P. Hill he must come up."

Then the great Confederate murmured, "Strike the tent."

Bibliography

Abernethy, Thomas P. *From Frontier to Plantation in Tennessee*. Chapel Hill, 1932.

Adams, Henry. *The Education of Henry Adams*. Boston, 1918.

———. *The Great Secession Winter, 1860–61*. Massachusetts Historical Society Papers, Vol. 43 (1910).

Agar, Herbert. *The People's Choice, from Washington to Harding: A Study in Democracy*. New York, 1933.

Alexander, E. P. *Military Memoirs of a Confederate*. New York, 1907.

Alfriend, Frank H. *The Life of Jefferson Davis*. Cincinnati, 1868.

Ambler, Charles Henry. *Thomas Ritchie: A Study in Virginia Politics*. Richmond, 1913.

Andrews, Eliza Frances. *War-Time Journal of a Georgia Girl*. New York, 1908.

Auchampaugh, P. G. *James Buchanan and His Cabinet on the Eve of Secession*. Lancaster, Pa., 1926.

Avary, Myrta Lockett, ed. *Recollections of Alexander H. Stephens*. New York, 1910.

Baldwin, Joseph G. *The Flush Times of Alabama and Mississippi*. Americus, Ga., 1908(?).

Barringer, Dr. Paul B. *The Natural Bent*. Chapel Hill, 1949.

Bartlett, Napier. *Military Record of Louisiana . . . A Soldier's Story of the Late War. . . .* New Orleans, 1875.

Basso, Hamilton. *Beauregard, the Great Creole*. New York, 1933.

Battles and Leaders of the Civil War. 4 vols. New York, 1887.

Beale, R. L. T. *History of the Ninth Virginia Cavalry*. Richmond, 1899.

Beard, Charles A. and Mary R. *The Rise of American Civilization*. New York, 1930.

Benton, Thomas Hart. *Thirty Years' View*. 2 vols. New York, 1854, 1856.

Black, Robert C., III. *The Railroads of the Confederacy*. Chapel Hill, 1952.

Blackford, William Willis. *War Years with Jeb Stuart*. New York, 1945.

Blanton, Wyndham B. *Medicine in Virginia in the Nineteenth Century*. Richmond, 1933.

Bowers, Claude. *The Tragic Era*. New York, 1929.

Boykin, E. M. *The Falling Flag: Evacuation of Richmond, Retreat and Surrender at Appomattox.* New York, 1874.

Bradbeer, William West. *Confederate and Southern State Currency.* Mount Vernon, N.Y., 1915.

Bradford, Gamaliel. *Confederate Portraits.* Boston, 1914.

————. *Lee, the American.* Boston, 1912.

————. *Wives.* New York, 1925.

Brooks, Van Wyck. *The World of Washington Irving.* New York, 1946.

Brown, William G. *The Lower South in American History.* New York, 1902.

Bruce, Kathleen. *Virginia Iron Manufacture in the Slave Era.* New York, 1930.

Bruce, Philip A., and others. *History of Virginia.* 6 vols. The American Historical Society. Chicago and New York, 1924.

Bruce, William Cabell. *Recollections.* Baltimore, 1931.

Bulloch, James D. *Secret Service of the Confederate States in Europe.* 2 vols. London, 1883.

Burge, Mrs. Thomas. *A Woman's Wartime Journal . . . as Recorded in the Diary of Dolly Sumner Lunt (Burge).* Ed. Julian Street. Macon, 1947.

Butler, Pierce. *Judah P. Benjamin.* Philadelphia, 1906.

Caldwell, J. F. F. *The History of a Brigade of South Carolinians. . . .* Marietta, Ga., 1951.

Campbell, John A. *Reminiscences and Documents Relating to the Civil War during the Year 1865.* Baltimore, 1887.

Capers, Gerald M. *The Biography of a River Town; Memphis: Its Heroic Age.* Chapel Hill, 1932.

Capers, Henry D. *Life and Times of C. G. Memminger.* Richmond, 1893.

Carolina Rice Plantation of the Fifties, A. New York, 1936. Thirty water colors and preface by Alice R. Huger Smith with chapters from the unpublished memoirs of D. E. Huger Smith and narrative by Herbert Ravenel Sass.

Carpenter, Jesse T. *The South as a Conscious Minority. 1789–1861. . . .* New York, 1930.

Cash, W. J. *The Mind of the South.* New York, 1941.

Casler, John O. *Four Years in the Stonewall Brigade.* Marietta, Ga., 1951.

Catton, Bruce. *Glory Road.* Garden City, 1952.

————. *Mr. Lincoln's Army.* Garden City, 1951.

Cavada, Frederick F. *Libby Life: Experiences of a Prisoner of War in Richmond, Va., 1863–64.* Philadelphia, 1865.

Chamberlayne, C. G., ed. *Ham Chamberlayne—Virginian.* Richmond, 1933.

Chase, P. H. *Confederate States of America Paper Money.* Bala-Cynwyd, Pa., 1936.

Chesnut, Mary Boykin. *A Diary from Dixie.* New York, 1929.

Christian, W. Asbury. *Richmond, Her Past and Present.* Richmond, 1912.

Claiborne, J. F. H. *Life and Correspondence of John A. Quitman.* New York, 1860.

Clay, Mrs. Clement C. *A Belle of the Fifties.* New York, 1905.

Coit, Margaret L. *John C. Calhoun, American Portrait.* Boston, 1950.

Cole, Arthur C. *The Irrepressible Conflict.* New York, 1927.

Commager, Henry Steele. *The Blue and the Gray: The Story of the Civil War as Told by Participants.* 2 vols. Indianapolis, 1950.

Commager, Henry Steele, and Nevins, Allan. *The Heritage of America.* Boston, 1939.

Confession, Trial and Execution of Nat Turner, The. Published by R. M. Stephenson, Southampton County, Va. Printed by John B. Ege, Petersburg, 1881.

Cooke, John E. *A Life of General Robert E. Lee.* New York, 1875.

——. *The Life of Stonewall Jackson.* Richmond, 1863.

——. *Wearing of the Gray.* New York, 1867.

Corbin, Diana Fontaine Maury. *Life of Matthew Fontaine Maury.* London, 1888.

Cotterill, Robert S. *The Old South.* Glendale, Calif., 1936.

Couch, William T., ed. *Culture in the South.* Chapel Hill, 1934.

Coulter, E. Merton. *The Confederate States of America: 1861–1865.* Vol. 7, *A History of the South.* Baton Rouge, 1950.

Couper, William. *One Hundred Years at V.M.I.* 2 vols. Richmond, 1939.

Craven, Avery Odelle. *The Coming of the Civil War.* New York, 1942.

——. *Edmund Ruffin, Southerner: A Study in Secession.* New York, 1932.

——. *The Growth of Southern Nationalism: 1840–1861.* Vol. 6, *A History of the South.* Baton Rouge, 1953.

——. *The Repressible Conflict.* Baton Rouge, 1939.

Craven, John J. *Prison Life of Jefferson Davis.* New York, 1866.

Cumming, Kate. *A Journal of Hospital Life.* Louisville, 1866.

Curry, J. L. M. *Civil History of the Government of the Confederate States.* Richmond, 1901.

Cutchins, John A. *A Famous Command: The Richmond Light Infantry Blues.* Richmond, 1934.

Dabney, R. L. *Life and Campaigns of Lieutenant-General Thomas J. Jackson.* New York, 1866.

Dabney, Virginius. *Liberalism in the South.* Chapel Hill, 1932.

Dame, William Meade. *From the Rapidan to Richmond. . . .* Baltimore, 1920.

Daniel, Frederick S. *Richmond Howitzers in the War.* Richmond, 1891.

Davis, Jefferson. *The Rise and Fall of the Confederate Government.* 2 vols. New York, 1881.

Davis, Reuben. *Recollections of Mississippi and Mississippians.* Boston and New York, 1889.

Davis, Varina Howell. *Jefferson Davis, ex-President of the Confederacy: A Memoir by His Wife.* 2 vols. New York, 1890.

Dawson, Sarah Morgan. *A Confederate Girl's Diary.* New York, 1913.

DeLeon, Thomas Cooper. *Belles, Beaux, and Brains of the Sixties.* New York, 1907.

——. *Four Years in Rebel Capitals.* Mobile, 1892.

Dictionary of American Biography. New York, 1928– .

Dietz, August. *The Postal Service of the Confederate States of America.* Richmond, 1929.

Dixon, Thomas. *The Victim: A Romance of the Real Jefferson Davis.* New York, 1914.

Dodd, William E. *The Cotton Kingdom.* New Haven, 1919.

——. *Jefferson Davis.* Philadelphia, 1907.

——. *Statesmen of the Old South.* New York, 1911.

Douglas, Henry Kyd. *I Rode with Stonewall.* Chapel Hill, 1940.

Drewry, W. S. *The Southampton Insurrection.* Washington, 1900.

DuBose, John W. *The Life and Times of William Lowndes Yancey. . . .* Birmingham, 1892.

Duke, Basil W. *Reminiscences of General Basil W. Duke.* Garden City, 1911.

Dyer, John P. *Fighting Joe Wheeler.* Baton Rouge, 1941.

Eckenrode, H. J., and Conrad, Bryan. *James Longstreet, Lee's War Horse.* Chapel Hill, 1936.

Eckenrode, H. J. *Jefferson Davis, President of the South.* New York, 1923.

Eaton, Clement. *A History of the Southern Confederacy.* New York, 1954.

Eggleston, George Cary. *A Rebel's Recollections.* New York, 1875.

Eisenschiml, Otto, and Newman, Ralph. *The American Iliad.* Indianapolis and New York, 1947.

Foote, Henry Stuart. *Casket of Reminiscences.* Washington, 1874.

——. *War of the Rebellion.* New York, 1866.

Freeman, Douglas Southall. *Lee's Lieutenants.* 3 vols. New York, 1942–44.

——. *R. E. Lee.* 4 vols. New York, 1934–35.

Fremantle, Lieutenant-Colonel Arthur James Lyon. *The Fremantle Diary.* Ed. Walter Lord. Boston, 1954.

Fuller, Claud E., and Steuart, Richard D. *Firearms of the Confederacy.* Huntington, W. Va., 1944.

Gaines, Francis P. *The Southern Plantation.* New York, 1925

Gildersleeve, John R. "History of Chimborazo Hospital, Richmond, Va., and Its Medical Officers during 1861–1865," *Virginia Medical Semi-Monthly,* July 8, 1904.

Gordon, John B. *Reminiscences of the Civil War.* New York, 1903.

Grant, Ulysses S. *Personal Memoirs.* New York, 1885–86.

Gregory, Mrs. Meg T. Unpublished letter on the presence of Butler's army between Richmond and Petersburg in 1864. Property of the Virginia Historical Society.

Grimes, Absalom C. *Absalom Grimes, Confederate Mail Runner.* New Haven, 1926.

Guedalla, Philip. *The Second Empire.* London, 1922.

Hamlin, Percy Gatling. *Old Bald Head (General R. S. Ewell).* Strasburg, Va., 1940.

Hanna, A. J. *Flight into Oblivion.* Richmond, 1938.

Harper's Pictorial History of the Great Rebellion. Ed. Alfred H. Guernsey and Henry M. Alden. 2 vols. New York, 1866–68.

Harris, William C. *Prison-Life in the Tobacco Warehouse at Richmond.* Philadelphia, 1862.

Harrison, Burton H. "The Capture of Jefferson Davis," *Century Magazine,* November 1883.

Harrison, Mrs. Burton H. *Recollections Grave and Gay*. New York, 1911.

Harwell, Richard B. *Confederate Belles Lettres*. Hattiesburg, Miss., 1941.

———, ed. *A Confederate Diary of the Retreat from Petersburg*. Emory, Ga., 1953.

———. *Confederate Music*. Chapel Hill, 1950.

———. "The Confederate Search for a National Song." Reprinted from Lincoln *Herald*, 1950.

———. "Propaganda for Secession. . . ." Reprinted from Lincoln *Herald*, 1952.

Headley, John W. *Confederate Operations in Canada and New York*. New York, 1906.

Heartsill, W. W. *1491 Days in the Confederate Army*. Ed. Bell Irvin Wiley. Jackson, Tenn., 1954.

Helper, Hinton Rowan. *The Impending Crisis of the South: How to Meet It*. New York, 1857.

Henderson, George F. R. *Stonewall Jackson and the American Civil War*. London, 1900.

Hendrick, Burton J. *The Lees of Virginia*. Boston, 1935.

———. *Lincoln's War Cabinet*. Boston, 1946.

———. *Statesmen of the Lost Cause: Jefferson Davis and His Cabinet*. Boston, 1939.

Henry, Robert Selph. *"First with the Most" Forrest*. Indianapolis, 1944.

———. *The Story of the Confederacy*. Indianapolis, 1931.

———. *The Story of Reconstruction*. Indianapolis, 1938.

Hesseltine, William Best. *Civil War Prisons: A Study in War Psychosis*. Columbus, O., 1930.

———. *The South in American History*. (Revised ed.) New York, 1943.

Hill, Louise B. *Joseph E. Brown and the Confederacy*. Chapel Hill, 1939.

Hodgson, Joseph. *Cradle of the Confederacy; or, the Times of Troup, Quitman, and Yancey. . . .* Mobile, 1876.

Hood, John B. *Advance and Retreat*. New Orleans, 1880.

Hopley, Catherine C. *Life in the South: From the Commencement of the War*. London, 1863.

Horan, James D. *Confederate Agent*. New York, 1954.

Horn, Stanley F. *The Army of Tennessee: A Military History*. Indianapolis, 1941.

Howard, McHenry. *Recollections of a Maryland Soldier and Staff Officer*. Baltimore, 1914.

Hume, Major Edgar Erskine. "Chimborazo Hospital, Confederate States Army, America's Largest Military Hospital," *Virginia Medical Monthly*, July 1934.

Huse, Caleb. *The Supplies for the Confederate Army*. Boston, 1904.

Jackson, Mrs. Mary Anna. *Memoirs of Stonewall Jackson*. Louisville, 1895.

James, Marquis. *The Life of Andrew Jackson*. Garden City, 1940.

Jeffrey, William H. *Richmond Prisons 1861–2*. St. Johnsbury, Vt., 1893.

Johns, Frank S., and Johns, Anne Page. "Chimborazo Hospital and J. B. McCaw, Surgeon-in-Chief," *Virginia Magazine of History and Biography*, Vol. 62, April 1954.

Johnston, Joseph E. *Narrative of Military Operations during the Late War between the States.* New York, 1872.

Johnston, Richard M., and Browne, William H. *Life of Alexander H. Stephens.* Philadelphia, 1878.

Jones, John B. *A Rebel War Clerk's Diary at the Confederate States Capital.* 2 vols. New York, 1935.

Jones, Virgil Carrington. *Ranger Mosby.* Chapel Hill, 1944.

Journal of the Congress of the Confederate States of America. 7 vols. Washington, 1904–5.

Kane, Harnett T. *The Lady of Arlington.* Garden City, 1953.

Kelln, Albert L. "Confederate Submarines," *Virginia Magazine of History and Biography,* July 1953.

Kennedy, John P. *Swallow Barn.* New York, 1851.

Kern, M. Ethel Kelley. *The Trail of the Three-Notched Road.* Richmond, 1929.

Lee, Robert E., Jr. *Recollections and Letters of General Robert E. Lee.* New York, 1905.

Leech, Margaret. *Reveille in Washington, 1860–1865.* New York, 1941.

Lewis, Lloyd. *Captain Sam Grant.* Boston, 1950.

———. *Sherman, Fighting Prophet.* New York, 1932.

Little, John P. *History of Richmond.* Richmond, 1933.

Loehr, Charles T. *History of the First Virginia Regiment.* Richmond, 1884.

Longstreet, A. B. *Georgia Scenes, Characters, Incidents. . . .* New York, 1843.

Longstreet, James. *From Manassas to Appomattox. . . .* Philadelphia, 1896.

Lonn, Ella. *Desertion during the Civil War.* New York, 1928.

———. *Foreigners in the Confederacy.* Chapel Hill, 1940.

———. *Salt as a Factor in the Confederacy.* New York, 1933.

Lossing, Benson J., ed. *Pictorial History of the Civil War in the United States of America.* 3 vols. Philadelphia, 1866–68.

Lytle, Andrew. *Bedford Forrest and His Critter Company.* New York, 1931.

McCarthy, Carlton. *Detailed Minutiae of Soldier Life in the Army of Northern Virginia, 1861–1865.* Richmond, 1899.

McClellan, H. B. *The Life, Character and Campaigns of Major-General J. E. B. Stuart.* Richmond, 1880.

MacDonald, Rose M. E. *Mrs. Robert E. Lee.* Boston, 1939.

McElroy, Robert. *Jefferson Davis: The Unreal and the Real.* 2 vols. New York, 1937.

McGuire, Judith W. *Diary of a Southern Refugee during the War.* Richmond, 1889.

McKim, Randolph H. *A Soldier's Recollections.* New York, 1910.

Macon, T. J. *Reminiscences of the First Company of Richmond Howitzers.* Richmond.

Malet, Rev. William W. *An Errand to the South in the Summer of 1862.* London, 1863.

Mallory, Stephen R. "The Last Days of the Confederacy," *McClure's Magazine,* December 1900–January 1901.

Marshall, Charles. *An Aide-de-camp of Lee.* . . . Ed. General Sir Frederick Maurice. Boston, 1927.

Mason, Virginia. *The Public Life and Diplomatic Correspondence of James M. Mason.* New York, 1906.

Maurice, Sir Frederick. *Statesmen and Soldiers of the Civil War: A Study of the Conduct of War.* Boston, 1926.

Maury, Major General Dabney H. *Recollections of a Virginian.* New York, 1894.

Meade, Robert Douthat. *Judah P. Benjamin: Confederate Statesman.* New York, 1943.

Mercer, Philip. *The Life of the Gallant Pelham.* Macon, 1929.

Meredith, Roy. *The Face of Robert E. Lee in Life and in Legend.* New York, 1947.

Midyette, Dayton Ralph, Jr. *Thomas Roderick Dew.* In the John P. Branch Historical Papers of Randolph-Macon College. Richmond, 1909. Vol. 3, No. 1.

Milton, George Fort. *Conflict: The American Civil War.* New York, 1941.

———. *The Eve of Conflict: Stephen A. Douglas and the Needless War.* Boston, 1934.

Moore, Albert Burton. *Conscription and Conflict in the Confederacy.* New York, 1924.

Moore, Edward A. *The Story of a Cannoneer under Stonewall Jackson.* New York, 1907.

Moore, Mrs. M. B. *The Geographical Reader for the Dixie Children.* Raleigh, 1863.

Morgan, James Morris. *Recollections of a Rebel Reefer.* Boston, 1917.

Morison, Samuel Eliot. *Oxford History of the United States,* Vol. II. London, 1927.

Munford, Beverley B. *Virginia's Attitude toward Slavery and Secession.* New York, 1911.

Munford, Robert Beverley. *Richmond Homes and Memories.* Richmond, 1936.

Nevins, Allan. *The Emergence of Lincoln.* 2 vols. New York, 1950.

———. *The Statesmanship of the Civil War.* New York, 1953.

Noll, Arthur Howard, ed. *Dr. Quintard, Chaplain C.S.A.* Sewanee, 1905.

Official Records of the Union and Confederate Armies. Washington, D.C., 1880–1901.

O'Flaherty, Daniel. *General Jo Shelby: Undefeated Rebel.* Chapel Hill, 1954.

Olmsted, Frederick Law. *Journey in the Back Country.* New York, 1860.

———. *Journey in the Seaboard Slave States.* New York, 1856.

Owen, William M. *In Camp and Battle with the Washington Artillery of New Orleans.* Boston, 1885.

Owsley, Frank L. *King Cotton Diplomacy.* Chicago, 1931.

———. *States' Rights in the Confederacy.* Chicago, 1925.

Parker, William Harwar. *Recollections of a Naval Officer, 1841–1865.* New York, 1883.

Parrington, Vernon L. *Main Currents in American Thought.* New York, 1927.

Patrick, Rembert W. *Jefferson Davis and His Cabinet.* Baton Rouge, 1944.

Pember, Phoebe Yates. *A Southern Woman's Story*. New York, 1879.

Pemberton, John C. *Pemberton, Defender of Vicksburg*. Chapel Hill, 1942.

Pendleton, Louis. *Alexander Stephens*. Philadelphia, 1908.

Phillips, Ulrich Bonnell. *Life and Labor in the Old South*. Boston, 1929.

———. *The Life of Robert Toombs*. New York, 1913.

Photographic History of the Civil War. 10 vols. New York, 1911.

Pickett, George E. *Soldier of the South . . . Pickett's War Letters to His Wife*. Boston, 1928.

Pickett, LaSalle Corbell. *Pickett and His Men*. Atlanta, 1899.

Pinkerton, Allan. *The Spy of the Rebellion*. New York, 1885.

Polk, William M. *Leonidas Polk, Bishop and General*. 2 vols. New York, 1893.

Pollard, Edward A. *A Life of Jefferson Davis. With a Secret History of the Southern Confederacy*. Chicago, 1869.

———. *The Lost Cause: A New Southern History of the War of the Confederates*. New York, 1866.

Potts, Frank. *The Death of the Confederacy*. Richmond, 1928.

Pressly, Thomas J. *Americans Interpret Their Civil War*. Princeton, 1954.

Pryor, Mrs. Roger A. *Reminiscences of Peace and War*. New York, 1904.

Putnam, Sallie A. Brock. *Richmond during the War*. New York, 1867.

Quarles, Benjamin. *The Negro in the Civil War*. Boston, 1953.

Rabun, James Z. "Alexander H. Stephens and Jefferson Davis," *American Historical Review*, January 1953.

Ramsdell, Charles W. "Lincoln and Fort Sumter," *Journal of Southern History*, Vol. III (1937).

Randall, J. G. *Civil War and Reconstruction*. New York, 1937.

———. *Lincoln, the President*. 2 vols. New York, 1945.

Ravenel, [Harriott Horry (Rutledge)]. *Mrs. St. Julien Ravenel. Charleston, the Place and the People*. New York and London, 1906.

Reagan, John H. *Memoirs, with Special Reference to Secession and the Civil War*. New York, 1906.

Review of the Slave Question, Extracted from the American Quarterly Review, December, 1832. By a Virginian: printed by T.W. White, opposite the Bell Tavern, Richmond, 1833.

Richards, Jacob F. *The Florence Nightingale of the Southern Army: Experiences of Mrs. Ella K. Newsom, Confederate Nurse. . . .* New York, 1914.

Richardson, James D., ed. *Messages and Papers of the Confederacy*. 2 vols. Nashville, 1906.

Richmond Directories.

Roberts, Joseph Clarke. *The Road from Monticello: A Study of the Virginia Slave Debates of 1832*. Durham, 1941.

Robertson, W. G. *A Biography of A. P. Hill*. Published serially in the Richmond *Times-Dispatch Sunday Magazine*, October 14–November 11, 1934.

Robinson, William Morrison, Jr. *The Confederate Privateers*. New Haven, 1928.

Roman, Alfred. *Military Operations of General Beauregard in the War between the States.* 2 vols. New York, 1884.

Rowland, Dunbar, ed. *Jefferson Davis, Constitutionalist, His Letters, Papers and Speeches.* 10 vols. Jackson, Miss., 1923.

Rowland, Eron. *Varina Howell: Wife of Jefferson Davis.* 2 vols. New York, 1931.

Royall, William L. *Some Reminiscences.* . . . Washington, 1909.

Russell, William Howard. *My Diary North and South.* 2 vols. London, 1863.

Sandburg, Carl. *Abraham Lincoln: The War Years.* 4 vols. New York, 1939.

Saxon, Lyle. *Fabulous New Orleans.* New York, 1928.

Schaaf, Morris. *The Sunset of the Confederacy.* Boston, 1912.

Scharf, J. T. *History of the Confederate States Navy.* New York, 1887.

Schlesinger, Arthur, Jr. *The Age of Jackson.* Boston, 1945.

Schwab, John C. *The Confederate States of America.* New York, 1901.

Scott, Mary Wingfield. *Houses of Old Richmond.* Richmond, 1941.

Sears, Louis Martin. *John Slidell.* Durham, 1925.

Seitz, Don. *Braxton Bragg, General of the Confederacy.* Columbia, S.C., 1924.

Semmes, Raphael. *Memoirs of Service Afloat during the War between the States.* Baltimore, 1869.

Shanks, Henry T. *The Secession Movement in Virginia.* Richmond, 1934.

Sherman, William T. *Memoirs of General W. T. Sherman.* 2 vols. New York, 1891.

Sigaud, Louis A. *Belle Boyd, Confederate Spy.* Richmond, 1944.

Simkins, Francis Butler. *The South Old and New.* New York, 1947.

———, and Patton, James Welch. *The Women of the Confederacy.* Richmond, 1936.

Simms, Henry H. *A Decade of Sectional Controversy 1851–1861.* Chapel Hill, 1942.

———. *Life of Robert M. T. Hunter.* Richmond, 1935.

Small, Abner R. *The Road to Richmond.* Berkeley, Calif., 1939.

Smith, Edward C. *The Borderland in the Civil War.* New York, 1927.

Sorrel, G. Moxley. *Recollections of a Confederate Staff Officer.* New York, 1917.

Southern Historical Society Papers. 49 vols. Richmond, 1876–   .

Stanard, Mary Newton. *Richmond, Its People and Its Story.* Philadelphia, 1923.

Steele, Matthew F. *American Campaigns.* Washington, 1909.

Stephens, Alexander H. *A Constitutional View of the Late War beween the States.* Philadelphia, 1868–70.

Stephenson, Nathaniel W. *The Day of the Confederacy.* New Haven, 1919.

———. "A Theory of Jefferson Davis," *American Historical Review,* October 1915.

Stiles, Robert. *Four Years under Marse Robert.* Washington, 1903.

Stovall, Pleasant A. *Robert Toombs, Statesman, Speaker, Soldier, Sage.* New York, 1892.

Stranger's Guide and Official Directory of the City of Richmond, The. Richmond, 1863.

Stuart, J. E. B. *Letters of General J. E. B. Stuart to His Wife, 1861.* Ed. Bingham Duncan. Atlanta, 1943.

Sturgis, Thomas. *Prisoners of War 1861–5.* New York, 1912.

Swiggett, Howard. *The Rebel Raider: A Life of John Hunt Morgan.* Indianapolis, 1934.

Sydnor, C. S. *A Gentleman of the Old Natchez Region: Benjamin L. C. Wailes.* Durham, 1938.

Tate, Allen. *Jefferson Davis: His Rise and Fall.* New York, 1929.

Tatum, Georgia Lee. *Disloyalty in the Confederacy.* Chapel Hill, 1934.

Taylor, Richard. *Destruction and Reconstruction: Personal Experiences of the Late War.* New York, 1879.

Taylor, Walter H. *General Lee: His Campaigns in Virginia, 1861–65. . . .* Norfolk, 1905.

Thomason, John W., Jr. *Jeb Stuart.* New York, 1934.

Thompson, Samuel B. *Confederate Purchasing Operations Abroad.* Chapel Hill, 1935.

Tilghman, Tench Francis. *The Confederate Baggage and Treasure Train Ends Its Flight in Florida.* Winter Park, Fla., 1939.

Trent, William P. *William Gilmore Simms.* Boston, 1892.

Trexler, Harrison A. *The Confederate Ironclad "Virginia" ("Merrimac").* Chicago, 1938.

Tucker, Nathaniel Beverley. *The Partisan Leader.* Ed. and intro. Carl Bridenbaugh. New York, 1933.

Turner, Frederick Jackson. *The United States 1830–1850.* New York, 1935.

Turner, Robert. *Recollections of the Secession Convention in Virginia.* Unpublished manuscript in the Virginia Historical Society, Richmond, Virginia.

Van Deusen, Glyndon G. *The Life of Henry Clay.* Boston, 1937.

Venable, A. L. *The Role of William L. Yancey in the Secession Movement.* Nashville, 1945.

Von Borcke, Heros. *My Memoirs of the Confederate War for Independence.* London, 1866.

Walker's Appeal. Boston, 1829.

Wallace, David Duncan. *South Carolina: A Short History. 1520–1948.* Chapel Hill, 1951.

Walthall, Ernest Taylor. *Hidden Things Brought to Light.* Richmond, 1933.

Watkins, Sam R. *"Co. Aytch": A Side Show of the Big Show.* Jackson, Tenn., 1952.

Weddell, Alexander Wilbourne. *Richmond, Virginia, in Old Prints. (1737–1887).* Richmond, 1932.

Weddell, Elizabeth Wright. *St. Paul's Church, Richmond, Virginia: Its Historic Years and Memorials.* 2 vols. Richmond, 1931.

Wertenbaker, Thomas J. *Patricians and Plebians in Virginia.* Charlottesville, 1910.

———. *The Planters of Colonial Virginia.* Princeton, 1922.

Wesley, Charles H. *The Collapse of the Confederacy.* Washington, 1937.

White, E. V. *The First Iron-Clad Naval Engagement in the World.* . . . Portsmouth, Va., 1906.
White, Laura. *Robert Barnwell Rhett, Father of Secession.* New York, 1931.
Wiley, Bell Irvin. *The Life of Johnny Reb.* Indianapolis, 1943.
————. *The Plain People of the Confederacy.* Baton Rouge, 1944.
————. *Southern Negroes 1861–65.* New Haven, 1938.
Wilkinson, John. *The Narrative of a Blockade-Runner.* New York, 1877.
Williams, Kenneth P. *Lincoln Finds a General.* 2 vols. New York, 1949.
Williams, Thomas Harry. *Lincoln and His Generals.* New York, 1952.
Willson, Beccles. *John Slidell and the Confederates in Paris.* New York, 1932.
Winston, Robert Watson. *High Stakes and Hair Trigger: The Life of Jefferson Davis.* New York, 1930.
Wise, John S. *The End of an Era.* Boston, 1927.
Woodward, W. E. *A New American History.* Garden City, 1938.
Worsham, John H. *One of Jackson's Foot Cavalry* . . . New York, 1912.
Wright, Mrs. D. Giraud. *A Southern Girl in '61: War-Time Memories of a Confederate Senator's Daughter.* New York, 1905.
Wright, Louis B. *The First Gentlemen of Virginia.* . . . San Marino, Calif., 1940.

PERIODICALS

Harper's Illustrated Weekly.
Liberator, The. May 7, June 25, July 2, October 1, October 8, 1831. Boston.
Magnolia Weekly. Richmond.
Record. Richmond.
Richmond *Dispatch.*
Richmond *Enquirer.*
Richmond *Examiner.*
Richmond *News Leader.* Bicentennial Supplement. September 8, 1937.
Southern Illustrated News. Richmond.
Southern Literary Messenger. Richmond.

Index